BARRON'S

ESSENTIAL WORDS FOR THE

TOEIC®

with MP3 CD

5TH EDITION

Lin Lougheed
Ed.D., Teachers College
Columbia University

BARRON'S

®TOEIC is a registered trademark of Educational Testing Service (ETS). This publication is not endorsed or approved by the ETS.

All inquiries should be addressed to:
Barron's Educational Series, Inc.
250 Wireless Boulevard
Hauppauge, New York 11788
www.barronseduc.com

ISBN: 978-1-4380-7445-0

Library of Congress Control Number: 2013951991

PRINTED IN THE UNITED STATES OF AMERICA
9 8 7 6 5 4 3

Contents

Introduction

What the Book Is About

This book teaches you vocabulary that will help you when you take the TOEIC (Test of English for International Communication). The TOEIC measures the English proficiency of people working in international business or planning to use English to communicate with others. Although the exam does not specifically test specialized vocabulary, the items on the exam are in specialized contexts.

This book will help you understand specialized contexts that are often used on the TOEIC. Each chapter focuses on a particular context that has appeared on the TOEIC. The contexts are specialized, but the words are not. The words are general vocabulary. They can be used in many contexts. You will learn these words in contexts that are used on the TOEIC.

How to Use This Book

This book contains 50 lessons, and each lesson introduces you to 12 new words in a specific context. If you study one lesson every day, in 50 days you can learn 600 new words. You will practice these words by doing exercises that look just like the questions on the TOEIC.

Word List

On the first page of each lesson, you will see a list of 12 words. For each word you will see the definition of the word and two sentences using the word in context.

This page

- Introduces you to the words for the lesson
- Shows you the words in context
- Serves as a reference anytime you need to check the meaning of a word

Word Families

On this page, you will see the verb, noun, adjective, and adverb forms of six words selected from the word list.

Example

verb	popularize
noun	popularity
adjective	popular

You will also see sentences using these words in context.

On this page, you will

- Learn more words
- Learn to recognize words in their different forms
- Learn about word endings that change words into nouns, verbs, adjectives, and adverbs

Words in Context

Next you will see a paragraph called Words in Context. You will have the opportunity to see and use the words for the lesson in context.

- Complete the paragraph using words from the word list.
- Read the paragraph over to see all the words for that lesson used in context.
- Return to the paragraph as often as you like to reinforce the meanings of the words.

Listening Comprehension

In this section, you will practice the words for the lesson by doing exercises that are just like the listening questions on the TOEIC.

Part 1—You will see a photo. You will choose the statement that best describes the photo.
Part 2—You will listen to a question or statement and choose the best response.
Part 3—You will listen to a conversation and answer three questions about it.
Part 4—You will listen to a talk and answer three questions about it.

You will practice the words for the lesson in context because the questions, conversation, and talk all use words from the word list for each lesson. You will also practice listening skills and test-taking skills that you will need when you take the TOEIC.

Reading Comprehension

In this section, you will practice the words for the lesson by doing exercises that are just like the reading questions on the TOEIC.

Part 5—You will choose the best word to complete each sentence.
Part 6—You will read a paragraph and choose words to complete it.
Part 7—You will read a passage, or two related passages, and answer comprehension questions.

You will practice the words for the lesson in context because the reading passages all use words from the word list for each lesson. You will also practice reading skills and test-taking skills that you will need when you take the TOEIC.

Strategies to Improve Your Vocabulary

One of the best ways to improve your vocabulary is to read, and read often. When you read, you

- See words in context
- Expose yourself to new words

The more you read, the more words you will see. The more words you see, the more you will learn. Reading can be a very enjoyable experience, so make sure you read things that are interesting to you. Then you will have fun, improve your vocabulary, and build skills you will need for the TOEIC, all at once. When you read, there are several strategies you can use to improve your vocabulary.

1. Analyze Word Parts

Words can be made of roots, prefixes (before the root), and suffixes (after the root).

Example

re (prefix) + *circula* (root) + *tion* (suffix) = *recirculation*

In English, many of these roots, prefixes, and suffixes come from Greek and Latin words. Learning the meanings of different roots, prefixes, and suffixes will help you increase your vocabulary.

Example

re means *again*

reunite	bring together again
reconsider	think about again
retrain	train again

This book will expose you to many words that use common roots, prefixes, and suffixes.

2. Recognize Prefixes

Prefixes add to or change the meaning of the root word in some way. Learning the meanings of different prefixes will help you expand your vocabulary.

Some common prefixes in English:

Prefix	Meaning	Examples
out-	more or better	outperform, outsell
over-	too much	overwork, overdo
re-	again	rewrite, regain
fore-	before, in front	foretell, forehead
pre-	before	prepay, pretest
inter-	between	international, interact
in-	not	incorrect, inconvenient
multi-	many	multicolored, multilevel

3. Recognize Suffixes

Suffixes can tell you whether a word is a noun, verb, adjective, or adverb. As you learn to recognize different suffixes, they will help you understand the meanings of new words.

Some common suffixes in English:

Verbs

Suffix	Examples
-ize	prioritize, authorize
-ate	refrigerate, hesitate
-en	lighten, widen
-fy	magnify, verify

Nouns

Suffix	Examples
-tion, -sion	nation, conclusion
-ment	government, arrangement
-ance, -ence	importance, independence
-er, -or	manager, refrigerator
-ity	ability, community
-ness	happiness, weakness
-ship	membership, friendship
-ee	employee, attendee

Adjectives

Suffix	Examples
-y	easy, wavy
-ous	mountainous, ridiculous
-able, -ible	presentable, terrible
-ic, -ical	athletic, musical
-ful	beautiful, wonderful
-less	careless, joyless
-ive	productive, creative
-ant, -ent	important, dependent

Adverbs

Suffix	Examples
-ly	easily, importantly

4. Recognize Word Families

Word families are related groups of words that have the same root but different suffixes.

Example

depend (verb)
depend*ence* (noun)
depend*able* (adjective)
depend*ably* (adverb)

By adding different suffixes to the original word, *depend*, new words are formed. The meaning of each word is similar to the others, but each one has a different grammatical form.

When you learn a new word, it is very easy to understand the other words that are part of the same word family. In each chapter of this book, you will see examples of word families.

5. Make Your Own Word Journal

When you read, you will come across many new words, and you will need an organized way to record them.

- Use a special notebook just for recording your new words.
- Make a new page each day or each time you read a new article or story.
- For each new word, write the word, a synonym, a definition, the original sentence where you found the word, and then make up your own sentence using the word.
- Every day, review the pages from the previous days.
- Photocopy the chart on the next page to make the pages for your word journal.

Example

New Word	Synonym	Definition	Original Sentence	My Sentence
consider	think about	To think carefully about something	After considering all the difficulties, they decided to go ahead with the project.	I considered different schools before I chose this one.

New Word	Synonym	Definition	Original Sentence	My Sentence

6. Keep a Daily Reading Log

It is important to read something in English every day, aside from class assignments. It is important to read things that are interesting to you. You will get more out of the experience this way. It is also important to read many different kinds of things. This keeps you from getting bored, and, more important, it helps you learn a wider variety of vocabulary.

- Read for 20–30 minutes each day.
- Read things that are interesting to you.
- Read on a variety of topics.
- Read books, magazines, newspapers, and web pages.

The following steps will help you read in a way that will improve your vocabulary:

1. Read without stopping. Do not stop to look up unknown words. You can understand the general idea of a passage without understanding every word.

2. Underline or highlight unknown words, or write them on a separate piece of paper.

3. Guess the meaning of unknown words. Use the context and your knowledge of prefixes and suffixes and word families to do this.

4. Choose five key words and write them in your reading log. These should be unknown words that are important for understanding the meaning of the passage.

5. Look up the five key words in your dictionary.

6. Write a one-paragraph summary of the passage. Try to use the five key words in your summary.

Photocopy the chart below to make pages for your reading log.

Title: _____

Date: _____

No. of pages read: _____

Source: (book, web, magazine, etc.) _____

Key words:

_____

_____

_____

_____

_____

Summary:

_____

_____

_____

_____

_____

_____

_____

_____

_____

_____

_____

_____

_____

_____

_____

_____

_____

_____

Study Contract

It takes a lot of discipline to learn a foreign language. You need to formalize your commitment by signing a contract with yourself. This contract will obligate you to spend a certain number of hours each week learning English for a certain period of time. Sign the contract below to make your commitment.

- Print your name below on line 1.
- Write the time you will spend each week studying English on lines 4–8. Think about how much time you have to study every day and every week and make your schedule realistic.
- Sign your name and date the contract on the last line.
- At the end of each week, add up your hours. Did you meet the requirements of your contract?

TOEIC STUDY CONTRACT

I, _____, promise to study for the TOEIC. I will begin my study with Barron's Essential Words for the TOEIC and I will also study English on my own.

I understand that to improve my English I need to spend time on English.

I promise to study English _____ a week.

I will spend _____ hours a week listening to English.
I will spend _____ hours a week writing English.
I will spend _____ hours a week speaking English.
I will spend _____ hours a week reading English.

This is a contract with myself. I promise to fulfill the terms of this contract.

Signed _____ Date _____

Strategies to Practice Your Vocabulary

Now that you have signed the contract, you are committed to studying English for a certain amount of time each week. The best way to do this is to pick a time when you will practice every day. Establishing a routine is part of developing good study habits. Here are some ways that you can practice the vocabulary you learn in this book.

1. Review Every Day

Every time you sit down to work with this book, you should look over the words from the previous lesson. Do the same every time you work with your Word Journal or Daily Reading Log.

- Review words from previous lessons
- Note words that you are unsure of
- Include these words in the following suggested practice activities

2. Read Out Loud

Saying your vocabulary words out loud is another way to reinforce them. You can read word lists out loud, and you can also read the passages that contain your vocabulary words. You can read out loud

- The word lists from each lesson in this book
- The Vocabulary in Context paragraphs in this book
- The passages you read for your Daily Reading Log
- The word lists in your Word Journal

3. Categorize Words

Make a list of words that you want to review. Be sure to include the words that have given you difficulty. Divide the words into categories. For example, you could make a list of things you have or do at home, things you have or do at an office, things you see or do at a store. Any one word might appear in more than one category.

- Choose a list of words to review
- Divide the list into categories
- Use the words from each category to write a paragraph
- Using the same words, think of new categories and make new lists

4. Associate Words

Choose a word from your list of words to review and list words you associate with it.

Examples

Word	search
Associations	Things you search for:
	keys
	money
	jobs
	parking spaces
Word	warning
Associations	Places where you see warnings:
	elevators
	electric wires
	subways
	cigarette packages

Extra Activities

In addition to studying this book, there are many ways that you can study on your own. You should listen to and read English as much as you can. You should also practice speaking and writing. Here are some ways you can practice your listening, reading, speaking, and writing skills in English. Check the ones you plan to try and add some ideas of your own.

Internet-Based Self-Study Activities

Listening
___ Podcasts on the Internet
___ News websites: CNN, BBC, NBC, ABC, CBS
___ Movies in English
___ YouTube
___ _____
___ _____

Speaking
___ Use Skype to talk with English speakers
___ _____
___ _____

Writing
___ Write e-mails to website contacts
___ Write a blog
___ Leave comments on blogs and YouTube
___ Post messages in a chat room
___ Use Facebook and Twitter
___ _____
___ _____

Reading
___ Read news and magazine articles online
___ Do Web research on topics that interest you
___ Follow blogs that interest you
___ _____
___ _____

Other Self-Study Activities

Listening
___ Listen to CNN and BBC on the radio
___ Watch movies and TV in English
___ Listen to music in English
___ _____
___ _____

Speaking
___ Describe what you see and do out loud
___ Practice speaking with a conversation buddy
___ _____
___ _____

Writing
___ Write a daily journal
___ Write a letter to an English speaker
___ Make lists of the things you see every day
___ Write descriptions of your family and friends
___ _____
___ _____

Reading
___ Read newspapers and magazines in English
___ Read books in English
___ Read graphic novels in English
___ _____

Examples of Self-study Activities

Whether you read an article in a newspaper or on a website, you can use that article in a variety of ways to practice reading, writing, speaking, and listening in English.

- Read about it.
- Paraphrase and write about it.
- Give a talk or presentation about it.
- Record or make a video of your presentation.
- Listen to or watch what you recorded. Write down your presentation.
- Correct your mistakes.
- Do it all again.

Plan a Trip

Go to *www.concierge.com*
Choose a city, choose a hotel, go to that hotel's website and choose a room, and then choose some sites to visit (*reading*). Write a report about the city. Tell why you want to go there. Describe the hotel and the room you will reserve. Tell what sites in that city you plan to visit and when. Where will you eat? How will you get around?

Now write a letter to someone recommending this place (*writing*). Pretend you have to give a lecture on your planned trip (*speaking*). Make a video of yourself talking about this city. Then watch the video and write down what you said. Correct any mistakes you made and record the presentation again. Then choose another city and do this again.

Shop for an Electronic Product

Go to *www.cnet.com*
Choose an electronic product and read about it (*reading*). Write a report about the product. Tell why you want to buy one. Describe its features.

Now write a letter to someone recommending this product (*writing*). Pretend you have to give a talk about this product (*speaking*). Make a video of yourself talking about this product. Then watch the video and write down what you said. Correct any mistakes you made and record the presentation again. Then choose another product and do this again.

Discuss a Book or a CD

Go to *www.amazon.com*
Choose a book or CD or any product. Read the product description and reviews (*reading*). Write a report about the product. Tell why you want to buy one or why it is interesting to you. Describe its features.

Now write a letter to someone recommending this product (*writing*). Pretend you have to give a talk about this product (*speaking*). Make a video of yourself talking about this product. Then watch the video and write down what you said. Correct any mistakes you made and record the presentation again. Then choose another product and do this again.

Discuss Any Subject

Go to *http://simple.wikipedia.org/wiki/Main_Page*
This website is written in simple English. Pick any subject and read the entry (*reading*).

Write a short essay about the topic (*writing*). Give a presentation about it (*speaking*). Record the presentation. Then watch the video and write down what you said. Correct any mistakes you made and record the presentation again. Choose another topic and do this again.

Discuss Any Event

Go to *http://news.google.com*
Google News has a variety of links. Pick one event and read the articles about it (*reading*).

Write a short essay about the event (*writing*). Give a presentation about it (*speaking*). Record the presentation. Then watch the video and write down what you said. Correct any mistakes you made and record the presentation again. Then choose another event and do this again.

Report the News

Listen to an English-language news report on the radio or watch a news program on TV (*listening*). Take notes as you listen. Write a summary of what you heard (*writing*).

Pretend you are a news reporter. Use the information from your notes to report the news (*speaking*). Record the presentation. Then watch the video and write down what you said. Correct any mistakes you made and record the presentation again. Then listen to another news program and do this again.

Express an Opinion

Read a letter to the editor in the newspaper (*reading*). Write a letter in response in which you discuss whether you agree with the opinion expressed in the first letter. Explain why (*writing*).

Pretend you have to give a talk explaining your opinion (*speaking*). Record yourself giving the talk. Then watch the video and write down what you said. Correct any mistakes you made and record the presentation again. Then read another letter to the editor and do this again.

Review a Book or Movie

Read a book (*reading*). Think about your opinion of the book. What did you like about it? What didn't you like about it? Who would you recommend the book to and why? Pretend you are a book reviewer for a newspaper. Write a review of the book with your opinion and recommendations (*writing*).

Give an oral presentation about the book. Explain what the book is about and what your opinion is (*speaking*). Record yourself giving the presentation. Then watch the video and write down what you said. Correct any mistakes you made and record the presentation again. Then read another book and do this again.

You can do this same activity after watching a movie (*listening*).

Summarize a TV Show

Watch a TV show in English (*listening*). Take notes as you listen. After watching, write a summary of the show (*writing*).

Use your notes to give an oral summary of the show. Explain the characters, setting, and plot (*speaking*). Record yourself speaking. Then watch the video and write down what you said. Correct any mistakes you made and record the presentation again. Then watch another TV show and do this again.

Lesson 1

Contracts

WORDS TO LEARN

abide by

agreement

assurance

cancellation

determine

engage

establish

obligate

party

provision

resolve

specific

Study the following definitions and examples.

1. **abide by** v., to comply with; to conform
   a. The two parties agreed to abide by the judge's decision.
   b. For years he has abided by a commitment to annual employee raises.

2. **agreement** n., a mutual arrangement, a contract
   a. The landlord and tenant were in agreement that the rent should be prorated to the middle of the month.
   b. According to the agreement, the caterer will also supply the flowers for the event.

3. **assurance** n., a guarantee; confidence
   a. We should not begin the work without the assurance of a signed contract.
   b. He spoke with assurance about the skills of his contract lawyer.

4. **cancellation** n., annulment; stopping
   a. Work on the project had to stop because of the cancellation of the contract.
   b. The cancellation clause appears at the back of the contract.

5. **determine** v., to find out; to influence
   a. After reading the contract, I was still unable to determine if our company was liable for back wages.
   b. The skill of the union bargainers will determine whether the automotive plant will open next week.

6. **engage** v., participate; involve
   a. Before engaging in a new business, it is important to do thorough research.
   b. He engaged us in a fascinating discussion about current business law.

7. **establish** v., to institute permanently; to bring about
   a. When this company was established, the owners signed contracts with all their employees.
   b. The contract establishes a relationship between the company and the service provider.

8. **obligate** v., to bind legally or morally
   a. The contractor was obligated by the contract to work 40 hours a week.
   b. I felt obligated to finish the project even though I could have exercised my option to quit.

9. **party** n., a person or group participating in an action or plan; the persons or sides concerned in a legal matter
   a. The parties agreed to a settlement in their contract dispute.
   b. The party that prepares the contract has a distinct advantage.

10. **provision** n., a measure taken beforehand; a stipulation
    a. Carefully read all the provisions of the contract before signing it.
    b. The contract contains a provision to deal with how payments are made if John loses his job.

11. **resolve** v., to deal with successfully; to declare; n., conviction
    a. The mediator was able to resolve the problem to everyone's satisfaction.
    b. The businessman resolved to clean out all the files by the end of the week.

12. **specific** adj., particular
    a. The customer's specific complaint was not addressed in his e-mail.
    b. In a contract, one specific word can change the meaning dramatically.

WORD FAMILIES

verb	agree	If both parties agree to the terms, we can finalize the contract.
noun	agreement	As soon as the labor agreement was signed, the factory resumed production of new cars and vans.
adjective	agreeable	The parties are agreeable to the terms.

verb	assure	I assure you that the contract was reviewed by our lawyer.
noun	assurance	What assurance is there that the company will stay in business during the life of the contract?
adverb	assuredly	He spoke assuredly about the terms of the contract.

verb	cancel	We can cancel the contract, but that will cause a number of problems.
noun	cancellation	A cancellation fee is usually included in a writer's contract in case the article isn't published.
adjective	canceled	The canceled contract ended up costing our company a good deal of money.

verb	obligate	The terms of the contract obligate us to work for at least one more month.
noun	obligation	According to the contract, the company has the obligation to provide child care for employees' families.
adjective	obligatory	Agreeing to the terms of the contract is obligatory if you want to work here.

verb	provide	Since the machine is very reliable, why don't we cancel the service contract they provided?
noun	provider	We must negotiate a new contract with our Internet service provider.
noun	provision	The provision for canceling the contract is in the last clause.

verb	specify	The contract specifies an annual salary raise.
noun	specification	The work was done according to the specifications of the contract.
adverb	specific	There is no specific part of the contract that prevents us from hiring extra help.

WORDS IN CONTEXT

Read the following passage and write the words in the blanks below.

abide by	cancel	establish	provide
agreement	determine	obligates	resolve
assurance	engaging	parties	specifies

Contracts are an integral part of the workplace. The purpose of a contract is to

(1) _____ an (2) _____ between two or more

(3) _____. The contract (4) _____ the terms and

(5) _____ the parties to follow them. Contracts often include the

amount that a client will pay contractors and what services will be provided.

For example, in your office, you may have a contract that provides

(6) _____ that your copier machine or phones will be repaired within

a certain amount of time. A contract often states ways to (7) _____

if the quality of work delivered is acceptable. Well-written contracts usually

(8) _____ ways to (9) _____ problems like these

when they happen. Before (10) _____ in a contract, both parties

should think carefully, as they will have to (11) _____ the conditions

specified in it. A contract usually specifies how the two parties can

(12) _____ it if either party fails to meet the terms.

WORD PRACTICE

LISTENING COMPREHENSION

TRACK
2

Part 1 Photo

Look at the picture and listen to the sentences.
Choose the sentence that best describes the picture.

1. Ⓐ Ⓑ Ⓒ Ⓓ

Part 2 Question—Response

Listen to the question and the three responses. Choose the response that best answers the question.

2. Ⓐ Ⓑ Ⓒ   3. Ⓐ Ⓑ Ⓒ

Part 3 Conversation

Listen to the dialogue. Then read each question and choose the best answer.

4. What problem do the speakers have with the computer company?
   (A) It won't renew the contract.
   (B) It can't repair the computer.
   (C) It sends incorrect bills.
   (D) It charges them for extra spare parts.

5. When will the contract run out?
   (A) In two months.
   (B) In nine months.
   (C) In one year.
   (D) In four years.

6. What does the woman suggest doing?
   (A) Asking the company to write a new contract.
   (B) Canceling the contract.
   (C) Renewing the contract.
   (D) Waiting until the contract runs out.

Part 4 Talk

Listen to the talk. Then read each question and choose the best answer.

7. Who is talking?
   (A) A lawyer.
   (B) An upset signer of the contract.
   (C) A secretary.
   (D) Someone who has canceled his agreement.

8. Which part of the contract are they looking at?
   (A) A cancellation clause.
   (B) The assurance of quality.
   (C) The agreement on payment.
   (D) A provision in case of bankruptcy.

9. When can the parties sign the contract?
   (A) In two days.
   (B) At the end of the week.
   (C) Next week.
   (D) In thirty days.

READING

Part 5 Incomplete Sentences

Choose the word that best completes the sentence.

10. The two sides were no closer to a final _____ at midnight than they were at noon.
    (A) agreement   (C) agree
    (B) agreeable   (D) agreed

11. Our union representative _____ members that our rights would be defended.
    (A) assured   (C) assuredly
    (B) assurance   (D) assure

12. If you _____ your reservation 48 hours in advance, you will not be billed.
    (A) oblige   (C) engage
    (B) cancel   (D) determine

13. I don't feel any _____ to give my boss more than two weeks notice when I leave.
    (A) oblige   (C) obliged
    (B) obligatory   (D) obligation

14. The _____ for terminating the contract were not discussed.
    (A) provide   (C) provider
    (B) provisions   (D) provisioning

15. The contract calls for the union to _____ who their bargaining representative will be.
    (A) specific   (C) specifying
    (B) specification (D) specify

Part 6 Text Completion

Choose the word or phrase that best completes the sentence.

Rental Property for Everyone

More and more people are investing in rental property these days. Whether you have a small apartment in your house to rent, or decide to invest in an apartment or office building, rental property n provide extra income for you and your family. What does every landlord need to know?

Leases

A lease is an _____ between a landlord and a tenant. Standard leases are available at most office

16. (A) agree
    (B) agreed
    (C) agreeable
    (D) agreement

supply stores, and many property owners find them quite satisfactory. Read the standard lease carefully to determine if it meets the needs of your situation. You may want to make some additional _____.

17. (A) provision
    (B) provisions
    (C) provider
    (D) providers

You may want to add a pet clause, for example, or make different specifications pertaining to the security deposit. If you decide to make changes to the standard lease, you should meet with a lawyer. The lease is the most important tool you have if you need to resolve a dispute with your tenant. When you have a lease written by a lawyer, you _____ that you have the protection you need.

18. (A) assure
    (B) will assure
    (C) are assuring
    (D) are assured

Part 7 Reading Comprehension

Questions 19–23 refer to the following letter and form.

Santos Office Cleaners
112 Main St.
Windsor, Ontario

December 15, 20—

Mr. James Harrison
17 Hartland Road
Windsor, Ontario

Dear Mr. Harrison,

We are very sorry that you have decided to cancel your cleaning service contract with us. In order to assure that we provide our customers with the best possible service, we always try to determine the reasons for contract cancellations. Please take a few minutes to fill out the enclosed form. This is for our information only; completing the form does not obligate you to buy any product or enter into any new agreement with our company. We appreciate your cooperation. If at any time in the future you decide to renew your contract with us, please don't hesitate to contact me.

Sincerely,

Rosa Santos

Rosa Santos
Owner

Santos Office Cleaners
Customer Questionnaire

Date contract signed: March 23, 20—

Type of facility:
☒ single office
☐ office building
☐ private home
☐ other

Frequency of service:
☐ daily
☒ weekly
☐ monthly
☐ other

Reason for contract cancellation (choose one):
☐ no longer need service
☐ signed contract with a different company
☒ payment dispute not satisfactorily resolved
☐ specific complaint not resolved
☐ other

Comments: I was always satisfied with the service provided by your employees. However, I am frustrated by your inability to resolve the payment issues.

---

19. What is the purpose of the letter?
    (A) To find out why Mr. Harrison no longer wants this service.
    (B) To ask Mr. Harrison to renew his contract.
    (C) To advertise new services provided by the company.
    (D) To offer the customer a better contract.

20. What is Ms. Santos's business?
    (A) Customer relations.
    (B) Cleaning service.
    (C) Contract review.
    (D) Conflict resolution.

21. Why did this customer cancel the contract?
    (A) The company damaged something in his office.
    (B) The employees provided unsatisfactory service.
    (C) He had a disagreement about his bill.
    (D) He doesn't want this type of service anymore.

22. The word *assure* in letter one, line 3, is closest in meaning to
    (A) guarantee.
    (B) discover.
    (C) prove.
    (D) advertise.

23. The word *specific* in form two, line 15, is closest in meaning to
    (A) personal.
    (B) important.
    (C) repeated.
    (D) particular.

Lesson 2

Marketing

Study the following definitions and examples.

1. **attract** v., to draw by appeal
    a. The display attracted a number of people at the convention.
    b. The new advertising attracts the wrong kind of customer into the store.

2. **compare** v., to examine similarities and differences
    a. Once the customer compared the two products, her choice was easy.
    b. The price for this brand is high compared to the other brands on the market.

3. **competition** n., a contest or struggle
    a. In the competition for afternoon diners, Hector's has come out on top.
    b. In order to keep up with the competition, we need to market our product better.

4. **consume** v., to absorb; to use up
    a. The business plans consumed all of Fritz's attention this fall.
    b. Marketing costs consume a good part of a company's budget.

5. **convince** v., to bring to believe by argument; to persuade
    a. The salesman convinced his customer to buy his entire inventory of pens.
    b. Before a business can convince customers that it provides a quality product, it must convince its marketing staff.

6. **currently** adv., happening at the present time; now
    a. Currently we do most of our advertising on the Internet.
    b. Currently, customers are demanding big discounts for bulk orders.

7. **fad** n., a practice followed enthusiastically for a short time; a craze
    a. The mini dress was a fad once thought to be finished, but now it is making a comeback.
    b. Classic tastes may seem boring but they have proven to resist fads.

8. **inspiration** n., a thing or person that arouses a feeling
    a. His work is an inspiration to the marketing department.
    b. Marta's high sales in Spain were an inspiration to other European reps.

9. **market** v., the course of buying and selling a product; n., the demand for a product
    a. When Omar first began making his chutneys, he marketed them door-to-door to gourmet shops.
    b. There was a good market for brightly colored clothing last year, but this year nobody seems interested in buying it.

10. **persuasion** n., the power to influence; a deep conviction or belief
    a. The seminar teaches techniques of persuasion to increase sales.
    b. Companies use different methods of persuasion to get people to buy their products.

11. **productive** adj., constructive; high yield
    a. Productive advertising results in many sales.
    b. Alonzo is excited about his productive marketing staff.

12. **satisfaction** n., happiness
    a. Your satisfaction is guaranteed or you'll get your money back.
    b. We will print the advertisement to your satisfaction.

WORD FAMILIES

verb	attract	The store's poor location did not help it attract customers.
noun	attraction	Having a clown in the toy store was a foolproof attraction for getting kids to enter.
adjective	attractive	Lou ran his store on an old-fashioned premise: quality merchandise at attractive prices.

verb	compare	She compared the prices before she made a decision.
noun	comparison	There was no comparison in the quality of the two brands.
adjective	comparable	To get an average for home costs, the agent sought prices on comparable homes.

verb	compete	In order to compete in today's market, companies need to advertise on the Internet.
noun	competition	A company must always be aware of what its competition is doing.
adjective	competitive	Companies keep their products competitive by making them available on the Internet as well as in stores.

verb	consume	The analyst was able to consume new information quickly.
noun	consumer	The government tracks consumer spending closely.
adjective	consumable	He ran a study of the use of consumable goods.

verb	market	The sales department disagreed about how to market their newest product.
noun	marketing	A good director of marketing can find a way to sell even an unattractive product.
adjective	marketable	Once the sales manager decided to change the packaging, the product became much more marketable.

verb	satisfy	The goal of marketing is to show that the product satisfies consumers' needs.
noun	satisfaction	Our highest priority is customer satisfaction.
adjective	satisfactory	All our products arrive in the stores in satisfactory condition.

WORDS IN CONTEXT

Read the following passage and write the words in the blanks below.

attract	consumers	fad	persuaded
compared	convinced	inspiration	product
competes	current	market	satisfied

Yassir is getting ready to realize his dream: opening a business that sells plants on the Internet. After completing a business plan that helped him to determine that there was demand for his (1) _____ in the (2) _____, Yassir is ready to start promoting his business. Having (3) _____ the bank that there was a market—that there were people willing to buy plants on the Internet—he needed to find these (4) _____.

Once he has an established base, Yassir, like other business owners, will have to continually (5) _____ new customers. At the same time, he must keep the customers he already has (6) _____. To this end, he has to make sure that his (7) _____ customers are happy with the products they buy. Yassir's job is to provide his customers with the (8) _____ to keep bringing him their business. To do this, he will have to (9) _____ consumers that he offers a good product at a fair price, especially when (10) _____ to the businesses with which he (11) _____. He hopes that Internet plant buyers are here to stay and not just part of a (12) _____.

WORD PRACTICE

LISTENING COMPREHENSION

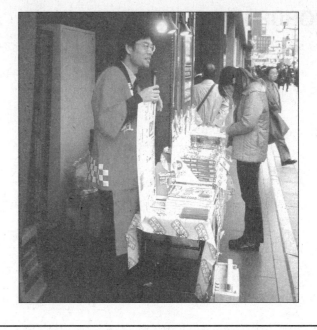

Part 1 Photo

Look at the picture and listen to the sentences.
Choose the sentence that best describes the picture.

1. Ⓐ Ⓑ Ⓒ Ⓓ

Part 2 Question–Response

Listen to the question and the three possible responses. Choose the response that best answers the question.

2. Ⓐ Ⓑ Ⓒ   3. Ⓐ Ⓑ Ⓒ

Part 3 Conversation

Listen to the dialogue. Then read each question and choose the best response.

4. Why does the store need to be more competitive?
   (A) There's currently a recession.
   (B) Productivity has dropped lately.
   (C) There's a new competitor nearby.
   (D) New employees have little experience.

5. How will the store attract more customers?
   (A) By giving them trial products.
   (B) By giving them discounts.
   (C) By selling new products.
   (D) By featuring happy customers in ads.

6. Who will the woman call?
   (A) A photographer.
   (B) A photocopy salesperson.
   (C) A customer.
   (D) A marketing executive.

Part 4 Talk

Listen to the talk. Then read each question and choose the best answer.

7. Who would listen to this talk?
   (A) Customers.
   (B) Competitors.
   (C) Students.
   (D) Salespeople.

8. What are they trying to identify?
   (A) Their weaknesses.
   (B) How to price their service.
   (C) Their strong points.
   (D) Who the competition is.

9. Where will the listeners be this afternoon?
   (A) At home.
   (B) In a workshop.
   (C) At a store.
   (D) With a client.

READING

Part 5 Incomplete Sentences

Choose the word that best completes the sentence.

10. Marketing specialists have conducted extensive studies of what _____ customers to a particular product.
    (A) attractive   (C) attracts
    (B) attraction   (D) attracting

11. Smart shoppers will _____ similar brands of an item before making a decision.
    (A) compare   (C) comparative
    (B) comparison   (D) comparable

12. If our work isn't to your _____, please notify us within 60 days.
    (A) satisfy   (C) satisfaction
    (B) satisfactory   (D) satisfied

13. Manufacturers like to know what features _____ find useful.
    (A) consumers   (C) consumption
    (B) consume   (D) consumable

14. Without good _____, good products can go unsold.
    (A) market   (C) marketed
    (B) marketable   (D) marketing

15. A careful analysis of the _____ products on the market indicated that our product lacked innovation and optional features.
    (A) compete   (C) competed
    (B) competing   (D) competition

Part 6 Text Completion

Choose the word or phrase that best completes the sentence.

Dear Valued Customer,

Smart consumers like yourself are concerned about your family's nutrition. Health is a top priority, and so is value. You want high-quality food products at competitive prices. That's why we are introducing Farm Fresh, our new line of 100% natural and organic frozen dinners. We know you'll love the great natural taste of Farm Fresh dinners such as Turkey and Wild Rice, Wild Salmon with Spring Greens, and Country Chicken with Vegetables. Farm Fresh dinners are _____ packaged with 100% recyclable materials.

16. (A) attract
    (B) attractive
    (C) attractively
    (D) attraction

But we don't have to use a lot of fancy words to convince you to enjoy Farm Fresh frozen dinners. We will let their great taste _____ you to keep coming back for more. Please use the enclosed

17. (A) convince
    (B) compete
    (C) consume
    (D) compare

coupons to buy up to six Farm Fresh dinners of your choice at 25% off the usual retail price. We know you _____ by the great taste and the great price.

18. (A) satisfy
    (B) satisfied
    (C) will satisfy
    (D) will be satisfied

Sincerely,

Rosa Martello
National Frozen Foods, Inc.

Part 7 Reading Comprehension

Questions 19–23 refer to the following report.

Catherine Cosmetics Company
Sales Department Meeting Report
March 29, 20—

We reviewed the sales figures for the past quarter. We are currently experiencing a significant drop in sales in our hair care products. This has been going on since the beginning of the year when we introduced the improved version of our top-selling hair care line, Catherine's Curls. Our advertising has not been successful in convincing more consumers to buy these products. We know there is a market for products such as these manufactured with 100% natural ingredients and no testing on animals. In fact, our competitors are doing quite well in this area and have been for a number of years. We know from our research that the popularity of all-natural cosmetic products is more than just a passing fad, and this is why we decided to branch out into this area. We have carefully compared our products to those of our three largest competitors. We have looked at product ingredients, packaging, target consumers, pricing, and sales strategies. Our product is similar, or even better, in all ways but one. Our packaging is significantly less eye-catching than that of our competitors, and it does not convey the important aspects of the products to the consumer, that is, that these products are entirely made with natural ingredients. Therefore, in order to attract more customers, we recommend employing a new designer to create better packaging for the Catherine's Curls line of products.

---

19. When did the sales department have a meeting?
    (A) At the beginning of the year.
    (B) In March.
    (C) A quarter of a year ago.
    (D) At the end of last year.

20. Which of the following might be part of the *Catherine's Curls* line of products?
    (A) Shampoo.
    (B) Hand lotion.
    (C) Nail polish.
    (D) Lipstick.

21. According to the report, why are fewer people buying *Catherine's Curls* products?
    (A) The prices are too high.
    (B) The ingredients aren't natural.
    (C) The packages aren't attractive.
    (D) The type of product is not popular.

22. The word *market* in line 6 is closest in meaning to
    (A) product
    (B) factory
    (C) purchase
    (D) demand

23. The word *fad* in line 10 is closest in meaning to
    (A) need
    (B) fashion
    (C) event
    (D) wish

Lesson 3

Warranties

WORDS TO LEARN

characteristic

consequence

consider

cover

expire

frequently

imply

promise

protect

reputation

require

variety

Study the following definitions and examples.

1. **characteristic** adj., revealing of individual traits; n., an individual trait
   a. That salesperson has an annoying characteristic—he always pushes his customers to buy the extended warranty.
   b. It is characteristic of this company to provide only a limited warranty with its products.

2. **consequence** n., that which follows necessarily
   a. The consequence of not following the service instructions for your car is that the warranty is invalidated.
   b. As a consequence of not having seen a dentist for several years, Lydia had several cavities.

3. **consider** v., to think about carefully
   a. The customer considered buying the computer until he learned that the warranty coverage was very limited.
   b. After considering all the options, Della decided to buy a used car.

4. **cover** v., to provide protection against
   a. The warranty covers the cost of all repairs for a period of one year.
   b. An extended warranty covers the product for a longer period of time.

5. **expire** v., to end
   a. Our contract with the cleaning company will expire next month.
   b. After the warranty expires, you will have to pay for repairs yourself.

6. **frequently** adv., occurring commonly; widespread
   a. Appliances frequently come with a one-year warranty.
   b. Warranties for this kind of appliance are frequently limited in their coverage.

7. **imply** v., to indicate by inference
   a. The salesperson implied that the warranty covered all damages to the iPad for one year.
   b. The warranty implies that repairs will take several weeks.

8. **promise** n., a pledge, a commitment; v., to pledge to do, bring about, or provide
   a. A warranty is a promise the manufacturer makes to the consumer.
   b. The sales associate promised that our new mattress would arrive by noon on Saturday.

9. **protect** v., to guard
   a. The warranty protects the consumer against a defective product.
   b. The warranty will protect you from spending a lot of money in repairs.

10. **reputation** n., the overall quality of character
    a. Even though the salesperson showed me a product I had never heard of, I bought it because of the good reputation of the manufacturer.
    b. The company knew that the reputation of its products was the most important asset it had.

11. **require** v., to deem necessary or essential
    a. A car warranty may require the owner to have it serviced by a certified mechanic.
    b. The law requires that each item clearly display the warranty information.

12. **variety** n., many different kinds
    a. There's a variety of standard terms that you'll find in warranties.
    b. A variety of unexpected problems appeared after the product had been on the market for about six months.

WORD FAMILIES

verb	characterize	A warranty is characterized by the length of its terms.
adjective	characteristic	It is characteristic of many companies to offer an extended warranty for a fee.
adverb	characteristically	A warranty characteristically provides for replacement or repair within certain time limits.

verb	consider	You should consider carefully whether a product will meet your needs.
noun	consideration	After long consideration, Heloise decided that the five-year warranty would be sufficient.
adjective	considerable	The fee for the extra year of protection was a considerable expense.

verb	imply	The salesperson implied that the cost of the extended warranty would be low.
noun	implication	The implication is that if you drop the product and it breaks, the repairs aren't covered by the warranty.
adjective	implicit	Correct use of the product by the consumer is implicit in the terms of the warranty.

verb	protect	Juan protected the warranty by taking excellent care of his lawn mower.
noun	protection	For your own protection, you should have a warranty that provides for a replacement product.
adjective	protective	Alfredo is very protective of the condition of his car and gets all the preventive maintenance his warranty requires.

noun	reputation	The good reputation of the manufacturer inspired Maria Jose to try the new product.
adjective	reputable	Because the company had a reputable name, I did not spend sufficient time reading the details of the warranty.
adjective	reputed	The new store is reputed to carry items that are not of the highest quality.

verb	require	The warranty requires that you send the product to an approved repair shop to have it fixed.
noun	requirement	The terms of the warranty divulge the legal requirement the manufacturer has to the consumer.
adjective	requisite	The warranty spelled out the requisite steps to take to request a replacement product.

WORDS IN CONTEXT

Read the following passage and write the words in the blanks below.

characteristics	covers	implies	reputations
consequences	expire	promise	required
consider	frequently	protect	variety

Warranties are a seller's (1) _____ to stand behind its products. Most major purchases such as computers or cars come with a warranty, as do smaller purchases such as stereos or other electronic housewares. Warranties are not (2) _____ by law, but are (3) _____ found on products. If you are making a purchase, you should (4) _____ the individual (5) _____ of a warranty, as not all warranties are the same. In fact, there is a great (6) _____ among them. Check the warranty to see what repairs it (7) _____ and for what amount of time. At the minimum, warranties are required to promise that the product will do what it (8) _____ that it will do; for example, that a blender will blend or a hair dryer will dry hair. Most warranties are good for a fixed time, then they (9) _____. You can (10) _____ yourself by buying products from companies with good (11) _____ and by taking good care of your new purchase. There are (12) _____ to not taking care of a product, as most warranties require that you use the product in a certain manner.

WORD PRACTICE

LISTENING COMPREHENSION

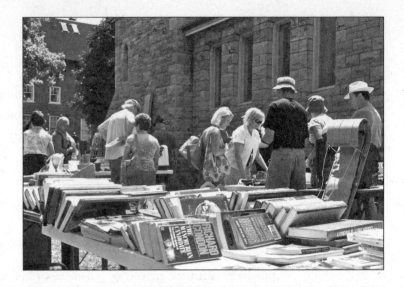

Part 1 Photo

Look at the picture and listen to the sentences.
Choose the sentence that best describes the picture.

1. Ⓐ Ⓑ Ⓒ Ⓓ

Part 2 Question–Response

Listen to the question and the three responses. Choose the response that best answers the question.

2. Ⓐ Ⓑ Ⓒ   3. Ⓐ Ⓑ Ⓒ

Part 3 Conversation

Listen to the dialogue. Then read each question and choose the best response.

4. How long is the basic warranty effective?
   (A) Thirty days.
   (B) Sixty days.
   (C) One year.
   (D) Two years.

5. What will happen if the woman uses an unapproved mechanic?
   (A) There are no consequences.
   (B) The warranty is no longer effective.
   (C) Protection is decreased by 50%.
   (D) She will have full coverage.

6. What does the woman decide to do?
   (A) Take her car to an approved mechanic.
   (B) Buy the extended warranty.
   (C) Refuse the basic warranty.
   (D) Buy a different car.

Part 4 Talk

Listen to the talk. Then read each question and choose the best answer.

7. What is the point of the talk?
   (A) Items under warranty must be fixed.
   (B) If an item is misused, the warranty may be invalidated.
   (C) Machines with unusual wear are difficult to repair.
   (D) Customers often don't understand warranties.

8. Who is the audience for this talk?
   (A) A factory repairperson.
   (B) A customer.
   (C) Someone who rents machines.
   (D) Buyers.

9. How can a customer receive money back for a defective product?
   (A) Follow the directions on the package.
   (B) Return it to the place of purchase.
   (C) Repackage it carefully.
   (D) Return it within 30 days.

READING

Part 5 Incomplete Sentences

Choose the word that best completes the sentence.

10. The timing belt _____ shows signs of wear after about 180,000 miles.
    (A) character   (C) characterize
    (B) characteristic (D) characteristically

11. Jacques and Louisa will only _____ purchasing appliances that come with a money-back guarantee.
    (A) consideration   (C) considering
    (B) consider   (D) considerable

12. If there is any _____ of the director's involvement, we need to follow up swiftly and thoroughly.
    (A) imply   (C) implicated
    (B) implicit   (D) implication

13. The level of _____ implied by the warranty was misleading.
    (A) protect   (C) protection
    (B) protective   (D) protector

14. It can be very helpful to consider the _____ of the manufacturer and the merchant when making a major purchase.
    (A) reputation   (C) reputing
    (B) reputable   (D) reputed

15. If the appliance breaks down within two years of purchase, the manufacturer is _____ to send you a replacement at no charge.
    (A) considered   (C) expired
    (B) protected   (D) required

Part 6 Text Completion

Choose the word or phrase that best completes the sentence.

One-Year Limited Warranty

This warranty _____ the purchaser from all malfunctions of the product due to defects in

16. (A) protects
    (B) protectors
    (C) protection
    (D) protective

materials or workmanship. Only the original purchaser of the product is covered. Resale of the product automatically invalidates this warranty. This warranty _____ the manufacturer to repair any

17. (A) require
    (B) requires
    (C) is requiring
    (D) has required

defective product or to refund the full purchase price to the purchaser, at the manufacturer's discretion. The manufacturer's liability does not exceed the purchase price of the product. This warranty does not imply that the purchaser has any rights in the case of a defective product beyond those stated herein. This warranty _____ one year from the date of purchase. A receipt or other proof of purchase is required

18. (A) should expire
    (B) might expire
    (C) will expire
    (D) can expire

in order to make claims under the terms of this warranty.

Part 7 Reading Comprehension

Questions 19–23 refer to the following two letters.

Kitchen Electronics, Inc.

October 12, 20—

Mrs. Sophie Bordeaux
118 Montrose Street
Stoneybrook, MI

Dear Mrs. Bordeaux,

We received the defective toaster which you returned to us asking for a full refund under the terms of the one-year warranty. Unfortunately, the warranty on the toaster expired a month ago. The terms of the warranty do not cover your product once it has expired. Consequently, we will not be able to send you a refund. However, we will be able to send you a refurbished toaster of the same model in exchange for the defective one if you desire. Please let us know if such an arrangement would be satisfactory to you.

Please don't hesitate to contact me if you have any questions. We appreciate your business.

Sincerely,

Matthew Bodine

Matthew Bodine
Customer Service Manager

November 1, 20—

Matthew Bodine
Customer Service Manager
Kitchen Electronics, Inc.
194294 Honeywell Boulevard
Victoria Springs, AL

Dear Mr. Bodine,

I have received your letter offering to send me a refurbished toaster in place of my defective one. I had not realized that my warranty had already expired. After considering the matter, I have decided to accept the refurbished toaster. Your company has a good reputation, and I frequently use your products. In fact, this is the first time I have ever had a problem with anything I have purchased from you. Therefore, I am sure that the refurbished toaster will work as well as a brand new one. However, I would like to be assured that the refurbished toaster will be protected by a warranty, just as a new toaster would be. If this is the case, then please send me the toaster as soon as possible. Thank you.

Sincerely,

Sophie Bordeaux

Sophie Bordeaux

---

19. Why did the customer return the toaster?
    (A) It doesn't work.
    (B) It was too expensive.
    (C) She wants a brand new one.
    (D) She prefers a different model.

20. When did she purchase the toaster?
    (A) A month ago.
    (B) Last October.
    (C) Exactly one year ago.
    (D) A little over a year ago.

21. What will she get in place of the returned toaster?
    (A) Nothing.
    (B) A refund.
    (C) A brand new toaster.
    (D) A different, repaired toaster.

22. The word *considering* in line 4 of the second letter is closest in meaning to
    (A) reading about
    (B) thinking about
    (C) talking about
    (D) worrying about

23. The word *frequently* in line 6 of the second letter is closest in meaning to
    (A) often
    (B) rarely
    (C) never
    (D) occasionally

Lesson 4

Business Planning

WORDS TO LEARN

address
avoid
demonstrate
develop
evaluate
gather
offer
primarily
risk
strategy
strengthen
substitution

Study the following definitions and examples.

1. **address** n., a formal speech; v., to direct attention to
   a. The article praised her address to the steering committee.
   b. Marco's business plan addresses the needs of small business owners.

2. **avoid** v., to stay clear of; to keep from happening
   a. To avoid going out of business, owners should prepare a proper business plan.
   b. Lloyd's errors in accounting could have been avoided by a business consultation with his banker.

3. **demonstrate** v., to show clearly and deliberately; to present by example
   a. Alban's business plan demonstrated that he had put a lot of thought into making his dream a reality.
   b. The professor demonstrated through a case study that a business plan can impress a lender.

4. **develop** v., to expand, progress, or improve
   a. Lily developed her ideas into a business plan by taking a class at the community college.
   b. The restaurant Wanda opened ten years ago has developed into a national chain.

5. **evaluate** v., to determine the value or impact of
   a. It's important to evaluate your competition when making a business plan.
   b. The lenders evaluated our creditability and decided to loan us money.

6. **gather** v., to accumulate; to conclude
   a. We gathered information for our plan from many sources.
   b. I gather that interest rates for small businesses will soon change.

7. **offer** n., a proposal; v., to propose; to present in order to meet a need or satisfy a requirement
   a. Devon accepted our offer to write the business plan.
   b. Jackie must offer her banker new statistics in order to encourage the bank to lend her money toward her start-up business.

8. **primarily** adv., first; most importantly
   a. We are primarily concerned with convincing the board of directors to apply for the second loan.
   b. The developers are thinking primarily of how to enter the South American market.

9. **risk** n., the chance of loss or damage
   a. The primary risk for most start-up businesses is insufficient capital.
   b. Expanding into a new market is a big risk.

10. **strategy** n., a plan of action
    a. A business plan is a strategy for running a business and avoiding problems.
    b. Let's develop a strategy for promoting our ice cream parlor.

11. **strengthen** v., make stronger or more powerful
    a. You can strengthen your plan by including the possibility of rising costs.
    b. We are working on a plan to strengthen sales over the next two quarters.

12. **substitution** n., replacement
    a. Your substitution of fake names for real ones makes the document seem insincere.
    b. There is no substitution for hard work and perseverance.

WORD FAMILIES

verb	avoid	It is best to avoid get-rich-quick schemes.
noun	avoidance	Your avoidance of these issues will not make them go away.
adjective	avoided	The avoided question became more important over time.

verb	demonstrate	A business plan demonstrates how the business will make money and pay expenses.
noun	demonstration	The business professor gave a demonstration of how to develop a business plan.
adjective	demonstrative	The failure of that business is demonstrative of what can happen when there is no business plan.

verb	develop	Our assignment is to develop a sample business plan.
noun	development	The plan is under development and will not be ready for a while.
noun	developer	The plan developers worked hard to make sure they had considered all the possibilities.

verb	evaluate	Please review these articles and evaluate their usefulness for our plan.
noun	evaluation	Yoko feared the professor's evaluation of her business plan.
noun	evaluator	The independent evaluator reviewed our business plan and gave us good feedback.

verb	strategize	Instead of going into a panic, let's strategize the best way to meet the deadline.
noun	strategy	The business plan lays out a strategy for future growth.
adjective	strategic	The handout outlined the strategic points to cover in a business plan.

verb	substitute	No amount of intelligence can substitute for good planning.
noun	substitution	The substitution of one amount for another made a big difference in their business plan.
adjective	substituted	The substituted amount was much larger than the original amount.

WORDS IN CONTEXT

Read the following passage and write the words in the blanks below.

address	develop	offered	strategy
avoid	evaluation	primary	strengthen
demonstrate	gathering	risks	substitute

Every business must (1) _____ a business plan. The business plan's (2) _____ purpose is to improve the entrepreneur's control over the business and to help him (3) _____ common mistakes. There is no (4) _____ for a well-prepared business plan. It is the way to (5) _____ the business and help it improve in all areas. The business plan documents the (6) _____ for growing the business. Think of the business plan as a road map that describes in which direction the company is going, what its goals are, and how it is going to get there.

In developing the plan, the entrepreneur will conduct research to determine a systematic and realistic (7) _____ of the company's chances for success in the marketplace. In creating the plan, the entrepreneur must research the company's target market and define its potential. The entrepreneur must be able to prove through research that customers in the market need the good or service that is (8) _____ and that a sufficient number of potential customers exists to support the business.

A business plan also looks at the (9) _____ the business faces. Chief among these is competitors. The business plan must analyze the company's competition by (10) _____ information on competitors' market share, products, and strategies. The plan should (11) _____ what distinguishes the entrepreneur's products or services from others already in the market. It is also common for businesses to fail because the owner fails to invest or seek sufficient capital to run the business. A good business plan should (12) _____ this issue as well.

WORD PRACTICE

LISTENING COMPREHENSION

TRACK
5

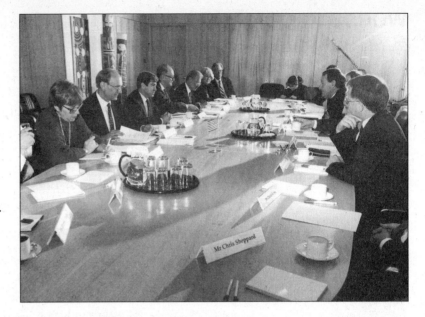

Part 1 Photo

Look at the picture and listen to the sentences.
Choose the sentence that best describes the picture.

1. Ⓐ Ⓑ Ⓒ Ⓓ

Part 2 Question–Response

Listen to the question and the three responses. Choose the response that best answers the question.

2. Ⓐ Ⓑ Ⓒ   3. Ⓐ Ⓑ Ⓒ

Part 3 Conversation

Listen to the dialogue. Then read each question and choose the best response.

4. How do the speakers feel about Alexa's business plan?
    (A) She has gathered too much data.
    (B) She has taken on too much risk.
    (C) She has made many obvious mistakes.
    (D) She is serious-minded and cautious.

5. How will the man help Alexa?
    (A) By doing market research.
    (B) By searching for an office.
    (C) By pointing out her mistakes.
    (D) By nominating her for an award.

6. According to the man, what is the most important strategy for success?
    (A) Investing in a good sound system.
    (B) Having a good business plan.
    (C) Eliminating all risk.
    (D) Studying the market.

Part 4 Talk

Listen to the talk. Then read each question and choose the best answer.

7. What is the topic of the talk?
    (A) Long-term growth plans.
    (B) An offer for a leveraged buyout.
    (C) How to minimize risk.
    (D) Where to borrow funds.

8. How will the company fund its growth?
    (A) Bank loans.
    (B) Profits.
    (C) Sale of stocks.
    (D) Owner investment.

9. When will the evaluation begin?
    (A) At the end of this year.
    (B) At the beginning of next year.
    (C) In two years.
    (D) In a few years.

READING

Part 5 Incomplete Sentences

Choose the word that best completes the sentence.

10. You cannot _____ learning how to use the new software as it will be needed in daily operations from now on.
    (A) avoid   (C) avoiding
    (B) avoided   (D) avoidance

11. I don't want to intrude, but would you like me to _____ how to use that machine?
    (A) demonstrate   (C) demonstrative
    (B) demonstration (D) demonstrator

12. While you are _____ your business plan, it is a good idea to keep a resource library of valuable materials.
    (A) develop   (C) developing
    (B) development   (D) developer

13. After you turn in your business plan, you will receive a written _____ of your work within two weeks.
    (A) evaluator   (C) evaluate
    (B) evaluative   (D) evaluation

14. If we think _____, we can come up with a plan that promises success.
    (A) strategize   (C) strategically
    (B) strategic   (D) strategist

15. It is now legal to _____ a generic brand drug for a prescription medicine if you have the patient's consent.
    (A) substitute   (C) substituting
    (B) substituted   (D) substitution

Part 6 Text Completion

Memo

To: Stephen Saunders, President
From: Willa Richardson, Marketing Department
Re: Changes in market

In order to address the changes that are currently taking place in the market, I believe we need to modify our business plan. I have been _____ data for the past several months. The information clearly shows

16. (A) substituting
    (B) addressing
    (C) avoiding
    (D) gathering

that younger and younger people are becoming interested in purchasing products such as ours. We need to develop a _____ to reach this younger age group. We need to redirect some of our resources

17. (A) strategy
    (B) strategize
    (C) strategic
    (D) strategically

toward this goal. I think if we make this a priority over the next year, we will be able to _____

18. (A) strong
    (B) strength
    (C) strengthen
    (D) stengthened

our position against our competitors. If we don't, we risk losing the market share that we already have. I would like to share the results of my research with you. It demonstrates the need to focus our energy toward this younger age group. Please let me know if we can meet this week to discuss it.

Part 7 Reading Comprehension

Questions 19–23 refer to the following article.

When developing a plan for a new business, the entrepreneur quite naturally wants to eliminate all risk. While it is impossible to avoid some risk, the goal is to minimize it as much as possible. How can we do this? Thorough research and careful planning are the keys. There are two parts to good research. First, you must demonstrate that there is a need for the product or service you plan to offer. Are there enough people out there who would be willing to pay for it? Second, you must look at your competition. What do you have to offer that your competitors do not? Is your product or service of better quality in some way? Is it cheaper or more easily available? Is there a niche in the market that your competitors are not addressing? If what you have to offer is identical to what your competitors are offering, your business is not likely to be successful. These are some things to consider when evaluating how well you can measure up against the competition. Once you have evaluated a need for your product or service and determined how yours will be different from your competitors', you are ready to begin the next part of your plan — financing.

19. What is this article mostly about?
    (A) Financing new businesses.
    (B) How to price products.
    (C) The need for research.
    (D) The best marketing strategies.

20. What does the author say about risk?
    (A) We should try to reduce it.
    (B) We must avoid it.
    (C) We can eliminate it with careful planning.
    (D) It is the key to success.

21. According to the article, what can lead to the failure of a new business?
    (A) Offering a cheaper product.
    (B) Selling the exact same product that the competitors sell.
    (C) Selling only to a niche in the market.
    (D) Offering only services and not products.

22. The word *addressing* in line 13 is closest in meaning to
    (A) focusing on
    (B) calling on
    (C) giving up
    (D) staying away from

23. The word *demonstrate* in line 6 is closest in meaning to
    (A) feel
    (B) create
    (C) remove
    (D) show

Lesson 5

Conferences

Study the following definitions and examples.

1. **accommodate** v., to fit; to provide with something needed
   a. The meeting room was large enough to accommodate the various needs of the groups using it.
   b. Because the deadline for reserving rooms was past, the hotel manager could not accommodate our need for more rooms.

2. **arrangement** n., a plan or organization
   a. The travel arrangements were taken care of by Sara, Mr. Billings's capable assistant.
   b. The arrangement of speakers was alphabetical to avoid any hurt feelings.

3. **association** n., an organization of persons or groups having a common interest; a relationship or society
   a. Membership in a trade or professional association provides business contacts and mutual support.
   b. Because of his association with the director of the conference, we were able to get good prices for the use of the rooms.

4. **attend** v., to go to; to pay attention to
   a. We expect more than 100 members to attend the annual meeting.
   b. The hotel manager attended to all our needs promptly.

5. **get in touch** v., to make contact with
   a. As soon as we arrive at the hotel, we will get in touch with the manager about the unexpected guests.
   b. The registration desk is a good central location for people to get in touch with each other.

6. **hold** v., to contain; to conduct
   a. This meeting room holds at least 80 people comfortably.
   b. She holds an annual seminar that is very popular.

7. **location** n., a position or site
   a. The location of the meeting was changed from the Red Room to the Green Room.
   b. Disney World was the perfect location for the annual meeting since many members could bring their families.

8. **overcrowded** adj., too crowded
   a. As soon as the guests entered the dining room for dinner, Sue Lin could see that the room would become overcrowded.
   b. To avoid being overcrowded, we limited the number of guests that members could bring.

9. **register** n., a record; v., to record
   a. According to the register, more than 250 people attended the afternoon seminar.
   b. Hotels ask all guests to register and give a home address.

10. **select** v., to choose from a group; adj., specially chosen
    a. The conference participant selected the marketing seminar from the various offerings.
    b. The winners were a select group.

11. **session** n., a meeting
    a. The morning sessions tend to fill up first, so sign up early.
    b. Due to the popularity of this course, we will offer two sessions.

12. **take part in** v., to join and participate in
    a. The format for the session is very informal, which makes it easier for people to take part in the discussion.
    b. We could not get enough people to take part in the meeting, so we canceled it.

WORD FAMILIES

verb	accommodate	The hotel staff was able to accommodate our many needs for the conference.
noun	accommodation	The accommodations at the hotel include a swimming pool, gym, and restaurant.
adjective	accommodating	The conference center manager was extremely accommodating and tried to make our stay pleasant.

noun	arrangement	Nobody could understand the seating arrangement.
verb	arrange	We will arrange the chairs in a circle.
adjective	arranged	The arranged flowers didn't look like those we chose from the catalog.

noun	association	Any association with the former company will put us in a negative light.
verb	associate	Do you think customers will associate the failed upstart with ours?
adjective	associated	The associated costs will put this project out of our reach.

verb	attend	Gillian attended the reception for visiting ambassadors.
noun	attendee	More than 500 attendees packed the ballroom.
noun	attendance	Attendance was low for this year's annual meeting.

verb	register	You can register for the conference by going to the conference website.
noun	register	The hotel's register showed that only half the attendees had arrived.
noun	registration	Registration is very easy because all the information and forms can be found on the conference website.

verb	select	Since there are overlapping workshops, participants will have to select which one most appeals to them.
noun	selection	His dinner selection of stuffed quail sounded better on the menu than it looked on the plate.
adjective	selective	The planning committee was very selective about who received invitations.

WORDS IN CONTEXT

Read the following passage and write the words in the blanks below.

accommodate	attending	location	select
arrangements	get in touch	overcrowded	sessions
associations	hold	register	take part in

Many (1) _____ and organizations hold annual conferences so that their members can (2) _____ with each other and (3) _____ educational programs. When planning a conference, event coordinators try to have a variety of (4) _____ so people (5) _____ can (6) _____ a workshop or meeting that best suits their needs. When making (7) _____ for a conference, they look for a site that will (8) _____ all their needs. They want to (9) _____ the conference at a place that is large enough for the number of people expected to attend, without the meeting rooms being (10) _____. Good event coordinators tour the site before making a final decision because brochures cannot show all the necessary details. Having meetings in a fun (11) _____ can really encourage people to (12) _____ for the meeting.

WORD PRACTICE

LISTENING COMPREHENSION

Part 1 Photo

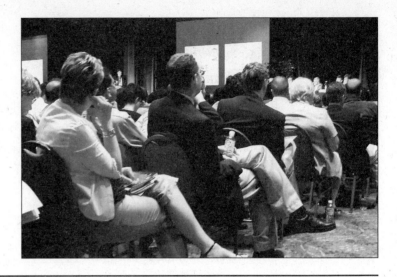

Look at the picture and listen to the sentences.
Choose the sentence that best describes the picture.

1. Ⓐ Ⓑ Ⓒ Ⓓ

Part 2 Question–Response

Listen to the question and the three responses. Choose the response that best answers the question.

2. Ⓐ Ⓑ Ⓒ   3. Ⓐ Ⓑ Ⓒ

Part 3 Conversation

Listen to the dialogue. Then read each question and choose the best response.

4. Why are they having difficulty arranging a site for the conference?
   (A) It's a busy time of year.
   (B) They procrastinated.
   (C) Their group is large.
   (D) The coordinator has been sick.

5. When will the conference take place?
   (A) At the end of this month.
   (B) Next month.
   (C) At the end of this year.
   (D) Next year.

6. How many people do they expect at the conference?
   (A) Two hundred.
   (B) Four hundred.
   (C) Five hundred.
   (D) Ten hundred.

Part 4 Talk

Listen to the talk. Then read each question and choose the best answer.

7. What is the topic of the talk?
   (A) Accommodating disabled people.
   (B) Legal responsibility for off-site events.
   (C) Arranging conferences.
   (D) Preparing convention catalogs.

8. What is true of the facility belonging to the speaker's company?
   (A) It is inconvenient for participants with disabilities.
   (B) It cannot accommodate hearing impaired attendees.
   (C) It is only available for certain types of events.
   (D) It is accessible to people with disabilities.

9. How should attendees request a special interpreter?
   (A) By asking for one at the time of registration.
   (B) By getting in touch with the head of the facility.
   (C) By registering ahead of the other attendees.
   (D) By requesting one when they arrive at a session.

READING

Part 5 Incomplete Sentences

Choose the word that best completes the sentence.

10. The banquet room can _____ up to 750 people for dinner.
    (A) select
    (B) hold
    (C) attend
    (D) arrange

11. Helen made the final _____ for use of the conference room with the hotel's general manager.
    (A) arranging
    (B) arrange
    (C) arrangement
    (D) arranged

12. For most people, Samco is _____ with computer chip production.
    (A) associate
    (B) associated
    (C) associating
    (D) association

13. We expect that fewer guests will _____ the evening gala.
    (A) attend
    (B) attending
    (C) attention
    (D) attendance

14. The association's members were asked to _____ for the special session well in advance because space in the lecture hall was limited.
    (A) register
    (B) registration
    (C) registering
    (D) registrar

15. By adding more class _____, the staff was able to please more members.
    (A) select
    (B) selective
    (C) selecting
    (D) selections

Part 6 Text Completion

All members of the Countywide Small Business Owners Association are invited to take part in our annual conference, to be held on March 31 at the Grand Hotel in Marysville.

The conference begins at 8:30 A.M. with an address by this year's guest, Cynthia Quinn, owner of Designs by Cynthia, Inc., and winner of numerous business and community awards. Morning small group sessions begin at 9:30. Attendees can _____ from a variety of session topics including Financing Your New

16. (A) select
    (B) selection
    (C) selective
    (D) selectively

Business; Selecting the Best Location; and Formulas for Success. Lunch will be served at 12:30, followed by afternoon small group sessions at 2:00.

This is the Association's most popular event, so _____ early to assure your place. Complete the

17. (A) will register
    (B) must register
    (C) registering
    (D) register

registration form and make your payment at csboa.com/conference_reg before March 1. Follow the same link to arrange your overnight _____ at the Grand Hotel and receive the special conference

18. (A) accommodate
    (B) accommodating
    (C) accommodations
    (D) accommodates

discount price.

Part 7 Reading Comprehension

Questions 19–23 refer to the following two e-mails.

To: Max Sullivan
From: Martha Reynolds
Subj: Conference

Max,

I have been working on the arrangements for our upcoming conference. I've looked into the City Convention Center, and I think it is the most convenient location. It is close to public transportation and hotels. The accommodations are also excellent. The rooms are large, and we can reserve up to ten meeting rooms. However, the price is almost 50% more than we agreed we could spend. The other choice is the Mayfield Hotel. Many associations hold their conventions there. It is a nice place, and the price is reasonable. However, it is not close to the subway. Also, it is much smaller than the Convention Center. I think we could only get three meeting rooms. Would that be enough? Please get in touch with me today to let me know what you think. I need to reserve a place soon.

Martha

To: Martha Reynolds
From: Max Sullivan
Subj: Re: Conference

Martha,

In regard to selecting a location for the conference, I think the Convention Center is better than the Mayfield Hotel. The hotel is much too small. Remember, we plan to hold at least five sessions at a time. We couldn't do that at the hotel. We expect more people to take part in the convention this year, so it is important to have a space that can accommodate everyone. About the price, I think we can rearrange the budget a bit in order to be able to pay for it. So go ahead and reserve the space at the Convention Center.

Max

---

19. What are these e-mails about?
    (A) The date of the conference.
    (B) The conference site.
    (C) The topics of the conference sessions.
    (D) The number of conference attendees.

20. How many meeting rooms will they need?
    (A) Only three.
    (B) At least five.
    (C) Up to ten.
    (D) Almost 50.

21. What does Max prefer about the Convention Center?
    (A) The price.
    (B) The location.
    (C) The size.
    (D) The people.

22. The words *get in touch* in line 16 of the first e-mail are closest in meaning to
    (A) offer
    (B) discuss
    (C) provide
    (D) contact

23. The word *selecting* in line 1 of the second e-mail is closest in meaning to
    (A) choosing
    (B) reserving
    (C) comparing
    (D) seeking

Word Review #1   Lessons 1–5 General Business

Choose the word that best completes the sentence.

1. Although negotiating a new contract was complicated, both parties came to an _____ that satisfied them.
   (A) address
   (B) reputation
   (C) agreement
   (D) implication

2. _____ conferences are a good way for employees to get in touch with people in similar organizations.
   (A) Associating
   (B) Associated
   (C) Associations
   (D) Association

3. When the family decided to open a restaurant, they had to find a _____ that would attract business.
   (A) locate
   (B) locator
   (C) locating
   (D) location

4. A _____ company will honor the terms set forth in its warranty.
   (A) repute
   (B) reputedly
   (C) reputation
   (D) reputable

5. The goal of marketing is to _____ customers, to persuade them to buy a product or service.
   (A) attract
   (B) specify
   (C) compare
   (D) consume

6. Once both parties have agreed to a contract, they have also agreed to abide by every _____ provision.
   (A) specify
   (B) specific
   (C) specification
   (D) specificity

7. Good business planning includes developing an overall _____, addressing likely objections, and demonstrating why potential buyers need the product or service.
   (A) strategy
   (B) strategic
   (C) strategically
   (D) strategize

8. When you register for out-of-town conferences, make room _____ as soon as you decide to attend.
   (A) accommodate
   (B) accommodations
   (C) accommodating
   (D) accommodated

9. Marketers must avoid making promises they can't keep while they _____ the quality of their product or service.
   (A) demonstrate
   (B) demonstration
   (C) demonstrative
   (D) demonstrable

10. A consultant must adhere carefully to his contract if he wants to _____ a good business reputation.
    (A) establish
    (B) establishment
    (C) established
    (D) establishing

Choose the one word or phrase that best completes each sentence.

Are you looking for a place _____ your next conference? The Littleton Convention Center offers a convenient location at

        11. (A) hold
            (B) holding
            (C) will hold
            (D) to hold

an affordable price. Whether your event is big or small, our site can accommodate your needs. We offer meeting rooms, several auditoriums, and a large exhibition hall. Catering services are also available. Get _____ touch with us at 555-0964 to

        12. (A) on
            (B) in
            (C) at
            (D) to

make arrangements for your event. We know you'll _____ with our services.

        13. (A) satisfy
            (B) satisfied
            (C) be satisfied
            (D) be satisfying

Smart _____ compare prices before they buy. That's why nine out of ten shoppers choose Star Brand

14. (A) presumers
    (B) consumers
    (C) assumers
    (D) resumers

household cleaning products. Star Brand products are the most efficient cleaning products around. They can clean even the toughest stains and dirt because they are _____ with bleach. Every Star Brand

        15. (A) strengthened
            (B) strengths
            (C) strongly
            (D) strong

product comes with the company promise: If you are not 100% satisfied, your money will be returned with no questions asked. Next time you are shopping for cleaning products, _____ Star Brand. We know you'll

        16. (A) consideration
            (B) considering
            (C) consider
            (D) considers

be happy you did.

When purchasing a new appliance, check to make sure that a warranty is included. This _____

17. (A) offer
    (B) offers
    (C) are offering
    (D) have offered

important protection to you, the consumer. If you decide to return a product that is under warranty, you will have _____ that any damage was not caused by misuse or mishandling. Also, make certain that

18. (A) demonstration
    (B) demonstrative
    (C) demonstrator
    (D) to demonstrate

you return a damaged product before the warranty _____. Companies do not have to accept products

19. (A) respires
    (B) inspires
    (C) expires
    (D) perspires

that are returned after the date stated in the warranty.

Lesson 6

Computers and the Internet

Study the following definitions and examples.

1. **access** n., the ability or right to enter or use; v., to obtain; to gain entry
   a. You can't gain access to the files unless you know the password.
   b. We accessed the information on the company's website.

2. **allocate** v., to designate for a specific purpose
   a. The office manager did not allocate enough money to purchase software.
   b. We will need to allocate more space on the website for advertising.

3. **compatible** adj., able to function together
   a. This operating system is not compatible with this model computer.
   b. Users of software applications want new versions to be compatible with current versions.

4. **delete** v., to remove; to erase
   a. The technicians deleted all the data on the disk accidentally.
   b. This button on the keyboard deletes the characters from the screen.

5. **display** n., what is visible on a monitor; v., to show
   a. The light on the LCD display is too weak.
   b. The web page does not display secure information such as passwords and credit card numbers.

6. **duplicate** v., to produce something equal; to make identical
   a. I think the new word processing program will duplicate the success of the one introduced last year.
   b. Duplicate the file and save it in another place.

7. **failure** n., an unsuccessful work or effort
   a. Your failure to inform us about the changed password cost the company a day's work.
   b. The repeated failure of her printer baffled the technician.

8. **figure out** v., to understand; to solve
   a. By examining all of the errors, the technicians figured out how to fix the problem.
   b. We figured out that it would take us at least ten minutes to download the file.

9. **ignore** v., not to notice; to disregard
   a. When the director is working at the computer, she ignores everything around her.
   b. Don't ignore the technician's advice when connecting cables.

10. **search** n., investigation; v., to look for
    a. Our search of the database produced very little information.
    b. If you search the Internet, I'm sure you'll find all the information you need.

11. **shut down** v., to turn off; to cease operations
    a. Please shut down the computer before you leave.
    b. We decided to shut down the blog after receiving so many bad comments.

12. **warning** n., an alert to danger or problems
    a. The red flashing light gives a warning to users that the battery is low.
    b. Flashing images on a web page are warnings to attract users' attention.

WORD FAMILIES

verb	access	In many cafés you can access the Internet free of charge.
noun	access	You need a password to gain access to the online database.
adjective	accessible	Some people are so busy that they are accessible only by e-mail.

verb	allocate	Maria didn't allocate enough time to train the new staff members on our computer system.
noun	allocation	We need to change our allocation of resources so that we can spend more money on building our website.
adjective	allocated	The allocated money was never spent on new computers.

verb	duplicate	As we introduce this year's new line of products, we hope to duplicate the success we had with last year's products.
noun	duplicate	You should delete all duplicates from your computer.
noun	duplication	We want our website to be completely original and to avoid the duplication of sites that are already online.

noun	failure	The power failure caused the system to shut down.
verb	fail	We failed to tell you that your records were deleted.
adjective	fallible	Everyone can make a mistake. Even a computer is fallible.

verb	ignore	Unfortunately, she ignored the warning about the virus.
noun	ignorance	His ignorance of this word processing program surprised everyone.
adjective	ignored	The ignored computer glitch caused the database to function improperly.

verb	warn	We were warned that our e-mail was not private.
noun	warning	The warning was written on the box.
adjective	warning	The warning signs were all there; we should have paid attention to them.

WORDS IN CONTEXT

Read the following passage and write the words in the blanks below.

access	deleted	failed	search
allocate	display	figure out	shut down
compatible	duplicate	ignore	warning

When I try to (1) _____ my computer, a (2) _____ pops up that says "Low Memory." From there, I can't (3) _____ what to do. The computer won't let me (4) _____ any of my files, so I can't (5) _____ for those that I could delete. I've already (6) _____ all of my (7) _____ files, and I can't believe that my remaining files are using up so much memory. I'd be happy to (8) _____ the computer's warning, but I have no option, since the (9) _____ is frozen on this message. Do you think I've (10) _____ to understand something about the operations of this computer? If you can, would you please (11) _____ a few minutes in your busy schedule to help me solve this dilemma? As I said before, I'm sure that my software is (12) _____ and is not the source of this problem.

WORD PRACTICE
LISTENING COMPREHENSION

Part 1 Photo

Look at the picture and listen to the sentences.
Choose the sentence that best describes the picture.

1. Ⓐ Ⓑ Ⓒ Ⓓ

Part 2 Question–Response

Listen to the question and the three responses. Choose the response that best answers the question.

2. Ⓐ Ⓑ Ⓒ   3. Ⓐ Ⓑ Ⓒ

Part 3 Conversation

Listen to the dialogue. Then read each question and choose the best response.

4. What happens when the man tries to access his
   e-mail?
   (A) The computer shuts down.
   (B) A warning appears on the screen.
   (C) He hears a beeping noise.
   (D) The screen turns black.

5. What will the man do now?
   (A) Turn off the computer.
   (B) Get a new monitor.
   (C) Use a different program.
   (D) Wait some more time.

6. What does the woman suggest doing?
   (A) Working harder.
   (B) Taking the computer back to the store.
   (C) Calling someone to fix the computer.
   (D) Ignoring the problem.

Part 4 Talk

Listen to the talk. Then read each question and choose the best answer.

7. What does the speaker suggest that listeners do?
   (A) Buy her software.
   (B) Read the manual.
   (C) Figure out the program by tinkering with it.
   (D) Consult the competitor's manual to check for
      compatibility.

8. What problems could users face?
   (A) Their warranties could be invalidated.
   (B) Their warning systems could malfunction.
   (C) Their computers could shut down without
      warning.
   (D) Their manuals could be inaccurate.

9. What does the speaker recommend doing with files?
   (A) Reading them.
   (B) Accessing them.
   (C) Deleting them.
   (D) Copying them.

READING

Part 5 Incomplete Sentences

Choose the word that best completes the sentence.

10. In order to _____ your e-mail messages, you must type in your password.
    (A) access
    (B) accessible
    (C) accessed
    (D) accessibility

11. After reviewing the schedule, I realized we had not _____ enough time for the software training.
    (A) allocate
    (B) allocated
    (C) allocating
    (D) allocation

12. The computer staff is responsible for making sure all system files are _____.
    (A) duplication
    (B) duplicated
    (C) duplicator
    (D) duplicate

13. _____ to maintain the website is the main reason why sales are down.
    (A) Fail
    (B) Failure
    (C) Failed
    (D) Fallible

14. She _____ the warning that the hard drive was full, and consequently they were unable to save the test data.
    (A) ignore
    (B) ignored
    (C) ignoring
    (D) ignorant

15. The computer will _____ you to save your work before quitting.
    (A) warning
    (B) warned
    (C) warn
    (D) warns

Part 6 Text Completion

MEMO

```
To:   All Office Staff
From: IT Department
Re:   Avoiding Computer Problems
```

We are here to help you with any problems you may have with your computer. Please make our job easier by observing the following guidelines.

• If you have problems seeing the _____, check to make sure that your

16. (A) keyboard
    (B) display
    (C) printer
    (D) controls

monitor is turned on.

• If your computer crashes, write down any warning message that appears. We can _____ a problem more easily if we have this information.

17. (A) figure out
    (B) to figure out
    (C) will figure out
    (D) figures out

• Please do not install any new software without our approval. Some software is not compatible with what is already on the computer and can cause problems.
• Some parts of the company website are _____ without a password. If you

18. (A) accesses
    (B) accessing
    (C) accessible
    (D) inaccessible

need a password, please let us know and we will assign you one.

Part 7 Reading Comprehension

Questions 19–23 refer to the following note.

Jim,

I have decided to get a new computer for my home office, and I need your advice to help me select the right one. I have allocated a certain amount of money from my budget for this. I think it is enough for a completely new system including computer, monitor, printer, and scanner. I would like to continue using the software I already use, so I need a system that is compatible with my current system and software. However, I think I should get a different brand. I have had nothing but trouble with the computer I have now. It often shuts down without warning, and sometimes I can't access my files. I haven't been able to figure out the reason for these problems, and no one has been able to fix it for me.

I plan to go to some stores this Saturday and Sunday to search for my new computer. Would you be able to go with me? If not, I'll call you before the weekend to get your advice. I have a big project coming up next month, so I would like to get my new computer up and running soon. Let me know if you can help me this weekend.

Janet

19. What does Janet want Jim to help her with?
    (A) Finding money to buy a computer.
    (B) Accessing her files.
    (C) Choosing a new computer.
    (D) Repairing her computer.

20. What does Janet plan to do this weekend?
    (A) Call Jim.
    (B) Go on a date with Jim.
    (C) Look for a new computer.
    (D) Figure out the reason for her problems.

21. When will Janet's big project begin?
    (A) Saturday.
    (B) Sunday.
    (C) Before the weekend.
    (D) Next month.

22. The word *allocated* in line 3 is closest in meaning to
    (A) earned
    (B) designated
    (C) borrowed
    (D) removed

23. The word *access* in line 10 is closest in meaning to
    (A) save
    (B) write
    (C) close
    (D) open

Lesson 7

Office Technology

WORDS TO LEARN

affordable

as needed

capacity

durable

in charge

initiative

physically

provider

recur

reduction

stay on top of

stock

Study the following definitions and examples.

1. **affordable** adj., able to be paid for; not too expensive
   a. The company's first priority was to find an affordable phone system.
   b. Obviously, the computer systems that are affordable for a Fortune 500 company will not be affordable for a small company.

2. **as needed** adv., as necessary
   a. The courier service did not come every day, only as needed.
   b. The service contract states that repairs will be made on an as-needed basis.

3. **capacity** n., the ability to contain or hold; the maximum that something can hold or do
   a. We need a small room that has the capacity to hold two photocopiers as well as shelves for paper and other supplies.
   b. The memory requirements of this software application exceed the capacity of our computers.

4. **durable** adj., sturdy, strong, lasting
   a. This printer is so durable that, with a little care, it will last another five years.
   b. The phone is very durable; I've dropped it several times and it still works well.

5. **in charge** adj., in control
   a. He appointed someone to be in charge of maintaining a supply of paper in the fax machine.
   b. Your computer should not be in charge of you, rather you should be in charge of your computer.

6. **initiative** n., the first step; an active role
   a. Employees are encouraged to take the initiative to discuss their technology needs with management.
   b. Our technology initiative involves an exciting new database system and will help us revolutionize our customer service.

7. **physically** adv., with the senses; of the body
   a. The computer screen is making her physically sick.
   b. Physically moving your screen from one place on the desk to another can help reduce same-position-strain syndrome.

8. **provider** n., a supplier
   a. The department was extremely pleased with the service they received from the phone provider.
   b. We need to find a new provider of supplies for our photocopier.

9. **recur** v., to occur again or repeatedly
   a. The need for repairs to the photocopier recurs too often.
   b. The managers did not want that particular error to recur.

10. **reduction** n., a lessening; a decrease
    a. The outlet store gave a 20 percent reduction in the price of the shelves and bookcases.
    b. The reduction in office staff has made it necessary to automate more job functions.

11. **stay on top of** v., to know what is going on; to know the latest information
    a. It's important to stay on top of supplies for the printers and reorder them before they run out.
    b. In this industry, you must stay on top of current developments.

12. **stock** v., to keep on hand; n., a supply
    a. Please stock the shelves with a large supply of ink and paper for the printers.
    b. The office's stock of toner for the photocopier was quickly running out.

WORD FAMILIES

verb	afford	Our office really needs new printers, but we can't afford to buy them this year.
noun	affordability	We looked into the affordability of buying a photocopier with a larger capacity.
adjective	affordable	A lot of office technology that was expensive in the past has now become more affordable.

verb	initiate	The company will initiate the use of smartphones this year.
noun	initiative	The manager, knowing how concerned his employees were, took the initiative to provide training for them on the new equipment.
adjective	initiation	The initiation of the new computer system was welcomed by the entire office staff.

noun	physique	Moving all that office equipment around will certainly help you develop a good physique.
adjective	physical	The physical presence of a computer engineer is much better than telephone tech support.
adverb	physically	Sitting at a computer all day may help you get your work done, but it isn't good for you physically.

verb	provide	The company provides a five-year warranty on its products.
noun	provider	As your provider of network services, I promise to give you the best prices and service.
noun	provision	Our provisions of supplies should last to the end of the quarter.

verb	recur	We don't want that problem to recur every month.
noun	recurrence	Every recurrence of the same problem costs us money.
adjective	recurring	Recurring problems waste time and money.

verb	reduce	Buying in bulk can help to reduce costs.
noun	reduction	Disconnecting the fax machine created a noticeable reduction in phone bills.
adjective	reducible	Although our system is working at capacity, the amount of information being processed is not reducible.

WORDS IN CONTEXT

Read the following passage and write the words in the blanks below.

affordable	durable	physical	reduce
as needed	in charge	provider	stays on top of
capacity	initiates	recurring	stock

Many companies have one person or a department that is (1) _____ of running the office. If you have ever worked for a company that doesn't have an office manager, you very quickly learn to appreciate the importance of the job. Who is in charge of placing orders? Who services the fax machine or printer? Who makes sure that the office is presentable for customers? Are the new conference tables and shelves (2) _____ enough to withstand heavy use? Are they (3) _____ for the office budget?

It is the office manager's responsibility to maintain an efficient and smooth-running office. He or she looks for ways to (4) _____ costs and minimize interruptions in the day-to-day operations. Whereas functional managers know the (5) _____ of their employees, the office manager knows the (6) _____ capacity of the office and the supplies and machines that are in the office.

The office manager (7) _____ the ordering of furniture and supplies, and (8) _____ changing office technology. Over time, he or she may notice (9) _____ problems that require changing a service (10) _____. Furniture and large items are ordered on an (11) _____ basis. Other frequently used materials, such as paper, folders, and mailing materials, are on an automatic ordering schedule and a (12) _____ of those supplies is on hand at the office.

WORD PRACTICE

LISTENING COMPREHENSION

Part 1 Photo

Look at the picture and listen to the sentences.
Choose the sentence that best describes the picture.

1. Ⓐ Ⓑ Ⓒ Ⓓ

Part 2 Question–Response

Listen to the question and the three responses. Choose the response that best answers the question.

2. Ⓐ Ⓑ Ⓒ   3. Ⓐ Ⓑ Ⓒ

Part 3 Conversation

Listen to the dialogue. Then read each question and choose the best response.

4. What is required for all new purchases?
   (A) A receipt.
   (B) A charge card.
   (C) Up-front payment.
   (D) Approval.

5. What is the purpose of this requirement?
   (A) To avoid delays.
   (B) To help save money.
   (C) To make purchasing a top priority.
   (D) To reduce steps in the ordering process.

6. What is the woman's opinion of this requirement?
   (A) It's annoying.
   (B) It's enjoyable.
   (C) It's a good idea.
   (D) It's boring.

Part 4 Talk

Listen to the talk. Then read each question and choose the best answer.

7. Why don't they order units on an as-needed basis?
   (A) They're more expensive.
   (B) The provider won't take individual orders.
   (C) Delivery time is too long.
   (D) Nobody takes the initiative to place the order.

8. What kind of provider could help them?
   (A) A less pushy provider.
   (B) A more aggressive provider.
   (C) One with better prices.
   (D) One with a website.

9. What does the speaker like about the suggested company's products?
   (A) The durability.
   (B) The quality.
   (C) The price.
   (D) The size.

READING

Part 5 Incomplete Sentences

Choose the word that best completes the sentence.

10. _____ is a major concern when choosing new equipment for the office.
    (A) Afford   (C) Affordable
    (B) Affording   (D) Affordability

11. The office manager took the _____ to order more printers without discussing the matter with his boss.
    (A) initiated   (C) initiative
    (B) initiating   (D) initiation

12. This phone has more capacity than my old one even though its _____ size is actually smaller.
    (A) physical   (C) physicality
    (C) physique   (D) physically

13. As promised in our last meeting, this contract _____ you with the best prices.
    (A) provide   (C) provision
    (B) provides   (D) provider

14. When a problem _____ frequently, it is time to reexamine the process.
    (A) recur   (C) recurring
    (B) recurrence   (D) recurs

15. The employee preferred to have a _____ in salary than to have to continue working with her outdated computer.
    (A) reducing   (C) reduce
    (B) reduction   (D) reduces

Part 6 Text Completion

Memo

To: Miriam Ketonen, Office Manager
From: Jason Roberts, Assistant Office Manager
Re: Photocopier

There have been recurring problems with the office photocopier, particularly with paper jams. I believe the problem is with the type of machine we have. A machine of this size simply does not have the capacity to handle the amount of copying we normally do. Obviously we can't _____ the number of copies we make. I suggest that it's time to order a larger and _____

16. (A) reduce
    (B) recur
    (C) stock
    (D) initiate

17. (A) durable
    (B) durables
    (C) more durable
    (D) most durable

machine. I have looked through the catalogs and discovered several that I think would suit our needs. I have selected the most _____ ones, as I know we have a limited amount of money

18. (A) costly
    (B) physical
    (C) attractive
    (D) affordable

to spend. I have attached their descriptions. Since you are in charge of making large purchases like this, I will need your approval before I go ahead and place the order. Let me know which of the machines you think is best, and I will fill out the purchase order.

Thanks.

Part 7 Reading Comprehension

Questions 19–23 refer to the following two letters.

Business Kitchens, Inc.
April 19, 20—

Dear Mr. Conner,

I am writing to follow up on our conversation of last Monday. You said you were looking for a new provider for kitchen supplies for your office, and that your particular need at this time was for a large-capacity coffeemaker. I have looked through the coffeemakers we have available, and believe I have found the best one to suit your needs. The primary advantage of the 300X Office Coffeemaker is that it reduces mess. The coffeemaker is filled with water daily. Then, to make a cup of coffee, the user simply inserts a premeasured package of coffee into the machine and presses the "on" button. The coffee is ready in one minute. There are no pots to clean or filters to change. The machine can make tea and other hot drinks as well. The 300X is also the most durable machine on the market.

I am enclosing a description of the machine and price information. We can also deliver refills of coffee and tea to you on a weekly or monthly basis. In addition, we stock other kitchen appliances such as microwave ovens and office-sized refrigerators. Please let me know if you are interested in purchasing such items.

Sincerely,

Laura Baker

Laura Baker
Sales Manager

Johnson Research Affiliates
April 26, 20—

Dear Ms. Baker,

Thank you for the information on the 300X Office Coffeemaker. I think it will meet our needs for large-capacity coffeemakers at an affordable price. Our office is large, so I would like to order two at this time. I don't think we will need the regular deliveries of coffee and tea. Our need for these varies so much from week to week that it is better to order them on an as-needed basis. My assistant is good at staying on top of these things, so we don't have to worry about running out. Currently we don't have a need for ovens or refrigerators although we may in the near future. I will keep you informed. Meanwhile, we will send you a purchase order for the coffeemakers. Thank you for your help.

Sincerely,

Matthew Conner

Matthew Conner
Office Manager

---

19. What will Mr. Conner buy now?
    (A) Coffeemakers.
    (B) Ovens.
    (C) Microcomputers.
    (D) Refrigerators.

20. What does he say that he likes about the product he has selected?
    (A) It reduces mess.
    (B) It is durable.
    (C) It has a good price.
    (D) It will be delivered regularly.

21. How often will he order refills?
    (A) Once a day.
    (B) Once a week.
    (C) Every month.
    (D) When he needs them.

22. The word *provider* in line 2 of the first letter, is closest in meaning to
    (A) consumer
    (B) supplier
    (C) maker
    (D) designer

23. The word *stock* in line 19 of the first letter, is closest in meaning to
    (A) have
    (B) repair
    (C) buy
    (D) use

Lesson 8

Office Procedures

WORDS TO LEARN

appreciation
bring in
casually
code
expose
glimpse
made of
out of
outdated
practice
reinforce
verbally

Study the following definitions and examples.

1. **appreciation** n., recognition; understanding; thanks
   a. In appreciation of your hard work on the Castcon project, the department will hold a casual lunch party on November third.
   b. Your appreciation of my efforts inspired me through the final stages of the construction.

2. **bring in** v., to hire or recruit; to cause to appear
   a. The company president wanted to bring in an efficiency consultant.
   b. The company brought in a new team of project planners.

3. **casually** adv., informally
   a. On Fridays, most employees dress casually.
   b. Martin spoke casually, as if he were chatting with friends.

4. **code** n., rules of behavior
   a. The new employees observed the unwritten code of conduct in their first week on the job.
   b. Even the most traditional companies are changing their dress code to something less formal.

5. **expose** v., to make aware; to give experience
   a. Mergers require that employees be exposed to different business practices.
   b. The new hires' week in each department exposed them to the various functions in the company.

6. **glimpse** n., a quick look
   a. The secretary caught a glimpse of her new boss as she was leaving the office.
   b. After one year with the company, he still felt as though he had only a glimpse of the overall operations.

7. **made of** v., consisting of; produced from
   a. This job will really test what you are made of.
   b. People say that the negotiator has nerves made of steel.

8. **out of** adj., no longer having; missing
   a. Orders should be placed before you run out of the supplies.
   b. The presenter ran out of time before he reached his conclusion.

9. **outdated** adj., obsolete; not currently in use
   a. The purpose of the seminar is to have employees identify outdated methods and procedures.
   b. Before you do a mailing, make sure that none of the addresses is outdated.

10. **practice** n., method of doing something; v., to repeat in order to learn
    a. The manager started her practice of weekly breakfast meetings more than twenty years ago.
    b. Bill practiced answering the telephone until he was satisfied.

11. **reinforce** v., to strengthen; support
    a. The financial officer's unconventional method of analyzing data was reinforced by the business journal article.
    b. Employees reinforced their learning with practice in the workplace.

12. **verbally** adv., in spoken form
    a. She verbally reprimanded the new hire in front of his entire team.
    b. The guarantee was made only verbally.

WORD FAMILIES

noun	appreciation	In appreciation for your hard work, we are giving you a top-priority project.
verb	appreciate	We appreciate the time that you have put into this project, but we need to see more positive results.
adjective	appreciated	The intern felt appreciated, like a member of the team.

noun	casualness	Her boss was unhappy with the casualness of her manner.
adjective	casual	The casual atmosphere at the office made everyone feel relaxed.
adverb	casually	The office dress code allows people to dress casually on Fridays.

verb	expose	As a matter of company policy, we try to expose all managers to the challenging work of telephone sales through hands-on experience.
noun	exposure	Exposure to the elements will corrode the container for the sensor.
adjective	exposed	Mr. Lee was exposed to Chinese business practices during his three-year assignment as a manager in Beijing.

noun	practice	He was surprised at the difference in office practices from one local office to another.
verb	practice	All managers are expected to practice caution in their spending until the end of the year.
adjective	practical	We need a practical solution to this common problem.

verb	reinforce	Reading the employee handbook will reinforce your understanding of office procedures.
noun	reinforcement	All employees need reinforcement from their supervisor.
adjective	reinforceable	The company dress code is reinforceable only if the managers follow it themselves.

adverb	verbally	No employees should be verbally reprimanded in front of their peers.
verb	verbalize	Well-established procedures are often difficult to verbalize.
adjective	verbal	The company operated on a practice of verbal and not written contracts.

WORDS IN CONTEXT

Read the following passage and write the words in the blanks below.

appreciation	casually	made of	practices
been exposed to	code	out of	reinforced
brought in	glimpse	outdated	verbalize

How many employees show any (1) _____ for their corporate culture? How many executives appreciate what their corporate culture is and what it is (2) _____? It is often (3) _____ by the office procedures and routines that have been established over the years. A manager made her mark twenty years ago by dressing (4) _____, thereby forever changing the dress (5) _____. A director bought from the competition when he ran (6) _____ stock and the practice soon became standard. These examples add to a company's culture.

Good employees know what the standard procedures are. This is an important element in recruiting new employees, as well as training workers. When training workers, it is often important to have them read the procedures, write their reactions, and (7) _____ their opinions about these practices. This promotes a sense of cooperation between those who establish the (8) _____ and those who must follow them.

Employees who have been with a company for many years may not be able to identify (9) _____ practices because they haven't (10) _____ anything else. What happens when a department needs an extra hand? Is a "temp" (11) _____, or is someone borrowed from another department? The new recruits often ask the questions that allow more senior employees to get a (12) _____ of the corporate culture.

WORD PRACTICE

LISTENING COMPREHENSION

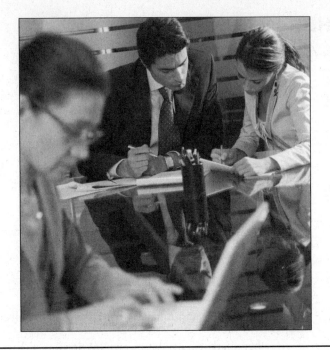

Part 1 Photo

Look at the picture and listen to the sentences.
Choose the sentence that best describes the picture.

1. Ⓐ Ⓑ Ⓒ Ⓓ

Part 2 Question–Response

Listen to the question and the three responses. Choose the response that best answers the question.

2. Ⓐ Ⓑ Ⓒ   3. Ⓐ Ⓑ Ⓒ

Part 3 Conversation

Listen to the dialogue. Then read each question and choose the best response.

4. What will the woman tell the man about?
   (A) Hiring policies.
   (B) Company practices.
   (C) How to make a schedule.
   (D) The employee's communication problems.

5. What problem has the man had?
   (A) No one can explain things to him clearly.
   (B) He never has time for anything.
   (C) No one has time to talk to him.
   (D) He isn't familiar with his coworkers.

6. How does the woman suggest he reinforce their discussion?
   (A) By talking to other employees.
   (B) By practicing what he hears.
   (C) By reviewing the schedule.
   (D) By looking at the handbook.

Part 4 Talk

Listen to the talk. Then read each question and choose the best answer.

7. Who is the speaker?
   (A) A software trainer.
   (B) A hardware salesman.
   (C) A new computer owner.
   (D) A scientist from R&D.

8. What will they do today?
   (A) Choose new software.
   (B) Review their computer skills.
   (C) Hire a specialist.
   (D) Take apart the CPU.

9. What will they do after the speaker finishes?
   (A) Spend a lot of time practicing.
   (B) Watch a television program.
   (C) Have lunch.
   (D) Attend a board meeting.

READING

Part 5 Incomplete Sentences

Choose the word that best completes the sentence.

10. Ms. Handa was unable to express her _____ for all that her colleagues had done for her.
    (A) appreciation   (C) appreciating
    (B) appreciated   (D) appreciates

11. Roger made a mistake when he greeted the client so _____ .
    (A) casual   (C) causality
    (B) casually   (D) casualness

12. _____ to more experienced staff members helps new employees learn the procedures.
    (A) Expose   (C) Exposing
    (B) Exposure   (D) Will expose

13. The _____ of answering each telephone call on the third ring requires a dedicated receptionist.
    (A) practices   (C) practiced
    (B) practical   (D) practice

14. Human Resources tries to _____ employees' understanding by offering workshops twice a year.
    (A) reinforce   (C) reinforced
    (B) reinforcing   (D) reinforcement

15. Senior employees are often asked to _____ office procedures.
    (A) verbally   (C) verbal
    (B) verbalize   (D) verbalizing

Part 6 Text Completion

> ### NOTICE—CASUAL FRIDAYS
>
> A number of staff members have expressed an interest in Casual Friday. I realize that this custom _____ in many offices
>
> 16. (A) practices
>   (B) practiced
>   (C) is practiced
>   (D) is practicing
>
> nowadays. I appreciate the fact that many of you have discussed this matter with me _____, and pointed out that our strict
>
> 17. (A) verb
>   (B) verbal
>   (C) verbally
>   (D) verbalize
>
> dress code is outdated. Because so many people have expressed an interest in dressing casually once a week, we will have Casual Friday in this office starting next week. While we want to be relaxed, we do not want to _____ our coworkers to styles of
>
> 18. (A) expose
>   (B) practice
>   (C) reinforce
>   (D) appreciate
>
> dress that may make them feel uncomfortable. So, while the dress code will be relaxed, it does not mean that you can wear anything you want. Shoes and shirts are required, and beach and gym attire are unacceptable.
>
> Amanda Jones, Director

Part 7 Reading Comprehension

Questions 19–23 refer to the following article.

When you bring in a new employee, it is important to make sure that he or she understands the usual office procedures as well as the codes of behavior. These things should be outlined clearly in the employee handbook. New employees should understand that they are expected to do more than just glimpse at the handbook and then hide it in a drawer. A thorough reading of it will help them understand many things they need to know about the workplace culture. Employees also appreciate verbal reinforcement. Supervisors should let them know when they have completed a job well, or if they are bending the rules too far. More experienced coworkers can be asked to support new employees while they are getting used to their new positions and explain procedures to them, but ultimately it is the supervisor's responsibility to make sure that the normal office practices are carried out. When everyone understands what is expected, then the office procedures run more smoothly. In fact, it is not a bad idea to review the codes and procedures with the entire staff from time to time. This can be done on a regular basis at staff meetings, or it can be part of a training session.

19. What should new employees do with the handbook?
    (A) Read it quickly.
    (B) Study it completely.
    (C) Hide it in a drawer.
    (D) Share it with coworkers.

20. What should the supervisor do when an employee breaks a rule?
    (A) Punish her.
    (B) Fire her.
    (C) Tell her.
    (D) Retrain her.

21. How can experienced coworkers help new employees?
    (A) By writing a new handbook.
    (B) By explaining office procedures.
    (C) By inviting them to staff meetings.
    (D) By telling the supervisor when a rule has been broken.

22. The words *bring in* in line 1, are closest in meaning to
    (A) invite
    (B) train
    (C) hire
    (D) meet

23. The word *codes* in line 3, is closest in meaning to
    (A) rules
    (B) lessons
    (C) mistakes
    (D) types

Lesson 9

Electronics

WORDS TO LEARN

device
facilitate
network
popularity
process
replace
revolution
sharp
skill
software
store
technically

Study the following definitions and examples.

1. **device** n., a tool or machine used for a specific task
   a. A cell phone is a small device that is easy to carry around.
   b. You can connect this device to your computer and use it to store your files.
2. **facilitate** v., to make easier
   a. The computer program facilitated the scheduling of appointments.
   b. The director tried to facilitate the transition to the new policy by meeting with all staff who would be affected.
3. **network** v., to connect; to broadcast; n., an interconnected group or system over a radio or TV; to engage in informal communication
   a. The recent graduate networked with her mother's coworkers.
   b. We set up a new network in my office to share files.
4. **popularity** n., the state of being widely admired, sought, or accepted
   a. After the new commercials began running, the popularity of the batteries increased significantly.
   b. This brand of computers is extremely popular among college students.
5. **process** v., to put through a series of actions or prescribed procedure; n., a series of operations or actions to bring about a result
   a. I've processed the data I collected and have gotten some interesting results.
   b. There is a process for determining why your computer is malfunctioning.
6. **replace** v., to put back in a former place or position; to take the place of
   a. I've replaced the hard drive that was malfunctioning.
   b. We have been looking for three months and we've found no one who can replace our former administrator.
7. **revolution** n., a sudden or important change in a situation
   a. We see a revolution in the computer field almost every day.
   b. Cell phones have caused a revolution in communication.
8. **sharp** adj., abrupt or acute; smart
   a. There was a sharp decline in calls to the help desk after we upgraded each employee's computer.
   b. The new employee proved how sharp she was when she mastered the new program in a few days.
9. **skill** n., a developed ability
   a. The software developer has excellent technical skills and would be an asset to our software programming team.
   b. Salman's job as designer of electronic tools makes good use of his manual dexterity skills.
10. **software** n., the programs for a computer
    a. This software allows me to integrate tables and spreadsheets into my reports.
    b. Many computers come pre-loaded with software.
11. **store** v., to keep
    a. You can store more data on a zip drive.
    b. You can store hundreds of songs on an iPod.
12. **technically** adv., with specialized skill or knowledge
    a. Technically speaking, the virus infected only script files.
    b. We find that our younger employees tend to be more technically skilled.

53

WORD FAMILIES

verb	popularize	The Internet has popularized last-minute travel.
noun	popularity	The popularity of the product was extremely short-lived, and it soon disappeared from the store shelves.
adjective	popular	The new computer program was extremely popular, and people asked for it at all the stores.

verb	replace	I'd like to replace my cell phone with a newer model.
noun	replacement	Look online to see if you can find an affordable replacement for this damaged computer.
adjective	replaceable	Make copies of all your files as they are not easily replaceable.

verb	revolutionized	Using diamond has revolutionized the pressure sensor industry during the last decade.
noun	revolution	The revolution in electronics technology has allowed products such as phones to get smaller and more portable.
adjective	revolutionary	The Internet is revolutionary in how it has changed the way we communicate.

noun	skill	Her marketing skills inspired Jason to return to school for his MBA.
adjective	skilled	Our carpenters are skilled in everything from cabinetry to furniture making.
adverb	skillfully	He negotiates so skillfully that both parties end up feeling that they've gotten what they wanted.

verb	store	I store the phone numbers of all my business contacts in my personal cell phone.
noun	store	We keep a store of computer supplies in that closet.
noun	storage	We need a computer with greater storage capacity.

noun	technician	Even a skilled technician couldn't repair that machine.
adjective	technical	At least a small amount of technical knowledge is required for most jobs these days.
adverb	technically	People who are technically trained have an easier time finding jobs.

WORDS IN CONTEXT

Read the following passage and write the words in the blanks below.

devices	popular	revolutionized	software
facilitated	processing	sharply	stored
networks	replaced	skills	technical

By the mid-1980s, virtually all U.S. businesses owned at least one computer. Prices of computers declined (1) _____ over the next few years, resulting in a surge in popularity. At the same time, offices started to rely on (2) _____, which (3) _____ the sharing and processing of data. Such data (4) _____ was made possible by improvements in both the hardware and software industries.

Today, virtually all office workers are trained to use the most (5) _____ word processing (6) _____ and most information is (7) _____ in computer files. In fact, electronics have completely (8) _____ the workplace. These days, workers rely on computers, cell phones, and other electronic (9) _____ to carry out their job responsibilities. The job (10) _____ needed today are very different from those needed in the past since now workers need to be comfortable with using electronics. Companies have to hire (11) _____ workers to maintain their computers and other electronic equipment. People who were hired to do boring, repetitive jobs in the past have been (12) _____ by computers, which can do such jobs faster and more cheaply.

WORD PRACTICE

LISTENING COMPREHENSION

TRACK
10

Part 1 Photo

Look at the picture and listen to the sentences.
Choose the sentence that best describes the picture.

1. Ⓐ Ⓑ Ⓒ Ⓓ

Part 2 Question–Response

Listen to the question and the three responses. Choose the response that best answers the question.

2. Ⓐ Ⓑ Ⓒ   3. Ⓐ Ⓑ Ⓒ

Part 3 Conversation

Listen to the dialogue. Then read each question and choose the best response.

4. Why can't the woman retrieve her file?
   (A) She doesn't know how.
   (B) She forgot its name.
   (C) It was accidentally deleted.
   (D) She can't remember where it's stored.

5. Why does she need the file?
   (A) To do her accounts.
   (B) To report the news.
   (C) To finish her proposal.
   (D) To get information about a store.

6. What does the man suggest the woman should do?
   (A) Figure it out herself.
   (B) Let him help her.
   (C) Improve her skills.
   (D) Get help from the IT department.

Part 4 Talk

Listen to the talk. Then read each question and choose the best answer.

7. What is the speaker's opinion of the process of downloading software?
   (A) Anyone can do it.
   (B) It requires technical skills.
   (C) It's easiest if you download from a remote server.
   (D) It's time-consuming.

8. Who is the intended audience for this talk?
   (A) Computer technicians.
   (B) Network managers.
   (C) New computer users.
   (D) Software writers.

9. What will the listeners do next?
   (A) Look at a chart.
   (B) Turn on their computers.
   (C) Connect to the Internet.
   (D) Type a web address.

READING

Part 5 Incomplete Sentences

Choose the word that best completes the sentence.

10. The _____ of the new computer network was apparent among the employees after only a few months.
 (A) popular
 (B) popularize
 (C) popularity
 (D) population

11. We will _____ all of our outdated software with the newest versions.
 (A) facilitate
 (B) process
 (C) store
 (D) replace

12. There is a _____ approach to software design integration that all the big software developers are currently learning.
 (A) revolutionized
 (B) revolutionary
 (C) revolution
 (D) revolt

13. While Fabio's _____ with computers surpasses that of the technicians, he is unable to communicate his personal needs to the office manager.
 (A) skill
 (B) skilled
 (C) skillful
 (D) skillfully

14. A smartphone is an electronic _____ that is used for much more than just making phone calls.
 (A) devise
 (B) division
 (C) device
 (D) deviance

15. The newspaper article on the development of new fiber-optic cables was so full of _____ language that nobody could understand it.
 (A) technical
 (B) technically
 (C) technicality
 (D) technique

Part 6 Text Completion

Computer technology has brought about a _____ in the workplace. Now employees

16. (A) revolted
 (B) revolution
 (C) revolutionary
 (D) revolutionize

all around the country do all or part of their jobs from home. This phenomenon is called telecommuting and has been made possible by the widespread use of the Internet. Telecommuting has become _____ among employees, although the reactions of

17. (A) sharp
 (B) technical
 (C) popular
 (D) replaceable

employers are mixed. Some like telecommuting and some don't. But most agree that it facilitates work for employees who live at a distance from the worksite. Telecommuting enables companies to keep skilled employees who move out of the area or who have family obligations that require them to stay close to home. _____ the regular nine-to-five

18. (A) It replaces
 (B) It will replace
 (C) Will it replace
 (D) Will it be replaced by

office job? Probably not entirely, but we are sure to see more and more of it in the future.

Part 7 Reading Comprehension

Questions 19–23 refer to the following two e-mails.

To: mary@acme.com
From: fred@acme.com
Subject: software training

Mary,

As you know, we have decided to replace our old software with a new program that will facilitate our work better. Although the new software is not technically difficult to use, it is significantly different from our old software. The entire staff will need to be trained to use it. Of course, not everyone can attend a training session together, because we need some staff members to be in the office at all times. The trainer suggests that each person attend one training session and one follow-up session. The sessions will last three to four hours each. The trainer can be here once a week. Please develop a training schedule so that everyone can be trained over the next two months. Thank you.

Fred

To: fred@acme.com
From: mary@acme.com
Subject: re: software training

Fred,

I have written up a schedule that will facilitate the training process. There will be eight weekly training sessions all together. Since we have four departments, the easiest way is to send one person from each department to each training session during the first month. Of course it will be a different person each week. We can repeat the process during the second month for the follow-up sessions. This way everyone will have a chance to develop his or her skills on the new software. I am attaching a copy of the schedule. Please let me know what you think.

Mary

---

19. What is true about the new software?
    (A) It's difficult to use.
    (B) It's very different from the old software.
    (C) It requires many months of training.
    (D) It's very expensive.

20. Which staff members will be trained to use the new software?
    (A) Just one from each department.
    (B) Fred and Mary only.
    (C) Only four of them.
    (D) All of them.

21. How many training sessions will each person attend?
    (A) One.
    (B) Two.
    (C) Four.
    (D) Eight.

22. The word *skills* in line 10 of the second e-mail is closest in meaning to
    (A) abilities
    (B) opportunities
    (C) tasks
    (D) ideas

23. The word *replace* in line 1 of the first e-mail is closest in meaning to
    (A) sell
    (B) change
    (C) keep
    (D) locate

Lesson 10

Correspondence

WORDS TO LEARN

assemble

beforehand

complication

courier

distribute

express

fold

layout

mention

petition

proof

revise

Study the following definitions and examples.

1. **assemble** v., to put together; to bring together
   a. Her assistant copied and assembled the documents.
   b. The mail room clerk read the directions before assembling the parts to the new postage printer.

2. **beforehand** adv., in advance, in anticipation
   a. To speed up the mailing, we should prepare the labels beforehand.
   b. The goods could have been shipped today had they given us the order beforehand.

3. **complication** n., difficulty, complex situation
   a. There was a complication with the delivery because the address was written incorrectly.
   b. Complications always arise when we try to cover too many topics in one letter.

4. **courier** n., a messenger, an official delivery person
   a. We hired a courier to deliver the package.
   b. The courier service will clear the goods through customs.

5. **distribute** v., to pass out to a variety of people
   a. We no longer distribute our newsletter by mail because everyone reads it online.
   b. We plan to distribute copies of the announcement throughout the building.

6. **express** adj., fast and direct
   a. It's important that this document be there tomorrow, so please send it express mail.
   b. Express mail costs more than regular mail service, but it is more efficient.

7. **fold** v., to bend paper
   a. Fold the letter into three parts before stuffing it into the envelope.
   b. Don't fold the document if it doesn't fit the envelope.

8. **layout** n., a format; the organization of material on a page
   a. We had to change the layout when we changed the size of the paper.
   b. The layout for the new brochure was submitted by the designer.

9. **mention** n., something said or written; v., to refer to
   a. There was no mention of the cost in the proposal.
   b. You should mention in the letter that we can arrange for mailing the brochures as well as printing them.

10. **petition** n., a formal, written request; v., to make a formal request
    a. The petition was photocopied and distributed to workers who will collect the necessary signatures.
    b. We petitioned the postal officials to start delivering mail twice a day in business areas.

11. **proof** v., to look for errors
    a. This letter was not proofed very carefully; it is full of typing errors.
    b. Please proof the memo one more time before you distribute it.

12. **revise** v., to rewrite
    a. The brochure was revised several times before it was sent to the printer.
    b. We will need to revise the form letter since our address has changed.

WORD FAMILIES

verb	complicate	Don't try to complicate things by making two-sided copies; single-sided will do.
noun	complication	There are a few complications with your layout, but they can be easily solved.
adjective	complicated	The revisions in the document made it more complicated, rather than simpler.

verb	distribute	We generally distribute the mail early in the morning.
noun	distribution	As soon as these envelopes are addressed, they will be ready for distribution.
noun	distributor	The distributor of our products just sent an e-mail informing us that he is closing down his business.

noun	mention	The mention of layoffs made us worry.
verb	mention	As I mentioned in my note to you, you should try to be less wordy and more concise in your writing.
adjective	mentionable	No one considered the mediocre design a mentionable achievement.

noun	petition	In order to be valid, the contents of the petition need to be printed at the top of each page that will contain signatures.
verb	petition	The welders petitioned the factory to install air conditioning.
noun	petitioners	The petitioners spent the night outside of the courthouse.

verb	proof	It is your responsibility to proof your own work before sending it out.
noun	proofreader	The proofreader did not find the errors.
gerund	proofing	Proofing a document is best done by starting at the end and reading backward.

verb	revise	After you revise the document, give it a new name so that we will still have access to both drafts.
adjective	revised	His revised memo was easier to read.
noun	revision	You may have to do three or four full revisions to this document before it is acceptable.

WORDS IN CONTEXT

Read the following passage and write the words in the blanks below.

assemble	courier	folding	petition
beforehand	distributed	layout	proofed
complicated	express	mention	revision

In small offices, it is often the executive assistant who must manage all of the printed material that the firm produces. The job responsibilities include typing and printing out the correspondence. These letters and memos must all be carefully (1) _____ to make sure they are error-free. If not, the errors should be corrected. If the meaning is not clear, the correspondence should be revised. This (2) _____ should be done (3) _____, not when the letter is ready to be sent.

Before putting correspondence into an envelope, the executive assistant must (4) _____ all the various attachments and other documents to be enclosed with the letter. When (5) _____ the correspondence, the assistant should make sure that when opening the envelope, the recipient sees the letterhead first.

Once prepared, the correspondence must be sent appropriately. Local, urgent mail could be hand-delivered by a (6) _____ service. Long-distance, urgent mail could be sent overnight or by (7) _____ mail. Or correspondence can be (8) _____ by a private delivery service instead of the mail system.

In addition to transmitting and receiving faxes, the executive assistant must work closely with company officials. When the company executives have to make a presentation, the executive assistant often becomes a graphic designer charged with the (9) _____, or the look of, the graphics and text for the printed materials used during the presentations. Did I (10) _____ that these duties generally involve learning extremely (11) _____ design software? It's a wonder that more executive assistants don't (12) _____ their bosses for a raise.

WORD PRACTICE

LISTENING COMPREHENSION

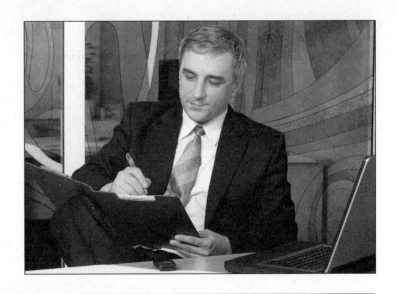

Part 1 Photo

Look at the picture and listen to the sentences.
Choose the sentence that best describes the picture.

1. Ⓐ Ⓑ Ⓒ Ⓓ

Part 2 Question–Response

Listen to the question and the three responses. Choose the response that best answers the question.

2. Ⓐ Ⓑ Ⓒ   3. Ⓐ Ⓑ Ⓒ

Part 3 Conversation

Listen to the short dialogue. Then read each question and choose the best response.

4. When will the meeting take place?
    (A) This afternoon.
    (B) Tomorrow.
    (C) In two days.
    (D) On Tuesday.

5. Why won't the woman help assemble the
    documents?
    (A) She's in a meeting.
    (B) She hurt her hand.
    (C) She's too busy.
    (D) She needs to revise them first.

6. What does the woman suggest that the man do?
    (A) Finish the work before the afternoon.
    (B) Do the work himself.
    (C) Ask another person for help.
    (D) Remember to fold all the documents.

Part 4 Talk

Listen to the talk. Then read each question and choose the best answer.

7. Where would you hear this talk?
    (A) A post office.
    (B) A grocery store.
    (C) A restaurant.
    (D) An assembly line.

8. What is the purpose of this talk?
    (A) To sell merchandise.
    (B) To inform customers of a new service.
    (C) To warn workers.
    (D) To recognize a new employee.

9. What time does the Courier Center close?
    (A) 2:00 P.M.
    (B) 4:00 P.M.
    (C) 6:00 P.M.
    (D) 8:00 P.M.

READING

Part 5 Incomplete Sentences

Choose the word that best completes the sentence.

10. I don't want to _____ matters, but have you considered using color to make your brochure stand out?
(A) complicate
(B) complication
(C) complicated
(D) complicating

11. It's worth _____ in the memo that we've finished the draft of the proposal.
(A) mentionable
(B) mentioning
(C) mentions
(D) mentioned

12. The signatures on the _____ weren't all legible because rain had caused the ink to run.
(A) petition
(B) petitioning
(C) petitioners
(D) petitioned

13. To send out business letters without _____ them is unprofessional.
(A) proofing
(B) proof
(C) proofreader
(D) proofread

14. The memo _____ to the entire staff yesterday afternoon.
(A) distributed
(B) was distributed
(C) was distributing
(D) distribution

15. After each _____, you need to reread what you've written and note your suggestions for changes.
(A) revise
(B) revised
(C) revision
(D) will revise

Part 6 Text Completion

MEMO

To: Production Staff
From: George Jones
Re: Document Preparation

In order to avoid extra work and waste of supplies, please observe the following guidelines when preparing documents for reproduction and distribution. The goal is to keep things simple and avoid _____ .

16. (A) mentions
(B) petitions
(C) revisions
(D) complications

• When you work on the final revision of a document, pay special attention to the layout. The presentation of material is as important as the content itself.
• Don't rush to the copier as soon as the final revision is complete. _____ each

17. (A) Proof
(B) Proofs
(C) To proof
(D) Proofing

document carefully beforehand.
• We have technology to help with the assembly of documents. The large copier on the second floor can _____ paper in addition to stapling. This will help you complete

18. (A) folder
(B) folded
(C) folds
(D) fold

tasks efficiently.
• If a document needs to be delivered the same day it is finished, please use a courier service.

Part 7 Reading Comprehension

Questions 19–23 refer to the following advertisement.

Do you run a small business? If so, you likely don't have a large enough staff to deal with developing, reproducing, and mailing all your documents and correspondence. Why not let Office Systems, Inc., take care of this work for you? We provide the following services:

Editing

Don't send out your documents until you are sure they are absolutely perfect. We provide revision and proofreading services on all documents, large or small.

Design and Production

Our professional graphic designers work with you to develop the best format and layout for your documents. We also provide copying and assembling services, including folding, stapling, and packaging.

Delivery

We can connect you with several different delivery services, including the postal system and private courier companies. Is your correspondence urgent? Our express delivery service gets it to the recipient within 24 hours or less, guaranteed.

Visit any one of our branches to open up an account with us today. You can download an application from our website and fill it out beforehand to make the process go more smoothly. Don't let the details of correspondence and document development complicate your life. Let Office Systems, Inc., handle it all for you.

Visit www.officesys.com to find the branch nearest you.

---

19. Who is the audience for this advertisement?
    (A) Editors.
    (B) Couriers.
    (C) Corporate directors.
    (D) Small business owners.

20. Which of the following is a service offered by Office Systems, Inc.?
    (A) Accounting.
    (B) Website development.
    (C) Assembling documents.
    (D) Reading letters.

21. How can a customer open an account with Office Systems, Inc.?
    (A) By visiting a company branch.
    (B) By sending an e-mail.
    (C) By completing an online questionnaire.
    (D) By writing a letter.

22. The word *revision* in line 6 is closest in meaning to
    (A) copying
    (B) rewriting
    (C) delivery
    (D) development

23. The word *beforehand* in line 16 is closest in meaning to
    (A) by hand
    (B) thoroughly
    (C) in advance
    (D) in person

Word Review #2   Lessons 6–10 Office Issues

Choose the word that best completes the sentence.

1. Who is in charge _____ hiring?
   (A) by
   (B) on
   (C) of
   (D) for

2. Most office furniture is bought more on the basis of _____ than comfort.
   (A) afford
   (B) affording
   (C) afforded
   (D) affordability

3. The office _____ samples of its products.
   (A) display
   (B) displayed
   (C) displaying
   (D) displayable

4. The staff expressed their _____ for the leadership of their boss.
   (A) appreciate
   (B) appreciated
   (C) appreciating
   (D) appreciation

5. Ms. Ming was pleased that the new employee showed such _____ .
   (A) initiate
   (B) initiative
   (C) initiated
   (D) initiating

6. Before you send the letter, you should _____ it to make sure there are no errors.
   (A) proof
   (B) fold
   (C) petition
   (D) assemble

7. We always use a private courier service for the _____ of our correspondence.
   (A) distributed
   (B) distribution
   (C) distributing
   (D) distributes

8. Many office supply businesses specialize in furniture that is as _____ as it is affordable.
   (A) duration
   (B) durable
   (C) durability
   (D) durableness

9. The office manager finally figured _____ why the new software wasn't working properly.
   (A) in
   (B) for
   (C) out
   (D) about

10. The letter from our accountant _____ that our petty cash spending was almost equal to budgeted items.
    (A) mention
    (B) mentioned
    (C) mentioning
    (D) mentionable

Choose the one word or phrase that best completes each sentence.

The use of computers _____ the workplace. Thirty years ago, many people had never touched a computer. Now almost

    11. (A) revolutionize
       (B) will revolutionize
       (C) had revolutionized
       (D) has revolutionized

everyone uses a computer for work. Computers facilitate work so that jobs can be completed more efficiently. Documents are easily duplicated and distributed with computers. The Internet has made it easy _____ for information. Computers have

    12. (A) search
       (B) to search
       (C) searching
       (D) can search

become very _____. Even the smallest businesses are able to buy them.

    13. (A) afford
       (B) affording
       (C) affordably
       (D) affordable

To: George Stanley
From: Marya Obermeyer
Subject: Photocopier issues

George,

We are almost out _____ paper for the photocopier. There is just one package left in the supply closet.

    14. (A) of
       (B) on
       (C) at
       (D) to

I would appreciate your ordering a new box today. In the future, please stay on top of things like this. The order should have been made much sooner.

Also, we will have to _____ the photocopy machine sometime in the near future. We need a new one

    15. (A) report
       (B) repeal
       (C) replace
       (D) repeat

that doesn't break down so often. Please start researching this and see if you can find one that is affordable. I would also like one that is not _____ to use.

    16. (A) complicate
       (B) complicated
       (C) complicating
       (D) complication

Marya

MEMO

To: All office staff
From: Office Manager
Re: New photocopier

We have finally purchased a new photocopier. _____, it is a great improvement over our old one. It can

                17. (A) Technical
                    (B) Technician
                    (C) Technicality
                    (D) Technically

_____ documents so you don't have to put them together yourself. It also folds documents for mailing.

18. (A) assemble
    (B) assume
    (C) assuage
    (D) assert

However, it does not correct mistakes in your writing. When making multiple copies of a document, please _____ it beforehand and correct any errors. This will save us a great deal in both paper and time.

19. (A) probe
    (B) proof
    (C) prove
    (D) prompt

Please let me know if you have any questions about using the new machine.

Lesson 11

Job Advertising and Recruiting

WORDS TO LEARN

abundant

accomplishment

bring together

candidate

come up with

commensurate

match

profile

qualifications

recruit

submit

time-consuming

Study the following definitions and examples.

1. **abundant** adj., plentiful; in large quantities
   a. The computer analyst was glad to have chosen a field in which jobs were abundant.
   b. The recruiter was surprised by the abundant number of qualified applicants.
2. **accomplishment** n., an achievement; a success
   a. The company was interested in hiring her because of her list of accomplishments.
   b. Finding the right applicant for the job is a big accomplishment.
3. **bring together** v., to join; to gather
   a. Every year, the firm brings together its top lawyers and its newest recruits for a training session.
   b. Our goal this year is to bring together the most creative group we can find.
4. **candidate** n., one being considered for a position, office, or award
   a. The recruiter will interview all candidates for the position.
   b. The president of our company is a candidate for the Outstanding Business Award.
5. **come up with** v., to plan; to invent; to think of
   a. In order to find good candidates for the position, we need to come up with a good advertising plan.
   b. How was the new employee able to come up with that cost-cutting idea after only one week on the job?
6. **commensurate** adj., in proportion to; corresponding; equal to
   a. Generally the first year's salary is commensurate with experience and education level.
   b. As mentioned in your packets, the number of new recruits will be commensurate with the number of vacancies at the company.
7. **match** n., a fit; a similarity; v.; to put together; to fit
   a. It is difficult to make a decision when both candidates seem to be a perfect match.
   b. A headhunter matches qualified candidates to suitable positions.
8. **profile** n., a group of characteristics or traits
   a. The recruiter told him that, unfortunately, he did not fit the job profile.
   b. As jobs change, so does the company's profile for the job candidate.
9. **qualifications** n., requirements, qualities, or abilities needed for something
   a. The job seeker had done extensive volunteer work and was able to add this experience to his list of qualifications.
   b. The applicant had so many qualifications that the company created a new position for her.
10. **recruit** v., to attract people to join an organization or a cause; n., a person who is recruited
    a. When the consulting firm recruited her, they offered to pay her relocation expenses.
    b. The new recruits spent the entire day in training.
11. **submit** v., to present for consideration
    a. Submit your résumé to the human resources department.
    b. The applicant submitted all her paperwork in a professional and timely manner.
12. **time-consuming** adj., taking up a lot of time; lengthy
    a. Even though it was time-consuming, all of the participants felt that the open house was very worthwhile.
    b. Five interviews later, Ms. Lopez had the job, but it was the most time-consuming process she had ever gone through.

WORD FAMILIES

noun	abundance	The company is growing fast and there is an abundance of job openings.
adjective	abundant	When jobs are scarce, job applicants are abundant.
adverb	abundantly	It was abundantly clear that the unemployment rate was not going to turn around anytime soon.

verb	accomplish	You can accomplish anything if you put your mind to it.
noun	accomplishment	The company is proud of our team's accomplishments.
adjective	accomplished	The accomplished artist had his paintings in all the major galleries.

noun	match	The former marketing director is a good match for this position in public relations.
verb	match	We need to match both job experience and personality for this position.
adjective	matching	The matching cushions look better on the chair.

verb	qualify	In order to qualify, you must have two years of work experience.
noun	qualifications	The manager made a list of qualifications for the vacant job position.
adjective	qualified	He applied for the position but he wasn't qualified for it.

verb	recruit	Large accounting firms recruit on college campuses every spring.
noun	recruitment	The company's recruitment resulted in ten highly qualified new employees.
noun	recruiter	As a recruiter, he traveled around the country speaking to recent college graduates.

verb	submit	Anyone who is interested in the position should submit a résumé and writing samples.
noun	submission	I'm very sorry, the submission date was last week. We can't take any more applications.
noun	submittal	The submittal of his resignation prompted his colleagues to apply for his job.

WORDS IN CONTEXT

Read the following passage and write the words in the blanks below.

abundant	candidates	match	recruit
accomplishments	coming up with	profile	submit
bring together	commensurate	qualifications	time-consuming

Recruiting employees is a (1) _____ and costly process. Therefore, employers want to (2) _____ the right person with the right job the first time around. There are many ways to (3) _____ good employees: advertising in newspapers and professional journals and online, recruiting on college campuses or at conferences, or getting referrals from headhunters.

Recruiting is a time for a company to brag about its (4) _____ and excite people about its future. Each company is trying to (5) _____ the best and the brightest, but they are not alone. Their competition is trying to do the same thing. When jobs are (6) _____ and there is low unemployment, employers may face higher demands from job seekers. Conversely, when the economy is slowing down and jobs are few, employers are in a better position for attracting the best (7) _____.

Employers look for certain characteristics and (8) _____ in their employees. (9) _____ a very specific (10) _____ that fits the company culture and the specific job requirements is a difficult job. Employers want to see a well-rounded candidate and someone who has related work experience. They are willing to offer a salary that is (11) _____ with that experience. Employers will make hiring and salary determinations based on the information candidates (12) _____ throughout the application and interview process.

WORD PRACTICE

LISTENING COMPREHENSION

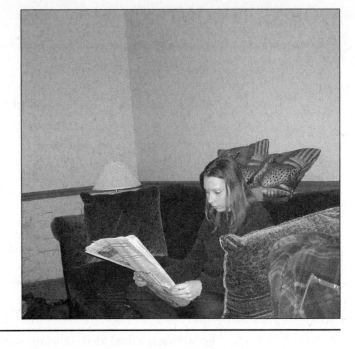

Part 1 Photo

Look at the picture and listen to the sentences.
Choose the sentence that best describes the picture.

1. Ⓐ Ⓑ Ⓒ Ⓓ

Part 2 Question–Response

Listen to the question and the three responses. Choose the response that best answers the question.

2. Ⓐ Ⓑ Ⓒ   3. Ⓐ Ⓑ Ⓒ

Part 3 Conversation

Listen to the dialogue. Then read each question and choose the best response.

4. What has the woman been doing lately?
   (A) Fixing her drain.
   (B) Earning money.
   (C) Looking for matches.
   (D) Searching for a job.

5. How long has she been doing this?
   (A) Two months.
   (B) Four months.
   (C) Five months.
   (D) Nine months.

6. What did she do yesterday?
   (A) She had an interview.
   (B) She read a review.
   (C) She helped someone.
   (D) She accepted a new position.

Part 4 Talk

Listen to the talk. Then read each question and choose the best answer.

7. What should the résumé include?
   (A) Your major in college.
   (B) Your grade point average.
   (C) A current reference.
   (D) A list of concrete achievements.

8. What is the employer looking for?
   (A) Employees with long-term career plans.
   (B) People to fill positions immediately.
   (C) Aggressive marketers.
   (D) People willing to accept minimum wage.

9. Who should apply for a position now?
   (A) Accountants.
   (B) Recruiters.
   (C) School teachers.
   (D) Apartment managers.

READING

Part 5 Incomplete Sentences

Choose the word that best completes the sentence.

10. Your résumé shows you have _____ a great deal in your last position.
    (A) accomplish   (C) accomplished
    (B) accomplishment   (D) accomplishing

11. This program is used to scan résumés and search for key words that _____.
    (A) match   (C) matching
    (B) matched   (D) will match

12. It is illegal to _____ candidates based on gender or ethnicity.
    (A) profile   (C) profiled
    (B) profiling   (D) will profile

13. The applicants who _____ will be flown to the corporate office and interviewed there.
    (A) ability   (C) application
    (B) qualify   (D) hesitation

14. After reading the job _____, she knew she was qualified for the position.
    (A) profile   (C) proofs
    (B) profit   (D) profess

15. After _____ all his materials, he had no option but to sit back and wait for some response.
    (A) submitting   (C) submission
    (B) submitted   (D) submit

Part 6 Text Completion

ATTENTION JOB SEEKERS!

Attend the National Recruiting Fair to be held next Saturday, May 11, at the Hinton Hotel. This fair _____ representatives of over 150 major national corporations. They are all looking

16. (A) bring together
    (B) brings together
    (C) brought together
    (D) to bring together

for qualified candidates to apply for thousands of currently available job openings. Attendees are advised to bring 15 copies of a current résumé that lists education, job experience, and professional _____. Many interviews will be conducted on site. Now you can stop that

17. (A) accomplishes
    (B) accomplished
    (C) accomplishing
    (D) accomplishments

_____ job search, making call after call and sending out résumé after résumé. All the

18. (A) time-consuming
    (B) submitting
    (C) recruiting
    (D) profiling

companies you want to work for will be together under one roof. You are sure to find the company that is the best match for you. Admission is free.

Part 7 Reading Comprehension

Questions 19–23 refer to the following two e-mail messages.

To: Marjorie Morgan
From: Bill Smithers
Subject: Recruiting

Marjorie,

We need to start looking at recruiting some new staff members over the summer. Our company has gotten lots of new contracts recently. We have abundant work and need to take on two or three new employees to help with it. We should advertise the positions as entry-level with room for promotion. We should choose the job candidates carefully as I don't want to have to end up firing anyone who turns out to be a bad match. I would like the new staff members to start work by June 10. Therefore, we should ask interested candidates to submit their applications before the end of April so that we can start interviewing in early May. Please come up with a recruiting plan and let me know. Thanks.

Bill

To: Bill Smithers
From: Marjorie Morgan
Subject: re: Recruiting
Attachment: ad draft

Bill,

Here is my plan for recruiting new staff members for this summer. I will place ads in our local newspapers, in two major national papers, and on the major websites by April 1. The deadline for submission of applications will be April 30. We will start interviews on May 8. In the ads I will carefully outline the qualifications we are looking for. I am attaching a draft of the ad. Please look it over and send me your comments. I want to make sure it contains all the details you want.

Marjorie

19. Why does Mr. Smithers need to hire new staff members?
    (A) He has recently fired several employees.
    (B) His company has a lot of work.
    (C) Marjorie Morgan is leaving her job.
    (D) Several employees have been promoted.

20. What does Mr. Smithers ask Ms. Morgan to do?
    (A) Interview job candidates.
    (B) Send him comments.
    (C) Make a plan to recruit new employees.
    (D) Read the major national newspapers.

21. What will happen by April 30?
    (A) Job candidates will submit their applications.
    (B) Interviews will begin.
    (C) Two or three new staff members will be hired.
    (D) The new staff members will begin working.

22. The word *candidates* in line 7 of the first e-mail is closest in meaning to
    (A) advertisements
    (B) descriptions
    (C) recommendations
    (D) applicants

23. The word *qualifications* in line 7 of the second e-mail is closest in meaning to
    (A) quantities
    (B) positions
    (C) abilities
    (D) salaries

Lesson 12

Applying and Interviewing

WORDS TO LEARN

ability

apply

background

call in

confidence

constantly

expert

follow up

hesitant

interview

present

weakly

Study the following definitions and examples.

1. **ability** n., a skill; a competence
   a. The designer's ability was obvious from her portfolio.
   b. The ability to work with others is a key requirement.

2. **apply** v., to look for; to submit an application
   a. The college graduate applied for three jobs and received three offers.
   b. Everyone who is interested should apply in person at any branch office.

3. **background** n., a person's experience, education, and family history
   a. Your background in the publishing industry is a definite asset for this job.
   b. The employer did a complete background check before offering him the job.

4. **call in** v., to ask to come; to beckon
   a. The young woman was so excited when she was called in for an interview that she told everyone she knew.
   b. The human resources manager called in all the qualified applicants for a second interview.

5. **confidence** n., a belief in one's abilities; self-esteem
   a. Good applicants show confidence during an interview.
   b. He had too much confidence and thought that the job was his.

6. **constantly** adj., on a continual basis; happening all the time
   a. The company is constantly looking for highly trained employees.
   b. Martin constantly checked his messages to see if anyone had called for an interview.

7. **expert** n., a specialist
   a. Our department head is an expert in financing.
   b. The candidate demonstrated that he was an expert in marketing.

8. **follow up** v., to take additional steps; to continue; n., the continuation of a previous action
   a. Always follow up an interview with a thank-you note.
   b. As a follow up, the candidate sent the company a list of references.

9. **hesitant** adj., reluctant; with reservation
   a. Marla was hesitant about negotiating a higher salary.
   b. The recent college graduate was hesitant about accepting his first offer.

10. **interview** n., a meeting for getting information; v., to ask a series of questions
    a. It is very important to act professionally during a job interview.
    b. We had to interview a lot of people before we found the right one for the job.

11. **present** v., to introduce; to show; to offer for consideration
    a. The human resources director presents each candidate's résumé to the department supervisor for review.
    b. The candidate presented her qualifications so well that the employer offered her a job on the spot.

12. **weakly** adv., without strength; poorly
    a. Her hands trembled and she spoke weakly at the interview.
    b. She wrote so weakly we couldn't read it.

WORD FAMILIES

verb	apply	Your chances are better if you apply for a job in the spring.
noun	applicant	The manager selected him from all the applicants.
noun	application	The department can't process your application until all documents have been received.

noun	confidence	It's refreshing to see a manager with so much confidence in her employees.
adjective	confident	Don't be too confident until you actually have an offer.
adverb	confidently	The applicant confidently walked into the interview, sat down, and began to talk about himself.

noun	expert	That company has an opening for an information technology expert.
noun	expertise	They hired her because of her Internet expertise.
adjective	expert	As an expert negotiator, she should have no problem getting the salary that she wants.

adjective	hesitant	The applicant was hesitant to explain his reason for leaving his last job.
noun	hesitation	Her hesitation about accepting the job made the department wonder if she was really interested.
verb	hesitate	Don't hesitate to call if you have any questions concerning the job.

verb	present	I'd like to present my résumé for your consideration.
noun	presentation	The applicant's presentation made a favorable impression.
adjective	presentable	The applicant was well dressed and presentable.

adverb	weakly	The applicant shook hands weakly, making me question her strength of character.
adjective	weak	She gave a weak description of her computer skills.
noun	weakness	Interviewers often ask candidates about their strengths and weaknesses.

WORDS IN CONTEXT

Read the following passage and write the words in the blanks below.

abilities	called in	experts	interview
apply	confidence	follow up	present
backgrounds	constantly	hesitant	weaknesses

How many times in your life will you search for a new job? The (1) _____ say probably more times than you think! Some people find the job search time-consuming and hard on their self- (2) _____. The best job hunters are those who never stop looking and don't dwell on their (3) _____. They network (4) _____: at meetings, at social gatherings, and with people they meet on the street. They (5) _____ periodically with contacts and acquaintances to keep up with new developments.

Good job hunters assess their (6) _____ all the time. Before they even (7) _____ for a position, they have researched the field and the specific companies they are interested in. They know where they could fit into the company and they tailor their résumés for each position. They try to show how their (8) _____ match the job opening. Therefore, they're prepared to answer almost any question they may be asked in an (9) _____. When they're finally (10) _____ to meet their prospective employers, they're ready.

At the interview, these job hunters know that they must (11) _____ themselves in the best way possible. This is their opportunity to shine. It is also their opportunity to see if this is truly the job that they want. If either party is (12) _____ at the interview, it may be a sign that it isn't a good fit.

WORD PRACTICE

LISTENING COMPREHENSION

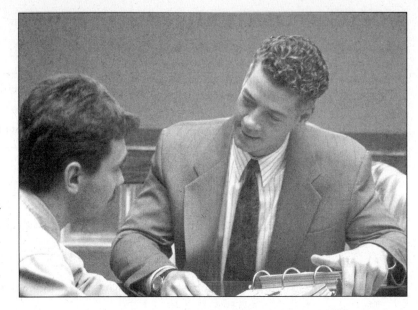

Part 1 Photo

Look at the picture and listen to the sentences.
Choose the sentence that best describes the picture.

1. Ⓐ Ⓑ Ⓒ Ⓓ

Part 2 Question–Response

Listen to the question and the three responses. Choose the response that best answers the question.

2. Ⓐ Ⓑ Ⓒ   3. Ⓐ Ⓑ Ⓒ

Part 3 Conversation

Listen to the dialogue. Then read each question and choose the best answer.

4. What do people think about the woman now?
    (A) She has no confidence.
    (B) She is an expert.
    (C) She is a beginner at networking.
    (D) Her computer skills are weak.

5. What was the woman hesitant to do?
    (A) Apply for a job.
    (B) Use a computer.
    (C) Give a presentation.
    (D) Go to a job interview.

6. What does the man want the woman to do?
    (A) Help him with a workshop.
    (B) Speak at a conference.
    (C) Give him some change.
    (D) Hire him.

Part 4 Talk

Listen to the talk. Then read each question and choose the best answer.

7. Who would call in to this hotline?
    (A) An expert in Salvo's product line.
    (B) An employer.
    (C) A human resources presenter.
    (D) A job seeker.

8. What is the purpose of this recording?
    (A) To inform callers about Salvo.
    (B) To explain to callers what they can do.
    (C) To present the company's philosophy.
    (D) To give background information about a
        product problem.

9. What kind of people is Salvo currently looking for?
    (A) Fashion designers.
    (B) Foreign language speakers.
    (C) Human resource experts.
    (D) Software users.

READING

Part 5 Incomplete Sentences

Choose the word that best completes the sentence.

10. So many well-qualified people _____ for the position that we won't be able to make a decision for several weeks.
    (A) applying   (C) applicant
    (B) application   (D) applied

11. As the interview continued, the applicant's _____ began to decline.
    (A) confidently   (C) confidence
    (B) confident   (D) confidential

12. The applicant's unique _____ enabled her to have almost any job that she wanted.
    (A) expertise   (C) expertly
    (B) experts   (D) expert

13. She spoke without _____, expressing self-confidence and projecting that she had a firm handle on the information.
    (A) hesitant   (C) hesitatingly
    (B) hesitate   (D) hesitation

14. During an interview, it is important to _____ your weaknesses in a way that shows you are working to improve them.
    (A) presentation   (C) presentable
    (B) present   (D) presenting

15. Her handshake had always felt like a dead fish and it was taken as a sign of a _____ character.
    (A) weak   (C) weakness
    (B) weakly   (D) weakening

Part 6 Text Completion

When you go on a job interview, the most important thing to remember is to present yourself well. Before you go, prepare yourself by dressing neatly and professionally. When you arrive, enter the interview room _____.

         16. (A) confident
             (B) confidently
             (C) confide
             (D) confidence

Look the interviewer in the eye when you shake hands. When you talk about yourself, do not be shy about your abilities. You are there to prove that you can do the job. Explain your work and educational background briefly and discuss the skills you have developed through experience. _____ to

         17. (A) No hesitation
             (B) Not hesitating
             (C) Don't hesitate
             (D) Doesn't hesitate

point out areas in which you have expertise. The worst thing you can do is discuss your experience weakly. Remember, if you believe in yourself, other people will, too. Don't forget to _____ the interview with a thank-you

        18. (A) call in
            (B) apply to
            (C) be ready for
            (D) follow up

note before a week has passed.

Part 7 Reading Comprehension

Questions 19–23 refer to the following letter.

Matilda Moreno,
Human Resources Director
Milestone Marketing, Inc.
1476 Honeycutt Avenue
Riverdale

Dear Ms. Moreno,

I am writing in response to your ad in last Sunday's newspaper. I am interested in applying for the marketing research assistant position. I have the background and abilities you are looking for. I have recently graduated from a four-year university program with a degree in Marketing. My work experience includes three months working as an intern for a local marketing firm, so I have on-the-job marketing experience in addition to my university training. I have also worked for the past two years as a part-time office manager while going to school. My experience at this job allowed me to develop important managerial and organizational skills.

I currently live in Deerfield but am interested in relocating to Riverdale. I will be visiting Riverdale during the first week of next month and am ready to come in for an interview any time during that week.

I am enclosing my résumé and three letters of reference. Please don't hesitate to contact me if you have any questions or need further information. I believe I am a good match for your company, and I am confident that I can do the job. I look forward to hearing from you.

Sincerely,

Samuel Rutherford

19. What kind of job is Mr. Rutherford looking for?
    (A) Office manager.
    (B) Human resources director.
    (C) Marketing research assistant.
    (D) Newspaper reporter.

20. When does he want to have an interview?
    (A) Sunday.
    (B) Next week.
    (C) Next month.
    (D) In three months.

21. What does he include with this letter?
    (A) A copy of his university degree.
    (B) Three reference books.
    (C) A job description.
    (D) His résumé.

22. The word *background* in line 2 is closest in meaning to
    (A) experience
    (B) location
    (C) position
    (D) age

23. The word *confident* in line 14 is closest in meaning to
    (A) afraid
    (B) lucky
    (C) glad
    (D) sure

Lesson 13

Hiring and Training

WORDS TO LEARN

conduct

generate

hire

keep up with

look up to

mentor

on track

reject

set up

success

training

update

Study the following definitions and examples.

1. **conduct** v., to hold, to take place
   a. We plan to conduct the training session in the auditorium.
   b. The interviews were conducted over a period of three weeks.

2. **generate** v., to create, to produce
   a. The new training program generated a lot of interest among employees.
   b. The job fair at the college campus should generate interest in our company.

3. **hire** n., an employee; v., to employ, to offer a job or position
   a. The new hire has integrated well with his colleagues.
   b. She was hired after her third interview.

4. **keep up with** v., to stay equal with
   a. The workers were told that they must keep up with the changes or they would find themselves without jobs.
   b. Employees are encouraged to take courses in order to keep up with new developments.

5. **look up to** v., to admire, to think highly of
   a. Staff members looked up to the director because he had earned their respect over the years.
   b. There are few people in this world that I look up to as much as I look up to you.

6. **mentor** n., a person who guides and instructs, a resource
   a. The mentor helped her make some decisions about combining career and family.
   b. One problem with many programs is that the mentors don't feel invested in the progress of the employees with whom they are working.

7. **on track** adj., on schedule; focused
   a. If we stay on track, the meeting should be finished at 9:30.
   b. You have a lot of work; if you can't stay on track, let me know immediately.

8. **reject** n., something that has been turned down; v., to turn down; to say no, to not accept
   a. We put the rejects in this box.
   b. Even though Mr. Lukin rejected their offer, they remained in contact.

9. **set up** v., to establish, to arrange
   a. Check with your supervisor to make sure that your office is all set up before you begin work.
   b. Set up a time and place for the meeting and then inform everyone who is involved.

10. **success** n., an accomplishment; the reaching of a goal
    a. The director's success came after years of hiring the right people at the right time.
    b. When the manager won an award, he attributed his success to his colleagues.

11. **training** n., the preparation or education for a specific job
    a. The new hire received such good training that, within a week, she was as productive as the other workers.
    b. The training is designed to prepare all workers, new and old, for the changes that the company will face.

12. **update** v., to make current
    a. He updated the employees on the latest personnel changes.
    b. We update the calendar weekly.

WORD FAMILIES

verb	generate	The newspaper article generated a lot of interest in working for our company.
noun	generation	The new job advertisements have resulted in the generation of hundreds of applications.
noun	generator	The personnel director was the generator of the ideas behind our new hiring policy.

verb	hire	The personnel director needed to hire 15 people within a week.
noun	hire	The new hire quickly gained a reputation for excellent work.
gerund	hiring	The hiring took the company much longer than expected.

verb	reject	The candidate rejected the offer the first time, but the second time she accepted it.
noun	rejection	Rejections are difficult, but you can learn something from them.
gerund	rejecting	Rejecting a job offer before you have it is not a smart thing to do.

verb	succeed	In order to succeed in this business, you must be persistent.
noun	success	Don't let success go to your head!
adjective	successful	The trainers were very successful with this last group of new hires.

verb	train	Even though you were trained on a Macintosh, you'll have to learn how to use a PC.
noun	trainer	The trainer stayed after the meeting to answer any questions.
noun	trainee	Each new employee spends six weeks as a trainee.

verb	update	One of the job responsibilities is to update the blog at least once daily.
noun	update	According to the latest update, they are ready to start interviewing the candidates.
adjective	updated	That schedule is old; let me get you an updated schedule.

WORDS IN CONTEXT

Read the following passage and write the words in the blanks below.

conducted	keep up with	on track	successfully
generate	look up to	rejected	training
hires	mentor	set up	update

After the ads have been placed, and the interviews have been (1) _____, decisions have to be made. Who should the company bring onboard? Job offers are extended and they are either accepted or (2) _____. For those who accept the offer, the job search has been completed (3) _____. But for both the employer and the new hire, the job has just begun.

Companies want new employees to (4) _____ new business and new ideas as soon as possible. Before they can do that, the new (5) _____ need some (6) _____. All companies have unique expectations and methods of operating. Company trainers conduct workshops and seminars for both experienced and new workers. All employees must prepare for the future and continuously (7) _____ themselves in their field. Nowadays, workers are expected to (8) _____ the latest trends and information. Otherwise, they fall behind.

Many companies (9) _____ a mentoring program for new employees. The (10) _____ is usually an experienced manager or employee and should be someone whom the new employee can (11) _____. Mentors often review goals and objectives with their mentorees and help them to stay (12) _____.

WORD PRACTICE

LISTENING COMPREHENSION

TRACK
14

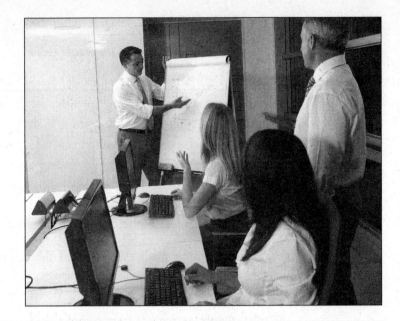

Part 1 Photo

Look at the picture and listen to the sentences.
Choose the sentence that best describes the picture.

1. Ⓐ Ⓑ Ⓒ Ⓓ

Part 2 Question–Response

Listen to the question and the three responses. Choose the response that best answers the question.

2. Ⓐ Ⓑ Ⓒ   3. Ⓐ Ⓑ Ⓒ

Part 3 Conversation

Listen to the dialogue. Then read each question and choose the best response.

4. What is the response to the training program?
   (A) Boredom.
   (B) Confusion.
   (C) Chaos.
   (D) Enthusiasm.

5. How long will the training program last?
   (A) One week.
   (B) Two weeks.
   (C) Three weeks.
   (D) Four weeks.

6. What will the woman do now?
   (A) Join a discussion.
   (B) Set up the room.
   (C) Look for seating.
   (D) Write a letter.

Part 4 Talk

Listen to the talk. Then read each question and choose the best answer.

7. Who is listening to this talk?
   (A) New workers.
   (B) Annual trainers.
   (C) Patients.
   (D) New mentors.

8. What will they do first?
   (A) Select participants for the program.
   (B) Think of traits of good teachers.
   (C) Generate a list of rules.
   (D) Hear an update on sales figures.

9. How long will they spend on the first activity?
   (A) Two minutes.
   (B) Three minutes.
   (C) Four minutes.
   (D) Five minutes.

READING

Part 5 Incomplete Sentences

Choose the word that best completes the sentence.

10. The presentation was _____ for the benefit of the new hires.
    (A) conduct   (C) conducting
    (B) conducted   (D) conductor

11. At next week's meeting we hope to _____ some new ideas for recruiting job applicants.
    (A) generated   (C) generates
    (B) generate   (D) generating

12. After he was _____, he continued to take classes to upgrade his skills.
    (A) hiring   (C) hired
    (B) hires   (D) hire

13. Unfortunately, not all candidates can be offered a job; some have to be _____.
    (A) rejected   (C) conducted
    (B) hired   (D) generated

14. The _____ of the program depends on the active participation of everyone.
    (A) successfully   (C) successful
    (B) succeed   (D) success

15. In all my years of _____, I have never seen such a motivated group of new hires.
    (A) trainee   (C) trains
    (B) training   (D) trainer

Part 6 Text Completion

MENTORING

In order to ensure the _____ of new hires, many companies have

      16. (A) success
          (B) succeed
          (C) successful
          (D) successfully

implemented a mentor program. This is a formal way to provide new hires with the guidance they need to understand their responsibilities, to _____, and to keep from falling behind. With a mentor in place, the

17. (A) set up
    (B) look up to
    (C) put up with
    (D) stay on track

new hire knows exactly whom to go to when confused about policies and procedures. In addition, many mentors conduct regular meetings with the people they are responsible for. This way they can make sure that no serious problems arise. A mentor does not necessarily replace formal _____

               18. (A) train
                   (B) trainer
                   (C) trained
                   (D) training

programs. In fact, they often go hand in hand. New hires may need a lot of support initially. Mentors are a good way to provide this.

Part 7 Reading Comprehension

Questions 19–23 refer to the following memo and e-mail message.

MEMO

To: All new hires
From: Edwin Mallory, Human Resources Director
Re: Training session

All new hires are required to attend a training session which will take place on Friday, October 12 from 9:30 A.M. until 3:30 P.M. The session will be conducted in Meeting Room 3, and lunch will be provided. During the session you will get an overview of company policies and procedures. You will also be updated on changes in the benefits package and learn about professional development opportunities you will be required to participate in so that you can keep up with changes in your field. Attendance at this training is mandatory for everyone hired since June of this year. There will be no excuses.

To: Edwin Mallory
From: Amelia Foote
Subject: Training session

Dear Mr. Mallory,

I just learned from your memo that I will be required to attend the training session on October 12. Unfortunately, I had already planned to be out of the office that week attending my niece's wedding. My supervisor has given me permission to take that time off, and I have already purchased my plane tickets. I didn't know about the date of the training session when I set up these plans, and it will be very difficult to change them now. My mentor suggested that I ask you for permission to miss this training session. I am willing to attend the next session instead. I hope you don't reject this offer. It is very important to me to be able to attend this family event. Thank you.

Amelia Foote

---

19. How long will the training session last?
    (A) Three hours.
    (B) Six hours.
    (C) Nine hours.
    (D) Twelve hours.

20. Who must attend the training session?
    (A) All company employees.
    (B) Only members of the Human Resources Department.
    (C) Mentors and supervisors.
    (D) All new hires.

21. Why doesn't Amelia Foote want to attend the training session?
    (A) She has an important family event.
    (B) She thinks it won't be useful.
    (C) She believes the next session will be better.
    (D) She doesn't have permission from her supervisor.

22. The word *conducted* in lines 3–4 of the memo is closest in meaning to
    (A) announced
    (B) informed
    (C) learned
    (D) held

23. The word *reject* in line 12 of the e-mail is closest in meaning to
    (A) consider
    (B) accept
    (C) say no
    (D) agree to

Lesson 14

Salaries and Benefits

WORDS TO LEARN

aware

basis

benefit

compensate

delicately

eligible

flexibly

negotiate

raise

retire

vested

wage

Study the following definitions and examples.

1. **aware** adj., knowing or noticing something
   a. The new staff member wasn't aware of the company's position on working a second job.
   b. Are you aware of the new employee's past work history?

2. **basis** n., the main reason for something; a base or foundation
   a. The manager didn't have any basis for firing the employee.
   b. On the basis of my ten years of loyalty to this company, I feel that I deserve three weeks vacation.

3. **benefit** n., an advantage provided to an employee in addition to salary; v., to take advantage of
   a. Although the analyst earned a better salary at his new job, his benefits were better at his previous job.
   b. We all benefit from the company's policy of semiannual reviews.

4. **compensate** v., to pay; to make up for
   a. The company compensates employees for overtime by paying double for extra hours.
   b. The company will compensate employees for any travel expenses.

5. **delicately** adv., with sensitivity
   a. Senior management is handling these contract negotiations delicately.
   b. The manager delicately asked about the health of his client.

6. **eligible** adj., able to participate in something; qualified
   a. Some employees may be eligible for the tuition reimbursement plan.
   b. I don't understand why I'm not eligible if I have been with the company for over a year.

7. **flexibly** adv., with the ability to change; loosely
   a. My manager thinks flexibly, enabling herself to solve many sticky problems.
   b. We need to respond flexibly if we want to keep customers in this competitive market.

8. **negotiate** v., to talk for the purpose of reaching an agreement, especially on prices or contracts
   a. You must know what you want and what you can accept when you negotiate a salary.
   b. The associate looked forward to the day that she would be able to negotiate her own contracts.

9. **raise** n., an increase in salary; v., to move up
   a. With his raise, Mr. Drvoshanov was able to afford to buy a new car.
   b. We need to raise the standard for timeliness.

10. **retire** v., to stop working; to withdraw from a business or profession
    a. She retired at the age of 64 but continued to be very active with volunteer work.
    b. Many people would like to win the lottery and retire.

11. **vested** adj., guaranteed as a right; involved
    a. The day that Ms. Weng became fully vested in the retirement plan, she gave her two weeks' notice.
    b. The company has a vested interest in the happiness of its employees.

12. **wage** n., the money paid for work done, usually hourly
    a. Hourly wages have increased by 20 percent over the last two years.
    b. The intern spends more than half of her wages on rent.

WORD FAMILIES

verb	base	We base promotions on seniority.
noun	basis	Salary raises are determined on the basis of performance alone.
adjective	basic	The basic problem with this job is that the wages are too low.

verb	benefit	In order to benefit from the plan, you must fill out the paperwork and submit it to the personnel office.
noun	benefits	The new employee's benefits went into effect three months after his start date.
adjective	beneficial	The service that the insurance has provided has been very beneficial.

verb	compensate	The company compensates its full-time employees well.
noun	compensation	Compensation will be based on your work performance over the past six months.
adjective	compensatory	Compensatory time is given in lieu of overtime pay.

adverb	flexibly	She approaches problems flexibly, looking at the situation from every different angle.
adjective	flexible	Younger workers tend to be more flexible with their work schedules.
noun	flexibility	His flexibility on benefits was one of the main reasons we were able to hire him at this time.

verb	negotiate	The employee prepared a list of her accomplishments to share with her supervisor so that she could negotiate a higher salary.
noun	negotiation	The director was very pleased that the negotiations brought about the end of the strike.
noun	negotiator	I should take lessons from Mr. Tarsa; he is such a skilled negotiator.

verb	retire	Many people don't know what to do with all their time when they retire from work.
noun	retirement	The administrator added more money to the fund for her retirement.
adjective	retired	The retired worker came back to the office from time to time to see his friends.

WORDS IN CONTEXT

Read the following passage and write the words in the blanks below.

aware	compensated	flexibility	retirement
basis	delicate	negotiated	vested
benefits	eligible	raise	wage

An important part of the job search often comes after an offer has been made. Papers should not be signed until you have successfully (1) _____ your salary and (2) _____. You want to make sure you will be adequately (3) _____ for your skills, work, and time. This is a (4) _____ and difficult area. You should be (5) _____ of what the salary ranges are at the company and in the field.

Some workers are not on a salary; rather they work for an hourly (6) _____. In some cases, workers who earn an hourly wage have more (7) _____ with the hours they work. The trade-off is that the worker may not receive any benefits. For those workers on a salary, the base salary that is negotiated is critical, because most subsequent pay raises come in small incremental amounts. Most companies have a review process either on an annual or semi-annual (8) _____. As a result of the review, an employee may receive a (9) _____.

Each employee has a unique situation. Health insurance coverage and (10) _____ plans may be essential to some employees, whereas they are not important to others. Many companies will offer benefits in such a way that it is to the employee's advantage to stay with the company for a longer period of time. Employees may not be (11) _____ to sign up for a retirement plan until they have been with the company for one year and employees are not fully (12) _____ in these plans until they have five years of service under their belts. Some bonus plans are paid out over a period of years. Vacation time increases after more years of service.

WORD PRACTICE

LISTENING COMPREHENSION

Part 1 Photo

Look at the picture and listen to the sentences.
Choose the sentence that best describes the picture.

1. Ⓐ Ⓑ Ⓒ Ⓓ

Part 2 Question–Response

Listen to the question and the three responses. Choose the response that best answers the question.

2. Ⓐ Ⓑ Ⓒ   3. Ⓐ Ⓑ Ⓒ

Part 3 Conversation

Listen to the dialogue. Then read each question and choose the best response.

4. Why is the man disappointed?
   (A) His health coverage is poor.
   (B) He asked for too much compensation.
   (C) He doesn't know how to negotiate.
   (D) He doesn't earn enough money.

5. How long has he been working at the company?
   (A) Two months.
   (B) Four months.
   (C) Six months.
   (D) Nine months.

6. What benefit does he get?
   (A) Life insurance.
   (B) Health insurance.
   (C) Paid vacation.
   (D) Regular raises.

Part 4 Talk

Listen to the talk. Then read each question and choose the best answer.

7. How often are raises given?
   (A) Once a year.
   (B) Twice a year.
   (C) At an employee's request.
   (D) Whenever an employee is eligible for a raise.

8. Where should employees go to learn more about wage increases?
   (A) The Employee Handbook.
   (B) Their paycheck stubs.
   (C) Their contract.
   (D) Their supervisor.

9. How many days of paid vacation does each employee get?
   (A) Five.
   (B) Ten.
   (C) Fourteen.
   (D) Forty-two.

READING

Part 5 Incomplete Sentences

Choose the word that best completes the sentence.

10. All temporary workers are paid on an hourly _____ and receive no benefits.
    - (A) base
    - (B) based
    - (C) basis
    - (D) basic

11. What is the company's policy on _____ for part-time workers?
    - (A) benefited
    - (B) beneficial
    - (C) benefits
    - (D) benefit

12. The tired employee hoped that she would be _____ for all the long hours she kept and weekends she worked.
    - (A) compensation
    - (B) compensates
    - (C) compensated
    - (D) compensate

13. Sometimes the manager is too _____ and his workers take advantage of him.
    - (A) flex
    - (B) flexible
    - (C) flexibly
    - (D) flexibility

14. If the _____ continue into the evening, we will break for dinner at six.
    - (A) negotiator
    - (B) negotiations
    - (C) negotiate
    - (D) negotiated

15. No one is sure what will happen to the company when the president finally _____.
    - (A) retires
    - (B) retirement
    - (C) retired
    - (D) retiree

Part 6 Text Completion

To all union members:

Your union has been working for you. You may _____ aware that we have been negotiating

16. (A) be
    (B) is
    (C) are
    (D) were

with management for improvements in the benefits package. Yesterday an agreement was reached on the following points:

1) All employees of the company will be _____ for an increase in wages every six

17. (A) flexible
    (B) beneficial
    (C) eligible
    (D) negotiable

months, following a performance review. Reasons for refusal to give a raise must be carefully documented according to union guidelines.

2) Employees _____ at one and a half times their usual hourly wages for overtime

18. (A) will compensate
    (B) are going to compensate
    (C) will be compensated
    (D) have to compensate

hours. Any time worked beyond 40 hours a week counts as overtime.

3) Part-time employees can now receive full health benefits. It is each employee's responsibility to complete and submit the application forms. Part-time employees are also guaranteed five days of paid vacation per year. These two benefits apply to employees who work a minimum of 20 hours per week on a permanent basis.

Part 7 Reading Comprehension

Questions 19–23 refer to the following e-mail message.

To: James Porter
From: Helene Bourassa
Subject: Re: Benefits questions

Dear James,

I will try to clarify for you your questions about retirement benefits.

Time of retirement: The time at which an employee can retire is calculated on the basis of age and number of years of service to the company. An employee of the company can retire with full benefits at age 55 if he or she has worked a minimum of 30 years for the company. Employees can retire at age 60 or above with 25 years of service to the company. Since you are younger than 60 years old and have worked for the company for 22 years, you won't be eligible to retire for another few years.

Benefits for your spouse: I know this is a delicate matter, but it is important to know about. If you die before your spouse, she will continue to receive full retirement benefits for the rest of her life.

Health insurance: Retirees are eligible to receive health insurance. There are several packages to choose from, and I will send you brochures about them. Your spouse will also be eligible for health coverage when you retire. If you happen to have any dependent children under the age of 21 and living at home, they, too, will be eligible for health coverage.

I hope this answers your questions. Please don't hesitate to contact me if you need any further information.

Helene

19. How old is James Porter?
    (A) Between 22 and 25.
    (B) 25.
    (C) Younger than 60.
    (D) Exactly 60.

20. Who can receive retirement benefits after James dies?
    (A) His children.
    (B) His wife.
    (C) All of his dependents.
    (D) Nobody.

21. Who can get health coverage when James retires?
    (A) His 19-year-old son who lives at home.
    (B) His 20-year-old daughter who lives with her spouse.
    (C) Any of his children who want it.
    (D) Only his wife.

22. The word *basis* in line 2 is closest in meaning to
    (A) solution
    (B) formula
    (C) amount
    (D) foundation

23. The word *delicate* in line 7 is closest in meaning to
    (A) sensitive
    (B) complicated
    (C) necessary
    (D) interesting

Lesson 15

Promotions, Pensions, and Awards

WORDS TO LEARN

achievement
contribute
dedication
look forward to
look to
loyal
merit
obviously
praise
promote
recognition
value

Study the following definitions and examples.

1. **achievement** n., an accomplishment; a completed act
    a. Your main achievements will be listed in your personnel file.
    b. Joseph's achievements in R&D will go down in company history.
2. **contribute** v., to add to; to donate, to give
    a. Make sure your boss is aware of the work you contributed to the project.
    b. All employees are asked to contribute a few minutes of their spare time to clean up the office.
3. **dedication** n., a commitment to something
    a. The director's dedication to a high-quality product has motivated many of his employees.
    b. We would never be where we are today if it weren't for many long hours and so much dedication.
4. **look forward to** v., to anticipate; to be eager for something to happen
    a. The regional director was looking forward to the new, larger offices.
    b. We look forward to seeing you at the next meeting.
5. **look to** v., to depend on; to rely on
    a. The workers always looked to him to settle their disagreements.
    b. The staff is looking to their supervisor for guidance and direction.
6. **loyal** adj., faithful; believing in someone or something
    a. You have been such a loyal advisor for so many years, I'm not sure what I'll do without you.
    b. Even though your assistant is loyal, you have to question his job performance.
7. **merit** n., excellence; high quality
    a. Employees are evaluated on their merit and not on seniority.
    b. Your work has improved tremendously and is of great merit.
8. **obviously** adv., clearly; evidently
    a. Her tardiness was obviously resented by her coworkers.
    b. He was obviously working hard to get the promotion.
9. **praise** n., the expression of approval or admiration; v., to express approval or admiration
    a. John received a lot of praise for the article he wrote about business trends.
    b. It never hurts to praise an employee for a job well done.
10. **promote** v., to give someone a better job; to support; to make known
    a. Even though the sales associate had a good year, it wasn't possible to promote him.
    b. The assistant director promoted the idea that the director was incompetent.
11. **recognition** n., credit; praise for doing something well
    a. The president's personal assistant was finally given the recognition that she has deserved for many years.
    b. Recognition of excellent work should be routine for every manager.
12. **value** v., to state the worth
    a. Employees value their colleagues' opinions.
    b. The expert valued the text at $7,000.

WORD FAMILIES

noun	achievement	His achievements were noticed by the vice president and he was sent to the London office.
verb	achieve	Making a list of your objectives will help you achieve them.
noun	achiever	Mr. Vadji always considered himself a high achiever.

verb	contribute	All employees were urged to contribute something useful at the staff meetings.
noun	contribution	Each of you has made a significant contribution to our team's success.
noun	contributor	As contributors to the company's outstanding year, all employees will receive an additional holiday bonus.

verb	dedicate	The manager dedicates too much time to reports and not enough time to the customer.
noun	dedication	Margo's dedication to the company was rewarded with a two-week trip to Hawaii.
adjective	dedicated	Before the change in management, he used to be a more dedicated worker.

adjective	loyal	He has been both a loyal coworker and a loyal friend.
noun	loyalty	Her loyalty to the company impressed even the owners.
adverb	loyally	The security officer loyally guarded the company's vault.

verb	promote	In order to move ahead in the company, you must promote yourself.
noun	promotion	Promotions are given to those who prove their worth.
noun	promoter	As the main promoter of the product, Ms. Ross was responsible for the marketing campaign.

WORDS IN CONTEXT

Read the following passage and write the words in the blanks below.

achievements	look forward	merits	promotions
contributions	look to	obvious	recognizes
dedicate	loyalty	praised	value

Congratulations. You have been chosen by your colleagues to receive the Keeler Award of Excellence. This prestigious award (1) _____ employees who have made extraordinary (2) _____ to the corporation over the years.

Your coworkers gave several reasons for selecting you. First, they mentioned your (3) _____ in the marketing department. You have increased sales for our company every year during the past four years. In addition, you have received four (4) _____ during the same period of time, taking on ever greater levels of responsibility, due to the (5) _____ of your work in developing our image in new markets. Your (6) _____ to the department is (7) _____ to everyone who works with you. The extra hours you regularly put in never go unnoticed. You are a mentor to your coworkers, who often (8) _____ you for advice. Your supervisor (9) _____ your high productivity.

The Keeler Award acknowledges an employee's (10) _____ with a $1,000 bonus. We (11) _____ to the opportunity to (12) _____ a rosebush in the company garden in each recipient's name.

The awards ceremony will be held on August 7 on the front lawn at 10:30 A.M. Again, congratulations.

WORD PRACTICE

LISTENING COMPREHENSION

Part 1 Photo

Look at the picture and listen to the sentences.
Choose the sentence that best describes the picture.

1. Ⓐ Ⓑ Ⓒ Ⓓ

Part 2 Question–Response

Listen to the question and the three responses. Choose the response that best answers the question.

2. Ⓐ Ⓑ Ⓒ   3. Ⓐ Ⓑ Ⓒ

Part 3 Conversation

Listen to the dialogue. Then read each question and choose the best response.

4. Why will the ceremony be held?
   (A) To honor Darrell.
   (B) To boast about production figures.
   (C) To celebrate the opening of a new office.
   (D) To present awards.

5. When will the ceremony be held?
   (A) Today.
   (B) Tuesday.
   (C) Tonight.
   (D) Tomorrow.

6. What is the speaker's opinion of Darrell?
   (A) He is loyal.
   (B) He is not productive.
   (C) He is unimpressive.
   (D) He is not a hard worker.

Part 4 Talk

Listen to the talk. Then read each question and choose the best answer.

7. Who is talking?
   (A) Two employees.
   (B) An award presenter.
   (C) Community volunteers.
   (D) A professor.

8. Who is the audience?
   (A) Students.
   (B) Customers.
   (C) Employees.
   (D) Citizens.

9. When did the company open?
   (A) 1965.
   (B) 1975.
   (C) 1985.
   (D) 1995.

READING

Part 5 Incomplete Sentences

Choose the word that best completes the sentence.

10. When he thought about his long career, he realized that his biggest _____ was in developing the new leaders of the company.
    (A) achiever   (C) achievement
    (B) achieved   (D) achieves

11. She has _____ so much time and energy to the project that her name should appear on the award.
    (A) contributes   (C) contributed
    (B) contribution   (D) contributor

12. Hard work and _____ will help you move up the corporate ladder.
    (A) dedicated   (C) dedication
    (B) dedicates   (D) dedicated

13. There is no reason to question her _____ to our company.
    (A) loyal   (C) loyalty
    (B) loyally   (D) laurels

14. A word of approval from Susan means a lot since she doesn't give out _____ very easily.
    (A) value   (C) dedication
    (B) praise   (D) contribution

15. Because you are a valued and dedicated employee, we are _____ you to director of the department.
    (A) promoting   (C) promotion
    (B) promote   (D) promoter

Part 6 Text Completion

Dear Harry,

We are pleased to inform you of your promotion within our company. Starting the first of next month, you will begin in your new position as manager of the Fulfillment Department. During your years as a member of the Fulfillment Department staff, you have made many _____ to the productivity and

16. (A) contribute
    (B) contributes
    (C) contributors
    (D) contributions

smooth operation of the department. We have always valued your dedication to your job, and now we are pleased to be able _____ your hard work and fine skills with this promotion. We know you

17. (A) recognize
    (B) to recognize
    (C) recognizing
    (D) will recognize

will do a wonderful job. The Personnel Department will contact you soon regarding the changes in your salary and benefits. We _____ welcoming you to your new position next month.

18. (A) look forward to
    (B) look in on
    (C) look for
    (D) look to

Sincerely,

Madeline Kovacs
President

Part 7 Reading Comprehension

Questions 19–23 refer to the following memo and e-mail message.

To: All company staff
From: Claude Dubois, Personnel Manager
Re: Annual Awards Ceremony

It is time to start getting ready for the company's annual awards ceremony. It will take place at the Merrimack Hotel on Friday, November 10. Up to 15 staff members will receive awards from the company president that evening. We look to you, our company staff, to help us select deserving award recipients. Please send in your nominations for colleagues who you think merit the recognition of an award. Obviously, we would like to see names of people who have contributed more than average to the company. Send me your nominations by e-mail before October 15 so that we can have the list finalized before November 5.
Thank you.

To: claude_dubois@starco.com
From: marilyn_freeland@starco.com
Subject: nomination

Hi Claude,

I would like to nominate my coworker, Janet McGhee, assistant manager of the research department, for an award. Her dedication to her job is far above average. She always works long hours to make sure she gets her job done. If she is working on an important project, she will come into the office on weekends if she thinks it's necessary to completing her job on time. The rest of us in the department always look to Janet as an example of how to get a job done right. If anyone deserves the recognition of an award for loyalty and dedication, it's Janet. I hope you will consider her as an award recipient.

Thank you.

Marilyn

19. When will the awards ceremony be held?
(A) October 15.
(B) November 5.
(C) November 10.
(D) November 15.

20. Who will suggest award recipients?
(A) The personnel manager.
(B) The company president.
(C) The assistant manager.
(D) The company staff members.

21. Why does Marilyn Freeland think Janet McGhee deserves an award?
(A) She works on important projects.
(B) She always works long hours.
(C) She looks to others as an example.
(D) She manages the research department.

22. The word *Obviously* in line 9 of the memo is closest in meaning to
(A) clearly
(B) quickly
(C) usually
(D) importantly

23. The word *dedication* in line 4 of the e-mail is closest in meaning to
(A) ability
(B) commitment
(C) knowledge
(D) attendance

Word Review #3   **Lessons 11–15 Personnel**

Choose the word that best completes the sentence.

1. Coming _____ with a good ad is time-consuming.
   (A) up
   (B) to
   (C) by
   (D) on

2. To _____ the best and the brightest, companies have to be willing to pay well.
   (A) recruit
   (B) recruits
   (C) recruiting
   (D) recruitment

3. A qualified candidate usually exudes _____.
   (A) confident
   (B) confidence
   (C) confidential
   (D) confidentially

4. Any applicant is wise to follow _____ an interview with a note or a phone call.
   (A) after
   (B) behind
   (C) up
   (D) with

5. Workers are promoted on their _____ and merits.
   (A) achieve
   (B) achieved
   (C) achiever
   (D) achievements

6. The benefits package is an important aspect of contract _____.
   (A) negotiate
   (B) negotiable
   (C) negotiations
   (D) negotiated

7. Some employees have to wait years before they are fully _____ in the company pension plan.
   (A) vest
   (B) vested
   (C) vesting
   (D) vests

8. Health _____ are very important for an employee who develops a serious medical problem.
   (A) benefit
   (B) benefits
   (C) beneficial
   (D) beneficiary

9. A _____ and hard-working employee can look forward to rapid promotions.
   (A) dedicate
   (B) dedication
   (C) dedicating
   (D) dedicated

10. An employee who does not meet expectations will _____ not get a promotion.
   (A) obvious
   (B) obviously
   (C) oblivious
   (D) obliviously

Choose the one word or phrase that best completes each sentence.

Thank you for your interest in working at Plytel Corporation. To apply for a position, please _____ a résumé

11. (A) submit
    (B) will submit
    (C) to submit
    (D) submitting

and a letter explaining your background and interest. We will keep your information on file for a year. If your qualifications match available openings, we will call you _____ for an interview. Please do not call us; we will

12. (A) on
    (B) in
    (C) to
    (D) at

contact you if we have a position suited to your _____.

13. (A) able
    (B) ably
    (C) enable
    (D) abilities

When your company has a job opening, it is important to hire the right person for the job. The job interview offers you, the employer, an opportunity to get to know each _____ and assess his or her ability to do the job. You will have

14. (A) expert
    (B) mentor
    (C) supervisor
    (D) candidate

many questions for the applicants, but you should also _____ ready for questions from them. In addition to

15. (A) be
    (B) do
    (C) have
    (D) will be

understanding the job duties, they may want to know about _____ offered by your company such as vacations

16. (A) beneficiaries
    (B) beneficial
    (C) beneficent
    (D) benefits

and health care.

Getting a promotion is a great honor. It means your company _____ your merits. When you are promoted to

17. (A) recruits
    (B) contributes
    (C) recognizes
    (D) dedicates

the position of supervisor, your work life changes. You are now in a position of responsibility. It is important to set a good example because your staff looks _____ you. If you carry out your job responsibilities _____, you will

18. (A) for
    (B) up to
    (C) down on
    (D) forward to

19. (A) confident
    (B) confidence
    (C) confidently
    (D) confidential

gain their respect. This is the key to success in your new position.

Lesson 16

Shopping

WORDS TO LEARN

WORDS TO LEARN

bargain

bear

behavior

checkout

comfort

expand

explore

item

mandatory

merchandise

strictly

trend

Study the following definitions and examples.

1. **bargain** v., to negotiate; n., an advantageous purchase
   a. She bargained for over an hour, finally reducing the price by half.
   b. Lois compared the sweaters carefully to determine which was a better bargain.

2. **bear** v., to have tolerance for; to endure
   a. Moya can't bear crowded stores so she does most of her shopping online.
   b. If you can bear with me, I'd like to stop in one more store.

3. **behavior** n., the manner of one's actions
   a. Annu is conducting a survey on whether consumer behavior differs between men and women.
   b. Suspicious behavior in a department store will draw the attention of the security guards.

4. **checkout** n., the act, time, or place of checking out, as at a hotel, library, or supermarket
   a. The line at this checkout is too long, so let's look for another.
   b. Get in the checkout line now and I'll join you with the last items.

5. **comfort** v., to calm somebody; n., a condition or feeling of pleasurable ease, well-being, and contentment
   a. Some people use shopping as a way to comfort themselves after a stressful day.
   b. I like to dress for comfort if I'm spending the day shopping.

6. **expand** v., to increase the size, volume, quantity, or scope of; to enlarge
   a. The new manager has significantly expanded the store's inventory.
   b. The shoe store is out of room, so the owners are thinking about expanding into the adjacent vacant building.

7. **explore** v., to investigate systematically
   a. The collector likes to explore antique shops looking for bargains.
   b. If you explore the Internet, you'll probably find the item you're looking for at a good price.

8. **item** n., a single article or unit
   a. The grocery store has a special checkout line for people who are purchasing fewer than ten items.
   b. Do you think I can get all these items into one bag?

9. **mandatory** adj., required or commanded; obligatory
   a. The jewelry store has a mandatory policy of showing customers only one item at a time.
   b. There is a mandatory limit of nine items for use of this checkout line.

10. **merchandise** n., items available in stores
    a. I am very impressed with the quality of the merchandise on this website.
    b. Helen wanted to make sure that the store had a wide variety of merchandise before she committed to buying a gift certificate.

11. **strictly** adv., rigidly, without flexibility
    a. Our store strictly enforces its return policy.
    b. Their high turnover rate is no surprise, considering how strictly the manager deals with them.

12. **trend** n., the current style; vogue
    a. The clothing store tries to stay on top of all the new trends.
    b. Mioshi followed market trends closely before she bought a clothing franchise.

WORD FAMILIES

noun	comfort	This car is designed with plush seats for your comfort and air bags for your safety.
adjective	comfortable	I prefer this sweater because it's more comfortable.
adverb	comfortably	I'd suggest buying the larger table, which comfortably seats six.

verb	expand	The bookstore expanded its selection by offering books in several foreign languages.
noun	expansion	The expansion of our sales territory into a new region will mean more stock will have to be ordered.
adjective	expanded	The expanded inventory is great, but it's hard to find room to store it.

verb	explore	Ms. Marce explored the bins of hardware, looking for the right size nails.
noun	exploration	The store designer's exploration of the art of different cultures gave the store an exotic look.
adjective	exploratory	We took an exploratory trip downtown to look for a site for our new store.

verb	mandate	Store policy mandates that all customers be greeted at the door.
noun	mandate	One of the company mandates is to treat all customers with respect.
adjective	mandatory	A credit card is mandatory for shopping online.

verb	merchandise	The purpose of this website is to merchandise a wide selection of office supplies at the lowest possible price.
noun	merchandise	Many stores make their merchandise available online as well as in the store itself.
noun	merchant	The merchants in this neighborhood organize a special sale every year during the holidays.

noun	strictness	Ms. Judd was appalled by the strictness of the store's policy not to renew her gift certificate after it had expired.
adjective	strict	Our store has a strict policy of no returns.
adverb	strictly	The no-food-or-drinks rule is strictly enforced in the bookstore.

WORDS IN CONTEXT

Read the following passage and write the words in the blanks below.

bargains	checkout	exploring	merchandise
bear	comfort	items	strictly
behavior	expand	mandatory	trend

Some people love to shop. Others can't (1) _____ shopping and only go when their clothes are completely worn out or their shelves are empty. No one can get away from shopping—unless you can do without eating! Consumption and consumer (2) _____ affects everything we do.

Some purchases are absolutely (3) _____. Everyone needs to eat, wear clothing, and sit on furniture. Other purchases are (4) _____ for luxury (5) _____. The vast majority of what most of us buy is somewhere in between essential items and frivolous items.

Most people shop by visiting stores on the weekend. It's fun to (6) _____ the number of places you shop in by (7) _____ new stores—even if you don't make a purchase.

Most shoppers are looking for (8) _____. Some people even check out all the aisles looking to see if the items they normally use have been marked down. Everyone loves finding that their favorite items are discounted to a lower price. A sale makes going to the (9) _____ counter a happier event.

A steadily growing (10) _____ is shopping from home. Instead of taking the time to go to stores, many people select (11) _____ from catalogs or websites. You can get almost everything, from books to clothing, without leaving the (12) _____ of your home.

106   ESSENTIAL WORDS FOR THE TOEIC

READING

Part 5 Incomplete Sentences

Choose the word that best completes the sentence.

10. It's hard to tell if these shoes will be _____ because the leather is so stiff.
    (A) comfort (C) comfortable
    (B) comfortably (D) comforting

11. Due to the store's success, the owners began to plan an _____ into a larger location.
    (A) expansion (C) expanse
    (B) expand (D) expanded

12. We _____ the entire store but still couldn't find the item we needed.
    (A) exploratory (C) explorer
    (B) exploration (D) explored

13. According to store policy, it is _____ to show photo identification when making a purchase with a credit card.
    (A) mandatory (C) expanded
    (B) exploratory (D) trendy

14. When you select _____ for the display windows, be sure to include seasonal gifts and clothing.
    (A) merchant (C) merchandise
    (B) merchants (D) merchandising

15. We _____ adhere to the store's policy of only specially ordering products that have been paid for in advance.
    (A) strictness (C) strictly
    (B) strict (D) strictest

Part 6 Text Completion

Attention Bargain Hunters!

Greene's Department Store is having its biggest sale ever. Every single item in the store is on sale at unbelievable prices. That's right—all merchandise, including clothes, shoes, toys, sports equipment, home furnishing, music, and music equipment, is 25 to 75 percent off the usual price.

* Have you always wanted _____ the underwater world? We have diving equipment

    16. (A) explore
        (B) explores
        (C) to explore
        (D) exploring

on sale at 50 percent off.

* Would you like to sleep in a more _____ bed? The prices of beds, mattresses, and

    17. (A) comfort
        (B) comforter
        (C) comfortable
        (D) comfortably

bedroom furniture have been reduced by 35 percent.

* Are you planning _____ your garden? Now it is more affordable than ever. All

    18. (A) will expand
        (B) can expand
        (C) expanding
        (D) to expand

garden plants and gardening equipment are on sale at discounts from 20 to 50 percent off the usual price.

Visit Greene's for the bargains of a lifetime. Sale ends Sunday.

Part 7 Reading Comprehension

Questions 19–23 refer to the following article.

DESIGNING RETAIL SPACE TAKES CAREFUL PLANNING. ATTENTION SHOULD BE PAID TO WHAT RESEARCH TELLS US ABOUT CONSUMER BEHAVIOR. STORES MUST BE DESIGNED WITH THE COMFORT OF SHOPPERS IN MIND. THE AISLES SHOULD BE WIDE ENOUGH TO ALLOW SHOPPERS TO MOVE THROUGH THEM COMFORTABLY. ITEMS SHOULD BE PLACED WHERE THEY CAN BE EASILY SEEN BY SHOPPERS. NOTHING SHOULD BE PUT ON HIGH SHELVES WHERE IT CANNOT BE REACHED. PLEASANT LIGHTING AND MUSIC ALSO CONTRIBUTE TO THE COMFORT AND GOOD FEELING OF SHOPPERS. SHOPPERS WHO FEEL HAPPY AND RELAXED WILL MAKE MORE PURCHASES.

WHEN ORGANIZING THE MERCHANDISE IN A STORE, THE TRENDS OF EACH SEASON SHOULD BE KEPT IN MIND. PICNIC AND BEACH EQUIPMENT SHOULD BE PROMINENTLY DISPLAYED IN THE SUMMER, FOR EXAMPLE, WHILE WARM CLOTHING SHOULD BE FEATURED IN THE WINTER. THEN, SHOPPERS WILL RETURN TO THE STORE BECAUSE THEY WILL SEE IT AS A PLACE THAT PROVIDES WHAT THEY NEED.

THERE SHOULD BE PLENTY OF CHECKOUT AISLES SO THAT LONG LINES ARE AVOIDED. MANY PEOPLE CANNOT BEAR LONG WAITS, AND LONG CHECKOUT LINES SCARE SHOPPERS AWAY FROM STORES. MANY STORES ARE NOW USING SELF-SERVICE CHECKOUT AISLES, ALTHOUGH THEY HAVE NOT YET BEEN COMPLETELY ACCEPTED BY SHOPPERS. THEY ARE OFTEN CONFUSING TO USE, AND MANY SHOPPERS FIND THEM IMPERSONAL. THE OLD-FASHIONED HUMAN CASHIER IS STILL POPULAR IN MOST RETAIL OUTLETS. THEREFORE, IT IS STILL CONSIDERED MANDATORY FOR STORES TO HAVE AT LEAST SOME FULL-SERVICE CHECKOUT LINES MANNED BY CASHIERS.

WHEN A STORE IS PROPERLY DESIGNED, SHOPPERS HAVE A PLEASANT EXPERIENCE AND WILL WANT TO RETURN. THIS HELPS THE BOTTOM LINE OF THE STORE OWNER WHICH IS, OF COURSE, INCREASED SALES.

19. According to the article, which shoppers buy more?
    (A) Those who have more money.
    (B) Those who can reach high shelves.
    (C) Those who feel comfortable in the store.
    (D) Those who shop in the summer.

20. What does the article say about self-service checkout aisles?
    (A) They are popular everywhere.
    (B) They aren't always easy to use.
    (C) They are personal.
    (D) They are mandatory.

21. According to the article, what is the most important thing for a store owner?
    (A) More sales.
    (B) Lighting and music.
    (C) Pleasant cashiers.
    (D) Wide aisles.

22. The word *behavior* in line 2 is closest in meaning to
    (A) questions
    (B) desires
    (C) interests
    (D) actions

23. The word *bear* in line 14 is closest in meaning to
    (A) tolerate
    (B) understand
    (C) refuse
    (D) decrease

Lesson 17

Ordering Supplies

WORDS TO LEARN

consistent

diversify

enterprise

essentially

function

maintain

obtain

prerequisite

quality

smooth

source

stationery

Study the following definitions and examples.

1. **consistent** adj., steady, regular, dependable
   a. If we order new paper and ink at the beginning of every month, we will have a consistent supply of these necessary items.
   b. We order from that supplier because of the consistent quality of their merchandise.
2. **diversify** v., to broaden, to make more varied
   a. The stationery department plans to diversify its offering of paper products.
   b. The consultant that we hired recommends that we don't diversify at this time.
3. **enterprise** n., a business; a large project
   a. The new enterprise quickly established an account with the office supply store.
   b. This enterprise has become unmanageable and is beginning to lose money.
4. **essentially** adv., necessarily, basically, finally
   a. Essentially, she wants to win the contract and put the competition out of business.
   b. After distributing all of the cartridges that were ordered, we were essentially left with none.
5. **function** v., to perform tasks; n., a purpose
   a. This room will function as the supply closet while the office is being painted.
   b. What is the function of this device?
6. **maintain** v., to continue; to support; to sustain
   a. I've been maintaining a list of office supplies that are in greatest demand.
   b. Trying to maintain two different stockrooms is too much work.
7. **obtain** v., to acquire
   a. I've been trying to obtain a list of supplies from the administrator for three weeks now.
   b. We can obtain all the supplies we need online.
8. **prerequisite** n., something that is required or necessary as a prior condition
   a. A prerequisite for ordering supplies is getting the approval of the office manager.
   b. Here are the prerequisites that you need to purchase before coming to class.
9. **quality** n., a distinguishing characteristic; a degree of excellence
   a. The most important qualities we look for in a supplier are reliability and quick response.
   b. I don't recommend ordering supplies from that website since the quality of their merchandise is usually poor.
10. **smooth** adj., without difficulties; deliberately polite and agreeable in order to win favor
    a. Thanks to our smooth transition to the new supplier, there was no interruption in shipments.
    b. Her smooth manner won her the appreciation of the manager but not her colleagues.
11. **source** n., the origin
    a. This website is a good source for paper and other office supplies.
    b. The source of this rare pottery that we are selling in our shop is a small village in India.
12. **stationery** n., writing paper and envelopes
    a. We do not have enough stationery, so please order some more.
    b. The new stationery featured the company's logo in blue ink at the top of the page.

WORD FAMILIES

noun	consistence	That store messes up our order with a consistence that is amazing.
adjective	consistent	The office manager is consistent about ordering supplies at the end of every month.
adverb	consistently	The office manager consistently orders supplies that we don't really need.

verb	diversify	That supplier has diversified its product line and is offering computer accessories as well as computers.
noun	diversity	We order from a website that offers a diversity of office and shipping supplies.
adjective	diverse	The wholesaler offered a more diverse range of computer accessories than I expected.

noun	essence	The essence of the problem lies in the lack of money allocated for supplies.
adjective	essential	Make sure we don't run out of essential supplies such as ink and paper.
adverb	essentially	Essentially, they want our business and will give us the price we ask for.

verb	function	She will function as office manager until a replacement is found.
noun	function	As assistant office manager you have two important functions: keep the supply closet stocked and maintain the office calendar.
adjective	functional	This machine isn't functional so I suggest buying a new one.

verb	maintain	If we maintain the organization of the supply closet, we will know what we have on hand and what we need to order.
noun	maintenance	The maintenance of this photocopier is costing us a great deal of money.
adjective	maintainable	We want to purchase equipment that is easily maintainable.

noun	smoothness	The smoothness of the ordering process encourages me to continue buying supplies from that website.
adjective	smooth	The vendor was so smooth on the phone that he had no difficulty in obtaining an appointment with the office manager.
adverb	smoothly	The meeting went smoothly, and we left with a lot of free samples to try out at the office.

WORDS IN CONTEXT

Read the following passage and write the words in the blanks below.

consistent	essential	obtain	smooth
diverse	functioning	prerequisite	source
enterprise	maintaining	quality	stationery

All businesses, large and small, must maintain an inventory of supplies. It is important to keep a (1) _____ supply of certain basic items that are used every day so that they are always on hand when needed. These include items such as (2) _____, printer ink and paper, pens, and staples. They are easy to (3) _____ from office supply stores, and can also be found online.

Some businesses require a more (4) _____ range of supplies. For example, businesses that ship their products usually need to keep cartons, Styrofoam peanuts, package tape, and shipping labels on hand at all times. These items can also be found at stores and websites that sell office and shipping supplies.

No matter what the type of business, the office administrator is in charge of ordering supplies and (5) _____ an inventory. Having the (6) _____ supplies on hand at all times is a (7) _____ for the (8) _____ and efficient (9) _____ of the (10) _____. The administrator should try to locate the cheapest (11) _____ of the supplies required, but also pay attention to the (12) _____ of the goods.

WORD PRACTICE

LISTENING COMPREHENSION

Part 1 Photo

Look at the picture and listen to the sentences.
Choose the sentence that best describes the picture.

1. Ⓐ Ⓑ Ⓒ Ⓓ

Part 2 Question–Response

Listen to the question and the three responses. Choose the response that best answers the question.

2. Ⓐ Ⓑ Ⓒ   3. Ⓐ Ⓑ Ⓒ

Part 3 Conversation

Listen to the dialogue. Then read each question and choose the best response.

4. What is the man looking for?
    (A) A diverse range of applicants.
    (B) A glassware merchant.
    (C) A pair of eyeglasses.
    (D) A warehouse.

5. How will he obtain more information about what
    he needs?
    (A) He'll write a letter.
    (B) He'll make a phone call.
    (C) The woman will tell him.
    (D) He'll visit a website.

6. When does the woman want to speak to the man
    again?
    (A) Today.
    (B) Tuesday.
    (C) Next week.
    (D) On the weekend.

Part 4 Talk

Listen to the talk. Then read each question and choose the best answer.

7. Who is listening to this talk?
    (A) Upper management at a stationery supplier.
    (B) Employees at a stationery supplier.
    (C) Upper management at Margatel.
    (D) Employees at Margatel.

8. What is the problem?
    (A) There was an order with a mistake.
    (B) The company lost a $50,000 client.
    (C) Employees got locked out of the office.
    (D) A worker slipped and fell.

9. When did Carla take the order?
    (A) January 14.
    (B) January 19.
    (C) January 21.
    (D) January 30.

READING

Part 5 Incomplete Sentences

Choose the word that best completes the sentence.

10. Many customers find that product _____ is confusing and deceptive.
    (A) diversify   (C) diversity
    (B) diverse   (D) diversified

11. He is starting a new _____: selling office supplies online.
    (A) enterprising   (C) enterprise
    (B) enterpriser   (D) enterprises

12. Your full participation is _____ to our timely completion of this project.
    (A) essence   (C) essential
    (B) essences   (D) essentially

13. We need to have a spare copier since the only one that is _____ is on its last leg.
    (A) functioned   (C) functional
    (B) functions   (D) function

14. In order to _____ our lead in the market, we'll have to find a cheaper source of industrial supplies.
    (A) maintainable   (C) maintaining
    (B) maintain   (D) maintainability

15. She talked so _____ that we ordered every single item that she had for sale.
    (A) smoothly   (C) smooth
    (B) smoothness   (D) smoothed

Part 6 Text Completion

Memo

To: All office staff
From: Luis Mendez, Office Manager
Re: Ordering office supplies

There has been a lot of confusion recently regarding the ordering of office supplies. In order to maintain a consistent stock of _____ supplies, from now on all supply orders must go through me. There are forms in my

16. (A) essence
    (B) essential
    (C) essentials
    (D) essentially

office that you may use to order the supplies that you need. I can _____ supplies for you within three

17. (A) maintain
    (B) function
    (C) diversify
    (D) obtain

days of receiving your order form if it is filled out properly. By following this procedure, the office will function more _____ , and we can be sure that we will always have quality supplies on hand when we need them.

18. (A) smooth
    (B) smoothly
    (C) smoother
    (D) smoothness

We will also avoid the problem of ordering supplies that we already have. Thank you for your cooperation.

Part 7 Reading Comprehension

Questions 19–23 refer to the following letter and memo.

April 12

Dear Business Owner,

The Supply Closet, Inc., is a new office supply store in your neighborhood. We opened last month right across the street from the post office. We are your local source for quality office supplies, including all office stationery, packing materials, folders, pens, note pads, and more. We provide you with the everyday items you need to keep your business functioning smoothly. In order to introduce ourselves to you, we are enclosing a coupon for 20 percent off your entire purchase during your first visit to the Supply Closet. Please visit us soon.

Sincerely yours,

Martha and Bill Heywood
Owners

Coupon expires June 30.

Memo

To: Gisela Freeman
From: James Riley
Re: New supply store

Please see the attached letter from the Supply Closet, Inc. I think we should try them out. I know we maintain an account with the Riverdale Supply Company, but I am not completely satisfied with them as a source for supplies. I would like to find a supplier with more diverse merchandise. I'd like you to visit the Supply Closet sometime this week and purchase some stationery. We need to do a big mailing at the beginning of May, so we'll need some manila envelopes and letter paper. You can use the coupon that came with the letter. Look at the items they have for sale and see how it compares with the Riverdale Supply Company. If it looks like they're a better source for supplies, we can start ordering from them regularly. Thank you.

---

19. When did the Supply Closet open?
    (A) March.
    (B) April.
    (C) May.
    (D) June.

20. What can a customer get during his first visit to the store?
    (A) A free pen.
    (B) An introduction.
    (C) A discount.
    (D) A stamp.

21. Why doesn't James Riley like the Riverdale Supply Company?
    (A) It's too near the post office.
    (B) It doesn't function smoothly.
    (C) It's far from the neighborhood.
    (D) It doesn't have a variety of merchandise.

22. The word *smoothly* in line 8 of the letter is closest in meaning to
    (A) easily
    (B) quickly
    (C) profitably
    (D) carefully

23. The word *maintain* in line 3 of the memo is closest in meaning to
    (A) open
    (B) pay
    (C) apply
    (D) keep

Lesson 18

Shipping

Study the following definitions and examples.

1. **accurately** adv., correctly; without errors
    a. To gauge these figures accurately, we first need to get some facts from the shipping department.
    b. The container company must balance the load accurately or there could be a disaster at sea.

2. **carrier** n., a person or business that transports passengers or goods
    a. Lou, our favorite carrier, takes extra care of our boxes marked "fragile."
    b. Mr. Lau switched carriers in order to get a price savings on deliveries out of state.

3. **catalog** n., a list or itemized display; v., to make an itemized list of
    a. The upcoming fall catalog shows a number of items from Laos that Mr. Lau has never before been able to offer.
    b. Ellen cataloged the complaints according to severity.

4. **fulfill** v., to finish completely
    a. All orders are fulfilled and ready for shipment within twenty-four hours.
    b. Her expectations were so high, we knew they would be hard to fulfill.

5. **integral** adj., necessary for completion
    a. Good customer relations is an integral component of any business.
    b. A dependable stream of inventory is integral to reliable shipping of orders.

6. **inventory** n., goods in stock; an itemized record of these goods
    a. The store closes one day a year so that the staff can take inventory of the stockroom.
    b. Their inventory has not changed much over the years.

7. **minimize** v., to reduce; to give less importance to
    a. The shipping staff minimized customer complaints by working overtime to deliver the packages quickly.
    b. To keep the customers happy and to minimize the effect of the carrier strike, we shipped orders directly to them.

8. **on hand** adj., available
    a. We had too much stock on hand, so we had a summer sale.
    b. The new employee will be on hand if we need more help with shipping orders.

9. **receive** v., get or accept something that is given
    a. You will receive your order within one week of the shipping date.
    b. When we received the package, the box was broken and some of the contents were missing.

10. **ship** v., to transport; to send
    a. Eva shipped the package carefully, since she knew the contents were made of glass.
    b. Very few customers think about how their packages will be shipped, and are seldom home when the packages arrive.

11. **sufficiently** adv., enough
    a. The boxcar was sufficiently damaged that it could not be loaded on the truck.
    b. We are sufficiently organized to begin transferring the palettes tomorrow.

12. **supply** n., stock; v., to make available for use; to provide
    a. By making better use of our supplies, we can avoid ordering until next month.
    b. Gerald supplied the shipping staff with enough labels to last a year.

WORD FAMILIES

noun	accuracy	His firm was well known for its accuracy in predicting how long shipping would take.
adjective	accurate	Don't forget to keep accurate records; you will need them when you have your annual inventory.
adverb	accurately	The in-depth shipping records made it possible for Max to accurately estimate when the mixing bowls would arrive in the store.

verb	fulfill	We take pride in fulfilling customers' unusual requests.
noun	fulfillment	Fulfillment of duties can be tedious, but job satisfaction demands attention to detail.

adjective	integral	This paperwork is integral to our ability to track packages.
verb	integrate	The new foreman is unable to integrate information about shipping perishables.
noun	integration	His full integration into the team could take weeks.

verb	minimize	To minimize any potential risk of injury, all workers must wear closed-toed shoes in the stockroom.
adjective	minimal	Luckily, the leak from the roof did only minimal damage to the inventory in the stockroom.
noun	minimum	The minimum is $50; orders of less will be assessed a shipping charge.

verb	ship	We ship all orders within 24 hours of your phone call.
noun	shipper	We can rely on our shipper to pack large, fragile items carefully.
noun	shipment	The shipment from the supplier was short a number of items, so we complained.

adverb	sufficiently	If you are sufficiently certain that the crate is in this room, I will check them one by one.
adjective	sufficient	The postage on that box is not sufficient to get it to its destination.
verb	suffice	Will this much Styrofoam suffice?

WORDS IN CONTEXT

Read the following passage and write the words in the blanks below.

accurate	fulfill	minimize	shipping
carrier	integral	on hand	sufficient
catalog	inventory	receive	supplies

For Mr. Park's Asian housewares store, shipping is an (1) _____ part of the business. Many customers need to send their purchases to friends or relatives who live far away. Other customers, who do not live near one of his stores, shop by (2) _____ and need their orders sent by mail.

(3) _____ is, of course, the process of getting goods delivered to a customer, but it is more than just getting a box in the mail. Goods must be packaged carefully to (4) _____ breakage and ensure that they arrive safely. Customers want to (5) _____ their orders in good condition. Staff members must keep (6) _____ records of the inventory shipped, and both Mr. Park and his customers need to be able to track the shipments online so that they can easily find the answers to these questions: When did a box leave the store? Who was the (7) _____ who delivered it? When did it arrive at its destination?

The shipping process must be tied to the store's (8) _____. When orders are taken, the shipping staff must know that there is (9) _____ inventory of the product on hand to (10) _____ the request. If a product is on order, the sales staff should advise the customer to expect a delay. When orders are shipped out, they must be deleted from the inventory records so Mr. Park knows exactly how many items are (11) _____ in his warehouse. It takes a good computer program to keep track of the additions and deletions to the inventory.

Sales staff must remember to charge for shipping and appropriate taxes. Mr. Park must keep good records on the cost of the shipping and packing materials and other (12) _____, the cost of the carriers, and staff time to assess whether he is billing enough to cover his shipping expenses.

WORD PRACTICE

LISTENING COMPREHENSION

TRACK
19

Part 1 Photo

Look at the picture and listen to the sentences.
Choose the sentence that best describes the picture.

1. Ⓐ Ⓑ Ⓒ Ⓓ

Part 2 Question–Response

Listen to the question and the three responses. Choose the response that best answers the question.

2. Ⓐ Ⓑ Ⓒ   3. Ⓐ Ⓑ Ⓒ

Part 3 Conversation

Listen to the dialogue. Then read each question and choose the best response.

4. What is the problem?
    (A) There aren't enough boxes.
    (B) The addresses were lost.
    (C) The packages need repair.
    (D) The wrong materials were shipped.

5. Who is responsible for the problem?
    (A) The woman.
    (B) The man.
    (C) The packers.
    (D) The suppliers.

6. When should the boxes be shipped?
    (A) Today.
    (B) Tomorrow.
    (C) By Friday.
    (D) On the weekend.

Part 4 Talk

Listen to the talk. Then read each question and choose the best answer.

7. What is the topic of the talk?
    (A) Company mottos.
    (B) High prices.
    (C) Customer loyalty.
    (D) A weak point in the catalog.

8. What is the company's basic philosophy?
    (A) Unsurpassed customer service.
    (B) A good catalog can sell anything.
    (C) Outperform the competition.
    (D) High quality at low cost.

9. When will the catalog show a comparison of prices?
    (A) January.
    (B) May.
    (C) September.
    (D) December.

READING

Part 5 Incomplete Sentences

Choose the word that best completes the sentence.

10. To assure that your order is _____ filled, it will be checked by a two-person team.
    (A) accurately
    (B) accurateness
    (C) accurate
    (D) accuracy

11. The suppliers have _____ the terms of our agreement and are now our supplier of choice.
    (A) fulfilling
    (B) fulfillment
    (C) fulfilled
    (D) fulfill

12. Scanning the shipment number is an _____ part of tracking these containers.
    (A) integral
    (B) integrate
    (C) integrating
    (D) integration

13. The customer ordered three cartons of paper but _____ only two.
    (A) received
    (B) relieved
    (C) deceived
    (D) perceived

14. To keep distribution costs low, we have selected only two _____ firms for the region.
    (A) ship
    (B) shipment
    (C) shipping
    (D) shipper

15. Based on their credit check, it seems likely that they have _____ funds to cover this order.
    (A) suffice
    (B) sufficient
    (C) sufficiently
    (D) sufficed

Part 6 Text Completion

PACKING GUIDELINES

In order to _____ breakage of merchandise and loss of shipments and to ensure accurate fulfillment

16. (A) minimum
    (B) minimize
    (C) minimal
    (D) minimally

of orders, please observe the following guidelines when preparing packages for shipment:

1) Check the order form carefully to make sure the item number matches the item number and description in the catalog.

2) Make sure that the address label has been _____ filled out, and particularly that names have

17. (A) acutely
    (B) accessibly
    (C) actively
    (D) accurately

been spelled correctly.

3) Each box must be _____ filled with packing material to protect the contents from damage.

18. (A) sufficiently
    (B) sufficient
    (C) suffice
    (D) suffuse

4) Packages must be ready to be picked up by the carrier before 3:30 P.M. daily.

Following these guidelines is of the utmost importance. Lost and damaged shipments cost the company valuable time and money.

Part 7 Reading Comprehension

Questions 19–23 refer to the following letter.

April 15

Customer Service Department
Fleetwood Fashions
21986 North Featherstone Avenue
Hiawatha, MN

Dear Customer Service,

I am writing about an order I made from the Fleetwood Fashions catalog over a month ago, which I have not yet received. When I called to order two new purses and several spring shirts, the customer service representative assured me that there was sufficient inventory on hand to fulfill the order. He told me that it would be shipped before the end of the week and that I would receive it within ten days. When I still had not received the shipment after 14 days, I called the company. The customer service representative checked the ordering information on the computer, and we discovered that my address had not been accurately recorded. He promised to reship the order with my correct address and told me I would receive it within ten days. That was over two weeks ago, and I still have not received the shipment. I cannot understand this. Perhaps the carrier that you use is not reliable. In any case, I am tired of waiting for my order and would like to cancel it. I am not sure whether I will make an order from your company again. This is unfortunate since it is one of the few places that carry dresses and shoes in my size and at a reasonable price. However, this is the second time I have had a problem with an order, and I don't want this to happen again. Please cancel my order #20857631. Thank you.

Sincerely,

Lucinda Walker

---

19. When did Lucinda Walker make an order from Fleetwood Fashions?
    (A) Last week.
    (B) Ten days ago.
    (C) Fourteen days ago.
    (D) Last month.

20. What did she order?
    (A) Purses.
    (B) Skirts.
    (C) Shoes.
    (D) Dresses.

21. What is the problem with her order?
    (A) The price is unreasonable.
    (B) The dress size is wrong.
    (C) She hasn't received it yet.
    (D) It contained the wrong merchandise.

22. The word *fulfill* in line 4 is closest in meaning to
    (A) pay for
    (B) complete
    (C) send
    (D) receive

23. The word *carrier* in line 10 is closest in meaning to
    (A) communication
    (B) employee
    (C) transporter
    (D) operator

Lesson 19

Invoices

WORDS TO LEARN

charge

compile

customer

discount

dispute

efficient

estimate

impose

mistake

promptly

rectify

terms

Study the following definitions and examples.

1. **charge** v., to demand payment; n., an expense or a cost
   a. The customer service representative was responsible for telling all existing customers that higher prices would be charged next month.
   b. The extra charge for gift wrapping your purchase will appear on your invoice.

2. **compile** v., to gather together from several sources
   a. I have compiled a list of the most popular items for sale on our website.
   b. The clerk is responsible for compiling the orders at the end of the day.

3. **customer** n., one who purchases a commodity or service
   a. Let's make sure all invoices sent to customers are kept in alphabetical order.
   b. As part of our customer satisfaction plan, let's offer a discount to customers who pay their invoices within a week.

4. **discount** n., a reduction in price
   a. Customers who pay their invoices before the end of the month receive a 5 percent discount.
   b. The discount on the sale items was not very big.

5. **dispute** v., argue about; question; disagree with
   a. Customers may dispute certain charges on an invoice.
   b. A customer called the company to dispute the no returns policy.

6. **efficient** adj., acting or producing effectively with a minimum of waste or unnecessary effort
   a. The accountant was so efficient in processing the customer receipts that she had the job done before lunch.
   b. Electronic invoicing has helped us to be efficient.

7. **estimate** v., to approximate the amount or value of something; to form an opinion about something; n., an approximation
   a. We estimated our losses this year at about five thousand dollars.
   b. In the owner's estimation, the high level of customer satisfaction was an adequate measure of how well the company was doing.

8. **impose** v., to establish or apply as compulsory; to force upon others
   a. The company will impose a surcharge for any items returned.
   b. We should not impose upon our staff by requiring them to work on weekends.

9. **mistake** n., an error or a fault
   a. I made a mistake in adding up your bill and we overcharged you twenty dollars.
   b. It was a mistake thinking that my boss would be reasonable when I explained my situation to him.

10. **promptly** adv., on time, punctually
    a. We always reply promptly to customers' letters.
    b. The new sales agent promptly offered a full refund for the damaged goods.

11. **rectify** v., to set right or correct
    a. He rectified the problem by giving the customer credit for the unused items that she returned.
    b. Embarrassed at his behavior, he rectified the situation by writing a letter of apology.

12. **terms** n., conditions
    a. The terms of payment were clearly listed at the bottom of the invoice.
    b. The terms of the agreement required that items be fully paid for before they would be shipped.

WORD FAMILIES

verb	discount	They discounted the price on the merchandise damaged in shipment.
noun	discount	There is a 20 percent discount on all the items for sale in the back room.
adjective	discountable	In most cases, damaged items are discountable.

verb	dispute	If a customer wants to dispute an item on an invoice, please let the manager know.
noun	dispute	It is not a good idea to get into a dispute with a customer about small charges on an invoice.
adjective	disputable	Customers tend to believe that late charges on an invoice are disputable.

noun	efficiency	The efficiency of our new billing system has resulted in almost all the invoices being paid on time.
adjective	efficient	We appreciate customers who are efficient about paying on time.
adverb	efficiently	If we work efficiently, we can get all these invoices sent out by the end of the day.

verb	impose	The government has decided to impose a larger sales tax on certain items, and this will be included on the invoice.
noun	imposition	The customer disputed the imposition of certain charges on the invoice.
adjective	imposing	The size of the amount due on the invoice was imposing.

verb	mistake	She mistook the amount on the invoice and overpaid.
noun	mistake	The manager called the supplier as soon as he saw the mistake on the invoice.
adjective	mistaken	The customer never received the invoice because of the mistaken address on the envelope.

noun	promptness	We appreciate the promptness with which you pay your bills.
adjective	prompt	I am happy to receive statements that thank me for my prompt payment.
adverb	promptly	Companies sometimes give discounts to customers who pay their bills promptly.

WORDS IN CONTEXT

Read the following passage and write the words in the blanks below.

charges	discount	estimated	promptly
compiled	dispute	imposed	rectified
customer	efficient	mistake	terms

Companies that sell items online through catalogs need to have an (1) _____ process for invoicing and billing customers. When a customer places an order, a list of items must be (2) _____ and an invoice generated. The invoice will list the items purchased, along with the cost of each item, and the quantity desired. (3) _____ that will be incurred in shipping the items to the (4) _____ are also added to the invoice. Sometimes shipping charges are simply (5) _____ based on the weight or value of the items ordered.

The invoice also shows the (6) _____ of payment. Payment is usually due within 30 days. Extra charges are often (7) _____ on overdue accounts. Customers are not always happy to see these extra charges and may (8) _____ them with the company. Many companies also offer a small (9) _____ if invoices are paid promptly.

Sometimes items get damaged or lost in transit, or customers discover that the wrong items have been shipped by (10) _____. They will usually contact the company to have the problem (11) _____. Such complaints should be dealt with (12) _____. If an item is missing, a replacement will be sent, usually at no additional charge to the customer.

WORD PRACTICE

LISTENING COMPREHENSION

Part 1 Photo

Look at the picture and listen to the sentences.
Choose the sentence that best describes the picture.

1. Ⓐ Ⓑ Ⓒ Ⓓ

Part 2 Question–Response

Listen to the question and the three responses. Choose the response that best answers the question.

2. Ⓐ Ⓑ Ⓒ   3. Ⓐ Ⓑ Ⓒ

Part 3 Conversation

Listen to the dialogue. Then read each question and choose the best response.

4. What do they need to order?
   (A) Computers.
   (B) Temporary workers.
   (C) Order forms.
   (D) Office supplies.

5. What does the man ask the woman to do?
   (A) Compile a list.
   (B) Clean the supply closet.
   (C) Read the invoice carefully.
   (D) Write a check.

6. When will the woman place the order?
   (A) Before noon.
   (B) Tonight.
   (C) Tomorrow.
   (D) Tuesday.

Part 4 Talk

Listen to the talk. Then read each question and choose the best answer.

7. What is the topic of the talk?
   (A) Late payments.
   (B) Billing customers.
   (C) Immediate payment.
   (D) Discounts.

8. How does immediate payment benefit the company?
   (A) The company doesn't have to use collections agencies.
   (B) The company doesn't have to charge late fees.
   (C) The company gains customers.
   (D) The company doesn't have to send a bill to the customer.

9. How much do immediate payments save per project?
   (A) 4 percent.
   (B) 14 percent.
   (C) 15 percent.
   (D) 50 percent.

READING

Part 5 Incomplete Sentences

Choose the word that best completes the sentence.

10. After we have _____ all of the necessary documents, we will begin our analysis of the data.
    (A) compile   (C) compiling
    (B) compiled   (D) compilation

11. Though he worked very _____ with machines and figures, he was slow and awkward with customers and coworkers.
    (A) efficient   (C) efficiency
    (B) efficiently   (D) efficacy

12. Although _____ expenses works well when applying for a contract, clients appreciate itemization on their invoices.
    (A) estimate   (C) estimating
    (B) estimator   (D) estimation

13. The customers usually pay their invoices promptly in order to avoid the _____ of late charges.
    (A) efficiency   (C) estimate
    (B) mistake   (D) imposition

14. The customer was angry at the _____ on her invoice.
    (A) mistakes   (C) mistakable
    (B) mistaken   (D) mistaking

15. The client would appreciate it if the invoice could be sent _____ so he can pay it before the end of the fiscal year.
    (A) promptly   (C) prompted
    (B) promptness   (D) prompt

Part 6 Text Completion

Invoices are an essential part of any business and should be given their due attention. Without invoices, after all, a business would not receive payment for services rendered. The _____ of the invoice must be stated clearly, that is, the customer needs to

16. (A) terms
    (B) orders
    (C) discounts
    (D) compilations

know exactly what he is being charged for and when the payment is due. If a customer discovers a mistake on the invoice, it should be rectified as soon as possible. If a final charge is much greater than the original estimate, the reason for this should be explained as clearly and simply as possible on the invoice. Some businesses _____ a late fee on late

17. (A) imposition
    (B) imposing
    (C) imposter
    (D) impose

payments. In such cases, this must also be made clear on the invoice. Finally, the invoice must be sent to the customer _____ in order to encourage timely payment.

18. (A) prompt
    (B) prompter
    (C) promptly
    (D) promptness

Part 7 Reading Comprehension

Questions 19–23 refer to the following invoice and letter.

CLARY CLOSETS
"Making your world more organized."

Invoice

To: Millicent Pensky
752 Montrose Avenue
Proctorville, VT

Date: November 10, 20–

Initial consultation fee	$ 75
Organizing four closets	$ 800
Supplies	$ 225
Total due	$1100

Thank you for doing business with us.

Please pay by November 30. A 10 percent late fee will be imposed on late payments.

November 15, 20—

Clary Closets
18 North Main Street
Chester, VT

Dear Ms. Clary,

I am writing to dispute the charges on the invoice I recently received from your company. The invoice contained several mistakes. First, I was told that I would not be charged an initial consultation fee if I decided to use your services. Since I did go ahead and hire you to organize my closets, I should not have to pay this fee. Second, the final charge for organizing my four closets was $250 higher than the original estimate. I think this is too much and that I should be charged no more than the original estimate. Finally, I was charged for supplies that you ordered without my authorization. I could have obtained these same supplies myself at a lower price. Since I did not authorize this charge, I think I should pay a lower price for the supplies.

I chose Clary Closets to organize my closets because several of my friends and business associates have been satisfied customers of yours. However, I find it difficult to believe that an organizing business can be so inefficient when it comes to invoices. Please rectify these mistakes and send me a corrected invoice promptly.

Sincerely,

Millicent Pensky

---

19. What did Ms. Pensky hire Ms. Clary to do?
    (A) Write invoices.
    (B) Collect fees.
    (C) Organize closets.
    (D) Buy supplies.

20. According to the terms of the invoice, how much will Ms. Pensky owe if she pays on December 1?
    (A) $110.
    (B) $1100.
    (C) $1110.
    (D) $1210.

21. How much was the original estimate?
    (A) $250.
    (B) $550.
    (C) $800.
    (D) $850.

22. The word *dispute* in line 1 of the letter is closest in meaning to
    (A) disagree with
    (B) add to
    (C) pay for
    (D) ask for

23. The word *rectify* in line 21 of the letter is closest in meaning to
    (A) explain
    (B) calculate
    (C) fix
    (D) see

Lesson 20

Inventory

Study the following definitions and examples.

1. **adjustment** n., a change in order to match
   a. With these adjustments to the numbers of screws and nuts, we are close to having an accurate count.
   b. An adjustment to the number of damaged items would help us align our figures.

2. **automatically** adv., independently, without outside prompting
   a. The computer automatically updates the inventory files when a sale is made.
   b. This door opens automatically so it's easier to carry large boxes out of the stockroom.

3. **crucial** adj., extremely significant or important
   a. Knowing how many products we have in stock is crucial to our shipping procedures.
   b. Inventory is a crucial process and must be taken seriously by all staff.

4. **discrepancy** n., a divergence or disagreement
   a. We easily explained the discrepancy between the two counts.
   b. Unless you catch the error immediately, the discrepancy gets entered into the computer and becomes very difficult to correct.

5. **disturb** v., to interfere with; to interrupt
   a. Let's see how many products we can count in advance of inventory so we disturb fewer customers.
   b. I hope I'm not disturbing you, but I need to ask you to move so I can record the products behind you.

6. **install** v., put equipment into place
   a. Since we installed the new software, taking inventory has become a lot easier.
   b. We'll need to get the new computers installed before we can take inventory.

7. **reflect** v., show; indicate
   a. The numbers on the computer log should accurately reflect the actual numbers in the warehouse.
   b. The way you handled the problems with the inventory reflects your professional attitude.

8. **run** v., to operate
   a. As long as the computer is running, you can keep adding new data.
   b. The new cash registers look complicated but they are actually quite easy to run.

9. **scan** v., to look over quickly; to automatically record data with a scanner
   a. Jasmine quickly scanned the list to see if any information was missing.
   b. When we take inventory, we have to scan each item number into the computer.

10. **subtract** v., to take away; to deduct
    a. Once you ring up an item, the computer automatically subtracts it from the inventory log.
    b. Whoever did the inventory forgot to subtract the items that arrived damaged and were never put into the stockroom.

11. **tedious** adj., tiresome by reason of length, slowness, or dullness; boring
    a. This may be tedious work but you will be glad the inventory is accurate when you hit the busy holiday sales season.
    b. Counting merchandise all weekend is the most tedious job I can imagine.

12. **verify** v., to prove the truth of
    a. I can't verify the accuracy of these numbers, since I was not present for inventory weekend.
    b. The inventory process verifies that you have accounted for all the items that are supposed to be in the store.

WORD FAMILIES

verb	adjust	After you've verified the quantities in the stockroom, I'll adjust the numbers in the computer.
noun	adjustment	While the adjustments are being made to the computer inventory, the computer will be off-line and unavailable for use.
adjective	adjustable	The height of the shelves is adjustable, which makes it easier to reach and count the merchandise.

noun	automation	Computers have brought a heightened level of automation into the retail industry.
adjective	automatic	The automatic updating of the inventory is convenient, but always a day behind.
adverb	automatically	After every cash register transaction, the computer automatically updates the inventory record.

verb	disturb	Count as many of the items on the salesroom floor as you can without disturbing the customers.
noun	disturbance	After considering all the options, Ellen decided that closing the store a day to do the annual inventory would cause the least amount of disturbance for customers.
adverb	disturbingly	The computer count and the physical count were disturbingly incongruous, which distressed the store manager.

verb	scan	Scan the aisles and see if you find the missing carton.
noun	scanner	We will install a scanner at two of the computer terminals.
adjective	scanned	These scanned documents need to be returned to their original owners.

verb	subtract	Subtract 50 from the total—I just found an unusable box.
noun	subtraction	If you feel confident doing basic addition and subtraction in your head, you don't have to carry the calculator with you.
adjective	subtracted	These subtracted figures don't add up to the total that was supposed to be subtracted.

noun	tedium	I can't bear the tedium of taking inventory.
adjective	tedious	Entering all the information about the inventory into the computer is a tedious job, but it has to be done.
adverb	tediously	We worked tediously on the inventory for the entire weekend.

WORDS IN CONTEXT

Read the following passage and write the words in the blanks below.

adjusted	discrepancies	reflect	subtracts
automatically	disturbances	running	tedious
crucial	installed	scanning	verifies

In a retail business, inventory has multiple meanings. Inventory means all the goods that a company has on hand or available to it in a warehouse. Inventory also means the process by which the business (1) _____ the number of goods. An accurate account of the inventory available is (2) _____.

Most retail businesses have (3) _____ cash registers that help keep count of inventory. (4) _____ these registers is easy, and they do an important job. When a customer makes a purchase, the computer system tied to the register (5) _____ the purchase from the inventory records. If a customer makes a return or an exchange, the inventory numbers will be (6) _____ by the computer (7) _____. That's why (8) _____ the bar code is so important in stores. If merchandise is broken or damaged in the stockroom or on the sales floor, the manager will ask the sales and stock help to change the stock holdings to (9) _____ the loss.

As good as the computer records may be, they are just an estimate. At least once a year, most businesses do an actual physical count of the inventory. This process can be (10) _____ but it is necessary as there are always (11) _____ between what the computer says you own and what your physical count says. Often stores close for a day, or at least close early, so that staff can perform the inventory without (12) _____.

WORD PRACTICE

LISTENING COMPREHENSION

Part 1 Photo

Look at the picture and listen to the sentences.
Choose the sentence that best describes the picture.

1. Ⓐ Ⓑ Ⓒ Ⓓ

Part 2 Question–Response

Listen to the question and the three responses. Choose the response that best answers the question.

2. Ⓐ Ⓑ Ⓒ   3. Ⓐ Ⓑ Ⓒ

Part 3 Conversation

Listen to the dialogue. Then read each question and choose the best response.

4. What information does the man want to verify?
   (A) The size of the bedspreads.
   (B) The number of bedspreads on hand.
   (C) The reason for the discrepancy.
   (D) The number of bedspreads the customer needs.

5. According to the computer, how many bedspreads are there?
   (A) Three.
   (B) Five.
   (C) Seven.
   (D) Eleven.

6. Where are the bedspreads?
   (A) In a box.
   (B) On a shelf.
   (C) On the bed.
   (D) In the stockroom.

Part 4 Talk

Listen to the talk. Then read each question and choose the best answer.

7. What happens every year in January?
   (A) They adjust the file drawers.
   (B) They record the audio portion.
   (C) They delete unnecessary computer files.
   (D) They do a physical count.

8. What is one problem with their work?
   (A) It consumes too much time.
   (B) Nobody appreciates it.
   (C) The hourly rate is low.
   (D) It's boring.

9. How many days does it take to complete the work?
   (A) Two.
   (B) Three.
   (C) Four.
   (D) Eight.

READING

Part 5 Incomplete Sentences

Choose the word that best completes the sentence.

10. The computer's inventory figures will be considered inaccurate until the store manager enters the data from the physical count and _____ the figures.
    - (A) adjustment
    - (B) adjusts
    - (C) adjustable
    - (D) adjusted

11. Inventory control cannot be performed _____, but must be done by physically counting the merchandise.
    - (A) automatically
    - (B) automatic
    - (C) automation
    - (D) automated

12. Do not _____ the staff when they are counting the items; they need to concentrate.
    - (A) disturb
    - (B) install
    - (C) reflect
    - (D) run

13. We need to take a physical count to _____ the numbers in the computer.
    - (A) very
    - (B) verifiable
    - (C) verification
    - (D) verify

14. In order to scan the bar code, you need to sweep the bar code directly in front of the _____.
    - (A) scan
    - (B) scanned
    - (C) scanning
    - (D) scanner

15. If we _____ the damaged merchandise from the inventory, our figures will accurately reflect what we have on hand.
    - (A) subtract
    - (B) subtracting
    - (C) subtracted
    - (D) subtraction

Part 6 Text Completion

Notice

Our new cash registers will be installed over the weekend so that we can start using them next week. The main reason we have bought these new machines is that they will make it easier to keep track of our inventory. When you _____ a customer's purchase into the

16. (A) scan
    (B) will scan
    (C) scanned
    (D) are going to scan

machine, it will automatically record the purchase in the inventory files of our computer. This will help us track sales and reorder items promptly. It will save us the _____ work

17. (A) tedious
    (B) tedium
    (C) tenacity
    (D) tenacious

of manually entering data into the computer and ensure that our numbers are accurate. All staff members are required to attend a training session on Friday afternoon during which you will learn how _____ the new cash registers. See you there.

18. (A) running
    (B) to run
    (C) runs
    (D) run

Part 7 Reading Comprehension

Questions 19–23 refer to the following memo.

```
To:   All store staff
From: Bill Jones, Manager
Re:   Next week

This is a reminder that we will be closing
the store for two days at the end of next
week,  Friday and Saturday, for inventory.
This is a long and tedious job, and we will
need the assistance of each and every one of
you to get it done. Therefore, no vacation
days will be granted during that time.
During the inventory process, we will ver-
ify the numbers in our computer files, clear
up any discrepancies we may find, and adjust
our records as necessary. We need to make
sure that our records accurately reflect the
stock that we actually have on hand. When
you report to work on Thursday, your super-
visor will give you your assignment. Some of
you will be required to work in the stock-
room taking a physical count, and others
will be asked to work in the office enter-
ing data on the computers. We won't reopen
the store until the following Tuesday since
Monday is a national holiday. I hope that
will give you a chance to rest up a bit
after the big job. Thank you in advance for
your assistance with this crucial work.
```

19. Why will the store close next week?
    (A) Everyone will be on vacation.
    (B) They need to count their stock.
    (C) The staff members need a rest.
    (D) There will be a computer training session.

20. Who will give the assignments?
    (A) The manager.
    (B) The assistants.
    (C) The supervisors.
    (D) The record keeper.

21. When will the store open again?
    (A) Monday.
    (B) Tuesday.
    (C) Thursday.
    (D) Friday.

22. The word *adjust* in line 10 is closest in meaning to
    (A) enter
    (B) write
    (C) change
    (D) create

23. The word *crucial* in line 24 is closest in meaning to
    (A) important
    (B) boring
    (C) difficult
    (D) lengthy

WORD REVIEW #4   **133**

Word Review #4   Lessons 16–20 Purchasing

Choose the word that best completes the sentence.

1. Most merchants are happy to find any way to
   _____ their customer base.
   (A) expand
   (B) expanding
   (C) expansion
   (D) expanded

2. All fashion _____ have a limited life span.
   (A) trend
   (B) trends
   (C) trendy
   (D) trending

3. It is a poorly run office that does not _____
   adequate office supplies.
   (A) maintain
   (B) maintained
   (C) maintaining
   (D) maintenance

4. Sometimes office policy doesn't allow the company
   to _____ less expensive supplies when they are
   available from someone other than a preferred
   provider.
   (A) obtain
   (B) obtained
   (C) obtaining
   (D) obtainable

5. A supplier who has chronic trouble _____ his
   obligations to a customer will quickly lose
   customers.
   (A) fulfill
   (B) fulfills
   (C) fulfilling
   (D) fulfillment

6. To _____ disruption, buyers should order well
   ahead of need.
   (A) minimum
   (B) minimal
   (C) minimize
   (D) minimally

7. It is wise to begin by _____ an inventory
   of equipment on hand.
   (A) compile
   (B) compiling
   (C) compiler
   (D) compilation

8. If the provider does not meet his client's demand, he
   should _____ the problem as soon as possible.
   (A) rectify
   (B) rectifier
   (C) rectifiable
   (D) rectification

9. If some supplies show a steady rise in consumption,
   the office manager should make an appropriate
   _____ in his standard order.
   (A) adjust
   (B) adjuster
   (C) adjusting
   (D) adjustment

10. Every time you remove an item from the shelves, you
    should _____ it from the inventory list.
    (A) compile
    (B) subtract
    (C) adjust
    (D) expand

Choose the one word or phrase that best completes each sentence.

Memo

To: Floor Managers
From: Head Manager
Re: Spring Sale

Our large Spring Sale begins next week. Before the store opens on Monday, all sale items should be placed on racks near the _____ area. This ensures that customers will see them right

      11. (A) catalog
         (B) merchandise
         (C) carrier
         (D) checkout

before they pay for their purchases. We expect large crowds in the store during the sale, so it will be important to _____ order. This means picking up any items that fall on the floor or end

      12. (A) pertain
         (B) maintain
         (C) remain
         (D) obtain

up on the wrong shelf, and making sure that all items are clearly marked with the correct price. Remember, a neat and organized store _____ more business.

      13. (A) receives
         (B) receiving
         (C) received
         (D) has received

To: Betsy Barnes
From: Lighting Limited Customer Service
Subject: Your order

Dear Betsy Barnes,

We have received your message about your recent order of a desk lamp with a glass shade. You state that the _____ arrived in damaged condition. We will be happy to replace the damaged merchandise at no extra

14. (A) ship
   (B) shipping
   (C) shipment
   (D) shippable

_____ to you. You will not have to pay anything. Simply place the damaged item back in the box and affix

15. (A) chase
   (B) chance
   (C) change
   (D) charge

the "postage paid" sticker to the outside. As soon as we receive it, a replacement lamp will be _____ sent

      16. (A) prompt
         (B) promptly
         (C) prompter
         (D) promptness

to you. We are sorry for any inconvenience this may have caused.

Manuel Gozanlez
Lighting Limited Customer Service Associate

To: Joanne Simmons
From: Bill Smithers
Subject: Supplies

Joanne,

It's time to order some supplies. We need several boxes of _____, including large and small

17. (A) stationery
    (B) invoice
    (C) bargain
    (D) inventory

envelopes as well as letter paper. Don't order this from XYZ Printers. I was not satisfied with the _____ of the paper in our last order. It tore very easily. Zippo Printers on Elm Street might

18. (A) quantity
    (B) quarry
    (C) quality
    (D) quandary

be a better source. Let's try them this time. It might be a good idea to get some ink cartridges, too. Why don't you check to see how many we have _____ hand? If we have just one or

19. (A) by
    (B) to
    (C) up
    (D) on

two boxes left, you should order more. Thanks.

Bill

Lesson 21

Banking

WORDS TO LEARN

accept

balance

borrow

cautiously

deduct

dividend

down payment

mortgage

restricted

signature

take out

transaction

Study the following definitions and examples.

1. **accept** v., to receive; to respond favorably
   a. He could not manage his bank account online because the website would not accept his password.
   b. Without hesitating, she accepted the job of teller.

2. **balance** n., the remainder; v., to compute the difference between credits and debits of an account
   a. His healthy bank balance showed a long habit of savings.
   b. It took him over an hour to balance his checkbook.

3. **borrow** v., to use temporarily
   a. Myra borrowed a pen so that she could sign the check.
   b. The couple borrowed money from the bank to buy a home.

4. **cautiously** adv., carefully, warily
   a. The bank manager spoke cautiously when giving out information to people she did not know.
   b. Act cautiously when signing contracts and read them thoroughly first.

5. **deduct** v., to take away from a total; to subtract
   a. If you choose, the bank will automatically deduct regular charges such as electric bills from your account.
   b. By deducting the monthly fee from her checking account, Yi was able to make her account balance.

6. **dividend** n., a share in a distribution
   a. The stockholders were outraged when their quarterly dividends were so small.
   b. The dividend was calculated and distributed to the group.

7. **down payment** n., an initial partial payment
   a. After Mary bought her car with a 30 percent down payment in cash, she was able to make her monthly payments online.
   b. Karl was disappointed when the real estate agent told him he needed a larger down payment on the house.

8. **mortgage** n., the amount due on a property; v., to borrow money with your house as collateral
   a. Due to low interest rates, Sheila moved quickly to find a good deal on a mortgage.
   b. Hiram mortgaged his home to get extra money to invest in his business.

9. **restricted** adj., limited
   a. The number of free withdrawals a customer can make from his or her account each month is restricted to five.
   b. Access to the safe deposit box vault is restricted to key holders.

10. **signature** n., the name of a person written by the person
    a. Once we have your signature, the contract will be complete.
    b. The customer's signature was kept on file for identification purposes.

11. **take out** v., withdraw; remove
    a. My checking account allows me to take out money at any bank branch without a fee.
    b. They took out the chairs in the bank lobby so now there is no place to sit.

12. **transaction** n., a business deal
    a. Banking transactions will appear on your monthly statement.
    b. The most common transactions can be made from your personal computer.

WORD FAMILIES

verb	accept	The bank will not accept a student ID as a valid form of identification.
noun	acceptance	The bank's acceptance of checks allows extra time for out-of-state checks to clear before they are credited to your account.
adjective	acceptable	Shorter banking hours are acceptable to customers because they can do their bank transactions at any hour online.

verb	caution	Our friends cautioned us against putting our money into an account that pays such a low interest rate.
adjective	cautious	The bank officer was cautious about approving Chen's loan because of his unfavorable credit history.
adverb	cautiously	We spent our money cautiously because we were not sure we would be able to borrow more.

verb	deduct	Remember to deduct the monthly bank fee from your statement.
noun	deductible	Taxes and health insurance payments are called deductibles because they are deducted from your paycheck.
noun	deduction	Deductions are made electronically every month and will appear on your statement.

verb	restrict	The bank's policies restrict the number of deductions you can make from your account without a penalty.
noun	restriction	The restrictions on who was eligible for a mortgage made it impossible for many low-income families to borrow money.
adjective	restricted	You can feel confident that your personal banking information is completely safe because of the restricted access to our website.

verb	sign	Once you have signed the mortgage contract, the bank will make a check payable to you.
noun	signature	Your signature can be electronically recorded to be verified later.

verb	transact	Our company transacts all its financial business at this bank.
noun	transaction	All parties concerned were pleased with the results of the business transactions.

WORDS IN CONTEXT

Read the following passage and write the words in the blanks below.

accept	cautious	down payment	signature
balance	deductions	mortgages	take out
borrow	dividends	restrict	transact

Banks are not only places in which to save money or to (1) _____ your financial business, but they are also institutions from which people can (2) _____ money. Every day, people look to banks for loans, such as (3) _____ for new homes. A loan is essentially a contract that binds the lender to a schedule of payments, so both parties should be (4) _____ and not enter into the arrangement without thinking. Banks will look at such factors as how much people have saved toward a (5) _____ in determining whether to make a loan.

Banks have different kinds of accounts. Some pay high quarterly (6) _____. Some accounts even severely (7) _____ the number of times, if any, that you can access your account, or the amount of cash you can (8) _____.

Today, electronic banking can be used to check the (9) _____ on an account, or to see if automatic (10) _____ have been made. This can all be done from your home or office computer. When you go to the bank, be sure to bring identification. Usually a bank will only (11) _____ a photo ID; a (12) _____ is not a valid ID.

WORD PRACTICE

LISTENING COMPREHENSION

TRACK
22

Part 1 Photo

Look at the picture and listen to the sentences.
Choose the sentence that best describes the picture.

1. Ⓐ Ⓑ Ⓒ Ⓓ

Part 2 Question–Response

Listen to the question and the three responses. Choose the response that best answers the question.

2. Ⓐ Ⓑ Ⓒ   3. Ⓐ Ⓑ Ⓒ

Part 3 Conversation

Listen to the dialogue. Then read each question and choose the best answer.

4. What does the man want to do?
   (A) Open a bank account.
   (B) Get a new driver's license.
   (C) Put his signature on file.
   (D) Cash a check.

5. According to the woman, what is required?
   (A) A photo ID.
   (B) An order form.
   (C) A large deposit.
   (D) A signed check.

6. When will the man's check clear?
   (A) In seven days.
   (B) In eight days.
   (C) In ten days.
   (D) In eleven days.

Part 4 Talk

Listen to the talk. Then read each question and choose the best answer.

7. Who is this talk for?
   (A) People who are looking for a job.
   (B) People who want to borrow money.
   (C) People who work in a bank.
   (D) People who want to open a bank account.

8. How big a down payment is required?
   (A) 10 percent.
   (B) 3 percent.
   (C) 1 percent.
   (D) 4 percent.

9. What is a requirement?
   (A) A new job.
   (B) An important address.
   (C) Money in the bank.
   (D) An accountant.

READING

Part 5 Incomplete Sentences

Choose the word that best completes the sentence.

10. I'm going to call the bank manager ahead of time to make certain that she will _____ a personal check to start a new account.
    (A) accept
    (B) accepted
    (C) acceptance
    (D) acceptable

11. We felt _____ about applying for such a large loan.
    (A) cautiously
    (B) caution
    (C) cautioning
    (D) cautious

12. Every month my automatic car loan payment shows up as a _____ on my monthly statement.
    (A) mortgage
    (B) deduction
    (C) dividend
    (D) restriction

13. The number of withdrawals at no charge from your savings account is _____ to three.
    (A) restricting
    (B) restricted
    (C) restrict
    (D) restriction

14. There is a counter in the bank lobby where customers can _____ their documents.
    (A) signing
    (B) signed
    (C) sign
    (D) signature

15. Many customers enjoy the convenience of carrying out their bank _____ online.
    (A) transacts
    (B) transacting
    (C) transacted
    (D) transactions

Part 6 Text Completion

Dear Customer,

Our records show that you qualify for our new automatic mortgage payment plan. Under this plan, your monthly mortgage payments _____ from your savings account automatically. Now you no longer

16. (A) deduct
    (B) deducted
    (C) are deducted
    (D) are deducting

have to worry about making your payments on time! We do it all for you. You must maintain a sufficient _____ in your account to cover the monthly payments. If you are interested in participating in this

17. (A) dividend
    (B) balance
    (C) transaction
    (D) down payment

plan, simply complete the enclosed form. Certain _____ apply to this plan, so read the explanation

18. (A) restrictions
    (B) restrictive
    (C) restricted
    (D) restricts

on the back of the form carefully. You may return the form in the enclosed envelope. Don't forget to sign it at the bottom. Your automatic deductions could begin as early as next month.

Part 7 Reading Comprehension

Questions 19–23 refer to the following two letters.

July 16, 20—

Customer Service Office
National Bank of Augusta
1398 State Street
Augusta, MD

Dear Customer Service Office,

I am a new customer at your bank. I opened an account with you last month, and I have recently received my first monthly statement. I find that there is a service charge on three of the checks that I wrote. I understood that this account had free checking, so I was surprised to see this charge. Perhaps it is a mistake. I am enclosing a copy of the statement. Please clarify this matter for me. Thank you.

Sincerely,

Marvin Gardner

August 3, 20—

Marvin Gardner
145 Merrywood Lane
Augusta, MD

Dear Mr. Gardner,

We recently received your letter asking about charges to your account. While it is true that your account has free checking, some restrictions apply. You may write five checks a month free of charge. After that, you must maintain a minimum average balance of $600 in your account in order to continue with free checking. Since your average account balance last month was only $435, you were entitled to only five free checks. A service charge was applied to the checks you wrote beyond that minimum. I hope this explanation is satisfactory to you.

Let me take this opportunity to make sure that you are aware of other services you can get with your account. You can arrange to have your monthly utility bills deducted from your account. You are also eligible to borrow small amounts of money from the bank at a low interest rate. If you are interested in these or any other services, please visit us at the bank, and an officer will be happy to explain all the details to you. Thank you for being a National Bank of Augusta customer.

Sincerely,

Eloise Lockwood
Customer Service Officer

19. Why did Mr. Gardner write this letter?
    (A) To pay his monthly utility bills.
    (B) To find out about borrowing money.
    (C) To ask a question about his monthly statement.
    (D) To order some free checks.

20. When did he open an account at the National Bank of Augusta?
    (A) May.
    (B) June.
    (C) July.
    (D) August.

21. How many checks did he write last month?
    (A) Three.
    (B) Five.
    (C) Six.
    (D) Eight.

22. The word *restrictions* in line 3 of the second letter is closest in meaning to
    (A) limitations
    (B) fees
    (C) customers
    (D) numbers

23. The word *deducted* in line 14 of the second letter is closest in meaning to
    (A) borrowed
    (B) attached
    (C) subtracted
    (D) added

Lesson 22

Accounting

WORDS TO LEARN

accounting

accumulate

asset

audit

budget

build up

client

debt

outstanding

profitably

reconcile

turnover

Study the following definitions and examples.

1. **accounting** n., the recording and gathering of financial information for a company.
   a. Good accounting is needed in all businesses.
   b. There are a number of good software programs to help with both personal and business accounting.

2. **accumulate** v., to gather; to collect
   a. They have accumulated more than enough information.
   b. The bills started to accumulate after the secretary quit.

3. **asset** n., something of value
   a. The company's assets are worth millions of dollars.
   b. A sophisticated accounting system is an asset to a company.

4. **audit** n., a formal examination of financial records; v., to examine the financial records of a company
   a. No one looks forward to an audit by the government.
   b. The independent accountants audited the company's books.

5. **budget** n., a list of probable expenses and income for a given period; v., to plan for expenses
   a. The department head was pleased that she received a 10 percent increase in her budget.
   b. The company will have to budget more money for this department next year.

6. **build up** v., to increase over time
   a. The firm has built up a solid reputation for itself.
   b. Be careful. Your inventory of parts is building up.

7. **client** n., a customer
   a. The accountant attracted many new clients through her website.
   b. Maintaining close contact with clients keeps the account managers aware of changing needs.

8. **debt** n., something owed, as in money or goods
   a. The company has been very careful and is slowly digging itself out of debt.
   b. The banks are worried about your increasing debt.

9. **outstanding** adj., still due; not paid or settled
   a. That client still has several outstanding bills.
   b. Clients with outstanding bills will not receive further service until the bills are paid.

10. **profitably** adv., advantageously
    a. The company used its accountant's advice profitably.
    b. We invested in the stock market profitably.

11. **reconcile** v., to make consistent
    a. The client uses his bank statements to reconcile his accounts.
    b. The accountant found the error when she reconciled the account.

12. **turnover** n., the number of times a product is sold and replaced or an employee leaves and another employee is hired
    a. We have had a low turnover of inventory this month and didn't bring in much money.
    b. Because of our high employee turnover we actually spend less money on salaries.

WORD FAMILIES

noun	accountant	The accountant was precise and hardworking.
noun	accounting	Accounting is a popular field of study.
noun	account	The client closed his bank account and withdrew all of his money.

verb	accumulate	The owner's goal was to accumulate as much wealth as possible.
noun	accumulation	The accumulation of goods may lead to an inventory problem.
adjective	accumulated	The sum of all your accumulated resources equals your total assets.

verb	audit	Some bookkeeping inconsistencies showed up when our records were audited.
noun	audit	If you keep your financial records carefully, you will always be ready for audit.
noun	auditor	The auditor will ask to see your recent spreadsheets.

verb	budget	There was no travel expense budgeted for the editorial department.
noun	budget	The boss asked for input on next year's budget.
adjective	budgetary	Due to budgetary constraints, we cannot hire additional staff at this time.

verb	build up	Over the years, our office has built up a solid list of clients.
noun	buildup	A buildup of debt will weaken the company's finances.

verb	profit	Our business has really profited from hiring an expert accountant.
noun	profit	After you enter your income and expenses, the spreadsheet will show your profit.
adjective	profitable	The accountant was able to show us where our business was profitable and where we were losing money.

WORDS IN CONTEXT

Read the following passage and write the words in the blanks below.

accounting	audited	clients	profitable
accumulated	budget	debt	reconcile
assets	building up	outstanding	turnover

Accounting information is pulled together or (1) _____ to help someone make decisions. A manager must come up with a (2) _____ to help control expenses. A retail store owner realizes that her (3) _____ have (4) _____ bills. A restaurant owner wants to know if it is (5) _____ to serve lunch. A nonprofit organization is being (6) _____ by the government. All of these people and organizations could use the services of an accountant.

Accountants and (7) _____ systems help a company stay on track. They raise flags when expenses are (8) _____ and keep an eye on the (9) _____ of inventory. They (10) _____ their clients' accounts to ensure that their clients' records are correct. Good accounting systems allow managers to come up with ways to improve their business.

The accountant prepares information for both internal and external use. Financial statements provide a quick look into the life of a business. They show how much (11) _____ the company is carrying and how much its (12) _____ are worth. The outside world uses this information to judge the health of the company.

WORD PRACTICE

LISTENING COMPREHENSION

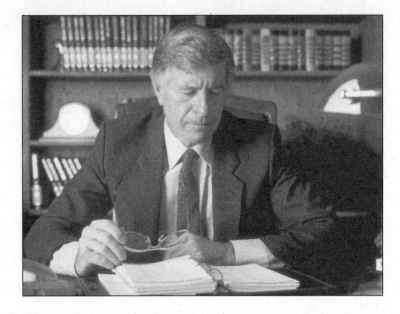

Part 1 Photo

Look at the picture and listen to the sentences.
Choose the sentence that best describes the picture.

1. Ⓐ Ⓑ Ⓒ Ⓓ

Part 2 Question–Response

Listen to the question and the three responses. Choose the response that best answers the question.

2. Ⓐ Ⓑ Ⓒ   3. Ⓐ Ⓑ Ⓒ

Part 3 Conversations

Listen to the dialogue. Then read each question and choose the best answer.

4. What time does the woman expect to return to the office?
    (A) By 1:00.
    (B) By 2:00.
    (C) By 4:00.
    (D) By 5:00.

5. What is the client's problem?
    (A) He doesn't understand his accountant.
    (B) He won't be in his office today.
    (C) He has a lot of debt.
    (D) He doesn't have a savings account.

6. What does the woman plan to do with the client today?
    (A) Show him a new budget.
    (B) Give him a present.
    (C) Ask him for more work.
    (D) Make a business deal with him.

Part 4 Talk

Listen to the talk. Then read each question and choose the best answer.

7. What is the topic of this talk?
    (A) How to start an accounting firm.
    (B) How to avoid client turnover.
    (C) How to have a profitable accounting firm.
    (D) How to get clients.

8. How can an accounting firm make more money?
    (A) By charging higher fees.
    (B) By getting recommendations from their clients.
    (C) By hiring new accountants.
    (D) By making a new list of clients.

9. According to the speaker, what is a firm's most valuable asset?
    (A) The staff.
    (B) Money.
    (C) Office space.
    (D) Equipment.

READING

Part 5 Incomplete Sentences

Choose the word that best completes the sentence.

10. The firm's _____ studied finance and business administration.
    (A) account   (C) accounted
    (B) accounting   (D) accountant

11. The account manager has _____ a tremendous amount of wealth in a very short time.
    (A) accumulated   (C) accumulating
    (B) accumulation (D) accumulates

12. We went over our records carefully in order to prepare for the meeting with the _____.
    (A) audit   (C) auditing
    (B) auditor   (D) audited

13. At the end of next week, all the division heads will meet to present one consolidated _____.
    (A) budgeting   (C) budgeted
    (B) budget   (D) budgets

14. I _____ some savings in my bank account before I made any investments in business.
    (A) building up   (C) built up
    (B) buildup   (D) build up

15. All the employees will benefit if the company's _____ continue to increase.
    (A) profited   (C) profits
    (B) profitable (D) profitably

Part 6 Text Completion

Wilson and Jones, Ltd.
Accountants

We specialize in small businesses.

Are you having trouble reconciling your accounts?
Do you need to improve your tax situation?
Do you want to get out of debt and make your business _____ ?

16. (A) profiting
    (B) profitable
    (C) profitably
    (D) profiteer

Wilson & Jones, Ltd., is a full-service accounting firm that can help small business owners like you with all aspects of your accounts. Our budget planning service will help you pay off _____ debts so that you can start accumulating savings. Our tax

17. (A) client
    (B) budget
    (C) turnover
    (D) outstanding

service provides tax planning assistance, tax return preparation, and preparation for audits. Our bookkeeping service guarantees that your accounts are always up to date. Call us today for an appointment. You'll be out of the red and free of _____ tomorrow.

18. (A) debate
    (B) doubt
    (C) debit
    (D) debt

Part 7 Reading Comprehension

Questions 19–23 refer to the following letter.

January 17, 20—

Buzzi Accountants
128 Waterford Drive
New Hanover, VA

Dear Ms. Buzzi,

I have just found out that my tax records will be audited by the government. I would like to hire someone from your firm to help me prepare for this. I run a small editing business which I started five years ago. I initially took out a loan from the bank to get my business started. My business has always been profitable, and I was able to repay the loan quickly. As of now, my business has no outstanding debts. My staff is quite small. I started out with one assistant, who is still with me. As I built up my client list, I hired a second assistant, who is also still working for me. Thus, I have not had a problem with staff turnover. In short, you can see that my business and financial situation are quite stable.

I have always prepared my taxes carefully, and I keep thorough records. I imagine that this audit will be fairly routine. However, I want to be sure that I am correctly prepared for it, and I feel that hiring an accountant is the best route to take. Please call me so that we can discuss the matter. I can be reached at my office Mondays, Wednesdays, and Fridays. One of my assistants is also usually in the office on Tuesdays and Thursdays and the occasional Saturday and will take messages for me.

I look forward to speaking with you.

Sincerely,

Jonathan Stein

---

19. Why does Mr. Stein want to hire an accountant?
    (A) To prepare his taxes.
    (B) To help with an audit.
    (C) To get him out of debt.
    (D) To help him stabilize his finances.

20. How many people work for Mr. Stein?
    (A) One.
    (B) Two.
    (C) Three.
    (D) Four.

21. When is Mr. Stein in his office?
    (A) Monday through Friday.
    (B) Tuesday and Thursday.
    (C) Monday, Wednesday, and Friday.
    (D) On occasional Saturdays.

22. The word *profitable* in the first paragraph, line 4, is closest in meaning to
    (A) large
    (B) in debt
    (C) interesting
    (D) earning money

23. The words *built up* in the first paragraph, line 6, are closest in meaning to
    (A) constructed
    (B) increased
    (C) employed
    (D) served

Lesson 23

Investments

WORDS
TO LEARN

aggressively

attitude

commit

conservative

fund

invest

long-term

portfolio

pull out

resource

return

wisely

Study the following definitions and examples.

1. **aggressively** adv., competitively, assertively
   a. Some people are risk takers and prefer to invest aggressively.
   b. His ideas were not well received because he spoke so aggressively.
2. **attitude** n., a feeling about something or someone
   a. The new fund manager's attitude changed quickly after the first big downturn in the market.
   b. Each investor should assess his or her own attitude toward investment.
3. **commit** v., to consign for future use, to promise
   a. It is a good idea to commit a certain percentage of your income to investments.
   b. The stockbroker committed herself to finding the best investments for each client.
4. **conservative** adj., cautious, restrained
   a. Her conservative strategy paid off over the years.
   b. Generally, older people should be more conservative in their investing than younger people.
5. **fund** n., an amount of money, an organization that manages money for a particular purpose
   a. If you have extra funds, talk to your stockbroker about the best place to put them.
   b. My stockbroker recommended investing in this fund.
6. **invest** v., to put money into a business or activity with the hope of making more money; to put effort into something
   a. The chief financial officer invested in the stock at a very good time.
   b. Don't invest all of your time in just one project.
7. **long-term** adj., involving or extending over a long period
   a. The CEO's long-term goal was to increase the return on investment.
   b. Long-term investments are not really affected by the daily ups and downs of the stock market.
8. **portfolio** n., a list of investments
   a. Investors are advised to have diverse portfolios.
   b. The investor's portfolio consisted of blue chip company stocks and government bonds.
9. **pull out** v., to withdraw, to stop participating
   a. A lot of people pulled out their money when it became clear that the bank was in trouble.
   b. He pulled out of the company and took all of his money with him.
10. **resource** n., assets; valuable things
    a. If you don't invest in petroleum resources now, you will find that the stock prices will get away from you.
    b. The company's most valuable resource was its staff.
11. **return** n., the amount of money gained as profit
    a. The 44 percent return on the new stock was far more than the stockbroker had anticipated.
    b. Some investors are satisfied with a 5 percent return, while others want to see a much larger return.
12. **wisely** adj., knowledgeably, smartly
    a. If you invest wisely, you will be able to retire early.
    b. Mary wisely followed her stockbroker's advice and took her money out of some bad investments.

WORD FAMILIES

noun	aggression	The act of aggression against our country caused a fear of war and had a negative effect on the stock market.
adjective	aggressive	The director's aggressive position on investing was frowned upon by the Board of Directors.
adverb	aggressively	I chose this stockbroker because he invests my money aggressively.

verb	commit	I've committed to donating a portion of my salary to charitable causes.
noun	commitment	The employee's commitment to working hard and saving her money was commendable.
adjective	noncommittal	I had hoped that the discussion would yield a definite answer from them, but they were noncommittal.

verb	conserve	Conserve your money now so you will be able to invest when the stock market gets better.
adjective	conservative	Some people are conservative investors and take few risks with their money.
adverb	conservatively	If you invest too conservatively, you may lose some chances for making money.

verb	fund	Private investors will fund the new business.
noun	fund	The stockbroker suggested investing funds in foreign companies.
noun	funder	We are looking for funders who can commit at least $50,000 each.

verb	invest	The company has been successful because it has invested wisely in its resources.
noun	investment	Some people like to manage their investments online by themselves, while others prefer to work with a stockbroker.
noun	investor	The fall in the stock market shook up the investors.

noun	wisdom	Common wisdom is to place your money in a variety of investments.
adjective	wise	The wise investor does her homework before parting with her money.
adverb	wisely	She planned her retirement wisely and was able to retire to her summer house.

WORDS IN CONTEXT

Read the following passage and write the words in the blanks below.

aggressive	conservative	long-term	resources
attitude	fund	portfolio	return
committed	invest	pull out	wise

Investment is a common, everyday occurrence. Companies (1) _____ time and money in finding and training their employees. Employees invest in their own training and education. Financial investment takes place at a corporate level and at an individual level. Whether an individual or a company, a decision must be made on the percentage of (2) _____ to have invested and the percentage to have in cash.

To avoid making stupid decisions, many people use financial advisors. Financial advisors help individuals and corporations make (3) _____ investment decisions. What kind of portfolio should be maintained? What should be in this (4) _____? At what point should an investor pull back or (5) _____ of the market? What kind of (6) _____ should the investor realistically expect? How much risk can an investor take (both emotionally and financially)? Investors who are (7) _____ to (8) _____ investments can more easily weather the ups and downs of a market. As one analyst commented, "If you're staying awake at night thinking about the stock market, you probably have too much invested."

Many employees have retirement plans at work. They decide what level of contribution to make to a certain (9) _____. These decisions and large company decisions depend to a large degree on (10) _____. Is the decision maker (11) _____ or (12) _____? That attitude often depends on the age of the investor or on the stage and the needs of the business.

WORD PRACTICE

LISTENING COMPREHENSION

TRACK
24

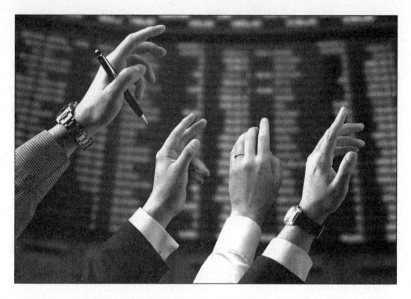

Part 1 Photo

Look at the picture and listen to the sentences.
Choose the sentence that best describes the picture.

1. Ⓐ Ⓑ Ⓒ Ⓓ

Part 2 Question–Response

Listen to the question and the three responses. Choose the response that best answers the question.

2. Ⓐ Ⓑ Ⓒ   3. Ⓐ Ⓑ Ⓒ

Part 3 Conversation

Listen to the dialogue. Then read each question and choose the best answer.

4. What does the man recommend?
   (A) Investing mainly in natural resources.
   (B) Investing in various industries.
   (C) Investing aggressively.
   (D) Investing in the basket industry.

5. How much money has the man made through
   his investments?
   (A) One million dollars.
   (B) Two million dollars.
   (C) Five million dollars.
   (D) Ten million dollars.

6. What will the woman do?
   (A) Take her money out of the stock market.
   (B) Hire an investment advisor.
   (C) Start a marketing business.
   (D) Follow the man's investment strategy.

Part 4 Talk

Listen to the talk. Then read each question and choose the best answer.

7. What is this talk about?
   (A) How to invest in the stock market.
   (B) How to choose a good college.
   (C) How to choose investments.
   (D) How to save money for college.

8. When should parents start saving money for college?
   (A) Two or three years from now.
   (B) When their children are small.
   (C) After they have had two or three children.
   (D) When their children are in high school.

9. How often should parents put money in the
   stock market?
   (A) Every month.
   (B) Every two or three months.
   (C) Every year.
   (D) Every two or three years.

READING

Part 5 Incomplete Sentences

Choose the word that best completes the sentence.

10. The stockbroker recommended investing some money more _____.
    (A) aggressive   (C) aggressively
    (B) aggression   (D) aggressor

11. All employees are encouraged to _____ a percentage of their earnings to the retirement fund.
    (A) committed   (C) commitment
    (B) commit   (D) committing

12. Because he had made such _____ investments, he lost very little money when the stock market went down.
    (A) conservative   (C) conservatively
    (B) conserved   (D) conserve

13. After months of study and research, the _____ decided to put his money into new facilities and materials.
    (A) investor   (C) investing
    (B) investment   (D) invested

14. A good financial analyst will advise investors on strategies that will generate higher _____.
    (A) returned   (C) returns
    (B) returning   (D) returnable

15. Is it _____ to consider funding a new project when we haven't even seen the returns from the last one?
    (A) wisdom   (C) wisely
    (B) wisest   (D) wise

Part 6 Text Completion

Many people try to save money by acting as their own investment advisors. This is not usually considered to be a wise choice. In the long term, it can actually end up costing the investor more money because of poor investment decisions. A professional investment advisor understands investment options more thoroughly than the layperson ever could. A good investment advisor becomes familiar with her clients' _____ toward investing and

16. (A) funds
     (B) returns
     (C) attitudes
     (D) resources

gives advice accordingly. The advisor makes certain recommendations to clients who are conservative investors and makes different recommendations to clients who prefer to invest more _____. The best way to create a strong investment _____ that matches

17. (A) aggressor
    (B) aggression
    (C) aggressive
    (D) aggressively

18. (A) portage
    (B) portrait
    (C) portfolio
    (D) portmanteau

your needs and preferred investing strategy is to work with a professional investment advisor.

Part 7 Reading Comprehension

Questions 19–23 refer to the following two e-mail messages.

To: Amelia Waddell
From: Peter Simpkins
Subject: Investment

Hi Amelia,

I wondered if you would give me the name of your investment advisor. My business is doing very well this year. In fact, I am now making a lot more money than I did when I had a job with a salary. I would prefer to invest my profits in the stock market as I'm sure I would earn more money that way than just letting it earn interest in a bank account. Of course, I want to invest wisely, so I am looking for professional advice. You know I tend to have a conservative attitude toward money, and I hope your advisor can help me make some safe investments. Please get back to me soon as I'd like to get started on this before the end of the month. Thanks.

Peter

To: Peter Simpkins
From: Amelia Waddell
Subject: Re: Investment

Hi Peter,

I would be happy to help you out. As a matter of fact, I just talked with my investment advisor this morning, and she mentioned that she is looking for more clients. Her name is Susannah Oliveros. I have been working with her for several years and have always been satisfied. I have gotten good returns on the investments I have made with her. I will call you this afternoon, and we can discuss all the details then. I will also give you her phone number so you can call her tomorrow. I know you will like her.

Amelia

19. Why did Peter write the e-mail message?
(A) He is looking for a job.
(B) He needs some investment advice.
(C) He lent some money to Amelia.
(D) He is looking for new clients.

20. Why does Peter have extra money to invest?
(A) He earned a lot of interest in his bank account.
(B) He has a high salary.
(C) His business is very profitable.
(D) He made money in the stock market last year.

21. When will Amelia call Peter?
(A) This morning.
(B) This afternoon.
(C) Tomorrow.
(D) Before the end of the month.

22. The word *wisely* in line 9 of the first e-mail is closest in meaning to
(A) smartly
(B) carefully
(C) quickly
(D) easily

23. The word *returns* in line 8 of the second e-mail is closest in meaning to
(A) goes back
(B) gives back
(C) suggestions
(D) profits

Lesson 24

Taxes

WORDS TO LEARN

calculation
deadline
file
fill out
give up
joint
owe
penalty
preparation
refund
spouse
withhold

Study the following definitions and examples.

1. **calculation** n., computation; estimate
   a. It took my accountant some time to complete the calculations on my income tax.
   b. According to my calculations, I'll owe less money on my income taxes this year.

2. **deadline** n., a time by which something must be finished
   a. The deadline for paying this year's taxes is just two weeks away.
   b. My best work is done with strict deadlines.

3. **file** v., to enter into public record
   a. If you file your taxes late, you will have to pay a fine.
   b. If you believe the tax preparer gave you incorrect information, you should file a complaint with her boss.

4. **fill out** v., to complete
   a. I usually ask someone to help me fill out my tax form.
   b. Don't forget to sign the tax form after you have filled it out.

5. **give up** v., to quit; to stop
   a. Bruce gave up paying an accountant to prepare his tax return and now does it himself with tax preparation software.
   b. Ms. Gomez gave up hope that she would ever receive a large tax refund.

6. **joint** adj., together; shared
   a. We opened a joint bank account five years ago.
   b. The couple no longer files joint tax returns.

7. **owe** v., to have a debt; to be obligated to pay
   a. People are often surprised to discover that they owe more money in income taxes at the end of the year.
   b. As the business grew, the owner paid back loans and owed less money.

8. **penalty** n., a punishment; a consequence
   a. Anyone who pays less than they should in taxes will face a penalty.
   b. Penalties are imposed to discourage underpayment of taxes by adding a percentage to the taxes you already owe.

9. **preparation** n., the act of making something ready
   a. Income tax preparation can take a long time.
   b. It is important to do some preparation on your own before hiring an accountant to work on your tax form.

10. **refund** n., the amount paid back; v., to give back
    a. With the tax refund, we bought two plane tickets.
    b. The government will refund any money that you overpaid.

11. **spouse** n., a husband or wife
    a. You can claim your spouse as a dependent on your tax return if he or she doesn't earn an income.
    b. My spouse prepares the tax return for both of us.

12. **withhold** v., to keep from; to refrain from
    a. My employer withholds money from each paycheck to apply toward my income taxes.
    b. Do not withhold any information from your accountant or he will not be able to prepare your tax form correctly.

WORD FAMILIES

verb	calculate	The tax software calculates your taxes for you.
noun	calculation	The calculation is no more difficult than high school math.
noun	calculator	In order to avoid making addition and subtraction errors, I suggest you use a calculator.

verb	file	Don't wait until the last minute to file your taxes.
noun	file	I keep all my tax information in one file.

adjective	joint	My husband and I filed a joint tax return.
adverb	jointly	Even though you are separated right now, you will save money if you and your wife file your taxes jointly.

verb	penalize	The government will penalize taxpayers who try to evade paying their fair share of taxes.
noun	penalty	For every dollar you owe in overdue taxes, a 10 percent penalty is imposed.
adjective	penal	Tax evasion is a penal offense.

verb	prepare	Most people wait until the last minute to prepare their tax returns.
noun	preparation	If you are organized, income tax preparation takes only a few hours.
adjective	preparatory	The preparatory work for doing my taxes is more time-consuming than filling out the forms.

verb	refund	The government should refund your overpaid taxes within a few weeks of filing your tax return.
noun	refund	If you have overpaid your income taxes, you will get a refund at the end of the year.
adjective	refundable	Sales tax that tourists pay in a foreign country may be refundable when they leave the country.

WORDS IN CONTEXT

Read the following passage and write the words in the blanks below.

calculated	fill out	owe	refund
deadline	gave up	penalized	spouse
filed	joint	prepares	withhold

Every year, my wife gathers all of our pay stubs and expense reports and

(1) _____ to fill out our tax forms. She tries to finish them in March,

well before the April 15th (2) _____. It's a time-consuming process.

There are receipts to find, records to organize, and forms to (3) _____.

When we first got married, we (4) _____ separate returns. But now she

marks me as her (5) _____ and files the (6) _____ return. It

saves us money and saves me time!

My wife is very proud of her accuracy. The government has never sent the

forms back with corrections. For several years now, we have received a

(7) _____. But this year, she (8) _____ the numbers over and

over again and found we had not paid enough taxes throughout the year. She didn't

want to (9) _____ any money. Finally, she (10) _____ and

sent in our check. Actually, it was my fault. I had changed jobs and didn't ask my

employer to (11) _____ enough money from my paychecks. I'm just glad

we found and corrected the mistake before we got (12) _____.

WORD PRACTICE

LISTENING COMPREHENSION

TRACK
25

Part 1 Photo

Look at the picture and listen to the sentences.
Choose the sentence that best describes the picture.

1. Ⓐ Ⓑ Ⓒ Ⓓ

Part 2 Question–Response

Listen to the question and the three responses. Choose the response that best answers the question.

2. Ⓐ Ⓑ Ⓒ   3. Ⓐ Ⓑ Ⓒ

Part 3 Conversation

Listen to the dialogue. Then read each question and choose the best answer.

4. Who usually prepares the man's taxes?
   (A) The man.
   (B) His wife.
   (C) The man and his wife together.
   (D) An accountant.

5. When did the man file his taxes last year?
   (A) One month before the deadline.
   (B) Two months before the deadline.
   (C) One month after the deadline.
   (D) Two months after the deadline.

6. What is the penalty for missing the deadline?
   (A) 1 percent.
   (B) 2 percent.
   (C) 9 percent.
   (D) 10 percent.

Part 4 Talk

Listen to the talk. Then read each question and choose the best answer.

7. Who is the speaker?
   (A) A tax preparer.
   (B) A government tax agent.
   (C) A tax filer.
   (D) An employer.

8. When can the refund check be expected?
   (A) In eighteen weeks.
   (B) Before six weeks.
   (C) In four weeks.
   (D) In ten weeks at the latest.

9. What does the speaker offer to do?
   (A) Calculate the amount to withhold from
       the paycheck.
   (B) Make an arrangement with the employer.
   (C) Show the listener a fee schedule.
   (D) Send in the tax payment.

READING

Part 5 Incomplete Sentences

Choose the word that best completes the sentence.

10. According to my _____, we owe a lot of money in taxes this year.
    (A) calculations   (C) calculators
    (B) calculated   (D) calculate

11. Those _____ on my desk contain all the information we'll need for preparing our taxes.
    (A) filed   (C) file
    (B) files   (D) filing

12. It is usually advantageous for spouses to file their income taxes _____.
    (A) joints   (C) joint
    (B) jointly   (D) jointed

13. We didn't know we had to claim the interest from our savings account and were _____ for the error.
    (A) penalize   (C) penalty
    (B) penalizing (D) penalized

14. The _____ of the forms took much less time than we expected.
    (A) preparatory   (C) prepared
    (B) preparation   (D) prepares

15. I didn't overpay my taxes this year, so I didn't get a _____.
    (A) calculation   (C) refund
    (B) deadline   (D) file

Part 6 Text Completion

**Smith & Johnson
Tax Preparation**

We take away the headaches of tax time.

_____ your own taxes can be frustrating and often leads to costly

16. (A) Prepare
    (B) Prepares
    (C) Preparing
    (D) Preparation

errors in calculations. Are you ready to give up trying to fill _____ your

17. (A) in
    (B) up
    (C) out
    (D) through

tax forms on your own? Smith & Johnson Tax Preparation can help you!

People who use professional tax preparers get larger refunds and avoid _____ for underpayment and missed deadlines.

18. (A) pennants
    (B) penalties
    (C) penumbras
    (D) peninsulas

Make tax time easier. Call us today. You owe it to yourself.

Part 7 Reading Comprehension

Questions 19–23 refer to the following letter.

April 1, 20—

Mr. Roger Earnshaw
2943 Northern Boulevard
New Orange, NH

Dear Mr. Earnshaw,

Enclosed are your completed tax forms, which I have prepared for you at your request. I am sorry to report that you will not receive the $500 refund that you expected. Instead, my calculations show that you owe $450 in taxes, as well as an additional penalty of $45 for underpayment of taxes. The reason for this is that you and your spouse have chosen not to file your taxes jointly this year. You may want to reconsider this for the future since, as you can see, it is more costly for married couples to file separately. If you and your spouse wish to continue to file separately, you may want to ask your employer to withhold a greater amount from your paychecks so that you don't end up owing money again next year. This will be even more important if you get the salary increase that you have been hoping for.

Write out a check for the taxes that you still owe and the penalty and mail it together with your tax forms before the April 15 deadline. Please let me know if I can be of any further assistance.

Sincerely,

Kathleen O'Hara
CPA

19. Who wrote the letter?
(A) A tax agent.
(B) A tax preparer.
(C) Mr. Earnshaw's spouse.
(D) Mr. Earnshaw's employer.

20. What is the total amount that Mr. Earnshaw owes?
(A) $45.
(B) $450.
(C) $495.
(D) $500.

21. What does Ms. O'Hara recommend to Mr. Earnshaw to improve his tax situation?
(A) Get married.
(B) File separately.
(C) Ask for a salary increase.
(D) Withhold more from his checks.

22. The word *jointly* in line 5 is closest in meaning to
(A) together
(B) apart
(C) on time
(D) finally

23. The word *deadline* in line 11 is closest in meaning to
(A) holiday
(B) schedule
(C) anniversary
(D) due date

Lesson 25

Financial Statements

WORDS TO LEARN

desire
detail
forecast
level
overall
perspective
project
realistic
target
translation
typically
yield

Study the following definitions and examples.

1. **desire** v., to wish
    a. We desire to have our own home.
    b. He desires to retire when he becomes forty.
2. **detail** v., to report or relate minutely or in particulars
    a. The business planner detailed the steps we should follow to write our financial statement.
    b. Fabio created a financial statement that detailed every expected expenditure for the next quarter.
3. **forecast** n., a prediction of a future event; v., to estimate or calculate in advance
    a. The financial forecast indicates a deficit in the next quarter.
    b. Analysts forecast a strong economic outlook.
4. **level** n., a relative position or rank on a scale
    a. We have never had an accountant work at such a sophisticated level before.
    b. If you expect your business to start earning at higher levels soon, your financial statement should show that.
5. **overall** adj., regarded as a whole; general
    a. The company's overall expectations were out of proportion.
    b. Our overall financial situation is not too bad.
6. **perspective** n., a mental view or outlook
    a. The budget statement will give the manager some perspective on where the costs of running the business are to be found.
    b. Joseph's accountant gave him some perspective as well as some data on how much he could expect to earn in his first year in business.
7. **project** v., to estimate or predict
    a. We need to project our earnings and expenses in order to plan next year's budget.
    b. The director projects that the company will need to hire ten new employees this year.
8. **realistic** adj., tending to or expressing an awareness of things as they really are
    a. Stefano found that an accurate accounting gave him a realistic idea of his business's financial direction.
    b. Realistic expectations are important when you review your financial statements.
9. **target** v., to establish as a goal; n., a goal
    a. We targeted March as the deadline for completing the financial statement.
    b. Most managers target desired income as the primary criterion for success.
10. **translation** n., something expressed in a different language or form
    a. The translation of the statement from Japanese into English was very helpful.
    b. The accountant was able to provide a translation of the financial terms into language we could all understand.
11. **typically** adv., acting in conformity to a type; characteristically
    a. Office expenses typically include such things as salaries, rent, and office supplies.
    b. Banks typically require a financial statement before they will lend money to a small business.
12. **yield** n., an amount produced; v., to produce
    a. Henry's budget gave him the desired yield: a better indication of his expected profit.
    b. The company's investment yielded high returns.

WORD FAMILIES

verb	desire	Our manager is trying to predict how many customers will desire our product over the next quarter.
noun	desire	Her desire for greater control of the business led her to discuss her need for more information with her accountant.
adjective	desirable	The category summary, while desirable, was time-consuming to prepare.

verb	detail	The statement details all of our income and expenses.
noun	detail	The budget report needs to be accurate down to the last detail.
adjective	detailed	The loan officer asked for a detailed financial statement.

verb	project	The budget summary helped us project our expenditures for the year.
noun	project	The financial project was time-consuming and challenging.
noun	projection	Maurice's projections for the upcoming fiscal year were not as helpful as we had hoped.

verb	realize	The plan helps her realize her dream of having the business turn a profit.
noun	reality	The financial statement reinforced the reality that our business is in deep trouble.
adjective	realistic	The accountant needs realistic numbers on which to base his plan.

verb	translate	We need to translate all of this information into a financial statement that shows the true condition of our business.
noun	translation	The translation of the document was provided at no charge.
adjective	translatable	The data was not translatable between programs and had to be entered by hand, which took hours.

noun	type	This type of business requires a lot of start-up money.
adjective	typical	Part of a category summary is defining the expenses that are typical of the business in question.
adverb	typically	Typically, we finish preparing the budget just in time to meet the deadline.

WORDS IN CONTEXT

Read the following passage and write the words in the blanks below.

desired	level	projected	translate
detailed	overall	realistic	typical
forecasts	perspective	target	yield

A business budget focuses on future profits and future capital requirements. A budget can help the business owner determine the amount of profit the business is expected to make, the amount of sales it will take to reach a goal, and what (1) _____ of expenses are attached to those sales. A business establishes a (2) _____, a goal to work toward. A business (3) _____ the sales that will be needed to reach this target.

Projecting or planning ahead is part of (4) _____ business planning. When creating a (5) _____ income statement, a business owner tries to determine how to reach the (6) _____ target. The annual profit must be sufficient to (7) _____ the owner a return for his or her time spent operating the business, plus a return on the investment. The owner's target income is the sum of a reasonable salary for the time spent running the business and a normal return on the amount invested in the firm.

After projecting the income needed, the business owner has to (8) _____ the target profit into a net sales figure for the forecasted period. The owner has to determine whether this sales volume is (9) _____. One useful technique is to break down the required annual sales into a daily sales figure to get a better (10) _____ of the sales required to yield the annual profit.

At this stage in the financial plan, the owner should create a (11) _____ picture of the firm's expected operating expenses. Many books and business organizations give (12) _____ operating statistics data, based on a percentage of net sales. The business's accountant can help you assign dollar values to anticipated expenses.

Developing a projected income statement is an important part of any financial plan, as the process forces the business owner to examine the firm's future profitability.

WORD PRACTICE

LISTENING COMPREHENSION

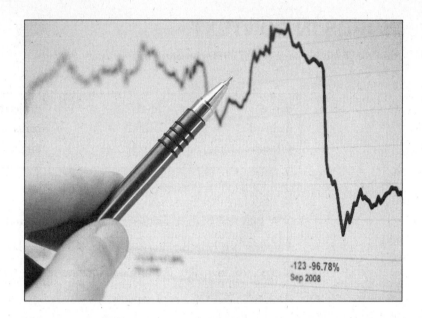

-123 -96.78%
Sep 2008

Part 1 Photo

Look at the picture and listen to the sentences.
Choose the sentence that best describes the picture.

1. Ⓐ Ⓑ Ⓒ Ⓓ

Part 2 Question–Response

Listen to the question and the three responses. Choose the response that best answers the question.

2. Ⓐ Ⓑ Ⓒ   3. Ⓐ Ⓑ Ⓒ

Part 3 Conversation

Listen to the dialogue. Then read each question and choose the best answer.

4. What is the woman doing?
    (A) Developing a project report.
    (B) Preparing a financial statement.
    (C) Making a weather forecast.
    (D) Writing an expense report.

5. When does she want to have this finished?
    (A) By noon.
    (B) Before 8:00.
    (C) By the end of the week.
    (D) Before the end of the year.

6. What does the man offer to do?
    (A) Write a check.
    (B) Sign a statement.
    (C) Solve her financial problems.
    (D) Correct her calculations.

Part 4 Talk

Listen to the talk. Then read each question and choose the best answer.

7. Who is this talk directed at?
    (A) Large companies.
    (B) Financial advisors.
    (C) Small business owners.
    (D) Finance companies.

8. When does a business typically become profitable?
    (A) During the first year.
    (B) After five years.
    (C) During the first five years.
    (D) After nine years.

9. According to the speaker, what is the first step to take when starting a small business?
    (A) Get an office with a key.
    (B) Write a financial statement.
    (C) Raise start-up funds.
    (D) Hire a project manager.

READING

Part 5 Incomplete Sentences

Choose the word that best completes the sentence.

10. Before we begin, I think we should all focus on the _____ outcome of this effort.
    (A) desirableness   (C) desired
    (B) desire   (D) desirability

11. The accountant can review all the _____ of the financial statement with you.
    (A) detailed   (C) details
    (B) detailing   (D) detail

12. The _____ figures for the next quarter will not be available until a week from tomorrow.
    (A) project   (C) projection
    (B) projected   (D) projects

13. The projected financial statement demonstrated to Susan that her business had a _____ chance of increasing its profit over the next two quarters.
    (A) realistic   (C) realistically
    (B) realist   (D) reality

14. To create our financial strategy, our consultant took the experiences of similar businesses and _____ relevant outcomes to our situation.
    (A) translatable   (C) translator
    (B) translation   (D) translated

15. Our business experienced a _____ fall in profits during the third quarter of the year.
    (A) typical   (C) type
    (B) typically   (D) typed

Part 6 Text Completion

Memo

To: Department Heads
From: Roy Jones, Manager
Re: Planning Meeting

As you know, our quarterly planning meeting will take place in two weeks. I want to let you know some of the topics that will be discussed, to give you a chance to prepare.

First, the overall economic situation in the country looks very good for the coming year. Economists _____ an increase in consumer spending, especially in our sector. Therefore, we should look into

16. (A) foreclose
    (B) forebode
    (C) forego
    (D) forecast

increasing production. I believe that a 15 percent increase by the end of the year is a realistic target.

Second, since the company plans to increase sales overseas, we will need to hire several _____.

17. (A) translators
    (B) translates
    (C) translations
    (D) transports

We will need to discuss how many we need and which languages should have priority.

These are the most important topics for the meeting. If anyone _____ to put a special item on

18. (A) desire
    (B) desires
    (C) will desire
    (D) have desired

the meeting agenda, please let me know by the beginning of next week.

Part 7 Reading Comprehension

Questions 19–23 refer to the following article and e-mail message.

Do you have a sound financial plan for your small business? You should. The majority of small businesses fail during the first five years, typically because they have not made realistic financial plans. A new business owner may start out with the necessary funds, a qualified staff, and office space and equipment. These things may not save the business from disaster, however, if the business owner hasn't set realistic targets and made plans to reach them. Everyone who contemplates starting a new business should sit down and write out all the details of a financial plan before doing anything else.

To: Shirley Haines
From: Matthew Rockwell
Subject: Financial planning
Attach: Financial Plans for Small Businesses

Shirley,

Have you seen the attached article on financial planning? It appeared in this week's issue of Small Business Owner magazine. It has given me a new perspective on things. I can't believe we have already been running our business for six months, but we still haven't sat down together to write out a financial plan. Overall, I believe our business is doing well, and we certainly have enough clients. But, I now understand that our future success depends on having a good financial plan. We need to project our earnings for the next year and set financial targets. We should get to work on this right away. Can we meet tomorrow afternoon? Three o'clock is a good time for me. Let me know soon.

Matthew

19. According to the article, why do most small businesses fail?
    (A) Lack of financial planning.
    (B) Lack of adequate office space.
    (C) Lack of qualified staff.
    (D) Lack of adequate funds.

20. Why did Matthew write the e-mail message?
    (A) He wants to start a small business with Shirley.
    (B) He is writing an article for a magazine.
    (C) He wants to make a financial plan.
    (D) He is looking for new clients.

21. When does Matthew want to meet with Shirley?
    (A) Tomorrow.
    (B) Next week.
    (C) In six months.
    (D) Next year.

22. The word *typically* in line 4 of the article is closest in meaning to
    (A) unfortunately
    (B) usually
    (C) really
    (D) sadly

23. The word *perspective* in line 4 of the e-mail is closest in meaning to
    (A) information
    (B) advice
    (C) goal
    (D) view

Word Review #5   Lessons 21–25 Financing and Budgeting

Choose the word that best completes the sentence.

1. The Small Business Administration will help you to arrange to _____ money to start a business.
   (A) borrow
   (B) borrowed
   (C) borrowing
   (D) borrower

2. When we _____ out a loan, we got very good terms.
   (A) take
   (B) took
   (C) taken
   (D) taking

3. Most people get nervous when someone is _____ their books.
   (A) audit
   (B) audits
   (C) audited
   (D) auditing

4. Sometimes it is difficult to pull _____ of bad investments.
   (A) through
   (B) out
   (C) at
   (D) to

5. I prefer _____ in social-conscience funds.
   (A) invest
   (B) investment
   (C) investing
   (D) investor

6. When the Dow is dropping, investors need to be _____.
   (A) resource
   (B) resources
   (C) resourceful
   (D) resourcefulness

7. Sometimes it is difficult to understand how the government _____ tax liability.
   (A) calculating
   (B) calculations
   (C) calculators
   (D) calculates

8. One decision with tax returns is whether to give _____ itemizing in favor of the standard deduction.
   (A) up
   (B) in
   (C) to
   (D) out

9. The company's _____ earnings over the next six months were exciting.
   (A) project
   (B) projects
   (C) projection
   (D) projected

10. Some parts of the tax code are so confusing that they need _____.
    (A) translate
    (B) translates
    (C) translated
    (D) translation

Choose the one word or phrase that best completes each sentence.

At Grover Investment Services, we understand that you work hard to earn your money, and it is important to invest it _____. This is where we come in. We offer our _____ a full range of investment services.

11. (A) wise
    (B) wisely
    (C) wizened
    (D) wisdom

12. (A) accountants
    (B) officers
    (C) spouses
    (D) clients

Whether you are a conservative or aggressive investor, we can help you develop an investment plan that suits your needs. At Grover, we are _____ to helping you get the best possible return for your money.

13. (A) commit
    (B) committee
    (C) committed
    (D) commitment

Call us today.

First-time home buyers may feel overwhelmed by the process of applying for a mortgage. However, the process of _____ money to buy a house is not very complicated. First, you will have to fill out a

14. (A) borrow
    (B) borrows
    (C) borrowed
    (D) borrowing

form giving information about your financial situation. You need to show that you have a good income. It is also important not to have a lot of _____. If you already owe a lot of money, the bank may

15. (A) debut
    (B) debt
    (C) doubt
    (D) dubbed

hesitate to lend you more. Then, you will have to make a _____, usually about 10 percent of the

16. (A) refund
    (B) target
    (C) down payment
    (D) forecast

total price of the house. The bank lends you the rest of the money for the purchase.

Many people use the services of an accountant to help _____ their tax forms. They consider it well

      17. (A) prepare
          (B) preparer
          (C) preparation
          (D) preparatory

worth the money. An accountant can help you avoid _____ for underpayment of taxes and, in

      18. (A) pennants
          (B) penalties
          (C) penitents
          (D) pendants

general, ensure that your tax form has been filled out correctly. But remember, accountants have deadlines too. Be sure to give all your tax information to your accountant early, then you can be sure that your taxes will be ready to _____ on time. No one wants to pay a fine for sending in his or her tax form too late.

      19. (A) file
          (B) fund
          (C) budget
          (D) invest

Lesson 26

Property and Departments

WORDS TO LEARN

adjacent

collaboration

concentrate

conducive

disruption

hamper

inconsiderately

lobby

move up

open to

opt

scrutiny

Study the following definitions and examples.

1. **adjacent** adj., next to
    a. My office is adjacent to the receptionist area on the third floor.
    b. The office manager found it very efficient to have the copier adjacent to the mail room.

2. **collaboration** n., the act of working with someone
    a. The manager had never seen such effective collaboration between two groups.
    b. We believe that it was our collaboration that enabled us to achieve such favorable results.

3. **concentrate** v., to focus; to think about
    a. In his quiet, corner office, the manager could finally concentrate and finish his work.
    b. We should concentrate our efforts on the last quarter of the year.

4. **conducive** adj., contributing to; leading to
    a. The new office arrangement is much more conducive to work than the dark, depressing space the company had before.
    b. Arranging chairs so that participants can see each other easily is conducive to open communication.

5. **disruption** n., interruption; disturbance
    a. If there are no disruptions, the office renovations will be finished this week.
    b. The strike caused a disruption in production at the factory.

6. **hamper** v., to impede or interfere
    a. When the weight of the freezing rain broke the telephone lines, the telemarketers' jobs were seriously hampered.
    b. The lack of supplies hampered our ability to finish on schedule.

7. **inconsiderately** adv., rudely; impolitely
    a. The manager inconsiderately scheduled the meeting for late Friday afternoon.
    b. Mr. Peterson inconsiderately disrupted the meeting by asking a lot of irrelevant questions.

8. **lobby** n., an anteroom, foyer, or waiting room
    a. The salesperson waited in the busy lobby for the buyer to see him.
    b. The reception area was moved from the lobby of the building to the third floor.

9. **move up** v., to advance, improve position
    a. As the employee moved up the corporate ladder, she never forgot where she started.
    b. In order to move up in the company, employees had to demonstrate their loyalty.

10. **open to** adj., receptive to; vulnerable
    a. What I valued most in my previous supervisor was that she was always open to ideas and suggestions.
    b. Since the junior executive was still on probation, he was open to much scrutiny and criticism.

11. **opt** v., to choose, to decide on
    a. The operations manager opted for the less expensive office design.
    b. If Mary opts to join that department, you will be working together.

12. **scrutiny** n., close, careful examination
    a. After a great deal of scrutiny, the manager decided that the employee's work had improved considerably.
    b. Jim left his old job because he found it difficult to work under the close scrutiny of his boss.

WORD FAMILIES

verb	collaborate	If we collaborate on this project, you will be sure to receive credit.
noun	collaboration	Collaboration often brings about results that no one could have predicted.
adjective	collaborative	The new project is a collaborative effort among several departments.

verb	concentrate	Some people find it difficult to concentrate when there is a lot of noise and activity around them.
noun	concentration	The concentration of a large percentage of the company's funds in just a few areas left several departments underfunded.
adjective	concentrated	With some concentrated effort, we should be able to finish this work by the deadline.

verb	disrupt	Try not to disrupt the meeting being held in the sales department.
noun	disruption	I'm sorry for the disruption, but this phone call is very important.
adjective	disruptive	Having to temporarily move the offices proved to be very disruptive and sales decreased during that quarter.

noun	inconsiderateness	The inconsiderateness of many of the customers caused several employees to quit their jobs.
adjective	inconsiderate	Would it be inconsiderate to ask to use your office while you are away?
adverb	inconsiderately	John inconsiderately looked through his coworker's mail before putting it on his desk.

verb	opt	When we moved offices, I opted for the one without a window.
noun	option	Presented with several options, we chose the one that required the least amount of effort.
adjective	optional	Attendance at tomorrow's meeting is optional for the people working in this department.

verb	scrutinize	The auditor carefully scrutinized the financial records.
noun	scrutiny	Employees under constant scrutiny tend to perform worse than those employees who have more freedom.
adjective	inscrutable	You can never tell what she is thinking, since her facial expressions are inscrutable.

WORDS IN CONTEXT

Read the following passage and write the words in the blanks below.

adjacent	conducive	inconsiderate	open to
collaboration	disruptive	lobby	opting
concentrate	hampered	move up	scrutinized

The layout of any office has an important influence on the atmosphere and operations in the company. The shipping department most likely will not be located next to the customer service department. The noise would be too (1) _____. Likewise, locating a kitchen (2) _____ to the (3) _____ would be (4) _____ of office visitors and clients. The marketing department is often situated close to the sales department due to their necessary (5) _____.

Employee productivity may be (6) _____ or improved by the arrangement of workers and departments. Employees vie for corner offices as they (7) _____ the corporate ladder. They want to be accessible to top management, but not so close that everything that they do is (8) _____. At the same time, many companies are (9) _____ for open work spaces versus traditional offices. Open spaces are more (10) _____ to team projects, where employees interact freely. However, some employees feel that such an environment makes it difficult to (11) _____. Employees know under which conditions they work the best. If employers are willing to listen and are (12) _____ suggestions, they can take advantage of office space and help employees to realize their full potential.

WORD PRACTICE

LISTENING COMPREHENSION

Part 1 Photo

Look at the picture and listen to the sentences.
Choose the sentence that best describes the picture.

1. Ⓐ Ⓑ Ⓒ Ⓓ

Part 2 Question–Response

Listen to the question and the three responses. Choose the response that best answers the question.

2. Ⓐ Ⓑ Ⓒ   3. Ⓐ Ⓑ Ⓒ

Part 3 Conversation

Listen to the dialogue. Then read each question and choose the best answer.

4. What does the man think of the current lobby?
    (A) People conduct a lot of conversations there.
    (B) It's quite pleasant.
    (C) More people should use it.
    (D) It's not a good place for conversations.

5. What might be disruptive to the business?
    (A) Loud conversations in the lobby.
    (B) Remodeling work.
    (C) The need to scrutinize plans.
    (D) A heavy workload.

6. When will the new lobby be finished?
    (A) This afternoon.
    (B) In two weeks.
    (C) Next month.
    (D) In four months.

Part 4 Talk

Listen to the talk. Then read each question and choose the best answer.

7. What is this talk about?
    (A) How to encourage collaboration.
    (B) How to increase productivity.
    (C) How to concentrate.
    (D) How to design an office.

8. What is the problem with a large, open office?
    (A) It isn't conducive to collaboration.
    (B) It doesn't include options.
    (C) Work is easily disrupted.
    (D) It isn't adjacent to a lobby.

9. Why is it important to have a large work room?
    (A) To allow staff members to work together.
    (B) To maintain a high level of activity.
    (C) To increase concentration.
    (D) To have a more attractive design.

READING

Part 5 Incomplete Sentences

Choose the word that best completes the sentence.

10. The data entry clerk is so accustomed to working by herself that I really doubt if she is capable of _____ on this project.
    - (A) collaborated
    - (B) collaborating
    - (C) collaborator
    - (D) collaborates

11. Sue always _____ so hard on her work that she forgets where she is.
    - (A) concentrated
    - (B) concentrates
    - (C) concentration
    - (D) concentrating

12. The constant flow of traffic by the researcher's desk proved to be very _____.
    - (A) disruptive
    - (B) disrupts
    - (C) disruption
    - (D) disrupted

13. The employee lounge is for everyone's enjoyment so please don't use it _____.
    - (A) inconsiderate
    - (B) inconsiderateness
    - (C) inconsiderately
    - (D) inconsideration

14. Some people always _____ for the easy way out.
    - (A) opt
    - (B) option
    - (C) optional
    - (D) options

15. After close _____ of the new offices, they decided to put the photocopier in a small room where no one would be bothered by the noise.
    - (A) scrutinize
    - (B) scrutinizing
    - (C) scrutiny
    - (D) scrutinized

Part 6 Text Completion

NOTICE

In order to maintain a professional office environment that is _____ to work,

16. (A) optional
    (B) conducive
    (C) inscrutable
    (D) collaborative

all staff members are asked to observe the following guidelines.

- Be _____ of your coworkers. When using an open work area, do not speak in

17. (A) concentrated
    (B) adjacent
    (C) considerate
    (D) hampering

loud voices or turn on radios.
- Remember that the lobby is the first place our clients see when they enter the office. Please cooperate by doing your best to keep this area clean and neat.
- Our clients are important. _____ your coworkers when they are meeting

18. (A) Not disrupt
    (B) Won't disrupt
    (C) Isn't disrupting
    (D) Don't disrupt

with clients.

Part 7 Reading Comprehension

Questions 19–23 refer to the following memo.

Memo

To: All office staff
From: P. Windermere, Office Manager
Re: Parking situation

As you may be aware, starting next week, the parking garage will be closed for repairs to the upper level due to damage caused by the heavy rains last month. There will be no parking allowed on any level of the garage while the repairs are taking place, as parked cars may hamper the work. Cars parked in the garage will be towed at the owner's expense. While the garage is closed, you may opt to park on the street or in the lot adjacent to the building. Remember that it is a private lot and a fee will be charged. I realize that the parking options will be limited, and I am open to any suggestions for solutions to this parking situation that any of you may have. Unfortunately, the repair work will take more than a few weeks. We cannot expect the garage to open again until two months from now. In the meantime, I thank you for your cooperation.

---

19. Why will the garage be closed?
    (A) It needs repairs.
    (B) The fees are too high.
    (C) Its parking options are limited.
    (D) Street parking is better.

20. What will happen to cars that are parked in the garage?
    (A) They will be charged a fee.
    (B) They will be repaired.
    (C) They will be towed.
    (D) They will be used for work.

21. When will the garage reopen?
    (A) In a week.
    (B) In just a few weeks.
    (C) In a month.
    (D) In two months.

22. The word *hamper* in line 5 is closest in meaning to
    (A) allow
    (B) interfere
    (C) encourage
    (D) contribute

23. The word *adjacent* in line 8 is closest in meaning to
    (A) distant
    (B) underneath
    (C) next to
    (D) across from

Lesson 27

Board Meetings and Committees

**WORDS
TO LEARN**

adhere to

agenda

bring up

conclude

go ahead

goal

lengthy

matter

periodically

priority

progress

waste

Study the following definitions and examples.

1. **adhere to** v., to follow; to pay attention to
    a. The chairman never adhered to his own rules.
    b. The best committee members are those who adhere to the time limits and speak only when they have something important to add.
2. **agenda** n., a list of topics to be discussed
    a. The board was able to cover fifteen items on the agenda.
    b. The agenda was sent out three weeks ago so that everyone could prepare for the meeting.
3. **bring up** v., to introduce a topic
    a. Just as the meeting was about to finish, the manager brought up a controversial issue.
    b. No one brought up the resignation of the director.
4. **conclude** v., to stop; to come to a decision
    a. The committee members concluded the meeting early so that they could finish their budgets.
    b. After long discussions, the board has concluded that the project has to be canceled.
5. **go ahead** v., to proceed with; n., permission to do something
    a. Five of the six members felt that they should go ahead with the plan.
    b. The manager was just waiting for the go ahead from her boss before mailing the report.
6. **goal** n., objective, purpose
    a. Employees are expected to analyze and evaluate their annual goals.
    b. The director had to report to the committee that his department would not reach its goal of 35 percent growth.
7. **lengthy** adj., long in time, duration, or distance
    a. After lengthy discussions, the chairperson was reelected for another term.
    b. The report was so lengthy that members had to take it home and read it over the weekend.
8. **matter** n., an item, issue, topic of interest
    a. If there are no other matters to discuss, we will conclude the meeting.
    b. This is not the place to bring up personal matters.
9. **periodically** adv., from time to time
    a. The group tried to meet periodically.
    b. Periodically, new members were nominated to the committee.
10. **priority** n., something of importance, something that should be done before other things
    a. Since the remaining issues were not a priority, the group decided to move them to the next week's agenda.
    b. The manager was ineffective because she was unable to set priorities.
11. **progress** n., a movement forward; v., to move forward on something, especially work or a project
    a. The executive committee asked each group to present a report showing their progress for the year.
    b. Progress is being made on the annual report; we expect to see a finished product by next week.
12. **waste** v., to use carelessly; n., the careless use of something
    a. Without a leader, the group members wasted time and energy trying to organize themselves.
    b. The meeting wasn't a waste of time, but the members had hoped to accomplish more than they did.

WORD FAMILIES

verb	adhere	The chairperson asked us to adhere to the items on the agenda.
noun	adherence	Your adherence to these guidelines would be appreciated.

verb	conclude	To conclude, we must all focus on the year ahead of us and the challenges that we will face.
noun	conclusion	Unfortunately, the conclusion of the meeting was that they needed to downsize their workforce.
adjective	conclusive	There is no conclusive evidence to back up the report.

verb	lengthen	Ms. Greene decided to lengthen the time allotted to the meeting to allow each person a chance to speak.
noun	length	Because of its length, we decided not to read the entire report at the meeting.
adjective	lengthy	A presentation that is too lengthy will only put the audience to sleep.

noun	period	The sales reports for the current period are excellent.
adjective	periodic	They received periodic updates from the overseas licensees.
adverb	periodically	The employee checked his messages periodically during the week-long seminar.

verb	prioritize	Once the team members learned to prioritize their work, they were much more productive.
noun	priority	The committee member has difficulties setting priorities for herself.
adjective	prior	The director did not give much attention to Ellen's proposal as he had several prior matters to attend to.

verb	progress	Everyone was surprised at how quickly the meeting had progressed.
noun	progression	The quick progression of events didn't surprise anyone.
adjective	progressive	The new president is very progressive and is always looking for ways to improve the business.

WORDS IN CONTEXT

Read the following passage and write the words in the blanks below.

adhered to	concluded	lengthy	priority
agenda	go ahead	matters	progress
brought up	goals	periodically	waste

Committee meetings are a frequent and necessary event at almost every company. In order for meetings to be productive and not viewed as a (1) _____ of time, they should be run efficiently. Critical to the success of any meeting is the (2) _____. Everyone who attends the meeting should be aware of the agenda and be prepared to discuss the (3) _____ at hand and the (4) _____ to be accomplished. To avoid (5) _____ discussions, time frames should be set and (6) _____.

The meeting is called to order by the chairperson. Attendance is taken and agenda items are (7) _____ one by one. In general, (8) _____ topics should be at the beginning of the agenda, to make sure that the attendees are able to discuss them fully and make timely decisions. Once the (9) _____ is given for a plan or project, a plan of action is developed. The committee must then (10) _____ check up on the (11) _____ of that plan. The meeting is (12) _____ without any outstanding issues and a date for the next meeting is set.

WORD PRACTICE

LISTENING COMPREHENSION

TRACK
28

Part 1 Photo

Look at the picture and listen to the sentences.
Choose the sentence that best describes the picture.

1. Ⓐ Ⓑ Ⓒ Ⓓ

Part 2 Question–Response

Listen to the question and the three responses. Choose the response that best answers the question.

2. Ⓐ Ⓑ Ⓒ   3. Ⓐ Ⓑ Ⓒ

Part 3 Conversation

Listen to the dialogue. Then read each question and choose the best answer.

4. What do the speakers say about the meeting?
   (A) They had a good time.
   (B) A lot was accomplished.
   (C) Important matters were discussed.
   (D) It was too long.

5. How long did the meeting last?
   (A) Two hours.
   (B) Three hours.
   (C) Four hours.
   (D) Nine hours.

6. What will the speakers do the next time there is a meeting?
   (A) Look at the agenda.
   (B) Accomplish more things.
   (C) Avoid attending it.
   (D) Plan it better.

Part 4 Talk

Listen to the talk. Then read each question and choose the best answer.

7. What is this talk about?
   (A) How to have a better staff meeting.
   (B) How to make speeches.
   (C) How to write an agenda.
   (D) How to develop guidelines.

8. What are the listeners asked to do?
   (A) Make long speeches.
   (B) Discuss personal matters.
   (C) Bring something to the meeting.
   (D) Follow the agenda.

9. What will happen at 4:30?
   (A) The meeting will end.
   (B) Goals will be discussed.
   (C) Guidelines will be presented.
   (D) A new item will be introduced.

READING

Part 5 Incomplete Sentences

Choose the word that best completes the sentence.

10. When using these facilities, please _____ to the rules posted by the door.
    (A) adhere
    (B) adhering
    (C) adherence
    (D) adhered

11. As the chairman stood to give his _____, everyone in the room was listening.
    (A) conclusion
    (B) conclude
    (C) conclusive
    (D) concluding

12. Nobody wanted to _____ the meeting, but it was necessary to have time to cover the entire agenda.
    (A) length
    (B) lengthen
    (C) lengthy
    (D) lengthened

13. The original members of the committee met _____ for lunch or dinner.
    (A) period
    (B) periods
    (C) periodically
    (D) periodic

14. As her first _____, the committee chairwoman wanted to attract new, energetic members to the group.
    (A) prior
    (B) priority
    (C) prioritize
    (D) prioritized

15. Even as they _____ through the hundreds of pages of supporting material, the committee was still not convinced that the project was justified.
    (A) progression
    (B) progressed
    (C) progresses
    (D) progressive

Part 6 Text Completion

Memo

To: Department Staff
From: Alison Roth, Department Manager
Re: Meeting

All members of the department staff are requested to attend a department meeting next Friday morning. As you know, we meet _____ to review our work of the past months and finalize

16. (A) period
    (B) periodic
    (C) periodical
    (D) periodically

plans for the coming months. The goal of this Friday's meeting is to set our priorities for the next six months. The meeting agenda is attached for your review. Let's agree to follow the agenda and not _____ other matters at this time so that we can finish the meeting in a timely manner. The most

17. (A) set back
    (B) go ahead
    (C) bring up
    (D) adhere to

important item on the agenda is the budget. We need to take a careful look at our spending practices. We _____ too much money over the past six months. Please come with ideas about how we can

18. (A) waste
    (B) have wasted
    (C) will waste
    (D) are wasting

use our funds more efficiently in the future. Please arrive at the meeting on time so that we can conclude before 12:00.

Part 7 Reading Comprehension

Questions 19–23 refer to the following agenda and e-mail message.

Perruche, Inc.

Annual Meeting
May 17, 20—
1:00 P.M.

Agenda

1. Progress report on overseas expansion   Robert Fleurat
2. Reducing waste in our plants   Madeline Costello
3. Reassessing our financial goals   Jean Duprey
4. Hiring and firing policies   Cynthia Weinstein
5. Looking ahead: priorities for the next decade   Samuel Lyon

---

To: Cynthia Weinstein
From: Samuel Lyon
Subject: Yesterday's meeting

Hello Cynthia,

We all missed you at yesterday's meeting. We were concerned that a medical emergency prevented your attendance but are glad to know that you are all right now. The meeting went well, and we were able to adhere to the agenda for the most part. There was only one small change. Jean gave his presentation on finance right after Robert since he had to leave early. Your secretary e-mailed a copy of your report to me, and I read it in your place. There were a few questions which will be submitted to you by e-mail. The meeting was not lengthy at all. In fact, even though we had scheduled three hours for the entire meeting, we actually concluded half an hour earlier than that. You see how efficient we have become. A copy of the meeting minutes will be e-mailed to you before 5:00 today. I hope to speak with you soon.

Samuel

---

19. What was the second item presented at the meeting?
    (A) Progress report on overseas expansion.
    (B) Reducing waste in our plants.
    (C) Reassessing our financial goals.
    (D) Hiring and firing policies.

20. Who read the report on hiring and firing policies?
    (A) Madeline Costello.
    (B) Jean Duprey.
    (C) Cynthia Weinstein.
    (D) Samuel Lyon.

21. What time did the meeting end?
    (A) 1:00.
    (B) 3:30.
    (C) 4:00.
    (D) 4:30.

22. The word *goals* in line 3 of the agenda is closest in meaning to
    (A) objectives
    (B) problems
    (C) needs
    (D) decisions

23. The words *adhere to* in line 3 of the e-mail are closest in meaning to
    (A) study
    (B) design
    (C) follow
    (D) understand

Lesson 28

Quality Control

WORDS TO LEARN

brand
conform
defect
enhance
garment
inspect
perceptive
repel
take back
throw out
uniformly
wrinkle

Study the following definitions and examples.

1. **brand** n., an identifying mark or label; a trademark
   a. Consumers often buy highly advertised brands of athletic shoes.
   b. All brands of aspirin are the same.
2. **conform** v., to match specifications or qualities
   a. The quality control manager insisted that every product that left the plant conform to the company's rigorous standards.
   b. Our safety standards conform to those established by the government.
3. **defect** n., an imperfection or flaw
   a. Because of a defect in stitching, the entire suit was thrown out.
   b. One way to sell a product with a defect is by labeling it as such and reducing the price.
4. **enhance** v., to make more attractive or valuable
   a. The reason behind quality control is to enhance the company's reputation for superior products.
   b. A stylish color enhances the appeal of a car.
5. **garment** n., an article of clothing
   a. Every garment must be carefully inspected for defects before it is shipped.
   b. The garment workers are accountable for production mistakes.
6. **inspect** v., to look at closely; to examine carefully or officially
   a. A quality control agent who does not inspect every product carefully can ruin his company's reputation.
   b. Children's car seats are thoroughly inspected and tested for safety before being put on the market.
7. **perceptive** adj., able to see or understand
   a. Dora always hires good workers because she is very perceptive about people's abilities.
   b. It takes a perceptive person to be a good manager.
8. **repel** v., to keep away; to fight against
   a. Umbrellas that do not repel water should never be passed through quality control.
   b. Faulty products repel repeat customers.
9. **take back** v., to return something; to withdraw or retract
   a. Good quality control significantly limits the number of products taken back for a refund.
   b. The quality inspector took the shoddy work back to the assembly line to confront the workers.
10. **throw out** v., to dispose of
    a. It is cheaper to throw out shoddy products than to lose customers.
    b. The factory decided to throw out hundreds of lightbulbs that might have been damaged, rather than lose customers.
11. **uniformly** adv., in the same way; consistently
    a. The products are checked to make sure they are uniformly packaged before they leave the factory.
    b. The food at chain restaurants is uniformly prepared so that customers will always find the same quality at each restaurant.
12. **wrinkle** n., a crease, ridge, or furrow, especially in skin or fabric
    a. A wrinkle that is ironed into a permanent-press product will annoy the consumer each time the garment is worn.
    b. A wrinkle in the finish can be repaired more economically before a sale than after.

WORD FAMILIES

noun	defect	Even a small defect can cause a product to fail.
adjective	defective	Good quality control employees will notice defective machinery before a serious breakdown occurs.

verb	inspect	We must inspect every product before we sell it.
noun	inspection	Each employee must conduct a careful inspection.
noun	inspector	The inspector leaves his identification number on the product to ensure accountability.

verb	perceive	The worker perceived that the stitching on the seams could not withstand normal strain.
noun	perception	Customers' perception of quality is often based on their experience with a given store or brand.
adjective	perceptive	Perceptive workers are excellent quality control inspectors.

verb	repel	A quality raincoat can repel rain and keep you dry.
noun	repellent	Testing insect repellent is never a pleasant task.
adjective	repellent	Testing stain removers can be repellent to workers because of the toxic fumes.

noun	uniform	The employees at this company are required to wear uniforms.
adjective	uniform	A successful company will ensure the uniform quality of its products.
adverb	uniformly	All of our company's products must be uniformly labeled.

verb	wrinkle	Linen is not a practical fabric because it wrinkles easily.
noun	wrinkle	Inspect garments carefully and remove any wrinkles that you find.
adjective	wrinkled	Garments become wrinkled after they have been tried on several times at the store.

WORDS IN CONTEXT

Read the following passage and write the words in the blanks below.

brand	enhance	perceive	throws out
conform	garment	repel	uniform
defects	inspect	take back	wrinkle

Alex is excited about his new job with Parapluie Rain Wear. As quality control manager, his job is to make sure that his company's goods (1) _____ to standardized quality criteria and are free from (2) _____. Before any (3) _____ leaves the factory, Alex must (4) _____ it. He knows that if he (5) _____ a damaged garment before a customer sees it, he will (6) _____ his company's reputation and increase the demand for its products. Alex must ensure that all products meet certain criteria: A customer who buys a raincoat that does not (7) _____ rain will probably (8) _____ the raincoat to the store and buy another (9) _____. The same is true if the seams are not sewn tightly or the color is not (10) _____. Alex knows that, in addition to keeping out rain, the product must be attractive to look at and to touch. It should not (11) _____ easily, and it should last a long time. Alex knows that it is important for customers to (12) _____ his company's goods as quality products so that his company will profit—and he can get a raise.

WORD PRACTICE

LISTENING COMPREHENSION

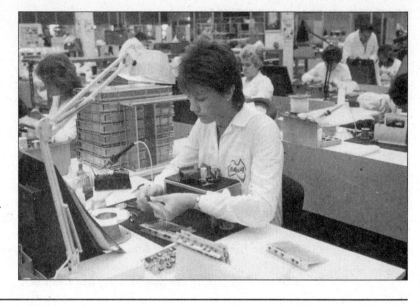

Part 1 Photo

Look at the picture and listen to the sentences.
Choose the sentence that best describes the picture.

1. Ⓐ Ⓑ Ⓒ Ⓓ

Part 2 Question–Response

Listen to the question and the three responses. Choose the response that best answers the question.

2. Ⓐ Ⓑ Ⓒ   3. Ⓐ Ⓑ Ⓒ

Part 3 Conversation

Listen to the dialogue. Then read each question and choose the best answer.

4. What does the company do with garments that have defects?
    (A) It exchanges them for better products.
    (B) It throws them out.
    (C) It stores them at the factory.
    (D) It sells them at a discount.

5. How many of the garments end up with defects?
    (A) 15 percent.
    (B) 16 percent.
    (C) 50 percent.
    (D) 60 percent.

6. What type of garment does the company manufacture?
    (A) Shirts.
    (B) Skirts.
    (C) Sweaters.
    (D) Uniforms.

Part 4 Talk

Listen to the talk. Then read each question and choose the best answer.

7. Who is this talk directed at?
    (A) Store employees.
    (B) Factory workers.
    (C) Product inspectors.
    (D) Customers.

8. When is a product inspected?
    (A) When it reaches the store.
    (B) Before it leaves the factory.
    (C) Before the customer takes it home.
    (D) When the customer returns it.

9. What can a customer do with a defective product?
    (A) Ask for a new product in exchange.
    (B) Send it back to the factory.
    (C) Show it to an inspector.
    (D) Return it to the store.

READING

Part 5 Incomplete Sentences

Choose the word that best completes the sentence.

10. _____ equipment on a new car is not only costly, but also dangerous.
    (A) Perceptive   (C) Defective
    (B) Enhanced   (D) Inspected

11. Rebecca is known as _____ #321 among her quality control coworkers.
    (A) inspect   (C) inspector
    (B) inspection   (D) inspecting

12. An employee who _____ his job as important performs better than one who wants only a paycheck.
    (A) perceives   (C) perceptive
    (B) perceived   (D) perception

13. Agnes was _____ by the odor of the waterproofing.
    (A) repel   (C) repelled
    (B) repellent   (D) repelling

14. Standardized products are _____ in appearance.
    (A) uniforms   (C) uniform
    (B) uniformly   (D) unformed

15. Sarah wants to return her dress to the store because it _____ too easily.
    (A) wrinkles   (C) wrinkle
    (B) wrinkly   (D) wrinkling

Part 6 Text Completion

Thank you for buying a Flexco product. Flexco is a top name in women's clothing, and the Flexco brand carries a reputation for excellence. Customer satisfaction is our top priority, and all Flexco garments carry the Flexco guarantee. All our products must _____ to high standards. They _____ by trained professionals

16. (A) conform
    (B) conforms
    (C) conforming
    (D) to conform

17. (A) inspect
    (B) inspected
    (C) are inspected
    (D) have inspected

before they leave the factory. If your purchase is defective in any way, you may take it _____ to the store for a complete refund.

18. (A) up
    (B) out
    (C) off
    (D) back

Part 7 Reading Comprehension

Questions 19–23 refer to the following letter.

October 10, 20—

Customer Service Department
Flexco Women's Clothing
234502 Anthony Place
Woodston, NY 12229

Dear Customer Service,

I am writing to express my extreme dissatisfaction with a recent purchase of a Flexco garment. Last week I went to our local department store to buy a gift for my wife. I chose a very hand-some Flexco raincoat and gave it to my wife on her birthday last Saturday. She was pleased with the gift and wore it yesterday because we had a big rainstorm. We were both surprised to find out that the raincoat is not water repellant at all. My wife returned from her walk very, very wet. In addition, the fabric of the coat became wrinkled in the rain. I bought the Flexco rain-coat for my wife because Flexco is one of her favorite brands. She already owns several Flexco dresses, skirts, and blouses. We never expected to be disappointed by a Flexco product.

I took the raincoat back to the store this morning. The manager there said that he did not see any defects in the coat, but he offered me a different coat in exchange. Since I understand that Flexco guarantees a complete refund on all its products, I did not accept the manager's offer. I hope that Flexco will stand by its guarantee. I am returning the raincoat with this letter, together with the receipt from the department store, and hope to receive a complete refund before the end of the month. Thank you for your attention to this matter.

Sincerely,

Thomas Jamison

19. Why did Mr. Jamison write this letter?
    (A) He wants to order more garments from Flexco.
    (B) He is unhappy with his purchase.
    (C) He is looking for a present for his wife.
    (D) He wants to express his appreciation of Flexco products.

20. What Flexco product did Mr. Jamison buy?
    (A) A dress.
    (B) A skirt.
    (C) A blouse.
    (D) A raincoat.

21. What happened when Mr. Jamison returned to the store?
    (A) He bought more garments.
    (B) He was offered a refund.
    (C) He was offered a new coat.
    (D) He noticed some defective clothes.

22. The word *wrinkled* in line 6 of the first paragraph is closest in meaning to
    (A) creased
    (B) wet
    (C) destroyed
    (D) dirty

23. The word *brands* in line 7 of the first paragraph is closest in meaning to
    (A) gifts
    (B) names
    (C) stores
    (D) styles

Lesson 29

Product Development

WORDS TO LEARN

anxious

ascertain

assume

decade

examine

experiment

logical

research

responsibility

solve

supervisor

systematically

Study the following definitions and examples.

1. **anxious** adj., worried
   a. The developers were anxious about the sales forecast for the new product.
   b. The graphic designers tried to be calm during their presentation, but you could tell they were anxious it would not be well received.

2. **ascertain** v., to discover; to find out for certain
   a. A necessary part of product development is to ascertain whether the product is safe.
   b. A customer survey will help to ascertain whether there is a market for the product.

3. **assume** v., to take upon oneself; to believe to be true
   a. The young man felt ready to assume the new responsibilities of his promotion.
   b. A company should assume nothing about the market but instead pay close attention to research results.

4. **decade** n., a period of ten years
   a. After a decade of trying, the company finally developed a vastly superior product.
   b. Each decade seems to have its own fad products.

5. **examine** v., to interrogate; to scrutinize
   a. Before marketing a new product, researchers must carefully examine it from every aspect.
   b. Good researchers have to examine every possible option, including some that seem bizarre.

6. **experiment** v., to try out a new procedure or idea; n., a test or trial
   a. Product developers must conduct hundreds of experiments in their research.
   b. After designing a new product, researchers continue experimenting to determine whether it has other uses.

7. **logical** adj., formally valid; using orderly reasoning
   a. It is only logical for a research and development team to concentrate on one or two new products at a time.
   b. In addition to logical thinkers, a good research and development team should include a few dreamers.

8. **research** n., the act of collecting information about a particular subject.
   a. Part of the research the team does is to determine whether similar products are already on the market.
   b. For toy manufacturers, research can be pure fun.

9. **responsibility** n., a task or duty; something for which one is responsible
   a. The product development department has a huge responsibility to be sure that the product is safe, even if used improperly.
   b. Another responsibility of product development is to ensure that there will be a demand for the product.

10. **solve** v., to find a solution, explanation, or answer
    a. Researchers find that every time they solve one problem, two more result.
    b. One of the biggest problems to solve is why people would want to own the new product.

11. **supervisor** n., an administrator in charge
    a. The department supervisor has to balance his department's responsibilities in order to keep the president satisfied with its progress.
    b. A good supervisor gets his team to work with him, not just for him.

12. **systematically** adv., methodically; following a system
    a. Once the creative development is completed, the department works systematically toward making the idea a reality.
    b. While creative thinking is necessary, analyzing a problem systematically is indispensable.

WORD FAMILIES

noun	anxiety	The level of anxiety was high when the experimental car underwent road tests.
adjective	anxious	If you feel anxious, sit down and try to relax.
adverb	anxiously	The stockholders anxiously awaited the release of the new drug that, if successful, would make their stocks more valuable.

verb	assume	Product developers should assume nothing that research does not support.
noun	assumption	Most consumers make the assumption that, unless they are warned otherwise, the products they buy are safe.
adjective	assumed	The assumed results should be kept confidential until the product is retested.

verb	experiment	The product developer had experimented with improving electronic equipment since she was in the sixth grade.
noun	experimentation	Hi-tech companies are constantly involved in experimentation with new products in order to stay ahead of their competitors.
adjective	experimental	The new computer was experimental, so you could try it at the store, but you couldn't buy one.

noun	logic	Most problems can be easily solved by the application of logic.
adjective	logical	It was logical to put Martha in charge of the project as she had spent so much time developing the idea.
adverb	logically	I thought Mr. Lee answered the question quite logically.

noun	responsibility	Although the ultimate responsibility falls on the supervisor, every employee shares it.
adjective	responsible	The researcher responsible for passing the defective product has joined the cafeteria workers' assembly line.
adverb	responsibly	Product designers must act responsibly when they consider how a product might be misused.

verb	supervise	It's important to carefully supervise the collection of research data to ensure its accuracy.
noun	supervisor	George hopes to be promoted to supervisor of his department.
noun	supervision	Many employees do better work when they are under less supervision.

WORDS IN CONTEXT

Read the following passage and write the words in the blanks below.

anxious	decade	logical	solve
ascertain	examining	researched	supervisor
assume	experiments	responsible	systematic

Michael was worried about his promotion. He needn't have been (1) _____ though. He had worked in the Product Development Division for nine and a half years, almost a (2) _____. He knew the department inside out. Now, however, he would be the director. As a member of the department, he only had to do what his (3) _____ told him. As the director, he would be the person (4) _____ for the success of his department. Fears are not always (5) _____; in fact, they are often illogical.

As his first task, he decided to conduct a (6) _____ analysis of the steps required to develop new products, and to organize the tasks into a logical order. The first step in developing new products would be to (7) _____ what kind of products the market needed and what problems existed with the products currently being used.

The second task would be to find out how best to examine these problems and determine what kind of research would be needed to (8) _____ the problems. It would be better to say, "reexamine these problems," since most of these unsolved problems had been thoroughly (9) _____ over the years.

The third task would be to look at the quality and characteristics of the competition's products. By (10) _____ the competition's products, he would know where he should improve. And the final task would be to decide how to gather the most substantial information from the fewest number of (11) _____. Michael smiled and sat back to read over his list. Confident that he had a good team and a good plan, he felt ready to (12) _____ his new job.

WORD PRACTICE

LISTENING COMPREHENSION

Part 1 Photo

Look at the picture and listen to the sentences.
Choose the sentence that best describes the picture.

1. Ⓐ Ⓑ Ⓒ Ⓓ

Part 2 Question–Response

Listen to the question and the three responses. Choose the response that best answers the question.

2. Ⓐ Ⓑ Ⓒ   3. Ⓐ Ⓑ Ⓒ

Part 3 Conversation

Listen to the dialogue. Then read each question and choose the best answer.

4. What does the woman want to do with the doll?
    (A) Make it less expensive.
    (B) Examine it.
    (C) Change it's color.
    (D) Add a noisemaker.

5. How much does the woman think that sales will increase?
    (A) 13 percent.
    (B) 15 percent.
    (C) 30 percent.
    (D) 40 percent.

6. What does the man suggest that the woman do?
    (A) Search for a bigger doll.
    (B) Research prices and sales.
    (C) Give the doll a new figure.
    (D) Hire more salespeople.

Part 4 Talk

Listen to the talk. Then read each question and choose the best answer.

7. Why is the product popular?
    (A) It has a low price.
    (B) People are familiar with it.
    (C) It is available everywhere.
    (D) Nobody is sure of the reason.

8. How long has the product been on the market?
    (A) Exactly two years.
    (B) Exactly twenty years.
    (C) More than twenty years.
    (D) About ten years.

9. Who buys the product?
    (A) Children.
    (B) Teenagers.
    (C) Men and women.
    (D) People of all ages.

READING

Part 5 Incomplete Sentences

Choose the word that best completes the sentence.

10. The product development team was _____ that the competition would produce a similar product and get it on the market before it did.
    (A) anxious
    (B) anxiously
    (C) anxiousness
    (D) anxiety

11. The designer made the _____ that people are attracted to boxes in primary colors.
    (A) assumption
    (B) assumed
    (C) assuming
    (D) assume

12. The _____ model of the new car drew attention wherever it was shown.
    (A) experiment
    (B) experimentation
    (C) experimental
    (D) experimenting

13. Our team came up with the most _____ solution to the problem.
    (A) logic
    (B) logical
    (C) logically
    (D) logician

14. The new employee accepted _____ for not discovering a trademarked toy exactly like his own company's.
    (A) responsible
    (B) responsibility
    (C) responsibly
    (D) response

15. Mr. Oh did not give the project adequate _____ and the product never made it to market.
    (A) supervisor
    (B) supervision
    (C) supervised
    (D) supervise

Part 6 Text Completion

In order to stay competitive in today's market, companies must continually work to develop new products. Through _____ research, a company can ascertain

16. (A) system
    (B) systemize
    (C) systematic
    (D) systematically

what consumers are interested in buying. Then products that match those interests can be developed. Nothing should _____ about consumer interests. Product

17. (A) assume
    (B) assumes
    (C) assumed
    (D) be assumed

developers need to _____ all the data carefully before spending money on a

18. (A) solve
    (B) examine
    (C) respond
    (D) experiment

new product. This is only logical. Consumers will buy products that meet their needs and desires. The money and effort spent on market research will be repaid many times over by a product that sells well.

Part 7 Reading Comprehension

Questions 19–23 refer to the following two letters.

February 12, 20–

Kathleen Hollinger
Product Development Department
New Age Systems, Inc.
475 Cutter Avenue
Sellingham, WA 90876

Dear Ms. Hollinger,

I understand that the company has an opening in the Product Development Department. I am interested in applying for this position. I have been working for New Age Systems for close to a decade. Currently I am a research assistant in the Marketing Department. During my time at New Age Systems, I have worked in several departments at the company and have had the opportunity to learn a great deal about its work. I feel that I am now ready to assume the responsibilities of a higher level position. I am anxious to speak with you about working in the Product Development Department. Thank you for your attention. I look forward to hearing from you.

Sincerely,

Dean Ayers

February 16, 20–

Dean Ayers
Marketing Department
New Age Systems, Inc.
475 Cutter Avenue
Sellingham, WA 90876

Dear Mr. Ayers,

Thank you for your letter expressing interest in applying for the position in the Product Development Department. Unfortunately, the position you are interested in has already been filled. However, I have communicated with your supervisor, and he speaks very highly of you. I have also examined your work record. It is clear that you would be a good asset to our department. I expect that we will have another opening before the end of this year. As soon as I have ascertained the availability of that position, I will be in contact with you. I look forward to meeting with you in the near future.

Sincerely,

Kathleen Hollinger
Manager, Product Development Department

---

19. How long has Mr. Ayers worked for New Age Systems, Inc.?
    (A) Almost ten years.
    (B) Exactly ten years.
    (C) Almost twenty years.
    (D) More than twenty years.

20. What job does Mr. Ayers have now?
    (A) Product developer.
    (B) Department head.
    (C) Marketing manager.
    (D) Research assistant.

21. What will Ms. Hollinger do?
    (A) Hire Mr. Ayers right away.
    (B) Ask Mr. Ayers to supervise a project.
    (C) Tell Mr. Ayers when a position becomes available.
    (D) Send Mr. Ayers a copy of his work record.

22. The word *assume* in line 9 of the first letter is closest in meaning to
    (A) teach
    (B) study
    (C) decide
    (D) accept

23. The word *examined* in line 7 of the second letter is closest in meaning to
    (A) looked at
    (B) brought up
    (C) taken back
    (D) given up

Lesson 30

Renting and Leasing

Study the following definitions and examples.

1. **apprehensive** adj., anxious about the future
   a. Most new home buyers are apprehensive about their decision.
   b. The mortgage lender was apprehensive about the company's ability to pay.

2. **circumstance** n., a condition; a situation
   a. Under the current economic circumstances, they will not be able to purchase the property.
   b. If the circumstances change in the near future and we have new properties, we will be sure to call you.

3. **condition** n., the state of something; a requirement
   a. Except for some minor repairs, the building is in very good condition.
   b. There are certain conditions that are unique to leasing a property.

4. **due to** prep., because of
   a. Due to the low interest rates, good office space is difficult to find.
   b. He didn't believe that the low prices were due only to the neighborhood.

5. **fluctuate** v., to go up and down; to change
   a. No one is very comfortable investing in real estate while property prices are fluctuating so much.
   b. Prime business areas fluctuate with local economies, crime rates, and cost of living indices.

6. **get out of** v., to escape; to exit
   a. The agent wasn't sure if the executives could get out of their prior real estate arrangement.
   b. The company wanted to get out of the area before property values declined even further.

7. **indicator** n., a sign, a signal
   a. If the economy is an accurate indicator, rental prices will increase rapidly in the next six months.
   b. The results of the elections were seen as an important indicator of the stability in the area.

8. **lease** n., a contract to pay to use property for an amount of time; v., to make a contract to use property
   a. With the lease expiring next year, they need to start looking for a new location as soon as possible.
   b. They decided to lease the property rather than buy it.

9. **lock into** v., to commit; to be unable to change
   a. The company locked itself into a ten-year lease that they didn't want.
   b. Before you lock yourself into something, check all your options.

10. **occupy** v., to dwell or reside in
    a. Tenants are usually allowed to occupy their space beginning on the first day of the month.
    b. Our company has occupied this office for more than five years.

11. **subject** adj., under legal power; dependent
    a. This contract is subject to all the laws and regulations of the state.
    b. The go-ahead to buy is subject to the president's approval.

12. **tenant** n., a person who rents property
    a. Property owners want tenants who are respectful of their neighbors and pay their rent on time.
    b. The new tenant wants to move in before the first of the month.

WORD FAMILIES

noun	apprehension	The air was thick with apprehension as the landlord met with the tenants.
adjective	apprehensive	The tenants were apprehensive about the conditions of their rental agreement.

adverb	circumstantially	The building owner circumstantially takes money out of the escrow account for emergency repairs.
noun	circumstance	Because of our circumstances, the rental agent kindly allowed us to get out of our lease early.
adjective	circumstantial	The judge's decision that the tenant was responsible for repairing the damage was based solely on circumstantial evidence.

verb	condition	The president conditioned her acceptance on two factors that were spelled out in the letter of agreement.
noun	condition	They decided to rent the space, under the condition that the price would not be raised for the next two years.
adjective	conditional	If you give a conditional go-ahead, we will start drawing up the plans.

verb	fluctuate	As interest rates began to fluctuate, many investors became nervous and took their money out of the real estate market.
noun	fluctuation	Construction is sensitive to any fluctuations in the economy.

verb	indicate	As was indicated in the terms of the lease, any changes to the property must be approved by the owners.
noun	indicator	The state of local schools is a good indicator of the health of the economy.
noun	indication	The management team had every indication that the tenants were planning to stay for the near future.

verb	occupy	The owner must make sure that the space is in good condition before the tenant occupies it.
noun	occupant	Most of the occupants of this building are doctors and lawyers.
noun	occupancy	The occupancy rate of the building has never fallen below 85 percent.

WORDS IN CONTEXT

Read the following passage and write the words in the blanks below.

apprehensive	due to	indicator	occupancy
circumstances	fluctuations	lease	subject
condition	get out of	lock into	tenant

Starting a new business is both an exciting and frightening undertaking. Most new business owners are (1) _____ about their ability to make all the decisions that arise during the course of opening a business. One of the first issues that will arise is whether to buy or (2) _____ property. In order to evaluate the options, business owners research the current real estate market. (3) _____ rates are a good (4) _____ of the overall business climate. Too many empty properties can be a sign that the local economy is not healthy.

Economic change is part of the business climate. There are often large (5) _____ in prices within a given city. These changes are (6) _____ many factors like the (7) _____ of the building, the surrounding neighborhood, access to public transportation, and business projections for the area.

Because there is so much uncertainty in starting a business, many owners do not want to (8) _____ themselves _____ a long-term lease. Many negotiate clauses in their contracts to (9) _____ a lease under certain (10) _____. They want to insure the prices and conditions of a property before making a large commitment. Leases often provide more flexibility than buying a property. They like to leave their options open. They don't like to be (11) _____ to the whims of the marketplace. Being a (12) _____ rather than a property owner has its advantages.

WORD PRACTICE

LISTENING COMPREHENSION

Part 1 Photo

Look at the picture and listen to the sentences.
Choose the sentence that best describes the picture.

1. Ⓐ Ⓑ Ⓒ Ⓓ

Part 2 Question–Response

Listen to the question and the three responses. Choose the response that best answers the question.

2. Ⓐ Ⓑ Ⓒ   3. Ⓐ Ⓑ Ⓒ

Part 3 Conversation

Listen to the dialogue. Then read each question and choose the best answer.

4. What does the man want to do?
   (A) Validate his signature.
   (B) Sign a contract.
   (C) Become a lawyer.
   (D) Get out of a lease.

5. What is he afraid of?
   (A) Wearing the wrong suit.
   (B) Paying too much money.
   (C) Making the wrong decision.
   (D) Being sued.

6. When does he have to make a decision?
   (A) Before 10:00.
   (B) Before the end of the month.
   (C) In four months.
   (D) In ten months.

Part 4 Talk

Listen to the talk. Then read each question and choose the best answer.

7. Who is the audience for this talk?
   (A) Customers and clients.
   (B) Landlords.
   (C) Lawyers.
   (D) Tenants.

8. What should a business owner do before signing
   a lease?
   (A) Make sure her business is successful.
   (B) Look at the neighborhood.
   (C) Get more customers.
   (D) Occupy the space.

9. What length of time does the speaker recommend
   for a lease?
   (A) Four years.
   (B) Five years.
   (C) Nine years.
   (D) Ten years.

READING

Part 5 Incomplete Sentences

Choose the word that best completes the sentence.

10. The president was _____ about adding more space to the factory.
    (A) apprehend
    (B) apprehensive
    (C) apprehension
    (D) apprehended

11. The financial _____ of our business don't allow us to lease an office with such a high monthly rent.
    (A) circumstances
    (B) circumstantial
    (C) circumstantially
    (D) circumstanced

12. The real estate agent couldn't determine how to best work with a company that placed so many _____ on everything that they did.
    (A) conditional
    (B) condition
    (C) conditioned
    (D) conditions

13. The buyer _____ with a nod of his head that he was placing a bid on the property.
    (A) indicates
    (B) indication
    (C) indicated
    (D) indicator

14. _____ as it does, I don't understand how anyone can depend on that country's market to provide a safe investment.
    (A) Fluctuated
    (B) Fluctuating
    (C) Fluctuation
    (D) Fluctuate

15. The lawyers signed the papers and the company took _____ of the new building.
    (A) occupied
    (B) occupants
    (C) occupancy
    (D) occupying

Part 6 Text Completion

FOR RENT

Large, sunny office in prime downtown location. We are seeking someone to take over the lease from the current occupant, who must leave due _____ unforeseen

16. (A) to
    (B) of
    (C) by
    (D) on

circumstances. The new _____ will take over the six months remaining on the

17. (A) circumstance
    (B) occupancy
    (C) tenant
    (D) owner

lease and will have the option to renew for an additional year. The office has been recently repainted and is in excellent _____. Call 567-0943 between 10:00

18. (A) fluctuation
    (B) indication
    (C) apprehension
    (D) condition

and 4:00 Monday through Friday to make an appointment to see the space.

Part 7 Reading Comprehension

Questions 19–23 refer to the following e-mail message.

To: Ted Van Dorn
From: Bernadette Riley
Subject: Office space
Date: April 10

Ted,

I have found the solution to our office problems. I know that you have been wanting to get out of the neighborhood where our office is currently located, but that you have been apprehensive about the cost of renting in a better neighborhood. I have found an office downtown that I am sure we can afford. It is a bit smaller than our current space, but I think it will be big enough. The best part is, the rent is the same as we are paying now. This is due to the fact that the office is not in excellent condition. However, I think it will be easy for us to paint it and make a few small repairs. The space will be available for occupancy on the fifteenth of next month. We have the option of signing a one- or two-year lease, so we won't have to lock ourselves into a long-term contract. However, in order to get the low rent, we have to sign by the thirtieth of this month. If you are interested in this, I can arrange for you to see the space this weekend. Let me know as soon as possible.

Bern

19. Why doesn't Ted like his current office?
    (A) It is in a bad location.
    (B) It is too expensive.
    (C) It isn't big enough.
    (D) It isn't in good condition.

20. When can Ted and Bernadette move into the new office?
    (A) April 10.
    (B) April 15.
    (C) May 10.
    (D) May 15.

21. What do they have to do before the end of this month?
    (A) Paint the office.
    (B) Sign the lease.
    (C) Change the locks.
    (D) Leave their old office.

22. The word *apprehensive* in line 3 is closest in meaning to
    (A) certain
    (B) relaxed
    (C) anxious
    (D) delighted

23. The word *condition* in line 7 is closest in meaning to
    (A) state
    (B) price
    (C) location
    (D) requirement

Word Review #6   Lessons 26–30 Management Issues

Choose the word that best completes the sentence.

1. The owner of the new company personally _____ every expense.
   (A) scrutiny
   (B) scrutinize
   (C) scrutinized
   (D) scrutinizing

2. Several employees will _____ on designing the office for efficiency.
   (A) collaborate
   (B) collaborated
   (C) collaborating
   (D) collaboration

3. When there is a problem with company policy, it should be _____ before the board of directors.
   (A) thrown out
   (B) moved over
   (C) brought up
   (D) taken back

4. The quality control department felt it was making good _____ when the number of defects declined.
   (A) progress
   (B) progressed
   (C) progressing
   (D) progressive

5. _____ goods can ruin the future of a new company.
   (A) Defect
   (B) Defects
   (C) Defective
   (D) Defection

6. The public's _____ of a company depends on how solidly the company stands behind its products.
   (A) perceive
   (B) perceptive
   (C) perceived
   (D) perception

7. The market research matched our _____.
   (A) assumes
   (B) assuming
   (C) assumed
   (D) assumptions

8. Determining the safeness of a particular appliance requires a _____ investigation of the electrical components.
   (A) system
   (B) systems
   (C) systematic
   (D) systematize

9. When _____ office space, it is wise to insist upon an option to renew.
   (A) lease
   (B) leasing
   (C) leased
   (D) lessor

10. Getting _____ a lease requires legal advice and could end up being quite expensive.
    (A) in
    (B) on
    (C) off of
    (D) out of

Choose the one word or phrase that best completes each sentence.

To: m_schwartz@donner.com
From: j_holmes@blitzen.com
Subject: board meeting

Mary,

We all missed you at yesterday's meeting, but you will be happy to know it went well.
We were able to adhere _____ the agenda and cover all topics in the allotted

11. (A) to
    (B) at
    (C) of
    (D) in

time. Wilbur gave a _____ explanation of the budget, and now I feel we all

12. (A) length
    (B) lengthy
    (C) lengthen
    (D) lengthily

understand it quite thoroughly. He plans to e-mail you a copy of his notes. The meeting
_____ on time, at 5:00. The next meeting is scheduled for June 16.

13. (A) had concluded
    (B) has concluded
    (C) concluded
    (D) concludes

John

Our job here in the Quality Control Department is to make sure that no garment leaves the
factory in less than perfect condition. This means that each garment _____ carefully

14. (A) inspects
    (B) is inspected
    (C) is inspecting
    (D) has inspected

by a trained garment inspector. We throw out all _____ garments. It is important to

15. (A) defect
    (B) defects
    (C) detective
    (D) defective

protect our _____ and make sure that the name of our company is always associated

16. (A) lobby
    (B) research
    (C) brand
    (D) wrinkle

with top-quality products.

Dear Mr. Wilcox,

Your lease for the office you _____ at 121 North Main Street will expire next month. I will be

              17. (A) occupy
                  (B) occupied
                  (C) occupant
                  (D) occupancy

very happy to have you renew the lease if you desire. You have occupied that space for a _____,

                      18. (A) month
                           (B) semester
                           (C) decade
                           (D) century

and during those ten years you have always been a reliable tenant. Unfortunately, _____ to

                    19. (A) because
                         (B) up
                         (C) ought
                         (D) due

rising costs everywhere, I will have to raise the rent on that space by 20 percent. I hope this won't cause you any hardship. Please let me know if you are still interested in renewing the lease, and I will have my assistant send one over to you.

Sincerely,

Amanda Brightwood

Lesson 31

Selecting a Restaurant

Study the following definitions and examples.

1. **appeal** n., the ability to attract
   a. A restaurant with good food and reasonable prices has a lot of appeal.
   b. The pleasing decor and friendly waiters are what give that restaurant its appeal.

2. **compromise** n., a settlement of differences; v., to settle differences
   a. The couple made a compromise and ordered food to take out.
   b. John doesn't like sweet dishes so I compromised by adding just a small amount of sugar.

3. **daringly** adv., bravely
   a. We daringly ordered the raw squid.
   b. Bob daringly asked to see the menu in French.

4. **delicious** adj., tasty, good to eat
   a. This restaurant is famous for its delicious soups.
   b. The fish stew wasn't as delicious as we had expected it to be.

5. **familiar** adj., often encountered or seen; common
   a. It's nice to see some familiar items on the menu.
   b. The chef blends the familiar tastes with the unusual.

6. **guide** n., one who leads, directs, or gives advice; a guidebook
   a. The guide led our tour group to a small restaurant only known to the locals.
   b. I don't know where to go, so why don't we consult the guide.

7. **majority** n., the greater number or part
   a. The majority of the group wanted to try the new Chinese restaurant.
   b. Claude was in the majority, so he was very pleased with the decision.

8. **mix** v., to combine or blend into one mass; n., a combination
   a. The daring chef mixed two uncommon ingredients.
   b. The mix of bright colors on the plate was very pleasing.

9. **rely** v., to have confidence in; to depend on
   a. You can rely on that website to give accurate restaurant reviews.
   b. I seldom rely on restaurant reviews when choosing a restaurant.

10. **secure** v., to get possession of; to obtain
    a. Despite the popularity of the restaurant, Max was able to secure reservations for this evening.
    b. The hostess secured us another chair, so we could eat together.

11. **subjective** adj., particular to a given person; highly personal; not objective
    a. Food preferences are subjective and not everyone agrees on what tastes good.
    b. The reviews on this website are highly subjective but fun to read.

12. **suggestion** n., a proposal; advice
    a. Can I make a suggestion about what to order?
    b. We followed the waiter's suggestion and ordered one of the specials.

WORD FAMILIES

verb	appeal	On a beautiful spring day, a sidewalk café appeals to many people.
noun	appeal	That restaurant has been around for a long time but it hasn't lost its appeal.
adjective	appealing	An ice-cold drink seems very appealing on a hot day.

verb	dare	I prefer familiar things and don't usually dare to try new restaurants.
adjective	daring	Kobi had more daring tastes than the rest of his family.
adverb	daringly	Jane daringly refused a fork and attempted to eat her entire meal with chopsticks.

noun	deliciousness	The deliciousness of the desserts is hard to resist.
adjective	delicious	All the comments on that blog agree that this restaurant serves the most delicious food in the city.
adverb	deliciously	The stew smells deliciously good.

verb	guide	The hostess guided us to our table.
noun	guidance	Li asked the waiter for guidance in selecting the wine.
noun	guide	I couldn't find any reviews for this restaurant in the online restaurant guide.

verb	mix	The chef never mixes sweet ingredients with salty foods.
noun	mixture	The texture of the vegetable mixture was too lumpy for my taste.
adjective	mixable	Oil and water are not mixable.

verb	rely	We will rely on the hostess's recommendations.
noun	reliability	The reliability of deliveries became a problem for the manager.
adjective	reliable	Hiring a reliable staff is the first priority for every restaurant manager.

verb	suggest	Can I suggest a good wine to go with the entrée?
noun	suggestion	Clark asked his boss for a suggestion for a good place to eat.
adjective	suggestible	The patrons were in a suggestible mood, and were easily convinced to have dessert.

WORDS IN CONTEXT

Read the following passage and write the words in the blanks below.

appeal	delicious	majority	secure
compromise	familiar	mix	subjective
daring	guidance	relies	suggestion

When Atul is trying to impress business contacts who are potential new clients, he takes them to the best restaurant in town. He hopes this will help (1) _____ a new contract for his telecommunications business.

It's hard to determine which restaurants are best. Atul (2) _____ on reviews that he finds on the Internet. He also asks his friends and colleagues for (3) _____. They are happy to make a (4) _____.

Food tastes are (5)_____. Although Atul likes to be (6) _____ and take risks, he knows that the food should (7) _____ to a variety of palates. He realizes that a dish that he enjoys may not taste (8) _____ to someone else. He wants the (9) _____ of his guests to be happy. He usually decides to (10) _____ on a restaurant that offers a menu with a (11) _____ of (12) _____ standards and some exciting specials.

WORD PRACTICE

LISTENING COMPREHENSION

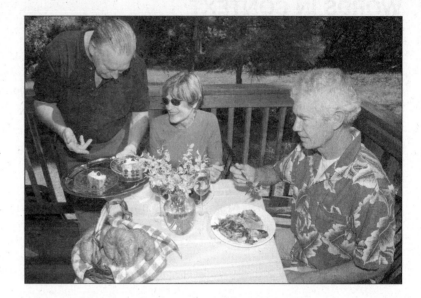

Part 1　Photo

Look at the picture and listen to the sentences.
Choose the sentence that best describes the picture.

1. Ⓐ Ⓑ Ⓒ Ⓓ

Part 2　Question–Response

Listen to the question and the three responses. Choose the response that best answers the question.

2. Ⓐ Ⓑ Ⓒ　　　3. Ⓐ Ⓑ Ⓒ

Part 3　Conversation

Listen to the dialogue. Then read each question and choose the best answer.

4. How often do restaurant reviews appear in the local newspaper?
   (A) Every day.
   (B) Every week.
   (C) Every month.
   (D) Every year.

5. What is the man's opinion of restaurant reviews?
   (A) They are appealing.
   (B) They are usually helpful.
   (C) They are very subjective.
   (D) They are mean.

6. Who recommends restaurants to the man?
   (A) His friends.
   (B) His mother.
   (C) His brother.
   (D) His coworkers.

Part 4　Talk

Listen to the talk. Then read each question and choose the best answer.

7. Where is the listener now?
   (A) At home.
   (B) In the bar.
   (C) At the restaurant.
   (D) In the parking lot.

8. What does the speaker suggest?
   (A) Driving to the restaurant.
   (B) Arriving early for drinks.
   (C) Making a reservation.
   (D) Bringing a big appetite.

9. What time is the reservation for?
   (A) 7:30.
   (B) 8:00.
   (C) 8:30.
   (D) 11:00.

READING

Part 5 Incomplete Sentences

Choose the word that best completes the sentence.

10. The colorful vegetables made the dish look _____.
    (A) appealed   (C) appeals
    (B) appealing   (D) appealingly

11. Even though the restaurant looked expensive, Pat _____ to order her meal without asking about the prices.
    (A) daring   (C) dared
    (B) daringly   (D) dares

12. If you need some _____ on what to order, be sure to consult your server.
    (A) guide   (C) guided
    (B) guides   (D) guidance

13. Your father is in the kitchen _____ a batch of his famous chocolate chip cookies.
    (A) mixture   (C) mix
    (B) mixed   (D) mixing

14. This website accepts reviews from anybody, so I would question their _____.
    (A) rely   (C) reliability
    (B) reliance   (D) relying

15. I have always found Lola's restaurant _____ to be very good, so I continue to seek her guidance.
    (A) suggestions   (C) suggestive
    (B) suggest   (D) suggestible

Part 6 Text Completion

ARE YOU LOOKING FOR A DELICIOUS LUNCH EXPERIENCE THAT WON'T EMPTY YOUR WALLET?

TRY THE BLUE SHUTTERS CAFÉ.

OUR VARIED MENU _____ TO ALL TASTES.

16. (A) appeal
    (B) appeals
    (C) appealed
    (D) are appealing

WE'RE FAMOUS FOR OUR HOMEMADE SOUPS, GARDEN-FRESH SALADS, AND FRESHLY BAKED BREADS AND PASTRIES.

TRY OUR HOMEMADE PIES IN ALL FLAVORS FROM _____ FAVORITES LIKE

17. (A) famously
    (B) famished
    (C) familiar
    (D) family

APPLE PIE TO EXOTIC CHOICES SUCH AS LOGANBERRY AND CHESTNUT MERINGUE.

BUT _____ ON OUR WORD ALONE. COME ON DOWN AND TRY FOR YOURSELF.

18. (A) no rely
    (B) not rely
    (C) not to rely
    (D) don't rely

WE'RE OPEN MONDAY THROUGH SATURDAY FROM 11:00 A.M. UNTIL 2:30 P.M.

READ ABOUT THE BLUE SHUTTERS CAFÉ IN THE RECENT EDITION OF THE LOCAL RESTAURANT GUIDE "RESTAURANTS OF RIVERDALE."

Part 7 Reading Comprehension

Questions 19–23 refer to the following restaurant review and e-mail message.

The Mountain View Restaurant is a charming dinner location that just opened up in Falls Village. The menu provides an interesting mix of both meat and vegetarian entrées. The chef, who trained in Paris, has introduced some exotic dishes such as Octopus Soufflé and Three Tuber Salad. For the less daring diner, the menu also abounds in such familiar choices as Baked Chicken and Pepper Crusted Steak. Whether you choose to rely on a familiar dish or decide to experiment with something exotic, you are sure to be delighted with your meal. All the selections I tasted were delicious, and the prices are quite reasonable. Don't forget to leave room for dessert. I especially suggest the chocolate cake. It's the best in town. Unfortunately, the charm of the menu selections is not matched by the charm of the décor. It is rather drab and uninspiring. If you visit the inn on a weekend evening, arrive by 6:00 since the restaurant does not take reservations, and it is difficult to get a table after 7:00 unless you are willing to wait half an hour or more.

To: Margaret Smithers
From: Anna Simpson
Subject: Dinner out

Hi Margaret,

Did you read the review of the Mountain View Inn in this Sunday's Falls Village Times? It sounds great. I usually read the restaurant reviews in that paper, and the majority of them are quite accurate. I rely on those reviews a great deal more than the ones in our local restaurant guide. I think we should try the inn. Are you free Saturday night? I think we should arrive at the time suggested in the paper. Then we can have a relaxed meal and still have time to go to an 8:30 movie afterward. Can you do it? Let me know before you leave work today.

Anna

19. What is the reviewer's opinion of the restaurant?
(A) The prices are too high.
(B) The food is very good.
(C) The décor is exotic.
(D) The menu is boring.

20. What does the reviewer recommend ordering?
(A) Octopus soufflé.
(B) Tuber salad.
(C) Baked chicken.
(D) Chocolate cake.

21. When does Anna want to arrive at the restaurant?
(A) Before 6:00.
(B) After 7:00.
(C) At 8:00.
(D) By 8:30.

22. The word *mix* in line 4 of the restaurant review is closest in meaning to
(A) style
(B) combination
(C) number
(D) course

23. The word *majority* in line 4 of the e-mail is closest in meaning to
(A) few
(B) some
(C) most
(D) several

Lesson 32

Eating Out

WORDS TO LEARN

appetite

complete

excite

flavor

foreign

ingredient

judge

mix-up

patron

predict

randomly

remind

Study the following definitions and examples.

1. **appetite** n., desire to eat
   a. The delicious smells coming from the restaurant kitchen increased my appetite.
   b. People generally have a good appetite after a long day of work.
2. **complete** v., to finish or make whole
   a. We ordered some dessert to complete our meal.
   b. Some restaurants want to hear their customers' opinions and ask them to complete a short evaluation form.
3. **excite** v., to arouse an emotion
   a. Exotic flavors always excite me.
   b. The new Asian restaurant has excited the interest of many people.
4. **flavor** n., a distinctive taste
   a. Fusion cooking is distinguished by an interesting mix of flavors.
   b. The cook changed the flavor of the soup with a unique blend of herbs.
5. **foreign** adj., of another country; unfamiliar
   a. It's fun to try the local food when traveling in a foreign country.
   b. The ingredients in this dish are foreign to me; I have never tried any of them before.
6. **ingredient** n., an element in a mixture
   a. The chef went to the farmer's market to select the freshest ingredients for tonight's menu.
   b. I was unfamiliar with some of the ingredients in the dish.
7. **judge** v., to form an opinion
   a. Hector was not familiar with Asian cooking, so he was unable to judge if the noodles were cooked correctly.
   b. The restaurant review harshly judged the quality of the service.
8. **mix-up** n., a confusion
   a. There was a mix-up in the kitchen so your order will be delayed.
   b. There was a mix-up about the ingredients and the dish was ruined.
9. **patron** n., a customer, especially a regular customer
   a. Once the word was out about the new chef, patrons lined up to get into the restaurant.
   b. This restaurant has many loyal patrons.
10. **predict** v., to state, tell about, or make known in advance
    a. I predicted this restaurant would become popular and I was right.
    b. Kona was unable to predict what time Andy, who is always late, would show up at the restaurant.
11. **randomly** adv., without any specific pattern
    a. We randomly made our selections from the menu.
    b. That chef chooses his spices randomly, but his dishes always taste great.
12. **remind** v., to cause to remember
    a. Ms. Smith was annoyed at having to remind the waitress to bring the check.
    b. I reminded the client that we are meeting for dinner tomorrow.

WORD FAMILIES

noun	appetite	I don't have much of an appetite tonight so I think I'll just order a salad.
noun	appetizer	We can order some appetizers to enjoy while we're waiting for the main course.
adjective	appetizing	All the dishes on the menu look so appetizing that it's hard to know which one to choose.

verb	complete	The meal could not be completed without dessert.
noun	completion	The coffee was the last item ordered and brought the meal to completion.
adverb	completely	The chef forgot that the dessert was in the oven and completely ruined it.

verb	excite	The chef knows how to excite his patrons.
noun	excitement	You can feel the excitement in the air.
adjective	excited	I am really excited about trying out this new restaurant.

verb	flavor	I like a chef who uses exotic spices to flavor the food.
noun	flavor	Some people don't like Mexican food because the flavors are too spicy.
adjective	flavorful	The special ingredients made the dish very flavorful.

verb	mix up	An inexperienced waiter can easily mix up orders.
noun	mix-up	We had a big mix-up in our plans and I ended up waiting for my friends at the wrong restaurant.
adjective	mixed up	Bob always gets mixed up when he tries to order food at a foreign restaurant.

verb	predict	I predict that this restaurant will be a success.
noun	prediction	The manager's prediction came true, and the chef was named to the "Top 100" list.
adverb	predictably	Predictably, because the waiter neglected to write down the order, he forgot some necessary items.

WORDS IN CONTEXT

Read the following passage and write the words in the blanks below.

appetites	flavor	judged	predict
complete	foreign	mix up	randomly
excite	ingredients	patrons	remind

The key to a happy meal is that everyone should enjoy eating what they ordered. Before the waiter takes your order, you can ask him for a recommendation or you can select (1) _____ from the menu. It's a good idea to ask the waiter for suggestions when eating at a (2) _____ restaurant as you might not be familiar with the food.

Good service is part of the overall enjoyment of the meal. The waiter should make the (3) _____ feel welcome and comfortable. Good waiters can (4) _____ what you need, like more water, without having to be asked for it. It's easy for a waiter to forget things, but you should not have to (5) _____ a waiter more than once to bring you something. Nor do you want the waiter to (6) _____ the food orders. You should get what you ordered, and your order should be (7) _____.

The quality of the food is the primary way restaurants are (8) _____. The food should taste and look wonderful. Your plate of food should (9) _____ all your senses and be fragrant and colorful. A chef can bring out a distinct (10) _____ in a dish, depending on the (11) _____ he or she uses. Well-prepared food can satisfy even the hungriest patrons with the biggest (12) _____ .

WORD PRACTICE

LISTENING COMPREHENSION

TRACK
33

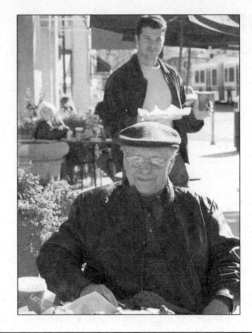

Part 1 Photo

Look at the picture and listen to the sentences.
Choose the sentence that best describes the picture.

1. Ⓐ Ⓑ Ⓒ Ⓓ

Part 2 Question–Response

Listen to the question and the three responses. Choose the response that best answers the question.

2. Ⓐ Ⓑ Ⓒ   3. Ⓐ Ⓑ Ⓒ

Part 3 Conversation

Listen to the dialogue. Then read each question and choose the best answer.

4. What are the speakers discussing?
   (A) The flavor of the food.
   (B) Their last vacation.
   (C) The restaurant décor.
   (D) The serving dishes.

5. What does the man want to do?
   (A) Take a rest.
   (B) Return to the restaurant.
   (C) Forget about the restaurant.
   (D) Get a new set of dishes.

6. What does the woman predict?
   (A) The restaurant will close soon.
   (B) The flavor of the dishes will improve.
   (C) The waiter will be very patient.
   (D) The restaurant will become popular.

Part 4 Talk

Listen to the talk. Then read each question and choose the best answer.

7. Who is speaking?
   (A) The kitchen assistant.
   (B) The head chef.
   (C) A patron.
   (D) A waitress.

8. What does the speaker offer?
   (A) To cook the meal.
   (B) To take the order.
   (C) To bring some free food.
   (D) To serve water.

9. When will the food be ready?
   (A) In 2 minutes.
   (B) In 8 minutes.
   (C) In 15 minutes.
   (D) In 50 minutes.

READING

Part 5 Incomplete Sentences

Choose the word that best completes the sentence.

10. Would you like to _____ your meal with an after-dinner drink?
    (A) complete
    (B) completed
    (C) completely
    (D) completion

11. I've had enough _____ for the day.
    (A) excite
    (B) exciting
    (C) excitement
    (D) excites

12. I can't figure out which ingredients the chef used to _____ this dish.
    (A) flavored
    (B) flavorful
    (C) flavors
    (D) flavor

13. I enjoy eating at _____ restaurants because I like to try food from different countries.
    (A) foreman
    (B) forepart
    (C) foreign
    (D) foremost

14. Unfortunately, on the day the restaurant opened there was a huge _____ in the kitchen.
    (A) mix-up
    (B) mixed up
    (C) mix up
    (D) mixing up

15. No one could have _____ how successful the restaurant would become.
    (A) reminded
    (B) excited
    (C) completed
    (D) predicted

Part 6 Text Completion

One of the joys of traveling abroad is taking the opportunity to try out different kinds of food. Travelers should always make a point of eating the local dishes. It is exciting to try out dishes made with unfamiliar ingredients and unusual _____. Daring travelers can order

16. (A) favors
    (B) flavors
    (C) fivers
    (D) fevers

_____ from the menu. Or, they can look at the dishes that other patrons are eating and

17. (A) random
    (B) randomly
    (C) randomize
    (D) randomness

order one that looks appealing. A traveler who doesn't speak the local language well can order by pointing to the dishes he wishes to order. That is the easiest way to avoid a mix-_____.

18. (A) up
    (B) in
    (C) of
    (D) out

Finally, dessert should not be forgotten. A sweet treat at the end of the meal will complete the experience of enjoying foreign cooking.

Part 7 Reading Comprehension

Questions 19–23 refer to the following advertisement.

Don't miss the Yorktown Festival of Food. This exciting annual event will take place May 10–16 at the Yorktown Fairgrounds.* Over 100 local restaurants will participate. Which are the best restaurants in town? You be the judge! The price of admission includes:

– Samples of food from all participating restaurants
– Cooking demonstrations by local chefs
– Copies of recipes of some of Yorktown's favorite dishes, including ingredients lists and preparation instructions
– A free Festival of Food chef's hat and apron

Fifty festival ticket holders will be randomly selected to enjoy a meal especially prepared for the festival by world-renowned chef Jean Pierre de la Farge, director of the Paris School of Cuisine. You could be one of them! Get your tickets today. An unforgettable experience is guaranteed.

Tickets are available at all participating restaurants and at the Yorktown Office of Tourism. Ticket prices are $15/day or $50 for the entire week.

*If rain is predicted, the event will take place in the Yorktown Sports Arena.

19. How often does the festival take place?
    (A) Once a day.
    (B) Once a week.
    (C) Once a month.
    (D) Once a year.

20. What can people do at the festival?
    (A) Try different kinds of food.
    (B) Cook a meal.
    (C) Judge a contest.
    (D) Buy hats and aprons.

21. What will fifty people win?
    (A) A ticket.
    (B) A cooking lesson.
    (C) A free meal.
    (D) A trip to Paris.

22. The word *randomly* in line 11 is closest in meaning to
    (A) quickly
    (B) by chance
    (C) beforehand
    (D) with determination

23. The word *predicted* in line 19 is closest in meaning to
    (A) heavy
    (B) expected
    (C) falling
    (D) problematic

Lesson 33

Ordering Lunch

WORDS TO LEARN

burden
commonly
delivery
elegance
fall to
impress
individual
multiple
narrow
pick up
reasonable
settle

Study the following definitions and examples.

1. **burden** n., a responsibility; something that is carried
    a. The secretary usually takes on the burden of ordering lunch for business meetings.
    b. The deliveryman's back ached from the heavy burden he carried.
2. **commonly** adv., usually, habitually
    a. The people who work in this building commonly order their lunch from the sandwich shop on the first floor.
    b. The restaurants in this area commonly serve office workers and are only open during the week.
3. **delivery** n., the act of conveying or delivering
    a. The caterer hired a courier to make the delivery.
    b. The restaurant is reluctant to make deliveries, but makes an exception for our office.
4. **elegance** n., refinement, beauty, grace
    a. The elegance of the restaurant made it a pleasant place to eat.
    b. A sandwich may lack elegance, but it makes a convenient and inexpensive lunch.
5. **fall to** v., to become one's responsibility
    a. The task of preparing the meal fell to the assistant chef when the chief chef was ill.
    b. The menu was in French, so ordering for us fell to Monique, who spoke French.
6. **impress** v., to affect strongly, often favorably
    a. I was impressed with how quickly they delivered our lunch.
    b. If you want to impress the new staff member, order her a nice lunch.
7. **individual** adj., by or for one person; special; particular
    a. We had the delivery man mark the contents of each individual order.
    b. The jaunty whistle of the delivery woman marked her individual style.
8. **multiple** adj., having, relating to, or consisting of more than one part
    a. The delivery person was not able to keep track of the multiple order, causing a food mix-up.
    b. It takes multiple steps to get into this building, which frustrates all our employees.
9. **narrow** v., to limit or restrict
    a. Etseko narrowed the restaurant possibilities down to three.
    b. This restaurant delivers only pizza and sandwiches, so that certainly narrows down the choices.
10. **pick up** v., to take on passengers or freight
    a. The delivery man picks up lunch orders on his motor scooter.
    b. If you ask me nicely, I will pick up the order on my way home.
11. **reasonable** adj., fairly priced, fair in quality
    a. I usually have lunch at the company cafeteria because of the convenient location and the reasonable prices.
    b. The lunches at this place are not top quality, but they're reasonable.
12. **settle** v., to make compensation for, to pay; to choose
    a. We settled the bill with the cashier.
    b. After much debate, we finally settled on the bistro on the corner.

WORD FAMILIES

verb	burden	The frequently complicated lunch orders unfairly burdened Jacques.
noun	burden	In addition to all her other responsibilities, Marie had the burden of picking up the daily lunch order.
adjective	burdensome	Keeping track of everybody's lunch orders can be a burdensome task.

verb	deliver	That restaurant delivers food at no extra charge.
noun	delivery	We all got very hungry waiting for the delivery to arrive.

noun	elegance	The elegance of the surroundings was accentuated by the wonderful meal the caterers delivered.
adjective	elegant	Delores set an elegant table that was sure to impress.
adverb	elegantly	The tasty appetizers were elegantly served from silver platters.

verb	impress	I am favorably impressed by how quickly the pizza was delivered.
noun	impression	She gave the impression that the food would be delivered within the hour.
adjective	impressionable	I have an impressionable child, so I don't like him to see deliverymen running red traffic lights.

verb	individualize	The take-out shop does not allow you to individualize your order by asking for substitutions.
noun	individual	The portions are large enough to feed two individuals.
adverb	individually	The individually marked boxes made it easy for us to claim our orders.

noun	reasonableness	Although the food is not fantastic, we eat here often because of the reasonableness of the prices.
adjective	reasonable	You can get a good meal for a reasonable cost at this café.
adverb	reasonably	They prepare Japanese dishes reasonably well at that restaurant.

WORDS IN CONTEXT

Read the following passage and write the words in the blanks below.

burdensome	elegant	individual	pick up
commonly	falls to	multiple	reasonably
delivered	impress	narrow	settled

As the office manager, it usually (1) _____ Lucia to order the food

for a working lunch or an office party. Lucia finds ordering food for a working

lunch to be especially (2) _____. First, in order to avoid placing

(3) _____ small orders from different food establishments, she must

(4) _____ down the choice to one kind of food. It's best to keep

the ordering as simple as possible since each (5) _____ has his or her

own tastes. The lunches that she orders most (6) _____ consist of

sandwiches and pizza.

Once she has (7) _____ on a good choice, she calls a restaurant on her

approved list. Usually she needs the food (8) _____ so she does not have

to leave the office and (9) _____ the order herself.

In case of a more formal lunch, where her boss is trying to (10) _____

new clients, for example, Lucia will call a catering service that can provide a

more (11) _____ meal. Even though the meal is a fancy one, it still must

be (12) _____ priced to fit the company's entertainment budget.

WORD PRACTICE

LISTENING COMPREHENSION

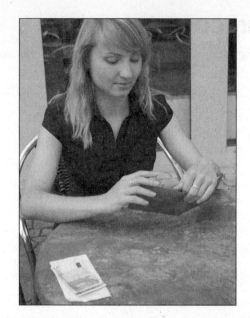

Part 1 Photo

Look at the picture and listen to the sentences.
Choose the sentence that best describes the picture.

1. Ⓐ Ⓑ Ⓒ Ⓓ

Part 2 Question–Response

Listen to the question and the three responses. Choose the response that best answers the question.

2. Ⓐ Ⓑ Ⓒ   3. Ⓐ Ⓑ Ⓒ

Part 3 Conversation

Listen to the dialogue. Then read each question and choose the best answer.

4. Why does the man want to have lunch at the office?
   (A) It is burdensome to leave the office.
   (B) He has a bad impression of the restaurant.
   (C) The office is more elegant than the restaurant.
   (D) He wants to show slides during lunch.

5. Who will the man have lunch with?
   (A) The woman.
   (B) The sales staff.
   (C) The regional manager.
   (D) The conference attendees.

6. What time will lunch be delivered?
   (A) Noon.
   (B) 1:00.
   (C) 1:30.
   (D) 2:00.

Part 4 Talk

Listen to the talk. Then read each question and choose the best answer.

7. What takes 10 minutes?
   (A) Delivering the order.
   (B) Selecting a meal from the list.
   (C) Getting the food ready to be picked up.
   (D) Making a group order.

8. How much does a delivery cost?
   (A) 15 percent.
   (B) 50 cents.
   (C) It's free.
   (D) 50 percent.

9. What kind of food can be ordered from the Parkside Café?
   (A) Rice.
   (B) Meat.
   (C) Sandwiches.
   (D) Ice cream.

READING

Part 5 Incomplete Sentences

Choose the word that best completes the sentence.

10. George no longer wants to be in charge of lunch orders because he finds that job too _____.
    (A) burdens
    (B) burdened
    (C) burden
    (D) burdensome

11. We _____ meet the delivery person in the lobby to pick up our orders.
    (A) common
    (B) comment
    (C) commonly
    (D) commonness

12. The _____ from that restaurant always arrive late.
    (A) delivers
    (B) deliveries
    (C) delivered
    (D) delivering

13. Despite being served in disposable containers, the meal had an _____ touch.
    (A) elegant
    (B) elegance
    (C) elegantly
    (D) elegancy

14. Our office manager was so _____ by the speed of the delivery, she decided to order from them again.
    (A) impressive
    (B) impressed
    (C) impression
    (D) impressionable

15. Let's order _____ so we can all get what we want for lunch.
    (A) individualize
    (B) individualist
    (C) individually
    (D) individual

Part 6 Text Completion

MEMO

To: All department staff
From: J. Holtzman, Manager
Re: Ordering Lunch

It has long been the practice in this department to order lunch to be served during department meetings. While this is a custom we all enjoy, it has become a _____ on our budget.

16. (A) burden
    (B) burglar
    (C) burnish
    (D) burnoose

Therefore, I have developed the following guidelines for ordering meeting lunches.

– We cannot afford to constantly order elegant lunches. Please limit your orders to common, everyday lunch choices such as sandwiches and salads.
– There are many restaurants in the area that offer take-out lunches. I will _____ the

17. (A) select
    (B) allow
    (C) enlarge
    (D) narrow

choices down to three or four places that have reasonable prices, then let you know which they are. Please order only from the restaurants on the approved list.
– We will no longer pay for delivery. All lunch orders must be _____ up in person.

18. (A) stood
    (B) taken
    (C) looked
    (D) picked

Thank you in advance for your cooperation.

Part 7 Reading Comprehension

Questions 19–23 refer to the following advertisement and e-mail message.

NOW OPEN

The Broad Street Eatery
1001 Broad Street
Phone: 298-0943

Serving breakfast and lunch
Monday–Saturday 6:30 A.M. – 2:30 P.M.

Don't settle for lunch choices that are
commonly found anywhere.

At the Broad Street Eatery,
we offer a tempting range of soups,
sandwiches, and salads for the discerning eater.

We specialize in take-out orders.
Call ahead for pick up.

We also offer free delivery on all orders over $30.
(There is a 10 percent delivery charge on smaller orders.)

To: Molly Anderson
From: Jerry Pinsky
Subject: New restaurant

Hi Molly,

Have you heard about the Broad Street Eatery? It's that new place that opened up last month just around the corner. I think we should order the lunch for this Friday's meeting from there. Some of the menu choices look quite elegant and I'm sure will impress our clients. Best of all, the prices are quite reasonable. I'll send you a list later of what I want you to order. Since the order will be large, I think you should call it in the day before the meeting. I'm sure we'll qualify for the free delivery, so you won't have to worry about picking it up. That will lighten your burden a bit. Thanks for your help with this.

Jerry

---

19. When should Molly place the lunch order?
    (A) Monday.
    (B) Thursday.
    (C) Friday.
    (D) Saturday.

20. If the order costs $45, how much will the delivery charge be?
    (A) $0.
    (B) $3.
    (C) $4.50.
    (D) $30.

21. What is Jerry's opinion of the restaurant?
    (A) It's too far away.
    (B) The prices are very high.
    (C) It should be open later.
    (D) The food looks good.

22. The word *commonly* in line 8 of the advertisement is closest in meaning to
    (A) usually
    (B) rarely
    (C) tastily
    (D) differently

23. The word *elegant* in line 5 of the e-mail is closest in meaning to
    (A) ordinary
    (B) expensive
    (C) pleasing
    (D) large

Lesson 34

Cooking as a Career

Study the following definitions and examples.

1. **accustom** v., to become familiar with, to become used to
   a. Chefs must accustom themselves to working long hours.
   b. It can be hard to accustom oneself to eating new types of food.

2. **apprentice** n., a student worker in a chosen field
   a. Instead of attending cooking school, Raul chose to work as an apprentice with an experienced chef.
   b. The cooking school has an apprentice program that places students in restaurants to gain work experience.

3. **culinary** adj., relating to the kitchen or cooking
   a. The chef was widely known for his culinary artistry.
   b. His interest in culinary arts drew him to a commercial foods program.

4. **demand** v., to require
   a. Theodore was always exhausted because his new job at the restaurant demanded so much of him.
   b. This style of cooking demands many exotic ingredients and a lot of preparation time.

5. **draw** v., to cause to come by attracting
   a. We hope the new restaurant will draw other business to the area.
   b. Matthew was drawn to a career in cooking.

6. **incorporate** v., to unite one thing with something else already in existence
   a. Coca incorporated the patron's suggestions into her new menu.
   b. Here are the fresh greens for you to incorporate into a salad.

7. **influx** n., a flowing in
   a. An influx of new chefs is constantly needed to fill open jobs.
   b. Due to the rise in popularity of cooking as a career, cooking schools report an influx of applications.

8. **method** n., a procedure
   a. Gloria perfected a simple method for making croissants.
   b. Many chefs borrow cooking methods from a variety of cultures and incorporate them into their cooking style.

9. **outlet** n., a means of release or gratification, as for energies, drives, or desires
   a. Even before he became a professional baker, Jacob used baking as an outlet for frustration.
   b. Many people find cooking to be a hands-on outlet for their creativity.

10. **profession** n., an occupation requiring considerable training and specialized study
    a. Cooking is considered as much a profession as is law or medicine.
    b. Lulu took up cooking as her profession and is very happy with her decision.

11. **relinquish** v., to let go; to surrender
    a. People find it hard to relinquish their accustomed food preferences and try something new.
    b. After Claude married Kiki, he had to relinquish his exclusive hold on the kitchen and learn to share the joys of cooking.

12. **theme** n., an implicit or recurrent idea; a motif
    a. The caterers prepared food for a party with a tropical island theme.
    b. The restaurant's food and decor demonstrated its southwestern theme.

WORD FAMILIES

verb	accustom	Shirley could not accustom herself to the fast pace of the restaurant kitchen.
noun	custom	It is the custom at this restaurant to offer free meals to patrons on their birthdays.
adjective	accustomed	Janet has become accustomed to cooking with a variety of spices.

verb	apprentice	Instead of attending cooking school, Michael decided to apprentice to a master chef.
noun	apprentice	The new group of apprentices will start working any day now.
noun	apprenticeship	The apprenticeship was a grueling period, but George learned a lot.

verb	demand	The head chef demands a lot from his assistants.
noun	demand	Pierre could not keep up with the many demands of the customers.
adjective	demanding	Working as a chef is a very demanding job.

verb	incorporate	Take these items and incorporate them into a stew.
noun	incorporation	The restaurant was the incorporation of every good idea the chef had thought of in his career.
gerund	incorporating	Chef Tao was famous for incorporating different cooking styles into one.

noun	method	The chef discovered a more efficient method of peeling boiled eggs.
noun	methodology	Even the order of adding ingredients is an unappreciated aspect of cooking methodology.
adjective	methodical	The head cook was not so artistic as methodical in preparing standard dishes.

noun	profession	The number of people choosing cooking as a profession has risen over the past decade.
adjective	professional	She was professional in her approach to dealing with the problem of late deliveries.
adverb	professionally	Although the customer was rude and loud, the waiter handled the situation very professionally.

WORDS IN CONTEXT

Read the following passage and write the words in the blanks below.

accustomed	demanding	influx	profession
apprenticeship	drawn	methods	relinquish
culinary	incorporate	outlet	themes

When people start thinking about careers, they may be looking for an (1) _____ for their creativity. Many people are (2) _____ to cooking as a career and see it as a (3) _____, not merely a trade. The restaurant business is (4) _____ and needs a constant (5) _____ of new talent.

Chefs (6) _____ ingredients and (7) _____ of cooking from around the world into successful menus. Most chefs offer meals that are variations on standard (8) _____. They will try to stretch their patrons' range of food tastes by taking food that is still recognized as traditional and infusing it with something new, like a rare spice or seasoning. People (9) _____ to certain tastes and textures aren't going to (10) _____ their preferences immediately.

Chefs attend (11) _____ school or train in restaurants with experienced chefs, in an (12) _____. For those of you who like hands-on creativity, being a chef might be a good choice.

WORD PRACTICE

LISTENING COMPREHENSION

Part 1 Photo

Look at the picture and listen to the sentences.
Choose the sentence that best describes the picture.

1. Ⓐ Ⓑ Ⓒ Ⓓ

Part 2 Question–Response

Listen to the question and the three responses. Choose the response that best answers the question.

2. Ⓐ Ⓑ Ⓒ   3. Ⓐ Ⓑ Ⓒ

Part 3 Conversation

Listen to the dialogue. Then read each question and choose the best answer.

4. According to the conversation, what do good chefs do?
   (A) Demand a lot from their assistants.
   (B) Manage their restaurants well.
   (C) Attract customers.
   (D) Influence new chefs.

5. What does the woman think of cooking as a career?
   (A) It pays well.
   (B) It's hard to manage.
   (C) It's not worth the effort.
   (D) It's very demanding.

6. What does the man plan to do?
   (A) Take more rests.
   (B) Eat at restaurants more often.
   (C) Become a chef.
   (D) Practice cooking

Part 4 Talk

Listen to the talk. Then read each question and choose the best answer.

7. Who is this talk for?
   (A) Cooking instructors.
   (B) People who work in the culinary arts.
   (C) People looking for a profession.
   (D) Career counselors.

8. What kind of people are attracted to the cooking profession?
   (A) Bored.
   (B) Demanding.
   (C) Exciting.
   (D) Creative.

9. What does the speaker recommend to become a professional chef?
   (A) Becoming an apprentice.
   (B) Reading cookbooks.
   (C) Visiting restaurants around the world.
   (D) Attending a culinary school.

READING

Part 5 Incomplete Sentences

Choose the word that best completes the sentence.

10. Susannah is having a hard time becoming _____ to the long hours of her job at the restaurant.
    - (A) custom
    - (B) customs
    - (C) accustoms
    - (D) accustomed

11. The student accepted a six-month _____ with a famous chef.
    - (A) apprentice
    - (B) apprenticed
    - (C) apprenticing
    - (D) apprenticeship

12. The patrons at this restaurant are often _____, but they make up for it by tipping well.
    - (A) accustomed
    - (B) drawn
    - (C) demanding
    - (D) culinary

13. I love this chef's cooking style, which _____ so many different tastes.
    - (A) incorporation
    - (B) incorporates
    - (C) incorporating
    - (D) incorporator

14. The experienced chef was _____ about the way he prepared his award-winning dish.
    - (A) method
    - (B) methodical
    - (C) methodically
    - (D) methodology

15. The _____ attitude of the staff is one of the keys to a restaurant's success.
    - (A) professional
    - (B) professionalism
    - (C) profession
    - (D) professionally

Part 6 Text Completion

More and more people are choosing to become professional chefs. The number of students enrolled in culinary schools is growing every year. People choose this career for different reasons. Some _____ to a cooking career because of a love of

16. (A) draw
    (B) are drawn
    (C) have drawn
    (D) are drawing

food. Others find that cooking is the perfect _____ for their creativity. People

17. (A) outlay
    (B) output
    (C) outage
    (D) outlet

traditionally think of Paris as the city where professional chefs are trained. However, fine culinary schools can be found all over the world. The _____ of a cooking

18. (A) demand
    (B) demands
    (C) demanders
    (D) demanding

career are great, but there are also many rewards.

Part 7 Reading Comprehension

Questions 19–23 refer to the following article.

Welcome to the National Institute of the Culinary Arts. You have chosen to enter a highly rewarding profession. People are drawn to this career for many different reasons, but you all have something in common—an appreciation of fine food. At the institute you will have the opportunity to study with some of the most highly skilled chefs in the world. In order to take the best advantage of this opportunity, you need to approach it with an open mind. Be ready to relinquish your old ideas about cooking and take in new ideas about the most artistic methods of preparing food. While at the institute, you will become accustomed to long hours, hard work, and also wonderful results. By the time you have finished with your coursework and are ready to start your apprenticeship, you will feel that you have accomplished much more than you ever expected to here at the institute. Please take the time to look over the following pages carefully as they contain all the information you need about course requirements, textbooks, apprenticeship opportunities, and the instructors at the institute.

19. Who is the audience for this article?
    (A) Students.
    (B) Instructors.
    (C) Working chefs.
    (D) Restaurant patrons.

20. What kind of place is the institute?
    (A) A restaurant.
    (B) A bookstore.
    (C) An art school.
    (D) A cooking school.

21. What does the writer ask the readers to do?
    (A) Start cooking.
    (B) Order more courses.
    (C) Keep reading.
    (D) Enjoy fine food.

22. The word *relinquish* in line 12 is closest in meaning to
    (A) let go
    (B) add to
    (C) share
    (D) discuss

23. The word *accustomed* in line 15 is closest in meaning to
    (A) interested in
    (B) tired from
    (C) bored by
    (D) used to

Lesson
35

Events

WORDS TO LEARN

assist

coordinate

dimension

event

exact

general

ideally

lead time

proximity

regulate

site

stage

Study the following definitions and examples.

1. **assist** v., to give help or support to
   a. Bonnie hired a secretary to assist her with the many details of the event.
   b. The hotel manager was able to assist us with some last-minute advice.

2. **coordinate** v., to adjust or arrange parts to work together
   a. Benet tried to coordinate all departments to make sure the event ran smoothly.
   b. The colors of the flowers were ordered to coordinate with the colors in the corporate logo.

3. **dimension** n., a measure of width, height, or length
   a. What are the dimensions of the ballroom?
   b. We need the dimensions of the meeting rooms before we can determine how many chairs each will hold.

4. **event** n., an organized occasion
   a. The spring conference is our biggest yearly event.
   b. This hotel is a popular place for events because of its beautiful location.

5. **exact** adj., characterized by accurate measurements or inferences
   a. We will need an exact head count by noon tomorrow.
   b. The exact measurements of the room are unknown, but we can guess.

6. **general** adj., involving only the main features rather than precise details
   a. We have a general idea of how many guests will attend.
   b. In general, about half the guests will bring their spouses.

7. **ideally** adv., perfectly; conforming to an ideal
   a. Ideally, the location for the concert would have plenty of parking.
   b. Lucy explained that ideally her wedding would take place on the beach, but she realized it might be difficult to arrange.

8. **lead time** n., the time between the initial stage of a project and the appearance of results
   a. The lead time for reservations is unrealistic.
   b. We will need to give the caterer enough lead time to cut the cake.

9. **proximity** n., the state, quality, sense, or fact of being near or next to; closeness
   a. The fans were worried by the proximity of the storm clouds.
   b. An important factor in selecting the site was its close proximity to a parking garage.

10. **regulate** v., to control
    a. The state strictly regulates the preparation of food for public consumption.
    b. The site staff closely regulates how many cars can be brought on the grounds.

11. **site** n., a place or setting
    a. Once we saw the site, we knew it would be perfect for the event.
    b. The manager of the site was most helpful.

12. **stage** v., to exhibit or present
    a. The gazebo outside was the perfect location from which to stage the cutting of the cake.
    b. A historic house can be the perfect site to stage a small reception.

WORD FAMILIES

verb	assist	Let me assist you with planning your next event.
noun	assistance	Dennis's idea of assistance is to call a professional firm for advice.
noun	assistant	In light of the number of events she had to run this year, Annu asked her boss for an assistant.

verb	coordinate	Ralph had a hard time coordinating the schedules of everybody involved in planning the event.
noun	coordination	Edna is a very good organizer, and coordination of events is one of her specialties.
noun	coordinator	The staff chose Marcel to be the coordinator for the company picnic.

noun	exactness	Exactness in all details is important when planning a large event.
adjective	exact	Everything went according to schedule so we were able to begin the speeches at the exact time that had been planned.
adverb	exactly	It is impossible to know ahead of time exactly how many people will attend an event.

verb	generalize	When we generalize, we must be aware of the many exceptions.
adjective	general	I need a general idea of what you want before I can provide specific answers.
adverb	generally	Although I cannot speak for every case, generally it is less expensive to buy in quantity.

verb	idealize	Rhoda idealized the location until she could no longer see any flaws in it.
adjective	ideal	A hotel with a large garden would be the ideal site for the reception.
adverb	ideally	Ideally, the site would be within our budget and have an outdoor area.

verb	regulate	The state will regulate the food-handling precautions.
noun	regulation	Please obey the state regulations regarding serving alcohol to minors.
adjective	regulatory	Even though it is private, the country club's kitchen is subject to the rules of regulatory agencies.

WORDS IN CONTEXT

Read the following passage and write the words in the blanks below.

assist	event	ideally	regulations
coordinated	exact	lead time	site
dimensions	general	proximity	stage

Planning an (1) _____ is not simple. There are hundreds of details that have to be (2) _____, whether it is a wedding or a business conference. Early in the planning process, you need to decide on the (3) _____. If you know where you want to (4) _____ the event, you should contact the site representative for an (5) _____ description of the facility. The staff will provide you with information about room (6) _____; food and beverage arrangements, including whether there are local (7) _____ or restrictions for serving alcoholic beverages; and required (8) _____ for reserving the site.

If you decide that the first site is not (9) _____ suited for your specific requirements, a guidebook will (10) _____ you in finding an alternative setting. In considering location, you should also think about its (11) _____ to public transportation.

With a (12) _____ idea of how many people will attend, and how much money you can spend, you can narrow down the available sites to the ones that best accommodate the needs of your group.

WORD PRACTICE

LISTENING COMPREHENSION

Part 1 Photo

Look at the picture and listen to the sentences.
Choose the sentence that best describes the picture.

1. Ⓐ Ⓑ Ⓒ Ⓓ

Part 2 Question–Response

Listen to the question and the three responses. Choose the response that best answers the question.

2. Ⓐ Ⓑ Ⓒ   3. Ⓐ Ⓑ Ⓒ

Part 3 Conversation

Listen to the dialogue. Then read each question and choose the best answer.

4. What are the speakers discussing?
(A) The wedding coordinator.
(B) The place for the wedding reception.
(C) The decorations for the reception.
(D) The wedding date.

5. Where does the man want to hold the wedding reception?
(A) At a hotel.
(B) In a park.
(C) At a club.
(D) In his backyard.

6. When do they have to sign the contract?
(A) Right now.
(B) Later today.
(C) This week.
(D) In four weeks.

Part 4 Talk

Listen to the talk. Then read each question and choose the best answer.

7. What event is being planned?
(A) A meeting.
(B) An awards ceremony.
(C) A formal dance.
(D) An office party.

8. When will the event take place?
(A) Next week.
(B) Next month.
(C) In the afternoon.
(D) Next weekend.

9. What kind of site are they looking for?
(A) One that is near the office.
(B) A small one.
(C) One that has a stage.
(D) An inexpensive one.

READING

Part 5 Incomplete Sentences

Choose the word that best completes the sentence.

10. Do you need our _____ with any of the evening's details?
    (A) assist
    (B) assisting
    (C) assistance
    (D) assistant

11. The event did not go off well because the _____ did a poor job of organizing it.
    (A) coordinator
    (B) coordination
    (C) coordinated
    (D) coordinates

12. _____ speaking, the event was poorly organized.
    (A) General
    (B) Generally
    (C) Generality
    (D) Generalizations

13. When the event planner saw the hotel ballroom, she knew that the size wasn't _____, but the price was right.
    (A) ideal
    (B) ideally
    (C) idealize
    (D) idealist

14. It was difficult to plan a tight schedule because we didn't know _____ when the guest speaker would arrive.
    (A) exact
    (B) exactor
    (C) exactly
    (D) exactness

15. Like restaurants, caterers are subject to _____ concerning safe food handling.
    (A) regulate
    (B) regulations
    (C) regulatory
    (D) regulating

Part 6 Text Completion

The most important part of planning an event is to give yourself plenty of _____.

16. (A) assistants
    (B) guest list
    (C) coordinators
    (D) lead time

You don't want to leave important details until the last minute. Ideally, you should give yourself several weeks to plan your event, or several months if it will be a large affair. The first step is to find a suitable _____ for your event. You want a place that is

17. (A) site
    (B) stage
    (C) assistant
    (D) regulation

pleasant and convenient. You also need a place that is the right size. If you have even a general idea of the number of guests you can expect to attend, it will be easy to calculate the _____ of the room that you will need. Many places that rent rooms for events

18. (A) dimities
    (B) dimmers
    (C) dimensions
    (D) diminishments

can also provide food and entertainment, and may also assist you with your plans.

Part 7 Reading Comprehension

Questions 19–23 refer to the following advertisement and e-mail message.

Hold your next event at the
Starlight Hotel
The grandest hotel in Weston

Are you planning a party, banquet, reception, or conference? We have the ideal location for you. We can accommodate groups of all sizes. Choose from any of our elegant event rooms:

The Garden View Room—holds up to 100 people
The Starlight Room—holds up to 200 people
The Banquet Hall—holds up to 250 people
The Stardust Ballroom—holds up to 350 people

We are ready to assist you with planning food, entertainment, invitations, and decorations.

We are conveniently located in the heart of the downtown entertainment district, in proximity to major bus and subway lines.

Contact Prisca Haines, Site Coordinator
      phone: 953-9172
      e-mail: p_haines@starlight.com

To: Prisca Haines
From: Peter Richards
Subject: Event room
Date: September 22

Dear Ms. Haines,

I saw the ad for event rooms at the Starlight Hotel in the Weston Daily News of September 20th. I am coordinating our company's annual awards banquet, which will be held on the 18th of next month. We would like to stage a simple but elegant affair. We don't expect more than about 75–85 guests. We would like to have a dinner followed by speeches and presentations of awards. Other than that, we don't plan to have any special entertainment. I would like to discuss the menu with you. Ideally, we would like to provide our guests with a choice of a meat entrée and a vegetarian entrée. I would like to know if your hotel kitchen can provide that, and which dishes you would specifically recommend.

Please call me before the weekend to discuss planning this event. I can be reached at 953-0955. Thank you.

Peter Richards

---

19. When will the company banquet take place?
    (A) This weekend.
    (B) September 20.
    (C) September 22.
    (D) October 18.

20. Which room will Ms. Haines probably recommend for the banquet?
    (A) The Garden View Room.
    (B) The Starlight Room.
    (C) The Banquet Hall.
    (D) The Stardust Ballroom.

21. What will Mr. Richards need assistance with?
    (A) The entertainment.
    (B) The decorations.
    (C) The invitations.
    (D) The food.

22. The word *ideal* in line 5 of the advertisement is closest in meaning to
    (A) large
    (B) perfect
    (C) beautiful
    (D) convenient

23. The word *coordinating* in line 3 of the e-mail is closest in meaning to
    (A) hosting
    (B) presenting
    (C) arranging
    (D) discussing

Word Review #7   Lessons 31–35 Restaurants and Events

Choose the word that best completes the sentence.

1. The aroma coming from the restaurant was so
_____ that the tourists did not hesitate
before entering.
   (A) random
   (B) subjective
   (C) appealing
   (D) reasonable

2. Because the menu was not in his native language,
the visitor asked the waiter for _____.
   (A) guide
   (B) guided
   (C) guiding
   (D) guidance

3. The waiter _____ that the customer would
enjoy the duck.
   (A) predict
   (B) predicted
   (C) predicting
   (D) prediction

4. Food critics are also expected to _____
a restaurant's service and atmosphere.
   (A) judge
   (B) judges
   (C) judging
   (D) judgment

5. My assistant usually picks _____ our lunch
order before noon.
   (A) over
   (B) on
   (C) off
   (D) up

6. Sometimes diners request _____, or
"separate," checks.
   (A) individuality
   (B) individually
   (C) individual
   (D) individualize

7. The most _____ customers seem to be
the worst tippers.
   (A) demand
   (B) demanded
   (C) demanding
   (D) demandingly

8. Food preparation is not just frying hamburgers;
it is a respected _____.
   (A) profess
   (B) professing
   (C) profession
   (D) professional

9. An event planner must _____ the entire
affair, not just choose the menu.
   (A) coordinated
   (B) coordinating
   (C) coordinator
   (D) coordinate

10. The planner must also ensure that participants
observe all local _____.
   (A) regulated
   (B) regulations
   (C) regulating
   (D) regulate

Choose the one word or phrase that best completes each sentence.

To: Robert Hughes
From: Betsy Wyman
Subject: re: places to eat

Hi Rob,

I got your message asking for ideas about places to take your clients to dinner. I have a great _____ for

11. (A) suggest
    (B) suggesting
    (C) suggestion
    (D) suggestible

you. The Waterfall Room is a fantastic restaurant that just opened on Maple Avenue. The atmosphere is pleasant and the food is very good. The menu features dishes from different countries, so it's a good place to eat if you like _____ food. They also have a dinner special that includes three courses and only costs $30. I really think

12. (A) foreign
    (B) appealing
    (C) random
    (D) exciting

this is the best place in town to enjoy an _____ meal at a reasonable price. Let me know how you like it.

13. (A) elegantly
    (B) elegance
    (C) elegies
    (D) elegant

Betsy

To: Sue Evans
From: Ron Smith
Subject: lunch tomorrow

Sue,

George will be out of the office all week, so it will _____ you to

14. (A) pick up
    (B) fall to
    (C) rely on
    (D) mix up

order the lunch for tomorrow's staff meeting. We always order from Sam's Deli. We'll need enough for 15 people. Look at their list of sandwiches and order three or four different kinds. _____ them to send a

15. (A) Reminding
    (B) To remind
    (C) Reminder
    (D) Remind

variety of desserts, too. People always like a sweet treat with their meal. Please make sure that the food _____ by noon tomorrow. Thanks.

16. (A) delivers
    (B) is delivered
    (C) is delivering
    (D) will deliver

Ron

Do you have what it takes to become a professional chef? The first requirement, of course, is an interest in the _____ arts. There is no point in becoming a chef if you don't love fine

17. (A) fine
    (B) visual
    (C) culinary
    (D) performing

food. You will also need to be willing to work long hours because this is a very _____

18. (A) demand
    (B) demander
    (C) demanded
    (D) demanding

profession. In addition, you will need leadership qualities. A working chef has _____

19. (A) to coordinate
    (B) coordinating
    (C) coordinates
    (D) coordinate

the work of everyone in the kitchen.

Lesson 36

General Travel

WORDS TO LEARN

agent

announcement

beverage

board

claim

delay

depart

embarkation

itinerary

luggage

prohibit

valid

Study the following definitions and examples.

1. **agent** n., a representative of a company
   a. The gate agent will make an announcement when it is time to board the plane.
   b. You can buy your ticket from the ticket agent at the train station right before you get on the train.

2. **announcement** n., a public notification
   a. Did you hear an announcement about our new departure time?
   b. I expect an announcement any time now about a snow emergency at the airport.

3. **beverage** n., a drink other than plain water
   a. The flight attendant offered all passengers a cold beverage during the flight.
   b. Hot and cold beverages as well as snacks are for sale in the train's café car.

4. **board** v., to enter a boat, plane, or train
   a. For security reasons, visitors are not allowed in the area of the airport where passengers board the planes.
   b. We will board the train for New York in ten minutes.

5. **claim** v., to take as rightful; to retrieve
   a. Please proceed directly to the baggage arrival area to claim your luggage.
   b. Lost luggage can be claimed at the airline office.

6. **delay** v., to postpone until a later time
   a. The bus was delayed due to inclement weather.
   b. The heavy traffic delayed our arrival at the train station.

7. **depart** v., to go away or leave; to vary from a regular course of action.
   a. After the wedding, the married couple departed for their honeymoon in Morocco.
   b. We're going to depart from our usual policy and allow you to leave work early one day a week.

8. **embarkation** n., the process of getting on a plane or ship
   a. Cruise passengers are given a pass for embarkation when they check in at the dock.
   b. The flight crew must check the passengers' documents before embarkation.

9. **itinerary** n., a proposed route for a journey, showing dates and means of travel
   a. He planned his itinerary after visiting several travel websites.
   b. I had to change my itinerary when I decided to add two more countries to my vacation.

10. **luggage** n., suitcases, baggage
    a. Airlines often limit the amount of luggage each person is allowed to carry.
    b. Traveling is a lot easier if you bring less luggage with you.

11. **prohibit** v., to forbid by authority or to prevent
    a. The bus company prohibits people without tickets from boarding the bus.
    b. Airline regulations prohibit the passengers from having beverages open during takeoff and landing.

12. **valid** adj., having legal efficacy or correctness
    a. I need to make certain that my passport is valid if we plan to go overseas this December.
    b. These tickets are no longer valid after the date printed on the back.

WORD FAMILIES

verb	announce	The captain announced that the flight would be landing in approximately 15 minutes.
noun	announcement	The flight attendant made an announcement reminding the passengers that this was a no-smoking flight.
noun	announcer	The announcer gave the instructions for boarding, in three languages.

verb	claim	International passengers must proceed to customs as soon as they claim their baggage.
noun	claim	If the airline has lost your luggage, you can file a claim with the insurance company.
noun	claimant	There was a long line of claimants waiting at the lost luggage office.

| verb | delay | Please don't delay me; I need to get to my gate immediately. |
| noun | delay | The delay in takeoff times was caused by a bad storm. |

verb	depart	The flight will depart from Gate 25.
noun	departure	The pilot always reminds the flight attendants to make sure that all passengers are ready for departure.
adjective	departed	The house felt empty without the departed guests.

verb	prohibit	Bus company regulations prohibit passengers from talking with the driver while the bus is moving.
noun	prohibition	The prohibition of many common items on airplanes can make it difficult for airplane travelers to pack their luggage.
adjective	prohibited	A passenger who carries a prohibited item onto an airplane may end up in the hands of security officers.

verb	validate	You can get your parking ticket validated at the concierge desk.
noun	validity	The agent will check the validity of your passport before you board the plane.
adjective	valid	Your ticket is no longer valid because it was issued over a year ago.

WORDS IN CONTEXT

Read the following passage and write the words in the blanks below.

agent	board	depart	luggage
announcements	claims	embarkation	prohibited
beverage	delayed	itinerary	valid

When Ms. Tan is planning a business trip, she prefers to act as her own travel (1) _____. If she is traveling to another country, first she checks her passport to make sure it is still (2) _____. Then she goes online and checks several travel websites to find out about airline flights and hotels. She likes to plan her own (3) _____, to choose when she will arrive at each place, how she will get there, and which hotels she will stay at. On the day her trip begins, she looks at the airline's website to make sure that her flight is on time and not (4) _____.

At the airport, Ms. Tan checks her suitcases at the check-in counter since she is (5) _____ from taking more than one piece of carry-on (6) _____ with her onto the plane. At the same time, she receives her (7) _____ card.

She will present this at the gate when it is time to (8) _____ her flight. She is told to be at the gate 15 minutes before the flight is to (9) _____. During the flight, the attendant may offer her a (10) _____, and a snack or meal. The captain will make (11) _____ during the flight to let the passengers know at what altitude they are flying, and when they may expect to arrive at their destination.

Once the flight has landed, Ms. Tan disembarks and must go through customs after she (12) _____ her baggage. After this, she will take a cab to the hotel where she is staying, so she can rest and prepare for her meeting the next day. She will also reconfirm her return flight a day or two before she leaves to return home.

WORD PRACTICE

LISTENING COMPREHENSION

Part 1 Photo

Look at the picture and listen to the sentences.
Choose the sentence that best describes the picture.

1. Ⓐ Ⓑ Ⓒ Ⓓ

Part 2 Question–Response

Listen to the question and the three responses. Choose the response that best answers the question.

2. Ⓐ Ⓑ Ⓒ   3. Ⓐ Ⓑ Ⓒ

Part 3 Conversation

Listen to the dialogue. Then read each question and choose the best answer.

4. Whom is the man speaking with?
   (A) A pilot.
   (B) A waitress.
   (C) A travel agent.
   (D) A flight attendant.

5. What does the woman offer the man?
   (A) Something to eat.
   (B) Something to read.
   (C) Something to drink.
   (D) Something to listen to.

6. When will they arrive?
   (A) In one hour.
   (B) In two hours.
   (C) In three hours.
   (D) In four hours.

Part 4 Talk

Listen to the talk. Then read each question and choose the best answer.

7. What do passengers have to show the flight attendant?
   (A) An embarkation card.
   (B) A passport.
   (C) A trip itinerary.
   (D) A boarding pass.

8. When will the flight leave?
   (A) At 1:15.
   (B) In twenty minutes.
   (C) At nine o'clock.
   (D) In five minutes.

9. What is not allowed before takeoff?
   (A) Talking on the phone.
   (B) Selling things.
   (C) Drinking.
   (D) Dining.

READING

Part 5 Incomplete Sentences

Choose the word that best completes the sentence.

10. The desk clerk _____ the change in gate numbers at least an hour ago.
    (A) announcement   (C) announcer
    (B) announcing   (D) announced

11. When it's time to _____ the flight, an announcement will be made.
    (A) boarded   (C) board
    (B) boarding   (D) boarder

12. As soon as John _____ his luggage, he went outside to look for a taxi.
    (A) boarded   (C) departed
    (B) claimed   (D) prohibited

13. The man had to _____ his travel plans because an emergency came up at work.
    (A) delay   (C) delayed
    (B) delaying   (D) delays

14. The train's _____ was delayed because of a problem on the track.
    (A) departed   (C) departs
    (B) departure   (D) depart

15. The airport applied a blanket rule that all passengers must be in possession of _____ tickets in order to enter the waiting area.
    (A) valid   (C) validate
    (B) validity   (D) validation

Part 6 Text Completion

Information for Travelers

* We make every effort to leave on time. To avoid _____, please plan to arrive at least one hour before your

    16. (A) delays
        (B) delights
        (C) deliveries
        (D) delusions

scheduled departure time. This is especially important because all passengers must pass through security control.

* Scissors, nail clippers, and other sharp instruments _____ on board. Leave these items at home or surrender

    17. (A) prohibit
        (B) prohibits
        (C) are prohibited
        (D) are prohibiting

them to the security officer in charge.

* Each passenger is allowed two small carry-on bags. Check your excess luggage with the attendant. You can claim it at the end of your trip.

* We request that passengers remain in the waiting area until the attendant _____ the embarkation time.

    18. (A) announce
        (B) announces
        (C) will announce
        (D) does announce

Please don't attempt to board ahead of time.

* Your comfort is our priority. Snack service is available on board. Please ask the attendant for pillows and blankets if you require them.

Thank you for traveling with us. Have a safe and happy trip.

Part 7 Reading Comprehension

Questions 19–23 refer to the following travel itinerary.

BREEZEWAY, INC.

Itinerary for: Edward Rochester

	April 15	Depart New York City — 10:30 P.M.
		*Solar Airlines flight 133
		Arrive Seattle, WA — 12:15 P.M.
		Hotel: Puget Inn
		1764 Capital Street
		Seattle, WA
	April 18	Depart Seattle — 8:05 A.M.
		**Train # 10
		***Arrive Vancouver, Canada 11:20 A.M.
		Hotel: Gas Town Hotel
		375 Alaska Avenue
		Vancouver, Canada
	April 20	Depart Vancouver — 11:30 P.M.
		*Solar Airlines flight 136
	April 21	Arrive New York City — 5:10 A.M.

* Please arrive at airport at least one hour ahead of scheduled departure time.
Plane will begin boarding 20 minutes ahead of scheduled departure time.
It is prohibited to bring firearms, explosive devices, or sharp instruments on board any Solar Airlines flight. There is no meal service on board any Solar Airlines flight. Beverages will be available for sale.

** Please arrive at train station 30 minutes before scheduled departure time.

*** A valid passport is required for entry into Canada.

---

19. How many nights will Mr. Rochester stay at the Puget Inn?
    (A) One.
    (B) Two.
    (C) Three.
    (D) Four.

20. What time can he get on the return flight to New York City?
    (A) 10:30.
    (B) 11:10.
    (C) 11:30.
    (D) 5:10.

21. What can he buy during the flight?
    (A) A meal.
    (B) A drink.
    (C) A passport.
    (D) A train ticket.

22. The word *itinerary* in line 2 is closest in meaning to
    (A) bill
    (B) ticket
    (C) advice
    (D) schedule

23. The word *prohibited* in line 20 is closest in meaning to
    (A) not encouraged
    (B) uncommon
    (C) permitted
    (D) not allowed

Lesson 37

Airlines

Study the following definitions and examples.

1. **deal with** v. phrase, to attend to; to manage; to see to
   a. Ticket agents must deal courteously with irate customers.
   b. Sick passengers, frightened children, and rude pilots are just a few of the things cabin attendants have to deal with.

2. **destination** n., the place to which one is going or directed
   a. The Great Barrier Reef is a popular tourist destination this year.
   b. Once you have determined your desired destination, we can work toward getting the best airfare.

3. **distinguish** v., to perceive a difference; to make noticeable or different
   a. Suki was able to distinguish between the different types of jets on the runway.
   b. This airline has distinguished itself as one of the most reliable in the business.

4. **economize** v., to be careful about spending money
   a. Since I like to economize when I travel, I always do a thorough Internet search for the best airline ticket prices.
   b. We decided to economize this year and take our vacation during the off season, when prices are lower.

5. **equivalent** adj., equal
   a. Carlos used the Internet to search for hotels of equivalent dollar value to the one recommended.
   b. The food the airline serves in coach class is equivalent to that served in first class.

6. **excursion** n., a pleasure trip; a trip at a reduced fare
   a. With some time between meetings in London, the company president enjoyed an excursion to Stonehenge.
   b. The finance officer was pleased to find an excursion for the entire consulting team.

7. **expense** n., something requiring payment
   a. A luxury vacation involves many expenses.
   b. If we keep our expenses down, we might have enough money to take a longer trip.

8. **extend** v., to make longer
   a. The delayed flight extended our wait in the airport.
   b. We enjoyed the beach so much that we extended our stay another day.

9. **prospective** adj., likely to become or be
   a. Airlines advertise on travel websites in order to attract prospective customers.
   b. I narrowed my list of prospective destinations to my three top choices.

10. **scenery** n., a view of the surrounding area; a landscape
    a. It is difficult to appreciate the natural scenery from an airplane seat.
    b. Many travelers visit this area because of the beautiful scenery.

11. **situation** n., the combination of circumstances at a given moment
    a. The airline suggested I check with the State Department regarding the political situation in the country I'm flying to.
    b. The vast number of different airfares available makes for a complicated situation.

12. **substantially** adv., significantly
    a. The airline I work for had a substantially higher rating for customer satisfaction than our competitors had.
    b. The airfares charged by different airlines are not substantially different.

WORD FAMILIES

verb	distinguish	I can't distinguish any difference in the two airlines, since their fares are the same.
adjective	distinguishable	The airline's planes were easily distinguishable by the bright logo on the planes' tails.
adverb	distinguishably	Even though that city looks farther away on the map, the flight there is not distinguishably longer.

verb	economize	We no longer fly first class, since our company is trying to economize.
adjective	economical	Without hesitation, we chose the more economical of the two airline tickets.
adverb	economically	The best way to plan a trip economically is to compare prices on the Internet.

noun	expense	To stay within our travel budget, we must keep all our expenses as low as possible.
adverb	expensively	The first-class seats are for those who travel expensively but with great style.
adjective	expensive	Only the most expensive fares were still available.

verb	extend	When people travel to an interesting destination for business, they often extend their trip by a few days in order to enjoy the place as a tourist.
noun	extent	Larry has traveled to Japan many times and the extent of his knowledge of that country is impressive.
adjective	extensive	Pamela is taking six months off from work in order to take an extensive tour of South America.

noun	prospect	The prospects of getting a seat on this evening's flight are not good.
adjective	prospective	Once you know the prospective dates for your trip, you can look on the Internet to see what flights are available.

noun	substance	I couldn't recognize the substance that was on my meal tray and that the airlines called dinner.
adjective	substantial	Ms. Qin found there was a substantial difference in the price quoted for the plane ticket, depending on which day she flew.
adverb	substantially	There is substantially no difference in the quality of food served in first class and in economy class.

WORDS IN CONTEXT

Read the following passage and write the words in the blanks below.

deal with	economical	expensive	scenery
destination	equivalent	extending	situation
distinguishable	excursion	prospective	substantial

If you travel, you most likely will have to (1) _____ flying. Flying is the quickest, most convenient means of travel between countries, and often between different parts of one country. Flying is (2) _____, but when all costs are taken into account for traveling any (3) _____ distance, air travel usually costs less than driving by car. It is also the most (4) _____ way to go in terms of time. You won't be able to enjoy the (5) _____ en route, as you would in a car, but you'll have more time to enjoy your surroundings when you arrive at your vacation (6) _____.

Airlines sell seats at a variety of prices through a system of requirements and restrictions. Full-fare tickets are the most expensive, but give you the most flexibility in terms of making changes. A (7) _____ traveler can buy a ticket up to takeoff time as long as a seat is available.

Fares change rapidly, and even travel experts find it difficult to keep up. The changing (8) _____ is due to many factors, including increased competition. As a general rule, the less you pay for the ticket, the more restrictions you can expect. If you are trying to save money, look for (9) _____ fares. These are (10) _____ to a special sale. Most excursion fares are for round-trip travel and have strict regulations and a minimum and maximum length of stay, so don't count on (11) _____ your vacation or staying less time than required. However, once you are on the plane, you are not (12) _____ from passengers who paid higher fares.

WORD PRACTICE

LISTENING COMPREHENSION

TRACK
38

Part 1 Photo

Look at the picture and listen to the sentences.
Choose the sentence that best describes the picture.

1. Ⓐ Ⓑ Ⓒ Ⓓ

Part 2 Question–Response

Listen to the question and the three responses. Choose the response that best answers the question.

2. Ⓐ Ⓑ Ⓒ   3. Ⓐ Ⓑ Ⓒ

Part 3 Conversation

Listen to the dialogue. Then read each question and choose the best answer.

4. What are the speakers discussing?
   (A) The length of the trip.
   (B) The schedule of the airline.
   (C) The cost of the ticket.
   (D) The quality of the airline.

5. How can the woman get a lower airfare?
   (A) By staying for just two days.
   (B) By flying to a different city.
   (C) By charging it as a work expense.
   (D) By changing the day of her arrival.

6. When does the woman want to arrive?
   (A) Sunday.
   (B) Monday.
   (C) Tuesday.
   (D) Wednesday.

Part 4 Talk

Listen to the talk. Then read each question and choose the best answer.

7. How can a client find out about tickets to another country?
   (A) Call back later.
   (B) Press two.
   (C) Use the computer.
   (D) Press one.

8. What can a client do by pressing three?
   (A) Make hotel reservations.
   (B) Purchase airline tickets.
   (C) Find out about excursion rates.
   (D) Connect with the agency's computer.

9. Why is there no information on excursions?
   (A) The excursion rates are no longer available.
   (B) The computer system is not working.
   (C) The situation has changed.
   (D) The excursions have all been reserved.

READING

Part 5 Incomplete Sentences

Choose the word that best completes the sentence.

10. Let me point out the features of our service that _____ our airline from our competitors.
    (A) distinguishably
    (B) distinguishable
    (C) distinguishing
    (D) distinguish

11. Let's shop around until we find a more _____ airfare.
    (A) economical
    (B) economize
    (C) economy
    (D) economically

12. We need to watch our _____, so we'll have to look for better prices on those airline tickets.
    (A) destinations
    (B) prospects
    (C) expenses
    (D) extents

13. I decided not to _____ my trip since I felt so tired by the time I finished my business meetings.
    (A) extended
    (B) extent
    (C) extensive
    (D) extend

14. If you wait until the last minute, the _____ of getting an airline ticket on a holiday weekend are not good.
    (A) prospective
    (B) prospectively
    (C) prospectors
    (D) prospects

15. Unless the airfares differ _____, you should book seats on the airline with which you have frequent flyer miles.
    (A) substance
    (B) substantially
    (C) substantial
    (D) substantiality

Part 6 Text Completion

Renovated City Airport Now Open

Frequent flyers will be happy to know that the renovations at City Airport are finally finished. The airport renovations were scheduled for completion at the end of last year, but the construction team fell behind schedule and _____ the deadlines twice. Now the work is completed, and travelers no longer have

    16. (A) extend
        (B) extended
        (C) have extended
        (D) had extended

to deal _____ the noise, dust, and inconvenience of construction work. Passengers can move more

   17. (A) to
      (B) for
      (C) with
      (D) from

easily and comfortably through the airport, and everything is easier to find. One of the biggest improvements in the renovated airport is the signs indicating the location of the various airlines' check-in counters. The new signs are much _____ than the old ones, and it is easier for passengers to find

     18. (A) distinguishable
        (B) more distinguishable
        (C) most distinguishable
        (D) the most distinguishable

the airlines they are looking for. In general, now that the work at the airport is finally over, the situation there has substantially improved.

Part 7 Reading Comprehension

Questions 19–23 refer to the following two e-mail messages.

To: Belinda Tuttle
From: Mark Wallaby
Subject: Re: Amazon Tours

Dear Ms. Tuttle,

In response to your request for information on guided tours in the Amazon region, I have found two excursions that may interest you. Both are led by reputable companies that are known for organizing interesting and educational trips at reasonable expense. One led by Jungle Tours, Inc. goes to all the destinations you are interested in visiting and lasts two weeks, the length of time you requested. However, it leaves on November 10th, a week earlier than the date you mentioned. I don't know whether or not you would be able to leave this early. There is a tour leaving on your designated date, run by Paradise Adventures. It doesn't, however, go to all the destinations you are interested in, and it lasts three weeks, not two, so you wouldn't return until December 8th. I don't know whether or not you would be able to extend the length of your vacation. If either of these two prospects interests you, let me know. Otherwise I will keep looking for a tour that will suit you.

Mark Wallaby
Southern Travel

To: Mark Wallaby
From: Belinda Tuttle
Subject   Re: Amazon Tours

Dear Mr. Wallaby,

Thank you for the information on trips to the Amazon. Unfortunately, I cannot change the dates of my vacation because of my work situation. The end of the year is a very busy time for accountants, and I will have a lot of work to deal with as soon as I return from my trip. On the other hand, I don't really need to economize, so I am flexible about the expense. The exact destinations don't really matter either. I will be happy just to visit that part of the world and get a chance to see the Amazon scenery I have heard so much about. So please keep looking and let me know what you find. Thank you for your efforts.

Belinda Tuttle

19. What is Mark Wallaby's job?
(A) Tour guide.
(B) Educator.
(C) Accountant.
(D) Travel agent.

20. When does Ms. Tuttle want to begin her vacation?
(A) November 10.
(B) November 17.
(C) December 1.
(D) December 8.

21. Why doesn't Ms. Tuttle like the tours suggested by Mr. Wallaby?
(A) They are too expensive.
(B) The companies have a bad reputation.
(C) They go to the wrong destinations.
(D) The dates don't fit her vacation time.

22. The word *situation* in line 3 of the second e-mail is closest in meaning to
(A) circumstances
(B) responsibilities
(C) requirements
(D) location

23. The word *scenery* in line 11 of the second e-mail is closest in meaning to
(A) culture
(B) climate
(C) landscape
(D) vegetation

Lesson 38

Trains

WORDS TO LEARN

comprehensive

deluxe

directory

duration

entitle

fare

offset

operate

punctually

relatively

remainder

remote

Study the following definitions and examples.

1. **comprehensive** adj., covering broadly; inclusive
   a. The conductor has a comprehensive knowledge of rail systems from all over the world.
   b. You can get a comprehensive travel package, including rail passes, if you visit the travel company's website.

2. **deluxe** adj., noticeably luxurious
   a. My parents decided to splurge on deluxe accommodations for their trip.
   b. The train station is not near any of the deluxe hotels, so we will have to take a taxi.

3. **directory** n., a book or collection of information or directions
   a. We consulted the directory to see where the train station was located.
   b. Mr. Scannel found the telephone number for the local train station in the telephone directory.

4. **duration** n., the time during which something lasts
   a. Mother lent me her spare jacket for the duration of the trip.
   b. Despite our personal differences, my roommate and I agreed to be as pleasant as possible for the duration of the train ride.

5. **entitle** v., to allow or qualify
   a. During the holiday rush, a train ticket entitled the passenger to a ride, but not necessarily a seat.
   b. The mess the train line made of Pedro's sleeping room reservations entitled him to a free upgrade to a better room.

6. **fare** n., the money paid for transportation
   a. The train fare has increased since I rode last.
   b. Pay your fare at the ticket office and you will get a ticket to board the train.

7. **offset** v., to counterbalance
   a. The high cost of the hotel room offset the savings we made by taking the train instead of the plane.
   b. By reducing her transportation costs once in the United States, Mrs. Sato offset the cost of getting to this country.

8. **operate** v., to perform a function
   a. The train operates on a punctual schedule.
   b. The train only operates in this area at the height of the tourist season.

9. **punctually** adv., promptly; on time
   a. Please be on time; the train leaves punctually at noon.
   b. The train usually arrives punctually; I can't imagine what is delaying it today.

10. **relatively** adv., somewhat
    a. The train is relatively empty for this time of day.
    b. The train station has been relatively busy for a weekday.

11. **remainder** n., the part that is left; leftover
    a. The Alaskan frontier has train service in the summer, but for the remainder of the year the tracks are impassable.
    b. We will move you to a less expensive room and credit the remainder of what you've already paid to your charge card.

12. **remote** adj., far away; not close to populated areas
    a. I was surprised to find train service to such a remote location.
    b. We took the train out of the city and found a remote hotel in the country for the weekend.

WORD FAMILIES

noun	comprehensiveness	Due to the comprehensiveness of the train system, the complete timetable was a thick document.
adjective	comprehensive	Due to the comprehensive reach of the rail system, the train can take you to every major city and many smaller ones.
adverb	comprehensively	The surveyors comprehensively studied the terrain before planning the site for the new train tracks.

verb	direct	We were unfamiliar with the city, so the hotel manager directed us to the train station.
noun	direction	The ticket agent at the train station gave us directions to the nearest restaurant.
noun	directory	On the Tourist Office website, you'll find a link to a thorough directory to local museums, parks, and other places of interest to visitors.

verb	operate	Trains don't operate in this town after the summer tourism season is over.
noun	operation	The train system is a massive operation with thousands of large and small stations across the country.
adjective	operational	As the operational expenses for the train system rose, the managers were forced to either cut services or raise prices.

noun	punctuality	The Swiss trains are legendary for their punctuality.
adjective	punctual	For a transportation service to have any credibility, it must be punctual.
adverb	punctually	The conductor arrived punctually at the train station.

verb	remain	It is safer for all passengers to remain in their seats until the train comes to a complete stop.
noun	remains	The waiter cleared off the remains of our meal after we left the dining car.
noun	remainder	After our exciting stay in New York, the remainder of the trip seemed dull.

noun	remoteness	The remoteness of the state park was part of its attraction, but since it's not served by a train line, I couldn't get to it.
adjective	remote	The remote cabin in the woods can only be reached by car; the nearest train station or airport is more than 100 miles away.
adverb	remotely	I wasn't remotely interested in taking a cross-country trip by train since I can't stand to be confined for a long time.

WORDS IN CONTEXT

Read the following passage and write the words in the blanks below.

comprehensive	duration	offset	relatively
deluxe	entitle	operate	remainder
directories	fares	punctual	remote

Trains are among the best ways to see a lot of a country in a (1) _____ short amount of time. In addition to the consideration of time, traveling by train allows you to really see the country you are passing through. You need only get to the station on time; after that, you can relax and watch from the window.

Most trains are on time and run on a (2) _____ schedule. Routes, schedules, and (3) _____ are listed in a timetable available at a train station, in many travel (4) _____, or posted on the Internet. Directories that are (5) _____ list all the trains, the cities they serve, the stations they depart from, and the class of services available. A few (6) _____ travel destinations are accessible only during the peak tourist season; the train does not (7) _____ there the (8) _____ of the year.

The fare is based on how far you travel and the quality of your accommodations. The basic fare buys you a seat for the (9) _____ of the trip. To be more precise, an unreserved seat guarantees a passenger transportation only; seats are allocated on a first-come, first-served basis. On busy holidays, it is possible that you could stand for at least some of your trip. For long trips, you will want to reserve a seat.

If you are traveling overnight, the cost of your room accommodation will depend on how (10) _____ your room is. Although taking the train is less expensive than flying, the savings may be (11) _____ by the cost of booking a sleeping room.

Travelers coming to the United States can take advantage of special rates not available in the United States. These passes (12) _____ the bearer to unlimited coach travel on trains for a fixed period of days, usually a month.

WORD PRACTICE

LISTENING COMPREHENSION

Part 1 Photo

Look at the picture and listen to the sentences. Choose the sentence that best describes the picture.

1. Ⓐ Ⓑ Ⓒ Ⓓ

Part 2 Question–Response

Listen to the question and the three responses. Choose the response that best answers the question.

2. Ⓐ Ⓑ Ⓒ   3. Ⓐ Ⓑ Ⓒ

Part 3 Conversation

Listen to the dialogue. Then read each question and choose the best answer.

4. What are the speakers discussing?
    (A) The operator of the train.
    (B) The comfort of the train ride.
    (C) The directions to the train station.
    (D) The time the train leaves.

5. How long will their train ride be?
    (A) Three and a half hours.
    (B) Five hours.
    (C) Ten hours.
    (D) Thirty hours.

6. What will they do now?
    (A) Eat some snacks.
    (B) Buy their train tickets.
    (C) Get on the train.
    (D) Buy something to read.

Part 4 Talk

Listen to the talk. Then read each question and choose the best answer.

7. What is an advantage of riding a high-speed train?
    (A) It is always on time.
    (B) It goes to many cities.
    (C) You can get off anytime you want.
    (D) It is cheaper than a plane.

8. What is true about a high-speed train?
    (A) It operates in most cities.
    (B) It is almost as slow as a traditional train.
    (C) It is almost as fast as a plane in some cases.
    (D) It is just as fast as a traditional train.

9. What is included in the cost of a high-speed train ticket?
    (A) A comfortable seat.
    (B) A movie.
    (C) A class.
    (D) A free meal.

READING

Part 5 Incomplete Sentences

Choose the word that best completes the sentence.

10. Do you have a _____ map that shows all the station stops west of the Mississippi?
    - (A) comprehension
    - (B) comprehensively
    - (C) comprehensive
    - (D) comprehensiveness

11. We got lost in the train station and had to ask for _____ to the gate that our train was leaving from.
    - (A) directions
    - (B) directed
    - (C) directory
    - (D) directs

12. The train has stopped because of a malfunction, but we expect it to be _____ again within minutes.
    - (A) operational
    - (B) operate
    - (C) operation
    - (D) operationally

13. John never arrives _____, so I am always anxious when we travel together for fear of missing a train.
    - (A) punctualness
    - (B) punctually
    - (C) punctual
    - (D) punctuality

14. Sylvia's family _____ with her in the station until she was ready to board the train.
    - (A) remains
    - (B) remainder
    - (C) remained
    - (D) remaining

15. With this traffic, there isn't even a _____ chance that we will get to the train station on time.
    - (A) remotely
    - (B) remote
    - (C) remoteness
    - (D) remotest

Part 6 Text Completion

Dear Henry,

I have made your train reservations for you. The tickets are enclosed. Your train leaves Sunday morning at 11:15. You should arrive at the train station on time since the trains all leave punctually. All the first-class tickets were sold out, so I wasn't able to get you deluxe accommodations. The tourist-class ticket I got you is considerably cheaper than a first-class ticket, so I hope the lower _____ offsets your

16. (A) far
    (B) fair
    (C) fore
    (D) fare

disappointment in not getting to ride first-class. I think you won't notice the difference since the trip is _____ short. I am sure you will be quite comfortable for the

17. (A) relatively
    (B) relation
    (C) relative
    (D) related

_____ of the ride. I will be waiting at the station for you when you arrive.

18. (A) duration
    (B) during
    (C) endure
    (D) endurance

I look forward to seeing you.

Eliza

Part 7 Reading Comprehension

Questions 19–23 refer to the following brochure.

Western Train Adventure

This comprehensive travel package includes round-trip train fare with sleeping car accommodations, deluxe hotel accommodations and meals at all overnight stops, and guided tours of selected cities along the way. In addition, your train ticket entitles you to three meals a day in the dining car or snack car while on board the train. We will travel through some remote areas with spectacular scenery. Every morning, a professional guide will provide information about the geology, natural history, and flora and fauna native to the areas we will travel through. You can spend the remainder of the day relaxing in your seat, chatting with your fellow passengers, or viewing movies. They will be shown twice a day in the lounge car, following lunch and dinner. An optional boat excursion to Victoria Island will be available at the western end of the trip for an extra fee. This special excursion is two days in duration and must be reserved and paid for two weeks prior to the trip departure date. The following trip departure dates are available:

June 7

June 28

July 21

August 8

Visit our website at *www.trainadventures.com* and make your reservation today!

---

19. Who is this information for?
    (A) Travel agents.
    (B) Tour guides.
    (C) Vacationers.
    (D) Business travelers.

20. Where can passengers watch movies?
    (A) In the dining car.
    (B) In the lounge car.
    (C) In the sleeping car.
    (D) In the snack car.

21. What is not included in the price of the travel package?
    (A) Hotel accommodations.
    (B) Meals.
    (C) Guided tours.
    (D) A trip to an island.

22. The word *comprehensive* in line 2 is closest in meaning to
    (A) inclusive
    (B) selected
    (C) reserved
    (D) popular

23. The word *entitles* in line 4 is closest in meaning to
    (A) suggest
    (B) reminds
    (C) expects
    (D) qualifies

Lesson 39

Hotels

Study the following definitions and examples.

1. **advanced** adj., highly developed; at a higher level
   a. Since the hotel installed an advanced computer system, all operations have been functioning more smoothly.
   b. Pablo has been promoted to assistant manager and he is happy with his advanced position.
2. **chain** n., a group of enterprises under a single control
   a. Budget-priced hotel chains have made a huge impact in the industry.
   b. The hotel being built in Seoul is the newest one in the chain.
3. **check in** v., to register at a hotel; to report one's presence
   a. Patrons check in at the hotel immediately upon their arrival.
   b. To know that the conference guests have arrived, we ask them to check in at the registration desk.
4. **confirm** v., to make definite
   a. Jorge contacted the hotel to confirm his room reservation.
   b. We automatically send an e-mail to let you know that your travel dates have been confirmed.
5. **expect** v., to consider probable or reasonable
   a. You can expect a clean room when you check in at a hotel.
   b. Mr. Kim expected that the bed linens would be changed daily.
6. **housekeeper** n., someone employed to do domestic work
   a. Eloise's first job at the hotel was as a housekeeper and now she is the manager.
   b. The desk clerk is sending the housekeeper to bring more towels to your room.
7. **notify** v., to report
   a. They notified the hotel that they had been delayed in traffic and would be arriving late.
   b. Lydia notified the hotel in writing that she was canceling her reservation.
8. **preclude** v., to make impossible; to rule out
   a. The horrible rainstorm precluded us from traveling any further.
   b. The unexpected cost of the room precluded a gourmet dinner for the travelers.
9. **quote** v., to give exact information on; n., a quotation
   a. We were quoted a price of $89 for the room for one night.
   b. Call ahead and get a price quote for a week-long stay.
10. **rate** n., the payment or price according to a standard
    a. The rate for the hotel room is too high considering how few services are available on-site.
    b. The sign in the lobby lists the seasonal rates.
11. **reservation** n., an arrangement to set something aside
    a. I know I made a reservation for tonight, but the hotel staff has no record of it in the system.
    b. It is difficult, if not impossible, to get reservations at this hotel at the height of the summer season.
12. **service** n., useful functions
    a. The hotel has a number of luxury services like the on-site gym, sauna, pool, and beauty salon.
    b. Mr. Rockmont called room service to order a late-night snack.

WORD FAMILIES

verb	advance	We are advancing steadily toward our goal of improving customer service at every hotel in the chain.
noun	advance	Clarissa booked the bridal suite in advance of the hotel's official opening.
adjective	advanced	All hotel employees who do well at their jobs will be given the opportunity to move up to an advanced position.

verb	confirm	It is wise to confirm your reservation before you leave for your trip.
noun	confirmation	The confirmation code given to Suzanne when she booked her room made it easy for her to resolve her problem.
adjective	confirmed	If you don't have a confirmed reservation, you may end up without a hotel room.

verb	expect	We expect to reach our destination by dinner.
noun	expectation	The guest's expectations were not met, so he complained to the manager.
adjective	expectant	The expectant travelers, loaded with luggage, left the hotel for their scheduled flight.

verb	notify	Please notify the front desk clerk if there are any problems with your room.
noun	notification	Written notification is required for any changes in reservations.

verb	quote	When customers ask for the room rate, just quote them the prices listed on this sheet.
noun	quotation	The quotation given to me didn't make sense, so I called again to verify it.
adjective	quotable	Our manager instructed us that the current room rates would be quotable only until the end of the month, when a rate increase would go into effect.

verb	reserve	We reserved a room well in advance.
noun	reservation	Seeing the crowds on the highway, I decided to pull over and telephone the hotel to make a reservation.
noun	in reserve	Like many other businesses, a hotel must keep some cash in reserve to pay for emergencies.

WORDS IN CONTEXT

Read the following passage and write the words in the blanks below.

advance	confirm	notify	rates
chains	expect	preclude	reservations
check in	housekeeper	quoted	service

People stay in hotels for business and personal travel. But with room rates being so high, many travelers are staying home. Since high costs can (1) _____ travel, smart travelers know they can save money and get the best (2) _____ for a room by making (3) _____ well in (4) _____ of the beginning of their trip. When you make a reservation, the hotel staff will ask you to (5) _____ them as soon as there is any change in your travel plans. To avoid any surprises, it's a good idea to call and (6) _____ the availability of your room and the rate you were (7) _____.

In selecting a hotel, first think about the kinds of (8) _____ you will need or like to have. You will naturally (9) _____ a comfortable, well-lit room and that a (10) _____ will make the bed and clean things up daily, even in the smallest hotels. Large hotel (11) _____ offer the most services, such as a pool, health club, or money exchange. The front desk clerks will tell you about such services when you (12) _____ at the hotel.

WORD PRACTICE

LISTENING COMPREHENSION

TRACK
40

Part 1 Photo

Look at the picture and listen to the sentences.
Choose the sentence that best describes the picture.

1. Ⓐ Ⓑ Ⓒ Ⓓ

Part 2 Question–Response

Listen to the question and the three responses. Choose the response that best answers the question.

2. Ⓐ Ⓑ Ⓒ   3. Ⓐ Ⓑ Ⓒ

Part 3 Conversation

Listen to the dialogue. Then read each question and choose the best answer.

4. When must a customer notify the hotel?
   (A) When he wants to leave a deposit.
   (B) When he will check in early.
   (C) When he expects to return to the hotel.
   (D) When he wants to cancel a reservation.

5. How much in advance should the customer notify
   the hotel?
   (A) Two to four hours.
   (B) Four hours.
   (C) Twenty-four hours.
   (D) Forty-four hours.

6. What does the man tell the woman to do?
   (A) Telephone the customer.
   (B) Send the customer a bill.
   (C) Charge the customer extra.
   (D) Get the customer's credit card number.

Part 4 Talk

Listen to the talk. Then read each question and choose the best answer.

7. Who is the speaker addressing?
   (A) New hotel employees.
   (B) Regular hotel customers.
   (C) Experienced hotel managers.
   (D) Hotel chain owners.

8. What is the goal of the hotel chain?
   (A) To get more customers.
   (B) To provide the best service.
   (C) To charge higher rates.
   (D) To hire more employees.

9. Where will the speaker take the listeners?
   (A) To the front door.
   (B) To the service entrance.
   (C) To the tour office.
   (D) To the dining room.

READING

Part 5 Incomplete Sentences

Choose the word that best completes the sentence.

10. We paid a lot of money for this room and we expect
an _____ level of service.
(A) advance
(B) advances
(C) advanced
(D) advancing

11. Gladys _____ her reservation by calling in
advance.
(A) confirmation
(B) confirmed
(C) confirming
(D) confirmative

12. The Chamber of Commerce had high _____ for
the amount of business the new hotel would bring to
the town.
(A) expectancy
(B) expected
(C) expect
(D) expectations

13. The hotel received the _____ of our early arrival
and had everything ready for us.
(A) notified
(B) notifies
(C) notification
(D) notify

14. I expect the rate that I was _____ over the phone
and I will not accept any changes.
(A) quoted
(B) quotation
(C) quotable
(D) quotes

15. Since we had made our _____ so far in advance,
we saved considerably on the room rate.
(A) reserve
(B) reservation
(C) reserved
(D) reservable

Part 6 Text Completion

Welcome to the Springflower Radford Hotel.
We are part of the Radford Hotel Group, one of the top hotel chains in the world.

Your comfort is important to us. When you check _____, please let us know if you will need

16. (A) in
(B) out
(C) up
(D) for

any special services during your stay.

A _____ will clean your room daily and supply you with fresh linens. Please notify her if you

17. (A) manager
(B) server
(C) housekeeper
(D) janitor

need any extra supplies for your room.

The exercise room and pool are available for the use of all guests. Exercise classes are offered daily.
Registration is required in _____. Please see the front desk clerk for more information.

18. (A) advancement
(B) advanced
(C) advancer
(D) advance

You can book city tours through us. See the front desk clerk for a price quote. If you have already made a
reservation for a city tour, we can confirm it for you.

Thank you for choosing a Radford Hotel. Have a pleasant stay.

Part 7 Reading Comprehension

Questions 19–23 refer to the following two letters.

June 10, 20—

Gisela Fried
Springflower Radford Hotel
2857 King Street
Hartsdale, WI

Dear Ms. Fried,

I am writing to let you know of the excellent service I received from your staff during my recent stay at the Springflower Radford Hotel. Although I had made an advance reservation for my stay, I had forgotten to confirm it. Thus, when I checked in at the hotel, there were no rooms available of the type I had wanted. Your kind and professional staff immediately found another, more luxurious, room for me. Although it was more expensive than the room I had reserved, they charged me the rate I had originally been quoted.

The excellent service continued throughout my stay and, indeed, exceeded my expectations. For example, the housekeeper cheerfully arrived to clean my room at 10:00 one evening after I had had problems with the bathtub overflowing. The staff at the front desk were always ready to answer my questions and were very helpful in assisting me to find my way around the city. All in all, my stay at the hotel was a very pleasant experience. I will certainly recommend this hotel to any of my friends who plan a visit to Hartsdale in the future.

Sincerely,

Andrew Wyatt

June 17, 20—

Andrew Wyatt
23 North Cuttersville Road
Creek Lake, MI

Dear Mr. Wyatt,

Thank you very much for your letter of June 10 notifying me of the fine service you received during your stay at the Springflower Radford Hotel. I am pleased to know that you had such a good experience as our guest. We at the Radford Hotel chain pride ourselves on the high quality of our service. As the hotel manager, I sometimes hear complaints about my staff, but it is just as important for me to hear about the fine work that they do.

I am enclosing a coupon for the hotel restaurant so that the next time you stay with us, you can enjoy a meal free of charge at the Springflower Restaurant.

Sincerely,

Gisela Fried

---

19. Why did Mr. Wyatt write the letter?
    (A) To complain about the hotel.
    (B) To ask for a rate quote.
    (C) To reserve a room.
    (D) To praise the hotel staff.

20. Who is Ms. Fried?
    (A) A hotel guest.
    (B) The hotel manager.
    (C) A housekeeper.
    (D) The front desk clerk.

21. What does Ms. Fried offer Mr. Wyatt?
    (A) A free meal.
    (B) A less expensive room.
    (C) A recommendation.
    (D) A job.

22. The word *rate* in the first letter, first paragraph, line 10 is closest in meaning to
    (A) time
    (B) place
    (C) price
    (D) speed

23. The word *notifying* in the second letter, first paragraph, line 2 is closest in meaning to
    (A) advertising
    (B) complaining
    (C) informing
    (D) scolding

Lesson 40

Car Rentals

Study the following definitions and examples.

1. **coincide** v., to happen at the same time
   a. My cousin's wedding coincided with a holiday weekend, so it was a perfect time to rent a car and go for a drive.
   b. Sean was hoping that the days for the special discount on car rentals would coincide with his vacation, but they did not.

2. **confusion** n., a lack of clarity, order, or understanding
   a. There was some confusion about which rental discount coupons applied to which car rental agency.
   b. To avoid any confusion about renting the car, Yolanda asked her travel agent to make the arrangements on her behalf.

3. **contact** v., to get in touch with
   a. Manuel contacted at least a dozen car rental agencies to get the best deal.
   b. Last night I was contacted by my travel agent who said he had found a better price on a car rental.

4. **disappoint** v., to fail to satisfy the hope, desire, or expectation of
   a. Leila was disappointed to discover that no rental cars were available the weekend she wished to travel.
   b. I hate to disappoint you, but I can't allow you to rent a car unless you have a major credit card.

5. **guarantee** v., promise
   a. The rental agency guarantees that all their cars are in good working order.
   b. By reserving a car ahead of time, you will be guaranteed the make and model of car that you want.

6. **intend** v., to have in mind
   a. I never intended to drive to Los Angeles until my brother suggested we do it together.
   b. Do you intend to return the car to this location or to another location?

7. **license** n., the legal permission to do or own a specified thing
   a. First, I'll need to see your driver's license and a major credit card.
   b. You will need a license in order to run this business.

8. **nervously** adv., in a distressed or uneasy manner
   a. As we approached the city Lonnie started driving nervously, so I volunteered to drive that part of the trip.
   b. I looked around nervously the entire time I was in the dark parking garage.

9. **request** v., ask for something politely or formally
   a. When Sonia reserved her rental car, she requested a luxury model.
   b. Most rental agencies request that you return the car with a full tank of gasoline.

10. **tempt** v., to be inviting or attractive to
    a. I am tempted by the idea of driving across the country instead of flying.
    b. Gina is tempted to rent the smaller car to save a few dollars.

11. **thrill** n., the source or cause of excitement or emotion
    a. The thought of renting a sports car gave John a thrill.
    b. Just taking a vacation is thrill enough, even if we are driving instead of flying.

12. **tier** n., a rank or class
    a. The car rental company had a few tiers of cars, each one costing more than the previous tier.
    b. If you are on a budget, I suggest you think about renting a car from our lowest tier.

WORD FAMILIES

verb	confuse	These long car rental contracts always confuse me.
noun	confusion	The crowds at the car rental office resulted in a lot of confusion.
adjective	confusing	Driving in an unfamiliar city can be quite confusing.

verb	coincide	This year, my vacation coincides with a national holiday, which will make renting a car more expensive.
noun	coincidence	By coincidence, I ran into an old friend in line waiting to rent a car.
adverb	coincidentally	Coincidentally, we are offering a special discount if you are over age 65.

verb	disappoint	The service at that car rental agency always disappoints me, so next time I plan to use a different agency.
noun	disappointment	The poor condition of the car we rented was an unexpected disappointment.
adjective	disappointing	The weather during our trip was so disappointing that we came home early.

noun	intention	I have every intention of paying by cash even though I reserved the car with my credit card.
adjective	intent	Intent on avoiding an accident, Zola drove cautiously through the rush hour traffic.
adverb	intently	The tourist intently studied the road map.

noun	nervousness	I hope my nervousness did not show when I was filling out the forms.
adjective	nervous	This was Jane's first time renting a car, so she was somewhat nervous.
adverb	nervously	Mr. Lane nervously parallel parked the rental car between two others in the parking garage.

verb	tempt	Can I tempt you to rent a larger car with a special discount?
noun	temptation	The temptation to drive the sports car fast was too great for Karl to resist.
adjective	tempting	As tempting as it sounds to drive to Florida, I think I'd rather fly.

WORDS IN CONTEXT

Read the following passage and write the words in the blanks below.

coincided	disappointment	license	tempted
confusing	guaranteed	nervous	thrill
contacted	intended	request	tier

When Yoko was planning her vacation, she went online to reserve a rental car at her vacation destination. Although she was (1) _____ to book a car once she arrived at her destination, Yoko was (2) _____ about not having a reservation. Her vacation (3) _____ with a holiday, so she knew many other people would also be renting cars. Yoko wanted to avoid the (4) _____ of finding that a car was not available at this time. By making a reservation ahead of time, she was (5) _____ to have a car available when she arrived at her destination.

There are a lot of car rental firms, so Yoko (6) _____ several of them to compare rates and requirements. While each company had different rates, they all had the same requirements: a valid driver's (7) _____ and a major credit card.

Yoko found the many different rates for renting cars (8) _____. Some companies offered substantial discounts provided that the car was reserved for a certain number of days. One company offered her a great daily rate, but it was based on a three-day rental. Since she only (9) _____ to rent the car for two days, the discount did not apply to her.

Another factor influencing the rate was the type of car. Rentals are based on a (10) _____ price system. The more luxurious or sporty, or the larger the car, the higher the daily rate. Since Yoko planned to (11) _____ only a small, basic car, she found a reasonable rate—although she would have liked the (12) _____ of driving a convertible.

WORD PRACTICE

LISTENING COMPREHENSION

TRACK
41

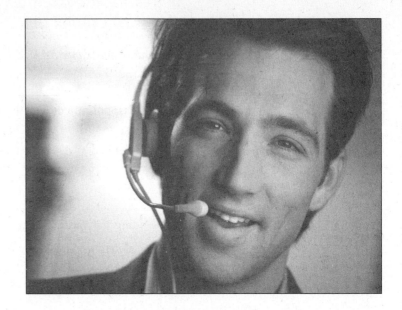

Part 1 Photo

Look at the picture and listen to the sentences.
Choose the sentence that best describes the picture.

1. Ⓐ Ⓑ Ⓒ Ⓓ

Part 2 Question–Response

Listen to the question and the three responses. Choose the response that best answers the question.

2. Ⓐ Ⓑ Ⓒ   3. Ⓐ Ⓑ Ⓒ

Part 3 Conversation

Listen to the dialogue. Then read each question and choose the best answer.

4. Whom is the man speaking with?
   (A) An insurance agent.
   (B) A police officer.
   (C) Another customer.
   (D) A car rental agent.

5. How much does insurance cost?
   (A) $4.
   (B) $9.
   (C) $13.
   (D) $30.

6. How will the man pay?
   (A) Cash.
   (B) Check.
   (C) Credit card.
   (D) Money order.

Part 4 Talk

Listen to the talk. Then read each question and choose the best answer.

7. Who is the audience for this talk?
   (A) People who work in travel agencies.
   (B) People who rent cars locally.
   (C) People who work in car rental agencies.
   (D) People who travel to other countries.

8. When should a traveler get an international driver's license?
   (A) After arriving in another country.
   (B) After contacting a local rental agency.
   (C) Before leaving on a trip.
   (D) When signing a car rental contract.

9. What should a traveler do when picking up a rental car?
   (A) Look for damage.
   (B) Sign a check.
   (C) Drive it right away.
   (D) Make an appointment.

READING

Part 5 Incomplete Sentences

Choose the word that best completes the sentence.

10. The constant road repair work made driving through the city _____.
    (A) confuse
    (B) confuses
    (C) confusion
    (D) confusing

11. I don't think it is a _____ that the special discount rate for renting a car expires right before the holiday weekend.
    (A) coincidental
    (B) coincidentally
    (C) coincidence
    (D) coincide

12. It was _____ to discover that the rental agency only had compact cars available, as we needed to rent a larger vehicle.
    (A) disappointing
    (B) confusing
    (C) tempting
    (D) thrilling

13. Our _____ is to rent a comfortable car and spend several weeks driving through the mountains.
    (A) intent
    (B) intently
    (C) intention
    (D) intend

14. Tito _____ drove the rental car through the crowded garage following the signs to the car rental return location.
    (A) nerve
    (B) nervousness
    (C) nervous
    (D) nervously

15. The new car rental company _____ me to try them by offering a discount coupon toward my next rental.
    (A) tempted
    (B) tempting
    (C) temptation
    (D) temptress

Part 6 Text Completion

> **Are you looking for a reliable rental car? Look no more.**
>
> **Riverton Rent-a-Car** offers the most reliable and economical rental cars in town.
>
> We _____ that you will find the car you want at **Riverton Rent-a-Car**. We have
>
> 16. (A) guarantees
>   (B) guarantee
>   (C) to guarantee
>   (D) guaranteeing
>
> several tiers of cars, from budget to luxury.
>
> Our rates start at $19.99 daily for a compact car, with several options available including two-door and four-door sedans and hatchbacks.
>
> Have you always wanted to experience the _____ of driving a luxury sports car?
>
> 17. (A) thrill
>   (B) thriller
>   (C) thrilled
>   (D) thrilling
>
> Live your dream by renting a sports car from **Riverton Rent-a-Car**. Daily and weekly rates are available. Contact us to find out more.
>
> *Rent a car from **Riverton Rent-a-Car**. You won't _____.*
>
> 18. (A) disappoint
>   (B) disappointed
>   (C) be disappointed
>   (D) are disappointed

Part 7 Reading Comprehension

Questions 19–23 refer to the following article.

Will your next trip involve a rental car? With a little careful planning, you can prevent some common headaches. If your travel plans coincide with a holiday, you need to plan well ahead of time. Car rental agencies are very busy at such times, and you won't be guaranteed a car unless you make your reservation well in advance. Contact the car rental agency and specify the kind of car you want and the dates you will need it. It's a good idea to call the agency again shortly before you begin your trip to confirm your reservation. This is the best way to avoid disappointment.

Another common problem that car renters face is extra charges. Some agencies add charges for options without letting the renter know about them. Sometimes renters aren't aware of this until they receive their credit card bill. Read the contract carefully before you sign it to make sure that you are paying only for what you requested. And don't be tempted to pay for things you don't need. It might be fun to drive a large, luxury car, but if you are traveling alone and are on a budget, it probably isn't worth paying for such a car.

19. Who is the audience for this article?
    (A) Car rental agents.
    (B) Travel agents.
    (C) Car renters.
    (D) Car owners.

20. What is a problem for holiday travelers?
    (A) Businesses are closed.
    (B) Rental agencies are very busy.
    (C) Rental rates go up.
    (D) People get headaches.

21. How can a car renter avoid paying extra charges?
    (A) Read the contract.
    (B) Confirm reservations.
    (C) Pay with a credit card.
    (D) Make a budget.

22. The word *disappointment* in the first paragraph, line 11, is closest in meaning to
    (A) expense
    (B) disagreement
    (C) cancellation
    (D) unhappiness

23. The word *requested* in the second paragraph, line 7, is closest in meaning to
    (A) tuned in
    (B) asked for
    (C) looked at
    (D) read about

Word Review #8   Lessons 36–40 Travel

Choose the word that best completes the sentence.

1. When _____ your luggage, be sure to check the name on the tag.
   (A) claim
   (B) claimed
   (C) claimant
   (D) claiming

2. The plane's _____ was delayed until the wings were defrosted.
   (A) depart
   (B) departed
   (C) departure
   (D) departing

3. Many airlines _____ courtesy discounts to senior citizens.
   (A) extend
   (B) extending
   (C) extension
   (D) extensive

4. It is easier to deal _____ making reservations if you are specific about your requirements.
   (A) in
   (B) from
   (C) out
   (D) with

5. Trains are generally more _____ than airlines.
   (A) punctuality
   (B) punctually
   (C) punctual
   (D) punctuate

6. Some travel agencies _____ on a very tight budget.
   (A) operating
   (B) operation
   (C) operates
   (D) operate

7. Even if you pay cash, you will have to show your credit card when you _____ to the hotel.
   (A) check in
   (B) fill out
   (C) pick up
   (D) pull out

8. Sometimes when you arrive, there is no room for you, even with a _____ reservation.
   (A) confirm
   (B) confirms
   (C) confirmed
   (D) confirmation

9. Without a reservation, renting a car could be a big _____.
   (A) disappoint
   (B) disappointed
   (C) disappointing
   (D) disappointment

10. No one will allow someone who doesn't have a _____ to rent a car.
    (A) licensed
    (B) license
    (C) licensing
    (D) licensee

Choose the one word or phrase that best completes each sentence.

DO YOU NEED TO _____? TRAINS ARE A GREAT WAY TO SAVE MONEY WHEN IT COMES TO

    11. (A) economy
        (B) economize
        (C) economist
        (D) economical

TRAVEL. TRAIN FARE COSTS CONSIDERABLY LESS THAN PLANE FARE IN MOST CASES. ON THE OTHER HAND, IF COMFORT IS MORE IMPORTANT TO YOU THAN SAVING MONEY, YOU WILL BE HAPPY TO KNOW THAT MOST TRAINS OFFER _____ ACCOMMODATIONS. WHEN YOU

    12. (A) deluxe
        (B) valid
        (C) remote
        (D) punctual

_____ YOUR TICKET, SIMPLY NOTIFY THE AGENT THAT YOU WANT A FIRST-CLASS SEAT.

13. (A) will reserve
    (B) reserving
    (C) reserved
    (D) reserve

To: Margaret Berdan
From: Spring Flower Hotel Management
Subject: Your reservation

Dear Ms. Berdan,

Thank you for making a reservation at the Spring Flower Hotel for the nights of May 11–14. We suggest that you call the hotel _____ your reservation 24 hours in advance. Payment in full is required at

    14. (A) confirm
        (B) confirming
        (C) to confirm
        (D) did confirm

the time you check _____, before we can give you your room key. Remember, your status as a

    15. (A) in
        (B) up
        (C) out
        (D) through

guest at the Spring Flower Hotel _____ you to unlimited use of the hotel fitness room and

    16. (A) entitle
        (B) entitles
        (C) entitled
        (D) is entitled

swimming pool. We look forward to seeing you.

Sincerely,

The Spring Flower Hotel Management Office

If you plan to pick up a rental car at the airport, it's best to reserve a car ahead of time. This is easy to do on the Internet or by phone. When you pick up your car, you will have to show a valid _____ that proves you have legal permission to drive. Read the contract carefully

17. (A) passport
    (B) ticket
    (C) itinerary
    (D) license

and make sure that the _____ it states is the same one you were originally quoted. You

18. (A) rate
    (B) route
    (C) riot
    (D) runt

don't want to have to pay more than you expected. Also remember that certain features, such as GPS navigation systems or DVD players, are optional. You must _____ them if you want them.

19. (A) recount
    (B) request
    (C) require
    (D) record

Lesson 41

Movies

WORDS TO LEARN

attainment

combine

continue

description

disperse

entertainment

influence

range

release

representation

separately

successive

Study the following definitions and examples.

1. **attainment** n., achievement
   a. The actress received a lot of attention for her many professional attainments.
   b. The attainment of an Academy Award validates a performer's career.

2. **combine** v., to come together
   a. The director combined two previously separate visual techniques.
   b. The new production company combines the talents of three of Hollywood's best known teams.

3. **continue** v., to maintain without interruption
   a. The film continues the story set out in an earlier film.
   b. The search for a star will continue until one is found.

4. **description** n., a representation in words or pictures
   a. The description of the film did not match what we saw on screen.
   b. The critic's description of the film made it sound very appealing.

5. **disperse** v., to spread widely, to scatter
   a. The reporters dispersed after the press agent cancelled the interview with the film director.
   b. The crowd outside the movie premiere would not disperse until they had seen the movie stars.

6. **entertainment** n., a diverting performance or activity
   a. The movie was provided for our entertainment.
   b. There was no entertainment for children of guests at the hotel.

7. **influence** v., to alter or affect
   a. The editor's style influenced a generation of film editors.
   b. The producer was able to influence the town council to allow her to film in the park.

8. **range** n., the scope
   a. The range of the director's vision is impressive.
   b. What is the price range you are willing to pay for a ticket to the premiere?

9. **release** v., to make available to the public; to give permission for performance
   a. The film was finally released to movie theaters after many delays.
   b. The producers of the film are hoping to release it in time for the holidays.

10. **representation** n., exemplification; symbolization
    a. The actor's representation of his character did not seem authentic.
    b. The film's representation of world poverty through the character of the hungry child was quite moving.

11. **separately** adv., apart
    a. Each scene of the movie was filmed separately from the others.
    b. The theater was very crowded so we had to sit separately.

12. **successive** adj., following in order
    a. The script went through successive rewrites.
    b. Somehow the successive images were interrupted and had to be edited again.

WORD FAMILIES

verb	attain	The film quickly attained a reputation as a "must-see" movie.
noun	attainment	The technical attainments in the movie's special effects were impressive.
adjective	attainable	The director's goal of having an unlimited budget was not attainable.

verb	continue	Continue giving out movie passes until I tell you to stop.
noun	continuation	The continuation of the film will be shown after the intermission.
adjective	continual	The actors' continual demands slowed down the pace of production.

verb	describe	Please describe the new movie theater to me.
noun	description	The description of Africa in the film was not as I remembered it.
adjective	descriptive	The writer's descriptive account of the war is shocking and saddening.

verb	entertain	The comedian worked hard to entertain the children in the hospital.
noun	entertainment	Movies are one of the most popular forms of entertainment.
adjective	entertaining	The light comedy was entertaining, if not memorable.

verb	represent	The actor represented the ideals of the culture.
noun	representation	We felt that the movie's representation of the effects of war was very realistic.
noun	representative	The actress couldn't attend the awards ceremony so she had a representative accept the award for her.

verb	separate	Some movie fans can't separate fantasy from reality and confuse an actor with the character he plays.
adjective	separate	Moviemaking combines several separate processes.
adverb	separately	The actors rehearsed their lines separately before filming the scene together.

WORDS IN CONTEXT

Read the following passage and write the words in the blanks below.

attain	descriptions	influence	represent
combines	disperse	range	separate
continues	entertaining	released	successive

The popularity of the movies began early in the 20th century and (1) _____ today. People of all ages find movies (2) _____. Movies are a worldwide phenomenon, as the internationalism of movie distribution has helped to (3) _____ ideas around the globe. One movie can quickly (4) _____ other movies. But why are movies so popular?

Movies are a kind of storytelling. They try to describe an idea or record an observation about our culture. These (5) _____ are recorded using moving visual images. Some movies portray the situation accurately and realistically, whereas other movies find visual symbols to (6) _____ those situations.

On the most simple level, movies are a succession of moving images. These (7) _____ images are captured on film. Directors film a wide (8) _____ of shots—long, medium, and close up—to create a visual composition. The visual images, along with plot, characterization, and sound, produce the desired narrative. The shots are joined together in any number of combinations in a process called editing.

Making a film is a massive, complex, and expensive task that (9) _____ art and business. It involves the talents of hundreds, and sometimes thousands, of artists, producers, and business people. It can take months, even years, for a film to be (10) _____ into a movie theater.

Like a novel, a movie is not just a story, but a story told a certain way. A film director may want to make a movie that tells a meaningful story or one that is primarily entertaining, and will use different filming techniques to (11) _____ that goal. It is impossible to (12) _____ what is told in a movie from how it is told. A director's artistic vision can range from improvised to carefully controlled. Think about the complexity of a movie the next time you see one.

WORD PRACTICE

LISTENING COMPREHENSION

TRACK
42

Part 1 Photo

Look at the picture and listen to the sentences.
Choose the sentence that best describes the picture.

1. Ⓐ Ⓑ Ⓒ Ⓓ

Part 2 Question–Response

Listen to the question and the three responses. Choose the response that best answers the question.

2. Ⓐ Ⓑ Ⓒ   3. Ⓐ Ⓑ Ⓒ

Part 3 Conversation

Listen to the dialogue. Then read each question and choose the best answer.

4. What are the speakers discussing?
   (A) The lighting in the theater.
   (B) The price of entertainment.
   (C) Shows on television.
   (D) An actor's acting style.

5. What type of movie does the woman prefer?
   (A) Comedy.
   (B) Drama.
   (C) Mystery.
   (D) Documentary.

6. How many movies has the actor made this year?
   (A) One.
   (B) Two.
   (C) Three.
   (D) Ten.

Part 4 Talk

Listen to the talk. Then read each question and choose the best answer.

7. Who is Ms. Moreno?
   (A) A director.
   (B) An actress.
   (C) A movie producer.
   (D) A movie reviewer.

8. What will Ms. Moreno do next week?
   (A) She will attend a performance.
   (B) She will start a trip around the world.
   (C) She will be interviewed.
   (D) She will start a new career.

9. When will the movie be released?
   (A) Next month.
   (B) In several weeks.
   (C) Next year.
   (D) In several years.

READING

Part 5 Incomplete Sentences

Choose the word that best completes the sentence.

10. Do you think this actor will _____ the heights of his famous father?
    (A) attain
    (B) attaining
    (C) attainable
    (D) attainment

11. A sequel is a _____ of a story set in motion by a previous film.
    (A) range
    (B) release
    (C) continuation
    (D) combination

12. Each director has a uniquely _____ style of storytelling.
    (A) descriptive
    (B) describe
    (C) description
    (D) descriptively

13. _____ is one of the fastest growing sectors of the economy.
    (A) Entertained
    (B) Entertainment
    (C) Entertain
    (D) Entertainingly

14. We were impressed by the director's _____ of the conflict between good and evil.
    (A) representative
    (B) represented
    (C) represents
    (D) representation

15. The actors left the hotel _____ in order to avoid attracting a lot of attention.
    (A) separate
    (B) separately
    (C) separation
    (D) separating

Part 6 Text Completion

The Silver Screen Movie House is a new entertainment option in the downtown area. The Silver Screen is not your typical movie house. It combines a movie theater with a coffeehouse, so that patrons can relax with coffee and snacks while they enjoy the show. In addition to a menu of delicious homemade sandwiches and tempting pastries, the Silver Screen offers a _____ of movies to suit all tastes. Everything from comedy to drama to action is on their schedule. Prices are

16. (A) ridge
    (B) rage
    (C) rouge
    (D) range

reasonable, and frequent customers can take advantage of the ticket special. A booklet of five tickets for the price of four is available, or individual tickets can be bought _____ for each show. The place tends to fill up for the evening

17. (A) separate
    (B) separator
    (C) separately
    (D) separation

show, but if you like quiet, you can stay later. The crowds _____ when the last movie is over, but the café stays open

18. (A) remain
    (B) settle
    (C) converge
    (D) disperse

until 1:00 A.M., so night owls can enjoy a quiet cup of coffee into the wee hours. We predict that the Silver Screen will soon attain the status of one of the most popular entertainment venues in the city.

Part 7 Reading Comprehension

Questions 19–23 refer to the following movie review and e-mail message.

The newly released romantic comedy, *West Wind*, opens this week at the State Street Cinema. The combination of a great script with superb acting talent results in a movie that you won't soon forget. The show is entertaining from start to finish, and you'll still be laughing when you leave the theater. If you've been bored to tears by movies recently, don't give up on the cinema yet. Give *West Wind* a try. You're sure to love it.

West Wind continues at the State Street Cinema through next week with shows at 5:15, 7:00, and 9:15 nightly.

To: Madeline Wrightwood
From: Dan Green
Subject: Let's go to the movies

Hi Maddy,

Have you seen the reviews of *West Wind*? I think it's a movie worth seeing. I don't usually go for romances, but you know how I love comedies, and the description of this one sounds really good. There's also an action movie playing next door, but I know you don't like that kind of movie, and I don't really, either.

I can't leave work before 5:15, so we should go to the second show. I'd like to invite you to have dinner afterward. I can make reservations at that restaurant you like for 9:00. We should make it there by then easily. Since we'll each be coming from work, we'll have to arrive at the theater separately. If you get there first, would you mind getting the tickets? Thanks. See you tonight.

Dan

19. What is the reviewer's opinion of the movie?
(A) It's sad.
(B) It's boring.
(C) It's funny.
(D) It's forgettable.

20. What kind of movie does Dan like?
(A) Action.
(B) Comedy.
(C) Romance.
(D) Drama.

21. What time does Dan want to go to the movies?
(A) 5:15.
(B) 7:00.
(C) 9:00.
(D) 9:15.

22. The word *entertaining* in line 5 of the movie review is closest in meaning to
(A) enjoyable
(B) educational
(C) lengthy
(D) describing

23. The word *separately* in the e-mail, second paragraph, line 7, is closest in meaning to
(A) connected
(B) jointly
(C) slowly
(D) alone

Lesson
42

Theater

WORDS TO LEARN
action
approach
audience
creative
dialogue
element
experience
occur
perform
rehearse
review
sell out

Study the following definitions and examples.

1. **action** n., the series of events that form the plot of a story or play
   a. The director decided that the second act needed more action and asked the playwright to review the work.
   b. The action on stage was spellbinding.

2. **approach** v., to go near; to move toward
   a. The performance approaches perfection.
   b. The director approached the play from an unusual angle.

3. **audience** n., the spectators at a performance
   a. The audience cheered the actors as they walked off the stage.
   b. The playwright expanded his audience by writing for film as well as for stage.

4. **creative** adj., imaginative or artistic
   a. The writer's creative representation of the Seven Deadly Sins was astounding.
   b. There are a number of creative people writing for the theater these days.

5. **dialogue** n., a conversation between two or more persons
   a. The actors performed the dialogue without using scripts.
   b. The written dialogue seemed great, but was hard to perform.

6. **element** n., fundamental or essential constituent
   a. The audience is an essential element of live theater.
   b. By putting together all the elements of theater into one play, he overwhelmed the critics.

7. **experience** n., an event or a series of events participated in or lived through
   a. The experience of live theater is very thrilling.
   b. Going to the theater was not part of Claude's experience growing up.

8. **occur** v., to take place; to come about
   a. The murder in the play occurs in the second act.
   b. It never occurred to me that the wife whom the character referred to was imaginary.

9. **perform** v., to act before an audience, to give a public presentation of
   a. The theater group performed a three-act play.
   b. Juan performed the role without forgetting any lines.

10. **rehearse** v., to practice in preparation for a public performance; to direct in rehearsal
   a. The players rehearsed for only three weeks before the show opened.
   b. The director rehearses with the actors ten hours each day.

11. **review** n., a critical estimate of a work or performance; v., writing a criticism of a performance
   a. The critic's influential review of the play was so negative that it sank the entire production.
   b. The newspaper sent a rank amateur to review the play.

12. **sell out** v., to sell all the tickets
   a. The Broadway opening sold out months in advance.
   b. We expect that this play will be a smash and sell out quickly.

WORD FAMILIES

verb	act	Roger's dream is to act in a Broadway play.
noun	action	There isn't much action in the play, but it is captivating nonetheless.
noun	actor	There are quite a few well-known actors in the cast.

verb	approach	The actress approached me with the idea for a new play.
noun	approach	The informal approach to the play was unconventional.
adjective	approachable	Despite his great fame, the director was friendly and approachable.

verb	create	The playwright created a realistic town and townspeople with the scenery and dialogue.
noun	creation	The creation of the elaborate costumes took months.
adjective	creative	The director is one of the most creative people I know.

verb	experience	The actor experienced great self-doubt before he became famous.
noun	experience	Directors bring their experience of the world onto the stage.
adjective	experienced	The experienced make-up artist transformed Maxine into an old woman in a matter of minutes.

verb	perform	The popular actress was hired to perform Shakespeare on a world tour.
noun	performance	I booked tickets for the performance the day they went on sale.
noun	performer	The performers each had three costume changes.

verb	rehearse	The cast had to rehearse the scene over and over again until the director was finally satisfied.
noun	rehearsal	The actors spent several months in rehearsal before they performed the play.
adjective	rehearsed	Lydia's acceptance speech for her award sounded more rehearsed than natural.

WORDS IN CONTEXT

Read the following passage and write the words in the blanks below.

action	created	experiences	rehearsal
approach	dialogue	occurs	reviews
audience	elements	performance	sell out

Many people find nothing as exciting as an evening of live theater. The theater combines great works of literature written for the stage, the talents of great actors, and the efforts of hundreds of skilled artisans who work to create a mood. This mood, (1) _____ by the actors, director, and playwright with the supporting (2) _____ of sets, lighting, and costumes, is what makes a theatrical (3) _____ magical. When the curtain goes up, this magic (4) _____ right before your eyes.

The director of a play will (5) _____ the work from his or her own artistic perspective. Each director has a different vision and this shapes how he or she directs the movement or (6) _____ between the characters. Directors use not only their theatrical training, but real-life experiences to create a meaningful, realistic evening. Actors also bring their own artistic and personal (7) _____ to their work. This is why every staging of a play is unique.

Plays construct another world before your eyes. Ordinary words turn into meaningful (8) _____. Costumes and sets can be realistic or symbolic. Everything in a play looks easy, but it takes many weeks of (9) _____ to get everything in place.

Watching a play from the (10) _____ is great fun. To find out if a play is good, read (11) _____ or ask friends for their opinions. When plays are really popular, the available seats can fill up quickly and the play will (12) _____.

WORD PRACTICE

LISTENING COMPREHENSION

TRACK
43

Part 1 Photo

Look at the picture and listen to the sentences.
Choose the sentence that best describes the picture.

1. Ⓐ Ⓑ Ⓒ Ⓓ

Part 2 Question–Response

Listen to the question and the three responses. Choose the response that best answers the question.

2. Ⓐ Ⓑ Ⓒ   3. Ⓐ Ⓑ Ⓒ

Part 3 Conversation

Listen to the dialogue. Then read each question and choose the best answer.

4. When did the review appear in the newspaper?
   (A) Today.
   (B) Yesterday.
   (C) Four weeks ago.
   (D) Five weeks ago.

5. What does the woman say about the play?
   (A) She has heard that it is funny.
   (B) Tickets are still on sale.
   (C) It got a bad review.
   (D) The dialogue is hard to understand.

6. What did the woman do last Friday?
   (A) She wrote a review.
   (B) She won a prize.
   (C) She saw a performance.
   (D) She bought tickets.

Part 4 Talk

Listen to the talk. Then read each question and choose the best answer.

7. When can a performance of *Romeo and Juliet* be seen?
   (A) Today.
   (B) On Thursday afternoon.
   (C) On Sunday morning.
   (D) On Thursday evening.

8. How can you get tickets to the play?
   (A) Call the Shakespeare Organization.
   (B) Call 656-9025.
   (C) Write to the theater.
   (D) Order them by e-mail.

9. Where can reviews of the play be read?
   (A) In a newspaper.
   (B) On a website.
   (C) In a magazine.
   (D) At the theater.

READING

Part 5 Incomplete Sentences

Choose the word that best completes the sentence.

10. The director's creativity showed in everything from her _____ to the literary quality of the play to the costumes and sets.
    (A) approaching   (C) approachable
    (B) approach   (D) approachability

11. Edward is a very talented _____ although he can't sing or dance well at all.
    (A) actor   (C) action
    (B) acts   (D) acting

12. As your director, I call upon you to bring your life _____ into your role.
    (A) experienced   (C) experiential
    (B) experiencing   (D) experience

13. I am not _____ enough to work in the theater, but I certainly enjoy attending it.
    (A) create   (C) creative
    (B) creativeness (D) creativity

14. I look forward to the annual _____ of *The Nutcracker* ballet.
    (A) performance   (C) perform
    (B) performer   (D) performable

15. There isn't much time left to _____ before the play opens.
    (A) rehearsals   (C) rehearsing
    (B) rehearse   (D) rehearsed

Part 6 Text Completion

To: Jack Sprague
From: Sabrina Clark
Subject: Play

Hi Jack,

I just saw that play that opened recently at the City Theater. You really ought to see it, too. I know you would enjoy the experience. The play combines _____ from both comedy and drama, so it's funny, but it

16. (A) elements
    (B) elemental
    (C) elementally
    (D) elementary

also has an important message. Some people say this play is boring because there isn't a lot of action, but I think the _____ is very creative. The actors say some really funny lines. The whole performance is

17. (A) analogue
    (B) prologue
    (C) dialogue
    (D) catalogue

superb; you can tell that the actors rehearsed a long time before the play opened. You should call the theater today to get a ticket because they will probably sell _____ soon. Let me know how you like the play.

18. (A) up
    (B) out
    (C) from
    (D) down

Sabrina

Part 7 Reading Comprehension

Questions 19–23 refer to the following theater review.

> Audiences have waited a long time for the opening of the play *Dusk to Dawn* at the City Theater. Unfortunately, the long wait only adds to the disappointment of seeing a mediocre play. It is an uncomfortable experience from start to finish. The action is slow and the dialogue boring. The performance by most of the cast is awkward and, on the night I attended at least, many of the actors forgot their lines. They obviously did not rehearse enough before opening night. The plot is trite. Theatergoers had been told to expect a fresh approach to the age-old boy-meets-girl romance story. Instead, we get a story that is dull enough to drive one to tears. Although the play is relatively short—under two hours—the performance is so tedious it seems to drag on for three or four hours. The audience made an audible sigh of relief when the final curtain dropped. Rather than the predicted sold out performances, I expect that the play will close very shortly. Unfortunately, the producers invested a lot of money in this play, which they are not likely to get back. My advice to would-be theatergoers: spend the weekend at the movies instead.

19. What is the reviewer's opinion of the play?
    (A) It's very sad.
    (B) It's boring.
    (C) It's too short.
    (D) It's romantic.

20. How long is the play?
    (A) Less than two hours.
    (B) Exactly two hours.
    (C) Three hours.
    (D) Four hours.

21. What does the reviewer predict about the play?
    (A) The performances will be sold out.
    (B) The producers will make a lot of money.
    (C) The play will be made into a movie.
    (D) The play will close in a short time.

22. The word *experience* in line 4 is closest in meaning to
    (A) act
    (B) wait
    (C) event
    (D) seat

23. The word *rehearse* in line 8 is closest in meaning to
    (A) plan
    (B) sleep
    (C) memorize
    (D) practice

Lesson

43

Music

Study the following definitions and examples.

1. **available** adj., ready for use; willing to serve
   a. In order to understand all the words to the opera, Sue Lin kept an Italian dictionary available at all times.
   b. The website has an amazing variety of music available for downloading.

2. **broaden** v., to make wider
   a. Dominique wants to broaden her knowledge of opera history.
   b. You will appreciate music more if you broaden your tastes and listen to several types of music.

3. **category** n., a division in a system of classification; a general class of ideas
   a. Jazz is one of many categories of music.
   b. The works of Mozart are in a category by themselves.

4. **disparate** adj., fundamentally distinct or different
   a. In the song, the disparate voices hauntingly join a blended chorus.
   b. Religious songs cut across disparate categories of music.

5. **divide** v., to separate into parts
   a. The music class was evenly divided between those who liked country and western music and those who did not.
   b. The broad topic of music can be divided into manageable parts, such as themes, styles, or centuries.

6. **favor** v., to be partial to
   a. Sam enjoys the works of several composers but he tends to favor Mozart.
   b. I'd favor an evening at a jazz concert over an evening at the opera any time.

7. **instinct** n., an inborn pattern that is a powerful motivation
   a. The student's ability to play the cello was so natural, it seemed an instinct.
   b. The music lover followed his instincts and collected only music that he enjoyed.

8. **lively** adj., full of energy
   a. Some people enjoy lively music, whereas others tend to prefer slower types of music.
   b. The lively dance was fun but very tiring.

9. **reason** n., the basis or motive for an action; an underlying fact or cause
   a. We'll never understand the reason why some music is popular and some is not.
   b. There is every reason to believe that Beethoven will still be popular in the next century.

10. **relaxation** n., the act of relaxing or the state of being relaxed; refreshment of body or mind
    a. Listening to soothing music before bedtime provides good relaxation.
    b. He played the piano for relaxation and pleasure.

11. **taste** n., the ability to discern what is excellent or appropriate
    a. Ella had the taste required to select a musical program for the visiting dignitaries.
    b. This music does not appeal to my tastes; but I'm old-fashioned.

12. **urge** v., to advocate earnestly
    a. His mother urged him to study the piano; the rest is musical history.
    b. Despite my reluctance, my friends urged me to attend an opera.

WORD FAMILIES

verb	broaden	Connie has a huge variety of music on her iPod because she is trying to broaden her musical tastes.
adjective	broad	We'll cover a broad range of music in the music appreciation class.
adverb	broadly	The orchestra director travels broadly in search of new musical talent.

verb	categorize	Some singers have a broad range of styles and are difficult to categorize.
noun	category	Most of the music Sam listens to falls into the category of classical music.
adjective	categorical	The sheet music follows the categorical system used in most libraries.

verb	divide	Louise can divide her musical tastes into two broad categories: rock and jazz.
noun	division	There are a lot of different styles of rock music, but the divisions between them aren't always distinct.
noun	divider	The room divider didn't effectively block sound and we could clearly hear the piano students as they practiced.

verb	favor	The music critic clearly favors some musicians over others.
adjective	favorite	The teenager had an extensive collection of music by all her favorite groups.
adjective	favorable	The favorable reviews of the group's new album helped to push the album up the sales charts.

verb	relax	After a long concert tour, the singer liked to relax by the pool.
noun	relaxation	Listening to music is an enduring form of relaxation.
adjective	relaxing	There is nothing more relaxing than listening to music.

verb	urge	My music teacher urged me not to give up the violin even though I was having such a hard time with it.
noun	urge	Richard gets the urge to play the guitar every time he passes a music store window.
adjective	urgent	It's urgent to order those concert tickets as soon as possible because they will sell out quickly.

WORDS IN CONTEXT

Read the following passage and write the words in the blanks below.

available	disparate	instinctive	relax
broad	divided	lively	taste
category	favorite	reason	urge

Everyone loves music, it seems. And there's little (1) _____ to wonder why. There is so much music (2) _____ from which to choose, and there is a (3) _____ of music to appeal to every (4) _____. The major groups of music are (5) _____ broadly into classical, popular, and jazz. Within these (6) _____ groups are many other subcategories. For example, such (7) _____ types of music as movie sound tracks, rhythm and blues, rock, and rap all fit within the category of popular music.

The (8) _____ to make and enjoy music may be (9) _____. Even small children enjoy music. Since they tend to be active, children often prefer (10) _____ music that they can move and dance to.

Another reason that music is so popular is the variety of settings in which one can enjoy his or her (11) _____ kind of music. You can go to a church to hear great religious music, or to a concert hall to hear a well-known classical symphony. On another night, you might go to a small club to listen to an up-and-coming jazz group while you enjoy a drink. A few nights later, you might go with some friends to join thousands of other people in a stadium to hear your favorite rock band play in your city on a world tour. And, back at your house or apartment, you can (12) _____ while listening to your favorite artists on your MP3 player.

WORD PRACTICE

LISTENING COMPREHENSION

Part 1 Photo

Look at the picture and listen to the sentences.
Choose the sentence that best describes the picture.

1. Ⓐ Ⓑ Ⓒ Ⓓ

Part 2 Question–Response

Listen to the question and the three responses. Choose the response that best answers the question.

2. Ⓐ Ⓑ Ⓒ   3. Ⓐ Ⓑ Ⓒ

Part 3 Conversation

Listen to the dialogue. Then read each question and choose the best answer.

4. What does the man say about the website that the woman recommended?
   (A) It matches his taste.
   (B) It is boring.
   (C) It has good music.
   (D) It is interesting.

5. Why is the man looking for music?
   (A) For relaxation.
   (B) For a music class.
   (C) For a dance party.
   (D) For a present.

6. What does the woman suggest that the man do?
   (A) Ask another friend for help.
   (B) Go to a store.
   (C) Read a book.
   (D) Change his musical tastes.

Part 4 Talk

Listen to the talk. Then read each question and choose the best answer.

7. What is the class about?
   (A) The history of music.
   (B) Playing musical instruments.
   (C) Music appreciation.
   (D) Reading music.

8. What does the speaker urge the listeners to do?
   (A) Buy the text right away.
   (B) Try a musical instrument.
   (C) Take a test.
   (D) Start listening to music every day.

9. How much will students pay for concert tickets?
   (A) $3.
   (B) $13.
   (C) $25.
   (D) $30.

READING

Part 5 Incomplete Sentences

Choose the word that best completes the sentence.

10. My friends have urged me to _____ my tastes to include more classical music.
    (A) divide
    (B) favor
    (C) broaden
    (D) categorize

11. I don't know how to _____ my taste in music.
    (A) categorize
    (B) categories
    (C) categorical
    (D) categorically

12. The string quartet received a _____ comparison to the best of the genre.
    (A) favor
    (B) favoritism
    (C) favorably
    (D) favorable

13. The piano teacher _____ his classes into beginning, intermediate, and advanced levels.
    (A) divide
    (B) divides
    (C) have divided
    (D) are dividing

14. After a hard day at work, we like to _____ to soothing music.
    (A) relaxation
    (B) relaxes
    (C) relaxing
    (D) relax

15. Sometimes I get an _____ to learn how to play a musical instrument.
    (A) urgent
    (B) urge
    (C) urges
    (D) urgently

Part 6 Text Completion

Music Library User's Guide

These days, it's easy to hear the music you like, anytime you want. Almost any piece of music you can think of is _____ online. You can download an entire album of songs

    16. (A) avowal
        (B) avuncular
        (C) available
        (D) avoidable

or choose just the songs that you like. With all the music that you _____ stored in your

    17. (A) favoring
        (B) favored
        (C) favors
        (D) favor

MP3 player, you can take it with you everywhere. Then you can choose to listen to the music that suits your mood. Whether you feel like listening to _____ songs, romantic music,

    18. (A) lively
        (B) liven
        (C) livelier
        (D) liveliness

or feel the urge to dance, you have the music that you want right there at your fingertips.

Part 7 Reading Comprehension

Questions 19–23 refer to the following review and e-mail message.

We were fortunate to have internationally acclaimed violinist Maria Rogoff play at Symphony Hall last Saturday night. Ms. Rogoff appears to have been born with a musical instinct. She played her violin quite naturally, as if it were an old friend. The selection of pieces she played was superb. She favored lively, interesting pieces that kept the audience enthralled during the entire performance. All in all, it was a thoroughly enjoyable and relaxing evening. Music lovers everywhere are urged to hear Ms. Rogoff play anytime there is an opportunity.

To: Polly Andrews
From: Gus Hall
Subject: Concert

Hi Polly,

Did you see the review of Maria Rogoff's concert in the Sunday paper? Can you believe they gave her such a good review? I didn't agree at all with what the reviewer said about her selection of pieces. In fact, I thought quite the opposite. And she made several mistakes in her playing. Did you notice? Oh, well. I prefer cello music anyhow. It is much more to my taste. Maybe that's the real reason I didn't enjoy the concert. By the way, there is another concert this Friday. A pianist will be playing at Symphony Hall. Do you want to go? I am pretty sure there are still tickets available. I think there is a performance on Thursday, too, but I have a meeting that night. Let me know if you can make it, and I'll order the tickets.

Gus

19. When was Maria Rogoff's concert?
    (A) Thursday.
    (B) Friday.
    (C) Saturday.
    (D) Sunday.

20. What is Gus's opinion of the music at the concert?
    (A) It was lively.
    (B) It was boring.
    (C) It was relaxing.
    (D) It was enthralling.

21. What instrument does Gus prefer?
    (A) Viola.
    (B) Cello.
    (C) Violin.
    (D) Piano.

22. The word *instinct* in line 5 of the review is closest in meaning to
    (A) preference
    (B) knowledge
    (C) parentage
    (D) nature

23. The word *relaxing* in lines 10–11 of the review is closest in meaning to
    (A) fun
    (B) exciting
    (C) peaceful
    (D) educational

Lesson 44

Museums

WORDS TO LEARN

acquire

admire

collection

criticism

express

fashion

leisure

respond

schedule

significant

specialize

spectrum

Study the following definitions and examples.

1. **acquire** v., to gain possession of; to get by one's own efforts
    a. The museum acquired a van Gogh during heavy bidding.
    b. The sculptor acquired metalworking skills after much practice.

2. **admire** v., to regard with pleasure; to have esteem or respect for
    a. Raisa, admiring the famous smile, stood before the Mona Lisa for hours.
    b. I admire all the effort the museum put into organizing this wonderful exhibit.

3. **collection** n., a group of objects or works to be seen, studied, or kept together
    a. The museum's collection contained many works donated by famous collectors.
    b. The museum's collection kept two full-time curators busy.

4. **criticism** n., an evaluation, especially of literary or other artistic works
    a. According to the criticism of the Victorian era, the painting was a masterpiece; now it is considered merely a minor work.
    b. The revered artist's criticism of the piece was particularly insightful.

5. **express** v., to give an opinion or depict emotion
    a. The sculptor was able to express his feelings better through the use of clay rather than words.
    b. The photograph expresses a range of emotions.

6. **fashion** n., the prevailing style or custom
    a. According to the fashion of the day, the languid pose of the sculpture was high art.
    b. The museum's classical architecture has never gone out of fashion.

7. **leisure** n., freedom from time-consuming duties; free time
    a. The woman took up painting in her retirement, when she had more time for leisure.
    b. Spending a day at an art museum is a form of leisure that many people enjoy.

8. **respond** v., to make a reply; to react
    a. You should respond to the invitation to attend the museum gala.
    b. The visitors who viewed those poignant photographs responded emotionally.

9. **schedule** v., to enter in a planner or diary
    a. We didn't schedule enough time to see all the exhibits that we were interested in.
    b. The museum is scheduling a collection of works by Japanese masters.

10. **significant** adj., meaningful; having a major effect; important
    a. The use of lambs to symbolize innocence is significant in Western art.
    b. The rash of new acquisitions represented a significant change in the museum's policies.

11. **specialize** v., to concentrate on a particular activity
    a. The art historian specialized in Navajo rugs.
    b. The museum shop specializes in Ming vases.

12. **spectrum** n., a range of related qualities, ideas, or activities
    a. The painting crosses the spectrum from symbolic to realistic representation.
    b. The whole spectrum of artistic expression was represented in the exhibit.

WORD FAMILIES

verb	admire	People from all around the world visit the museum to admire the great works of art on display.
noun	admiration	I have great admiration for anyone who can create art.
adjective	admired	Monet is one of the most admired artists of the Impressionist movement.

verb	collect	The enthusiast began to collect Shaker furniture in the 1960s.
noun	collection	The collection at the museum is small, but it includes several significant pieces.
noun	collector	The avid collector spent weekends at estate sales looking for rare art objects.

verb	criticize	The sculptor was criticized for his lack of perspective.
noun	critic	The art critic gave the show a poor review, which saddened the exhibition team.
noun	criticism	The writer's elegant essays on the use of light in Flemish painting were landmarks in art criticism.

verb	respond	When Mr. Hon did not respond to the invitation to the opening, we assumed he was not able to attend.
noun	response	The response to the request for assistance was overwhelming.
adjective	responsive	The director was not responsive to any of the staff's suggestions, which made them both annoyed and anxious.

verb	schedule	The museum has scheduled a lecture series to accompany the special exhibit.
noun	schedule	Several local artists are featured on the gallery's winter schedule.
adjective	scheduled	There are several scheduled events at the museum this weekend.

verb	specialize	The art student decided to specialize in French and English paintings of the 1860s.
noun	specialist	The curator is a specialist in native Caribbean art.
adjective	specialized	The museum hired specialized personnel to adjust the humidity and light for the display of ancient books.

WORDS IN CONTEXT

Read the following passage and write the words in the blanks below.

acquire	criticism	leisure	significant
admire	expressing	responded	specialize
collected	fashion	schedule	spectrum

Museums are places to view and (1) _____ the great works of art. All large cities, and even many small cities, have good art museums in which you will find a wide (2) _____ of paintings, sculptures, drawings, and prints.

Museums attempt to collect and display a broad range of examples of how, throughout time, men and women have (3) _____ to what they have seen, thought, and felt by (4) _____ themselves through materials like stone, clay, and paint, or ink and paper. The artist imposes an order on these materials that is (5) _____. Some styles of art or particular objects are in (6) _____ for only a while, and others earn positive (7) _____ over time and are seen as enduring classics. Museums collect the best of these works for the public to see.

When you go to a museum, be sure to (8) _____ plenty of time to see the art without feeling rushed. If you are lucky enough to live near a museum, you can come back again at your (9) _____. Some museums show a broad collection of art from different times and cultures, often (10) _____ and donated by their generous patrons. Other museums (11) _____ in displaying art from a certain period, say from the ancient world, or by a certain group or nationality of people, such as Native Americans.

The operations of many museums are paid for by the government, and these museums are often free to the public; other museums must charge each person upon entry. These fees help the museum operate and (12) _____ more works.

WORD PRACTICE

LISTENING COMPREHENSION

Part 1 Photo

Look at the picture and listen to the sentences.
Choose the sentence that best describes the picture.

1. Ⓐ Ⓑ Ⓒ Ⓓ

Part 2 Question–Response

Listen to the question and the three responses. Choose the response that best answers the question.

2. Ⓐ Ⓑ Ⓒ   3. Ⓐ Ⓑ Ⓒ

Part 3 Conversation

Listen to the dialogue. Then read each question and choose the best answer.

4. What are the speakers discussing?
   (A) A drawing.
   (B) A sculpture.
   (C) A painting.
   (D) A photograph.

5. What does the man like about it?
   (A) The size.
   (B) The color.
   (C) The style.
   (D) The subject.

6. What does the woman say about the museum?
   (A) The admission fee is too expensive.
   (B) They should acquire more works.
   (C) It's not very interesting.
   (D) The collection is varied.

Part 4 Talk

Listen to the talk. Then read each question and choose the best answer.

7. When does the lecture series at the museum begin?
   (A) Next month.
   (B) Next week.
   (C) This month.
   (D) This week.

8. How can you find out the schedule of guided tours?
   (A) Visit the main gallery.
   (B) Press two.
   (C) Go online.
   (D) Speak with an operator.

9. What is the topic of the print exhibit?
   (A) Fashion.
   (B) Sculpture.
   (C) African art.
   (D) Nineteenth-century art.

READING

Part 5 Incomplete Sentences

Choose the word that best completes the sentence.

10. The museum was lucky to be given a collection of works by such an _____ artist.
    (A) admiration
    (B) admire
    (C) admired
    (D) admires

11. Mimi owns some beautiful pottery and is always looking for new pieces to add to her _____.
    (A) leisure
    (B) spectrum
    (C) collection .
    (D) schedule

12. The curator's _____ of the museum's fund-raising plan seemed shortsighted.
    (A) criticism
    (B) critic
    (C) critical
    (D) criticize

13. We have been asked to _____ to the proposal by the end of the month.
    (A) responsive
    (B) response
    (C) respond
    (D) responding

14. The museum offers a _____ of guided tours.
    (A) schedules
    (B) scheduled
    (C) scheduling
    (D) schedule

15. After becoming a _____ in Egyptian tomb painting, the art historian lost her interest in other kinds of art.
    (A) specialize
    (B) specialist
    (C) specially
    (D) special

Part 6 Text Completion

Thank you for visiting the Museum of History. This brochure has been developed to provide you with information to make your visit more enjoyable.

Viewing the Exhibits

Our main exhibits are located on the first and second floors of the museum. They cover all aspects of local history up to the present and are organized in chronological order. You are invited to join one of our regular guided tours at no extra charge, or you can visit the exhibits on your own and view them at your _____.

16. (A) lesion
    (B) legion
    (C) ledger
    (D) leisure

Group Tours

School groups and other groups that wish to visit the museum may _____ special group tours.

17. (A) schedule
    (B) scheduling
    (C) to schedule
    (D) have schedule

Please contact the Museum Tour Office for more information.

Museum Bookstore

The Museum Bookstore is located on the first floor next to the cafeteria. This store specializes in books about local history. Gift items are also for sale. In _____ to the requests of many of our visitors, the

18. (A) responsible
    (B) responsive
    (C) response
    (D) respond

bookstore hours have been extended. It is now open daily from 10:00 A.M. until 6:00 P.M.

Part 7 Reading Comprehension

Questions 19–23 refer to the following brochure.

Most visitors to our city spend time visiting some of the many museums that we are famous for. The City Art Museum, Museum of History, National University Museum of Scientific Research, and the Hall of Presidents are among the most popular destinations for museumgoers. The National Transportation Museum, currently undergoing renovations, is scheduled to reopen next year with a larger number of exhibits and extended hours.

Visitors to the City Art Museum can admire the collection of paintings by local artists as well as famous works of art from around the world. The museum's collection covers a wide spectrum of artists and styles, and critics have called it one of the most significant in the world. Art classes offered at the museum provide both the serious and the casual student of art with opportunities to explore the world of artistic expression. The Museum of History features rotating exhibits focusing on various aspects of our nation's history, and a permanent collection of portraits of our nation's presidents. This summer's special exhibit focuses on the history of fashion. The National University Museum of Scientific Research specializes in exhibits on research undertaken at the university. It also features a special hands-on exhibit for children.

All museums have the same entrance price: $10 for adults and $5 for children. A special $35 weekly pass, available at any museum, allows the holder entrance to all city museums for a week. This pass is especially recommended to visitors from out of town as it provides the opportunity to visit all the museums at their leisure.

19. Who is this brochure for?
    (A) Museum employees.
    (B) Historians.
    (C) Students.
    (D) Tourists.

20. Where can portraits of presidents be seen?
    (A) City Art Museum.
    (B) Museum of History.
    (C) National University Museum.
    (D) Hall of Presidents.

21. What is the price of a one-day museum ticket for an adult?
    (A) $3.50.
    (B) $5.
    (C) $10.
    (D) $35.

22. The word *admire* in the second paragraph, line 1, is closest in meaning to
    (A) look at
    (B) look to
    (C) look up
    (D) look for

23. The word *significant* in the second paragraph, line 4, is closest in meaning to
    (A) large
    (B) varied
    (C) interesting
    (D) important

Lesson 45

Media

WORDS TO LEARN

assignment

constantly

constitute

decision

disseminate

impact

in-depth

investigate

link

politician

subscribe

thorough

Study the following definitions and examples.

1. **assignment** n., something, such as a task, that is assigned
   a. This assignment has to be turned in before midnight.
   b. When the reporter is on assignment, research piles up on her desk.

2. **constantly** adv., continually
   a. An advantage of Internet news reports is that they can be constantly updated.
   b. People constantly look to the news to keep up-to-date on what is going on in the world.

3. **constitute** v., to be the elements or parts of
   a. All the different news sources constitute the media industry.
   b. A talented staff, adequate printing facilities, and sufficient distribution points constitute a successful newspaper.

4. **decision** n., judgment or choice
   a. The court made the decision to allow the newspaper to print the controversial story.
   b. Newspaper editors often have to make quick decisions about which stories to publish.

5. **disseminate** v., to scatter widely; to distribute
   a. The Internet disseminates news more quickly than newspapers, TV, or the radio can.
   b. The computer virus was disseminated through the newsroom by reporters sharing terminals.

6. **impact** n., a strong, immediate impression
   a. The story of the presidential scandal had a huge impact on the public.
   b. The impact of the news coverage is yet to be known.

7. **in-depth** adj., in complete detail; thorough
   a. The newspaper gave in-depth coverage of the tragic bombing.
   b. Ivan's in-depth story on the spread of the disease received praise from many of his colleagues.

8. **investigate** v., to uncover and report hidden information
   a. Reporters need to thoroughly investigate the facts before publishing their stories.
   b. Michelle's editor sent her to the capital to investigate the story behind the government scandal.

9. **link** n., an association; a relationship
   a. The computer links will take you to today's headlines.
   b. The father-daughter team of reporters is just one example of many family links at this newspaper.

10. **politician** n., a person involved in government activities
    a. The news media cover the activities of all the major politicians.
    b. The politician refused to talk to reporters about her private life.

11. **subscribe** v., to receive a periodical regularly on order
    a. Jill subscribes to a gardening magazine.
    b. Many people have stopped subscribing to newspapers because they prefer to read the news online.

12. **thorough** adj., exhaustively complete
    a. The reporters were thorough in their coverage of the event.
    b. The story was the result of thorough research.

WORD FAMILIES

noun	constancy	The reporter's constancy in writing thorough news reports earned her a loyal following of readers.
adjective	constant	The constant ringing of the telephone distracted Susan from writing her report.
adverb	constantly	The editor constantly asks the reporters to recheck their facts.

verb	decide	The editor decided not to publish the story because the facts were unreliable.
noun	decision	The decision to lay off several reporters was made for financial reasons alone.
adjective	decisive	Newspaper editors must be decisive when determining which stories go on the front page.

verb	investigate	Alban was excited about his first chance to investigate a story.
noun	investigation	The investigation into the president's past was covered by the media worldwide.
adjective	investigative	After turning up details in the crime that even the police had missed, Helen became well known as an investigative reporter.

noun	politician	More and more politicians are using the Internet as a way to communicate with their supporters.
noun	politics	Anyone who chooses a career in politics has to learn how to speak with news reporters.
adjective	political	Many blogs focus on political news and opinions.

verb	subscribe	I subscribe to the local newspaper to stay current.
noun	subscription	Buying a subscription to the magazine was much less expensive than buying individual issues.
noun	subscribers	The magazine went out of business because it did not have enough subscribers.

noun	thoroughness	A newspaper cannot survive long without a reputation for thoroughness.
adjective	thorough	Toshi is famous for her thorough and fair reporting of the issues.
adverb	thoroughly	The reporter thoroughly checked all his facts to avoid any potential embarrassment.

WORDS IN CONTEXT

Read the following passage and write the words in the blanks below.

assignments	decisions	in-depth	political
constant	disseminated	investigative	subscribes
constitutes	impact	links	thoroughly

Chen likes to go online to read the news. Lemma turns on the television to find out what's going on in the world. Eve (1) _____ to several newspapers, which arrive at her house daily. Kobi, who is especially interested in (2) _____ news, listens to radio talk shows that (3) _____ cover government issues. All these people are touched by the media.

What is the media? What (4) _____ the media? The media consists of all the ways that news and information is (5) _____ to a mass audience. The media covers everything from hard news, which is (6) _____ reporting, to stories that are purely entertaining, such as whether your favorite movie star was on the "Best Dressed/Worst Dressed" list. Whether in print or broadcast on TV, the stories are the product of the reporting of many journalists who write the stories, and editors who give out the (7) _____, assess the quality of the writing and research, and make the (8) _____ about where and when the stories run.

The news has an immediate (9) _____. The Internet puts global news onto the personal computer on your desk. Almost all browsers have (10) _____ to up-to-the-minute news stories from various news services. You can get (11) _____ news updates from a variety of sources via your personal computer, providing you with the most up-to-date and (12) _____ coverage.

WORD PRACTICE

LISTENING COMPREHENSION

TRACK
46

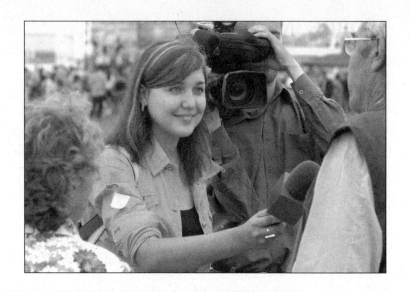

Part 1 Photo

Look at the picture and listen to the sentences.
Choose the sentence that best describes the picture.

1. Ⓐ Ⓑ Ⓒ Ⓓ

Part 2 Question–Response

Listen to the question and the three responses. Choose the response that best answers the question.

2. Ⓐ Ⓑ Ⓒ   3. Ⓐ Ⓑ Ⓒ

Part 3 Conversation

Listen to the dialogue. Then read each question and choose the best answer.

4. According to the woman, why are newspapers better than TV news shows?
   (A) Newspaper editors are decisive.
   (B) Newspaper coverage is more thorough.
   (C) Newspaper stories are more interesting.
   (D) Newspapers cover better stories.

5. How long has the woman worked as a newspaper reporter?
   (A) Four years.
   (B) Thirteen years.
   (C) Fourteen years.
   (D) Thirty years.

6. What is the man's job?
   (A) Investigative reporter.
   (B) TV news reader.
   (C) Journalism teacher.
   (D) Journalism student.

Part 4 Talk

Listen to the talk. Then read each question and choose the best answer.

7. What is the topic of the news report?
   (A) A speech made by the country's president.
   (B) The state of the national economy.
   (C) Fraud committed by a company president.
   (D) An industry report.

8. At what time can this news report be heard?
   (A) 5:00.
   (B) 12:00.
   (C) 6:00.
   (D) 10:00.

9. Why won't Mary Milo report the news tonight?
   (A) She is sick.
   (B) She got a new job.
   (C) She is away on vacation.
   (D) She has another assignment.

READING

Part 5 Incomplete Sentences

Choose the word that best completes the sentence.

10. It is very easy to find the latest _____ news online.
    (A) politics   (C) political
    (B) politician   (D) polite

11. By _____ asking questions, Harry was able to get the information he wanted for his report.
    (A) constant   (C) consistence
    (B) constancy   (D) constantly

12. Georgette _____ to stop subscribing to the newspaper because she felt the quality of the reporting had deteriorated.
    (A) decision   (C) decides
    (B) decided   (D) decisive

13. The reporters followed the official _____ by interviewing all the witnesses to the crime.
    (A) investigate   (C) investigative
    (B) investigation   (D) investigational

14. I need to renew my _____ for cable television, but I can't find the form.
    (A) subscribing   (C) subscriber
    (B) subscription   (D) subscribe

15. The editor was impressed with how _____ the reporter was in getting the details from his sources.
    (A) thorough   (C) thoroughly
    (B) thoroughness   (D) thoroughbred

Part 6 Text Completion

Stay on top of what's happening in today's world by _____ to *News Story Weekly*, the

16. (A) subscribe
    (B) to subscribe
    (C) subscribing
    (D) should subscribe

weekly news magazine that is read by politicians, corporate executives, and ordinary citizens like you.

News Story Weekly provides you with _____ coverage of the week's most important

17. (A) depth
    (B) in-depth
    (C) deepen
    (D) deepened

news, both national and international. *News Story Weekly* thoroughly investigates worldwide events that have an impact on your life and delivers this news to your mailbox every week.

People who care about what's happening in the world read *News Story Weekly*. Shouldn't you be one of them? *News Story Weekly* is _____ throughout the country to readers from

18. (A) assigned
    (B) constituted
    (C) investigated
    (D) disseminated

all walks of life.

To subscribe to *News Story Weekly*, call our offices at 888-685-9321, or visit us online at *www.nsw.com*.

Part 7 Reading Comprehension

Questions 19–23 refer to the following two letters.

April 12, 20—

Michelle Richards
News Story Weekly
346 Howard Avenue
White River, NH

Dear Ms. Richards,

I am a journalist and an avid reader of *News Story Weekly*.
It has long been my dream to write for your magazine.
I graduated from National University a year ago with a
degree in journalism. For the past six months I have been
working as an investigative reporter for the *Bluefield Daily*,
my hometown newspaper. This newspaper is disseminated
throughout the state. I work on assignments involving
local politics.

In my opinion, *News Story Weekly* is the top news magazine
in the country. It has had a great impact on my life. I
started reading it at an early age, and it inspired me to
pursue a career as a reporter. If there is a position available
for a reporter at *News Story Weekly*, I would be interested
in applying for it. I believe that my educational background
and work experience qualify me for such a position. I am
enclosing several of my articles that appeared in the
Bluefield Daily as writing samples. I have letters of reference available if you need them. I look forward to hearing
from you.

Sincerely,

Mark Conway

April 19, 20—

Mark Conway
1255 Park Place, Apt. 10
Bluefield, MA

Dear Mr. Conway,

Thank you for your letter of April 12 inquiring
about a position as a reporter. We are constantly
looking for reporters to work for our magazine,
and we currently have an opening for a reporter
to cover regional news. You seem to be well-
qualified, and we would welcome your application. I would need to see your reference letters
as well as a resume. The closing date for this
position is May 15. We will make our choice after
that date and let you know what we decide by
the first of June. Thank you for your interest in
News Story Weekly.

Sincerely,

Michelle Richards

19. Why did Mark Conway write the letter?
    (A) To express an opinion about the news.
    (B) To get a subscription to *News Story Weekly*.
    (C) To offer Ms. Richards an assignment.
    (D) To apply for a job as a reporter.

20. What did Mark Conway enclose with his letter?
    (A) Newspaper articles.
    (B) A resume.
    (C) Letters of reference.
    (D) His university diploma.

21. When will Mark Conway know Michelle Richards's
    decision?
    (A) April 12.
    (B) April 15.
    (C) May 15.
    (D) June 1.

22. The word *impact* in the first letter, second paragraph,
    line 2 is closest in meaning to
    (A) interest
    (B) influence
    (C) difference
    (D) education

23. The word *constantly* in the second letter, line 2 is
    closest in meaning to
    (A) always
    (B) sometimes
    (C) rarely
    (D) infrequently

Word Review #9   Lessons 41–45 Entertainment

Choose the word that best completes the sentence.

1. Movies are probably the most popular form of
   _____ in the United States.
   (A) category
   (B) experience
   (C) admiration
   (D) entertainment

2. Television has seriously _____ society.
   (A) influence
   (B) influenced
   (C) influencing
   (D) influential

3. Actors can spend too much time _____
   as well as too little.
   (A) rehearse
   (B) rehearsed
   (C) rehearsing
   (D) rehearsal

4. Even when a show is sold _____, it is
   sometimes possible to get a ticket.
   (A) up
   (B) to
   (C) off
   (D) out

5. Orchestra music is wonderfully conducive to
   _____.
   (A) relaxation
   (B) relaxed
   (C) relaxes
   (D) relax

6. There is no good or bad music, only that which does
   or does not appeal to your _____.
   (A) taste
   (B) tastes
   (C) tasted
   (D) tasting

7. New _____ are one of the most exciting
   aspects of museum work.
   (A) acquire
   (B) acquisitions
   (C) acquires
   (D) acquisitive

8. Sometimes I look at a famous painting and wonder
   why it is considered more _____ than the
   ones on either side of it.
   (A) signify
   (B) signified
   (C) significant
   (D) significantly

9. The Internet _____ information faster than
   any other medium.
   (A) disseminate
   (B) disseminates
   (C) dissemination
   (D) disseminating

10. In any news medium, the only news is what the
    editor _____ is news.
    (A) decide
    (B) decides
    (C) decision
    (D) decisions

Choose the one word or phrase that best completes each sentence.

Because of DVD players and cable TV, it is no longer necessary to leave home in search of
_____. Families can watch movies in the comfort of their own living rooms. Nevertheless,

11. (A) entertain
    (B) entertained
    (C) entertaining
    (D) entertainment

going out to the movies is still a popular way to spend a weekend evening. Many people enjoy going
to movie theaters because they like to see new movies as soon as they _____. They may also

12. (A) release
    (B) released
    (C) are released
    (D) will be released

prefer to spend an evening out in the _____ atmosphere of a public place rather than quietly

13. (A) lively
    (B) lovely
    (C) levelly
    (D) lividly

at home.

If you are looking for an activity that the whole family can enjoy, consider visiting one of our city's fine
museums. It is the perfect way to _____ fun with education. Depending on your family's

14. (A) separate
    (B) combine
    (C) rehearse
    (D) subscribe

interests, you might _____ to visit a science, history, or art museum. If your children are older,

15. (A) deride
    (B) derive
    (C) decide
    (D) decline

they will want to visit exhibits that particularly interest them and take the time to give each one a
_____ look. Younger children have a shorter attention span. Museums with interactive exhibits

16. (A) thorough
    (B) through
    (C) thought
    (D) though

are best for them.

The new play, *Sunflower Sunset*, opened at the Westwood Playhouse last night. A lot of effort went into this production. The actors _____

17. (A) rehearse
    (B) rehearsed
    (C) will rehearse
    (D) are rehearsing

for months, and an elaborate set was constructed. Unfortunately, this effort could not save the dull dialogue. It was easy to see that the _____ was bored—snoring was heard throughout the theater,

18. (A) audio
    (B) audition
    (C) audience
    (D) audacity

and many people left before the end of the play. The actors made a fine effort with their _____, but the best acting in the world cannot

19. (A) perform
    (B) performer
    (C) performable
    (D) performance

save a poorly written play.

Lesson 46

Doctor's Office

WORDS
TO LEARN

annually

appointment

assess

diagnose

effective

instrument

manage

prevent

recommendation

record

refer

serious

Study the following definitions and examples.

1. **annually** adv., once a year
   a. Everyone should get a physical exam annually.
   b. A number of tests are provided annually by my insurance plan.
2. **appointment** n., arrangements for a meeting; a position in a profession
   a. To get the most out of your appointment, keep a log of your symptoms and concerns.
   b. The psychiatrist holds an academic appointment at the university hospital as well as having a private practice.
3. **assess** v., to judge or evaluate
   a. It is a good idea to have a doctor assess your health every one or two years.
   b. The physical therapist assessed the amount of mobility Ms. Crowl had lost after her accident.
4. **diagnose** v., to recognize a disease; to analyze the nature of something
   a. After considering the patient's symptoms and looking at his test results, the doctor diagnosed the lump as benign.
   b. She diagnosed the problem as a failure to follow the directions for taking the medication.
5. **effective** adj., producing the desired result; in force
   a. Howard was pleased to find that the diet recommended by his doctor was quite effective.
   b. The new policies, effective the beginning of the fiscal year, change the amount charged to see the physician.
6. **instrument** n., a tool for precise work; the means whereby something is achieved
   a. The pediatrician tried not to frighten the children with her strange-looking instruments.
   b. The senior physician carried his instruments in a black leather bag.
7. **manage** v., to handle; to deal with; to guide
   a. The head nurse's ability to manage her staff through a difficult time caught the hospital administrator's attention.
   b. By carefully managing their limited resources, the couple found the money for the elective surgery.
8. **prevent** v., to keep from happening; to hinder
   a. By encouraging teenagers not to smoke, doctors are hoping to prevent many cases of cancer.
   b. His full caseload prevented the doctor from taking on new patients.
9. **recommendation** n., advice; endorsement
   a. It is important to follow the doctor's recommendations if you want to improve your health.
   b. The professor gave her former student a recommendation when he applied for a job at the hospital.
10. **record** n., an official copy of documents
    a. Ms. Han typed a written request for her medical records.
    b. The official records kept in the city archives showed that an unusually high number of babies are born in the summer months.
11. **refer** v., to direct for treatment or information; to mention
    a. I was referred to this specialist by the family practice nurse.
    b. As soon as Agnes referred to the failed treatment, everyone's mood soured.
12. **serious** adj., very bad or very important; not funny
    a. Sara's illness is serious but the doctors say they can treat it.
    b. The patient felt nervous when he saw the serious expression on the doctor's face.

WORD FAMILIES

verb	assess	He was able to assess her health problems with the help of her detailed medical history.
noun	assessment	The specialist's assessment of the patient's condition was consistent with the general practitioner's.
adjective	assessable	That medical condition is not assessable by this laboratory test.

verb	diagnose	Her symptoms are overlapping, making it difficult to diagnose the exact cause of her chest pain.
noun	diagnosis	Phil did a much better job of taking care of himself once his father had a diagnosis of lung cancer.
adjective	diagnostic	The new X-ray suite has all the latest diagnostic equipment.

verb	prevent	By stopping smoking now, you may be able to prevent lung cancer.
noun	prevention	He made a career of disease prevention through mass vaccinations.
adjective	preventive	Eloise took preventive steps against gum disease by more thorough toothbrushing.

verb	recommend	I recommend that you have this test annually starting at age 40.
noun	recommendation	Against my doctor's recommendation, I decided to purchase the generic brand of medication.
adjective	recommendable	There is nothing particularly recommendable about this therapy over the other therapy I mentioned.

verb	record	The doctor records the patient's description of her symptoms in the patient's medical chart.
noun	record	When you apply for health insurance, the insurance company will probably want to look at your medical records.
adjective	recorded	After office hours there is a recorded message on the doctor's answering machine that gives an emergency telephone number.

noun	seriousness	Martha's doctor tried to make her understand the seriousness of her condition.
adjective	serious	Mr. Kim was relieved to find out that his disease was not serious.
adverb	seriously	The doctor spoke seriously with Arthur about the need to lose weight.

WORDS IN CONTEXT

Read the following passage and write the words in the blanks below.

annually	diagnosing	manage	record
appointment	effective	preventing	refer
assessment	instruments	recommend	serious

Sooner or later, everyone needs to go to the doctor's office. In fact, it's in your best interest to see your doctor at least (1) _____. The better he or she knows you and your health, the more (2) _____ your doctor can be. Most people need help in (3) _____ routine medical problems they are experiencing, such as symptoms of colds and the flu, allergies, rashes, and earaches. Other times, people visit a doctor for help in (4) _____ health problems from ever occurring, such as lowering their risk of heart attack or stroke by dieting or exercising.

When you arrive for your (5) _____, the doctor's office staff will have ready a (6) _____ of all your visits, so that the doctor has a complete reference of your health. The visit will begin with an (7) _____ of your general health and a discussion of any problems that concern you.

The doctors may use a variety of (8) _____ to get a closer look at you. The doctor will (9) _____ your problem and (10) _____ a treatment plan. The doctor may prescribe medication, (11) _____ you to a specialist more experienced in treating your condition, or order tests to gain more information. In (12) _____ cases, he or she may send you to the hospital for care.

WORD PRACTICE

LISTENING COMPREHENSION

TRACK
47

Part 1 Photo

Look at the picture and listen to the sentences.
Choose the sentence that best describes the picture.

1. Ⓐ Ⓑ Ⓒ Ⓓ

Part 2 Question–Response

Listen to the question and the three responses. Choose the response that best answers the question.

2. Ⓐ Ⓑ Ⓒ   3. Ⓐ Ⓑ Ⓒ

Part 3 Conversation

Listen to the dialogue. Then read each question and choose the best answer.

4. What does the doctor recommend that the man do?
   (A) Research diagnostic methods.
   (B) Visit patients.
   (C) See a specialist.
   (D) Check into the best hospital.

5. When does the doctor say that the man should
   do this?
   (A) This afternoon.
   (B) Before 10:00.
   (C) This month.
   (D) In ten months.

6. What does the man ask the doctor to give him?
   (A) An appointment.
   (B) A new diagnosis.
   (C) A special treatment.
   (D) A copy of his record.

Part 4 Talk

Listen to the talk. Then read each question and choose the best answer.

7. What kind of job is being advertised?
   (A) Doctor.
   (B) Office manager.
   (C) Director.
   (D) Office assistant.

8. How can someone apply for this job?
   (A) Send in a résumé.
   (B) Make an appointment.
   (C) Telephone the office.
   (D) Submit records.

9. What is a benefit of the job?
   (A) An annual doctor's appointment.
   (B) Three weeks of vacation a year.
   (C) A yearly salary raise.
   (D) Health insurance.

READING

Part 5 Incomplete Sentences

Choose the word that best completes the sentence.

10. Luckily, the test results show no _____ damage from the accident.
    (A) assess
    (B) assessment
    (C) assessing
    (D) assessable

11. This is not an easy _____ to make without the benefit of numerous test results.
    (A) diagnosis
    (B) diagnose
    (C) diagnostic
    (D) diagnosed

12. The most effective way to treat illness is to _____ it from occurring in the first place.
    (A) refer
    (B) assess
    (C) manage
    (D) prevent

13. Gabriela did not consistently follow her doctor's _____ and her condition did not improve.
    (A) recommendations
    (B) recommendable
    (C) recommended
    (D) recommending

14. Jane's doctor asked her to _____ everything she ate for a week.
    (A) records
    (B) record
    (C) recording
    (D) recorded

15. Public health officials are just now realizing the _____ of this disease.
    (A) seriousness
    (B) serious
    (C) seriously
    (D) series

Part 6 Text Completion

Welcome to the office of Dr. Shaw. The following office policies are in effect.

– Please check in with the receptionist when you arrive. If you were given a referral, please tell the receptionist the name of the doctor who _____ you.

    16. (A) will refer
        (B) did refer
        (C) referred
        (D) refers

– We recognize that sometimes unexpected situations occur and you must cancel your _____. Cancellations must be made 24 hours ahead of time or

    17. (A) record
        (B) assessment
        (C) appointment
        (D) recommendation

you will be charged a fee.

– Please don't call us to find out the results of _____ tests. We will call

    18. (A) diagnose
        (B) diagnosis
        (C) diagnosed
        (D) diagnostic

you when the results are ready.

– Effective January 1, all bills must be paid in full at the time of your visit. We accept all major credit cards.

Part 7 Reading Comprehension

Questions 19–23 refer to the following article.

Caring for Your Health

Your health is one of your most valuable assets, so caring for it properly is very important. Regular visits to the doctor can help prevent any health problems from becoming serious. You should visit your doctor annually if you are in good health. If you have certain health conditions or if your doctor recommends it, you may need more frequent appointments.

It is important to have a doctor you can trust. The best way to find one is to get a recommendation from a trustworthy person such as a friend or relative. Call to make an appointment several weeks or even a month ahead of time. When you call, you can also ask a few questions about the doctor's background, such as which university he got his degree from and how long he has been practicing in the area. You will also want to find out which hospital the doctor is affiliated with. When you arrive for your appointment, make sure you bring a copy of your medical records with you.

When you meet with the doctor, you will want to ask him what his approach to treatment is and what diagnostic tools he uses. This way you can find out something about his skills, as well as whether or not he is a person you can talk to and feel comfortable with. Also, take a look around the office. Is it comfortable and organized? Do the instruments look clean and well-maintained?

If your appointment goes well and you feel comfortable with the doctor, then don't forget to make an appointment for your next physical before you leave the office. If you have any doubts, look around for another doctor. Having a good doctor is an essential part of your health care plan.

---

19. Who is this article for?
    (A) Patients.
    (B) Doctors.
    (C) Hospital staff.
    (D) Medical equipment salespeople.

20. How often should a healthy person visit the doctor?
    (A) Once a month.
    (B) Twice a month.
    (C) Once a year.
    (D) Twice a year.

21. What is the best way to find a good doctor?
    (A) Look in the phone book.
    (B) Call the hospital.
    (C) Go to a university.
    (D) Ask a friend.

22. The word *records* in the second paragraph, line 6, is closest in meaning to
    (A) plans
    (B) documents
    (C) descriptions
    (D) instructions

23. The word *instruments* in the third paragraph, line 4, is closest in meaning to
    (A) equipment
    (B) furniture
    (C) environment
    (D) clothing

Lesson 47

Dentist's Office

WORDS TO LEARN

aware

catch up

distraction

encouragement

evident

habit

illuminate

irritate

overview

position

regularly

restore

Study the following definitions and examples.

1. **aware** adj., having knowledge
   a. I was not aware that flossing my teeth could prevent a buildup of plaque.
   b. My dentist made me aware that I should have an appointment twice a year.

2. **catch up** v., to bring up to date
   a. My dentist likes to take time to catch up before she starts the examination.
   b. The dental assistant caught up on her paperwork in between patients.

3. **distraction** n., the act of being turned away from the focus
   a. To provide a distraction from the noise, Luisa's dentist offered her a pair of earphones.
   b. My dentist is kind enough to provide distractions like television, which take my mind off the procedure.

4. **encouragement** n., inspiration or support
   a. The perfect checkup was certainly encouragement to keep up my good dental hygiene.
   b. Let me offer you some encouragement about your crooked teeth.

5. **evident** adj., easily seen or understood; obvious
   a. The presence of a wisdom tooth was not evident until the dentist started to examine the patient.
   b. Unfortunately, his poor dental hygiene is evident from a distance.

6. **habit** n., a customary manner or practice
   a. The toddler's father stressed the importance of toothbrushing in hopes of establishing a good habit.
   b. The patient had a habit of grinding his teeth during his sleep.

7. **illuminate** v., to provide or brighten with light
   a. The dark recesses of the mouth can only be seen clearly when illuminated with a lamp.
   b. Let me turn on more lights to properly illuminate the back teeth.

8. **irritate** v., to chafe or inflame, to bother
   a. The broken tooth rubbed against my tongue, irritating it.
   b. Hannah's gums are irritated by foods that are very cold or very hot.

9. **overview** n., a summary; a survey; a quick look
   a. I did a quick overview of your teeth and they look in good shape.
   b. An overview of your dental records shows a history of problems.

10. **position** n., the place where something is; the way in which something is placed or arranged
    a. Let me tilt your head to a more comfortable position for you.
    b. The position of the chair can be adjusted to a range of heights.

11. **regularly** adv., occurring at fixed intervals
    a. She brushes regularly after every meal.
    b. I have to remind my son regularly to brush his teeth.

12. **restore** v., to bring back to an original condition
    a. The cleaning restored the whiteness of my teeth.
    b. I will talk to my dentist about whether she knows any procedure to restore the parts of my teeth that I have ground away.

WORD FAMILIES

verb	distract	The child is frightened by the instruments. Try to distract his attention while I get ready.
noun	distraction	The soothing background music was a pleasant distraction from the drilling sounds at the dentist's office.
adjective	distracted	The distracted patient left the office without paying her bill.

verb	encourage	My dentist has been encouraging me to see a specialist about my gum problem.
noun	encouragement	Although the cleaning routine recommended by the dentist was tedious, with some encouragement, Richard was able to follow it regularly.
adjective	encouraging	It was encouraging to find out that I had no serious problems at my last dental checkup.

noun	evidence	The dentist found evidence of decay on my wisdom tooth.
adjective	evident	My lack of dental hygiene was evident without a checkup.
adverb	evidently	Proper flossing evidently worked, since my gums are now in good health.

noun	habit	I'm trying to start the habit of flossing at least once a day.
adjective	habitual	His habitual coffee drinking stained his teeth.
adverb	habitually	Jack is habitually late for his appointments, which forced the receptionist to scold him.

verb	irritate	My dentist was late for my appointment, which irritated me, especially since he did not apologize.
noun	irritation	I have an irritation on the inside of my mouth that won't heal.
adjective	irritating	Matthew decided to visit the dentist because of an irritating gum problem.

noun	regularity	Visiting the dentist with regularity is an important part of maintaining good dental health.
adjective	regular	Many dental problems can be avoided by following a regular cleaning routine.
adverb	regularly	I haven't been visiting the dentist regularly.

WORDS IN CONTEXT

Read the following passage and write the words in the blanks below.

aware	encourage	illuminates	position
catch up	evident	irritates	regularly
distraction	habit	overview	restores

At least twice a year, Toshiro makes an appointment with his dentist. He's

(1) _____ that taking good care of his teeth and seeing a dentist can

help prevent the buildup of tartar and plaque that could cause serious problems later.

The dentist starts the appointment by looking over Toshiro's chart, which details

all the work that has been done on his teeth, as a way to (2) _____ on

Toshiro's dental health. Toshiro brushes (3) _____, but is not

consistent about flossing. His dentist is trying to (4) _____ a better

flossing (5) _____ by demonstrating some easy-to-use techniques.

When the dentist is ready to look into Toshiro's mouth, she adjusts the height and

(6) _____ of the chair to make sure she can see all of Toshiro's teeth.

A bright light (7) _____ Toshiro's eyes, but (8) _____

the dark places in the back of his mouth. The dentist does a quick

(9) _____ of Toshiro's mouth, looking for any obvious problems, such

as a cavity or a broken tooth. The dentist asks if Toshiro has been having any

problems, like tooth pain, bleeding, or soreness.

Sometimes, problems in the mouth are quite (10) _____ and can be

seen by the dentist's trained eye. But other times, the dentist will take X-rays to make

certain there are no problems in areas she cannot see, such as under the gum line or

inside a tooth.

The dentist then goes to work, repairing any damage. She then

(11) _____ the natural color to his teeth with a thorough cleaning.

The noise of the drills and cleaners can upset some patients, so Toshiro's dentist is

kind enough to supply earphones to provide a (12) _____.

WORD PRACTICE

LISTENING COMPREHENSION

Part 1 Photo

Look at the picture and listen to the sentences.
Choose the sentence that best describes the picture.

1. Ⓐ Ⓑ Ⓒ Ⓓ

Part 2 Question–Response

Listen to the question and the three responses. Choose the response that best answers the question.

2. Ⓐ Ⓑ Ⓒ   3. Ⓐ Ⓑ Ⓒ

Part 3 Conversation

Listen to the dialogue. Then read each question and choose the best answer.

4. What does the dentist recommend that the patient do?
   (A) Visit her office more regularly.
   (B) Shop at a certain store.
   (C) Review his records.
   (D) Talk about his concerns.

5. What does the patient want?
   (A) Shinier teeth.
   (B) A cup of coffee.
   (C) A copy of his records.
   (D) Fillings in his cavities.

6. When does the patient want an appointment?
   (A) This afternoon.
   (B) Tonight.
   (C) Next week.
   (D) Next month.

Part 4 Talk

Listen to the talk. Then read each question and choose the best answer.

7. What product is advertised?
   (A) False teeth.
   (B) A tooth whitener.
   (C) Chewing gum.
   (D) A toothbrush.

8. What are the customers asked to do?
   (A) Use the product for just two days.
   (B) Change their cleaning habits.
   (C) Use the product every night.
   (D) Visit the dentist.

9. Where can the product be bought?
   (A) At a store.
   (B) At the dentist's office.
   (C) From a sales representative.
   (D) Online.

READING

Part 5 Incomplete Sentences

Choose the word that best completes the sentence.

10. The dentist tells jokes while he is working in order to _____ patients from their fears.
    - (A) encourage
    - (B) illuminate
    - (C) restore
    - (D) distract

11. My dentist always _____ me to floss more regularly.
    - (A) encouraging
    - (B) encouragement
    - (C) encourages
    - (D) encourage

12. It was _____ from the X-rays that I needed dental work.
    - (A) evident
    - (B) evidently
    - (C) evidence
    - (D) evidential

13. Knowing his _____ tidiness, I'm not surprised to learn that David flosses three times a day.
    - (A) habit
    - (B) habitual
    - (C) habitually
    - (D) habitualness

14. An _____ at the gum line can be nothing serious or the symptom of a larger problem.
    - (A) irritate
    - (B) irritable
    - (C) irritation
    - (D) irritability

15. _____ visits to the dentist are necessary for maintaining good dental health.
    - (A) Regularly
    - (B) Regular
    - (C) Regulate
    - (D) Regulates

Part 6 Text Completion

The state of dental health in our nation is a cause for concern according to Dr. James Hibbard, president of the National Society of Dentists. Dr. Hibbard expressed his concerns in an article appearing this week in Our Dental Health magazine, which is distributed among dentists and other health care workers throughout the country. "Most people don't have good dental _____," he says. When people aren't

16. (A) habit
    (B) habits
    (C) habitual
    (D) habitually

careful about keeping their teeth clean, Dr. Hibbard warns, the result is _____ gums, cavities, and

17. (A) irritate
    (B) irritant
    (C) irritated
    (D) irritation

even tooth loss. "Dentists should be firmer about _____ their patients to maintain their dental

18. (A) encourage
    (B) encourages
    (C) encouraging
    (D) to encourage

health. Dentists need to do more education with their patients, and patients need to follow their dentists' advice," recommends Dr. Hibbard.

Part 7 Reading Comprehension

Questions 19–23 refer to the following advertisement and e-mail message.

ATTENTION DENTISTS!

You know how important it is to have the best equipment for your office. So why settle for less? Evidence shows that outdated, under-functioning equipment can reduce a dentist's efficiency by 50 percent or more. The Acme Dental Supply Company offers state-of-the-art dental equipment at affordable rates.

– Our special lighted dental mirrors illuminate all tooth surfaces better than any other light on the market. These mirrors are on sale this week at just $150 per set of three. That's 25 percent off the usual price.

– Our automated patient chairs automatically adjust their positions so that you can always work comfortably, without back or shoulder strain. Available in several models and colors.

– Our Dental Office Systems computer software streamlines record keeping so that you will never fall behind with your paperwork. Full version available at $500. Upgrade is $175.

– Our special edition Dental Office CD set provides hours of soothing music that will keep your patients relaxed. You can focus on your work without being distracted by patient anxiety. Choose from String Quartet, Contemporary Jazz, or Sounds of Nature. $35 per boxed set.

To: pdaly@dentaloffice.com
From: drbarb@dentaloffice.com
Subject: office equipment
attach: Acme Dental Supply

Peter,

Take a look at the attached ad. I think we should order a few things. I like the lighted mirrors and probably could use five or six sets, but let's spend no more than $300 on them for now, so I can see how well they work first. We probably need the upgrade for the record keeping software, too. It will help you stay caught up with the patient records. I think we could do without those CDs, though, don't you? We do better with the radio. You might as well go ahead and order paper, envelopes, and anything else you need for the front office at the same time.

Thanks,

Barbara

Barbara Hendricks, DDS

---

19. Who is Peter Daly?
    (A) A dentist.
    (B) A dental equipment salesman.
    (C) A dental patient.
    (D) A dentist's office manager.

20. How many sets of mirrors will Dr. Hendricks order now?
    (A) Two.
    (B) Three.
    (C) Five.
    (D) Six.

21. Which Acme product is sold to relax patients?
    (A) Computer games.
    (B) Automated chairs.
    (C) Special lights.
    (D) CD sets.

22. The word *illuminate* in the first letter, second paragraph, line 1 is closest in meaning to
    (A) smooth
    (B) light
    (C) clean
    (D) repair

23. The word *distracted* in the first letter, fifth paragraph, line 4 is closest in meaning to
    (A) interested
    (B) entertained
    (C) bothered
    (D) introduced

Lesson 48

Health Insurance

WORDS TO LEARN

alternative

aspect

concern

emphasize

incur

personnel

policy

portion

regardless

reimburse

suit

treatment

Study the following definitions and examples.

1. **alternative** adj., allowing a choice; other
   a. To lower the cost of health insurance, my employer chose an alternative method of insuring us.
   b. I'd like to discuss alternative treatments before I agree to anything.

2. **aspect** n., a feature element; an appearance
   a. The right to choose their own doctor is an important aspect of health coverage for many people.
   b. The aspect of HMOs that people most dislike is the lack of personal service.

3. **concern** n., anxiety; worry
   a. Whenever I have health concerns, I call my doctor.
   b. The rising cost of health care is of great concern to many people.

4. **emphasize** v., to stress
   a. The nurse emphasized the importance of eating a balanced diet.
   b. The new insurance plan emphasizes wellness by providing reimbursement for health club memberships.

5. **incur** v., to become subject to
   a. I incurred substantial expenses that my health plan does not cover.
   b. Dominic incurs the cost of a co-payment at each doctor's visit.

6. **personnel** n., a group of employees or workers
   a. The office manager insisted that she needed more personnel to finish the project on time.
   b. The employee went to see the director of personnel about taking an extended leave of absence.

7. **policy** n., a set of rules and regulations
   a. Company policy did not provide for overtime pay.
   b. The company's insurance policy did not cover cosmetic surgery.

8. **portion** n., a section or quantity within a larger thing; a part of a whole
   a. A portion of my benefits is my health care coverage.
   b. I am keeping a record of the portion of my income I spend on health care.

9. **regardless** adv., in spite of
   a. Regardless of the cost, we all need health insurance.
   b. I keep going to the same doctor, regardless of the fact that she does not take my pain seriously.

10. **reimburse** v., pay back money spent for a specific purpose
    a. The insurance company may not reimburse you for the entire cost of your medical care.
    b. The insurance company reimbursed Donald for the cost of his trip to the emergency room.

11. **suit** v., to be appropriate; to satisfy
    a. This insurance plan doesn't suit our family as it doesn't cover well-baby care.
    b. I have finally found a health plan that suits my needs.

12. **treatment** n., care provided for a medical condition
    a. Karl's health greatly improved under his new doctor's treatment.
    b. The treatment that the doctor recommended was expensive and not really effective.

WORD FAMILIES

verb	concern	It concerns me that we haven't been able to find a suitable health insurance plan.
noun	concern	A good doctor will pay attention to any and all concerns the patient expresses about his or her health.
adjective	concerned	I am concerned about the limited benefits this insurance plan offers.

verb	emphasize	The plan representative emphasized the need for a second medical opinion.
noun	emphasis	The emphasis of the health plan is on staying well.
adjective	emphatic	Hassan made an emphatic appeal to the medical insurance director.

verb	regard	We regard this health insurance plan as one of the best options available.
adjective	regardful	The company was not regardful of the needs of most of the employees when it chose this health insurance plan.
adverb	regardless	I took the job regardless of the poor health benefits the company offers.

verb	reimburse	The insurance company should reimburse you within one month.
noun	reimbursement	Paula was disappointed with the small reimbursement she received from her insurance company.
adjective	reimbursable	Before you pay for an expensive treatment, you should check with your insurance company to find out if it is reimbursable.

verb	suit	I'm dropping my health plan because it does not suit my needs.
adjective	suitable	Not every kind of health insurance is suitable for every family.
adverb	suitably	The errors on my insurance statement were caught and suitably fixed.

verb	treat	The best way to treat a cold is to stay in bed for a few days.
noun	treatment	Sam does not like to take drugs and prefers to use natural treatments.
adjective	treatable	The doctor told Marya that her condition was treatable with diet and exercise.

WORDS IN CONTEXT

Read the following passage and write the words in the blanks below.

alternatives	emphasize	policy	reimbursement
aspect	incurs	portion	suitable
concerns	personnel	regardless	treatment

The cost and availability of health insurance is one of the greatest (1) _____ of company (2) _____. A covered employee should be familiar with the terms and conditions of the insurance (3) _____. Although the insured pays a (4) _____ of the cost of his or her coverage, the employer generally covers most of the cost.

Health insurance policies vary widely. A doctor may recommend a particular (5) _____ for a medical condition, but it is the responsibility of the patient to make sure that it is covered by his or her insurance. Also, in some cases the insurance company pays the doctor directly, whereas in others the patient pays and then receives (6) _____ from the insurance company later.

Although the company or association negotiates the most (7) _____ terms they can, most experts (8) _____ that employees should be on the lookout for (9) _____ that might better suit their needs. (10) _____ of the cost of premiums, the most important (11) _____ of good health insurance is that it meets the needs of the insured and (12) _____ the least possible cost for necessary procedures.

WORD PRACTICE

LISTENING COMPREHENSION

Part 1 Photo

Look at the picture and listen to the sentences.
Choose the sentence that best describes the picture.

1. Ⓐ Ⓑ Ⓒ Ⓓ

Part 2 Question–Response

Listen to the question and the three responses. Choose the response that best answers the question.

2. Ⓐ Ⓑ Ⓒ   3. Ⓐ Ⓑ Ⓒ

Part 3 Conversation

Listen to the dialogue. Then read each question and choose the best answer.

4. What will happen if the man sees a specialist without a referral?
   (A) He will be dropped from his health plan.
   (B) He will see only a portion of the bill.
   (C) He won't be provided with good care.
   (D) He will pay a higher percentage of the cost.

5. When can the man get an appointment with his primary care provider?
   (A) In three days.
   (B) In ten days.
   (C) In two weeks.
   (D) In three weeks.

6. What does the woman recommend to the man?
   (A) See a specialist soon.
   (B) See his primary care provider first.
   (C) Get a treatment for his headache.
   (D) Get a special procedure.

Part 4 Talk

Listen to the talk. Then read each question and choose the best answer.

7. Why has a new health plan been chosen?
   (A) To help people save money.
   (B) Because the old plan is no longer available.
   (C) To get more benefits.
   (D) Because people are interested in alternative medicine.

8. Who will the new plan be available to?
   (A) Only people who earn a low salary.
   (B) Anyone who is interested.
   (C) Only people who have special health concerns.
   (D) Just those who have worked at the company for a long time.

9. When will the new health plan be in effect?
   (A) Today.
   (B) In two weeks.
   (C) In several months.
   (D) Next year.

READING

Part 5 Incomplete Sentences

Choose the word that best completes the sentence.

10. The insurance company will _____ you for the cost of any treatment that is on their list.
    (A) reimburse
    (B) reimburses
    (C) to reimburse
    (D) reimbursing

11. You should investigate to see if there are any _____ to costly hospital stays.
    (A) alternate
    (B) alternatively
    (C) alternatives
    (D) alternating

12. It _____ me that our company is not willing to look for an alternative to our current health insurance plan.
    (A) concern
    (B) concerned
    (C) concerns
    (D) concerning

13. I'm really pleased that my health plan provider is paying for my gym membership as a way to _____ its concern for my health.
    (A) emphasis
    (B) emphasize
    (C) emphatic
    (D) emphasizing

14. I _____ health insurance as an indispensable job benefit.
    (A) regardless
    (B) regardful
    (C) regarding
    (D) regard

15. This insurance policy is not _____ for our family because it doesn't cover the cost of health care for our children.
    (A) treatable
    (B) suitable
    (C) emphatic
    (D) regardful

Part 6 Text Completion

Memo

To: All personnel
From: Human Resources Office
Re: Health Insurance

Many of you have expressed an interest in certain types of health care _____ such as

16. (A) treat
    (B) treats
    (C) treatments
    (D) treatable

acupuncture and massage. In response to this, we have negotiated a new health insurance _____ with our provider, and benefits now include a discount on visits to acupuncturists,

17. (A) policy
    (B) police
    (C) politic
    (D) polite

massage therapists, and naturopaths. In order to take advantage of this discount, you need only to present your insurance card on your first visit to an approved provider. Please be advised that this discount is allowed only on visits to providers from the approved list. Please notify this office if you would like a copy of the list of approved _____ health care providers.

18. (A) alter
    (B) alternate
    (C) alternative
    (D) alternatively

Part 7 Reading Comprehension

Questions 19–23 refer to the following notice.

Workshop

Did you know that full medical coverage is available to all company employees and their families, regardless of position or salary? If you need to know more, attend the workshop that will be held in Conference Room 3 next Friday at 11:00. All aspects of our health care policy will be explained. This workshop will be particularly useful to new personnel, although all are welcome. However, you must register to attend. Please contact the Human Resources Office before 5:00 Thursday.

We will go over the various alternative plans available to company employees and discuss what criteria you need to consider in selecting the plan that best suits your needs. We will explain exactly what is covered and what is not under each alternative, and what portion of each doctor's visit or treatment that must be paid out of pocket. We will leave time at the end for a question-and-answer session to make sure that all your concerns are addressed. This workshop will last two hours.

---

19. What is the workshop about?
    (A) Choosing a doctor.
    (B) Health insurance.
    (C) Alternative medicine.
    (D) Planning a medical treatment.

20. Who can attend the workshop?
    (A) Anyone.
    (B) New personnel only.
    (C) The Human Resources staff.
    (D) Only employees with families.

21. What time will the workshop end?
    (A) 11:00.
    (B) 1:00.
    (C) 2:00.
    (D) 5:00.

22. The word *suits* in the second paragraph, line 3, is closest in meaning to
    (A) depends
    (B) satisfies
    (C) expresses
    (D) emphasizes

23. The word *concerns* in the second paragraph, line 8, is closest in meaning to
    (A) assignments
    (B) answers
    (C) benefits
    (D) worries

Lesson 49

Hospitals

accompany

admit

authorize

designate

escort

identify

mission

pertinent

procedure

result

statement

surgery

Study the following definitions and examples.

1. **accompany** v., to go with
   a. It is a good idea to ask a friend or relative to accompany you to a doctor's appointment when serious treatments will be discussed.
   b. Detailed instructions accompany most medications.

2. **admit** v., to permit to enter
   a. The injured patient was admitted to the unit directly from the emergency room.
   b. The staff refused to admit the patient until he had proof of insurance.

3. **authorize** v., to approve
   a. The doctor suggested that she check with her insurance company to make sure it would authorize a lengthened hospital stay.
   b. We cannot share the test results with you until we have been authorized to do so by your doctor.

4. **designate** v., to indicate or specify
   a. The labels on the bags designated the type of blood they contained.
   b. On her admittance form, Grandmother designated Aunt Tessa as her chief decision-maker.

5. **escort** n., a person accompanying another to guide or protect
   a. Let's see if there is an escort available to take you to the parking garage.
   b. You cannot leave the unit on your own; you'll have to wait for an escort.

6. **identify** v., to ascertain the name or belongings of
   a. The tiny bracelets identified each baby in the nursery.
   b. Your medical records are all marked with your patient number to identify them in case of a mix-up.

7. **mission** n., an inner calling to pursue an activity or perform a service
   a. The hospital chaplain took as his mission to visit every patient admitted each day.
   b. The nurse explained that the mission of everyone in the unit was to make sure the patients got well as soon as possible.

8. **pertinent** adj., having relevance to the matter at hand
   a. You should mention any pertinent health issues to the staff before you are admitted for surgery.
   b. The patient's health record contained pertinent information, like the dates of all his inoculations.

9. **procedure** n., a series of steps taken to accomplish an end
   a. The surgical procedure can now be done in half the amount of time it took even five years ago.
   b. Call the hospital to schedule this procedure for tomorrow.

10. **result** n., an outcome
    a. Your lab results won't be ready for hours.
    b. The scientific results prove that the new procedure is not significantly safer than the traditional one.

11. **statement** n., an accounting showing an amount due; a bill
    a. The billing statement was filed with the insurance company last month.
    b. Check with your doctor's office for an original statement; we cannot process a faxed copy.

12. **surgery** n., a medical procedure that involves cutting into the body
    a. The development of medical technology has made surgery much easier on the patient.
    b. Miranda had to stay in the hospital for several days following the surgery.

WORD FAMILIES

verb	admit	The patients lined the hospital corridors waiting to be admitted.
noun	admittance	Your admittance to the hospital is dependent on your showing proof that you can pay the bills.
noun	admission	Take these records down to Admissions and have them duplicate the files for you.

verb	authorize	Your doctor has to authorize these tests before we can proceed with them.
noun	authority	Before major surgery, it is a good idea to give decision-making authority to a close relative in case something happens to you.
noun	authorization	The nurse could not submit an authorization over the phone; it had to be done in writing.

verb	designate	The hospital administrator designated a team to create an emergency preparedness plan.
noun	designation	The designation of the hospital as one of the best in the region certainly helped its marketing efforts.
noun	designator	The national health service is the sole designator of which hospitals will get the grants.

verb	identify	If you identify your valuables, the nurse will give them back to you.
noun	identification	Please remember to bring some form of identification with you when you check in at the hospital.
adjective	identifiable	The red cross on the hospital's helicopter landing pad was identifiable from the air.

noun	pertinence	The doctor was not certain about the pertinence of many of the details in the patient's long medical history.
adjective	pertinent	The doctor will ask you for pertinent information, such as medications that you are currently taking.

noun	surgery	I have been feeling much better ever since I had surgery done on my back.
noun	surgeon	You will have an appointment with the surgeon so that she can explain the procedure to you.
adjective	surgical	It is important to keep surgical equipment absolutely clean.

WORDS IN CONTEXT

Read the following passage and write the words in the blanks below.

accompany	designated	mission	results
admission	escort	pertinent	statement
authorization	identification	procedures	surgeon

Hospitals have a (1) _____ to provide patients with high-quality medical care. Everyone on staff will make sure that you get the best possible treatment for your condition.

When you arrive at the hospital, you should have with you all the (2) _____ information needed to be admitted, like your insurance information and copies of X-rays and other test (3) _____, even if they were taken at another facility. Bring your insurance card and any referral or (4) _____ form from your doctor. You should also have some form of (5) _____ with a photo. You will also need to sign an agreement regarding treatment consent. Once you arrive, there is usually a concierge who will assist you with the (6) _____ process.

Some (7) _____ are simple and don't require an overnight stay in the hospital. You are given a while to rest and recover, and the (8) _____ may discuss home care with you before you leave the hospital. Then an (9) _____ takes you to the lobby and makes sure there is someone waiting for you to (10) _____ you home. Driving yourself, even after a simple surgery, is usually not recommended. After you leave the hospital, you will receive a (11) _____ from the hospital for the charges your insurer does not cover. Your insurance policy will outline any amount for which you may be responsible.

You will find that smoking is not permitted in any hospital building. Often, hospitals have (12) _____ smoking areas outside for patients, families, and staff who wish to smoke.

WORD PRACTICE

LISTENING COMPREHENSION

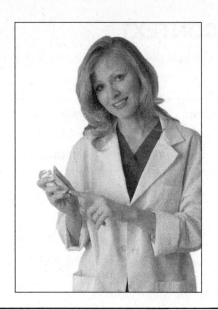

Part 1 Photo

Look at the picture and listen to the sentences.
Choose the sentence that best describes the picture.

1. Ⓐ Ⓑ Ⓒ Ⓓ

Part 2 Question–Response

Listen to the question and the three responses. Choose the response that best answers the question.

2. Ⓐ Ⓑ Ⓒ   3. Ⓐ Ⓑ Ⓒ

Part 3 Conversation

Listen to the dialogue. Then read each question and choose the best answer.

4. What is the woman's complaint?
   (A) The records weren't delivered on time.
   (B) Her husband didn't get an identification card.
   (C) The computer system broke down.
   (D) Her husband's records got mixed up.

5. Who is the man?
   (A) A hospital administrator.
   (B) A hospital patient.
   (C) A doctor.
   (D) A nurse.

6. Why was the woman's husband in the hospital?
   (A) For a surgical procedure.
   (B) To change his medications.
   (C) For tests.
   (D) To visit a friend.

Part 4 Talk

Listen to the talk. Then read each question and choose the best answer.

7. Who is the speaker?
   (A) A doctor.
   (B) A lab technician.
   (C) A nurse.
   (D) An insurance agent.

8. When will the surgery take place?
   (A) In eight days.
   (B) In a week.
   (C) In ten days.
   (D) In 23 days.

9. What will the listener do with the paperwork?
   (A) Prepare it.
   (B) Give it to the nurse.
   (C) Take it to the lab.
   (D) Submit it to the insurance company.

READING

Part 5 Incomplete Sentences

Choose the word that best completes the sentence.

10. Before my father was _____ to the hospital, he had to undergo a series of tests.
    (A) admit
    (B) admitted
    (C) admittance
    (D) admissions

11. Will your insurance company _____ a visit to a specialist?
    (A) authorize
    (B) authorization
    (C) authority
    (D) authorizing

12. As a precaution, it's wise to _____ someone in your family to make health care decisions for you in case there is a time that you cannot.
    (A) designation
    (B) designate
    (C) designator
    (D) designated

13. Your X-rays will have your name and social security number printed on them, so we can easily _____ them as yours.
    (A) identifiably
    (B) identification
    (C) identifiable
    (D) identify

14. The inability to move my elbow was an unfortunate and unexpected _____ of the surgery I had last month.
    (A) statement
    (B) procedure
    (C) result
    (D) mission

15. The billing statement from the hospital _____ by a detailed explanation of what the patient owed and what the insurance company would pay.
    (A) was accompanied
    (B) was accompanying
    (C) accompanied
    (D) accompanies

Part 6 Text Completion

CITY HOSPITAL ADMISSIONS PROCEDURES

- When you arrive, check in with the nurse on duty at the front desk.
- All patients must have signed _____ from a doctor before entering the hospital.

    16. (A) author
        (B) authorize
        (C) authority
        (D) authorization

Please give the signed form to the nurse.

- The nurse will also need to see a form of identification and proof of insurance. We cannot _____ anyone to the hospital without these. There will be no exceptions.

17. (A) submit
    (B) admit
    (C) remit
    (D) omit

- The nurse will complete the pertinent paperwork and assign you to a room.
- Please wait in the designated area. A hospital staff member _____ you to your room.

    18. (A) escorts
        (B) will escort
        (C) is escorting
        (D) has escorted

- Family members are not permitted to accompany patients to their rooms. They must wait until the usual visiting hours to see their loved ones. A schedule of visiting hours is posted in the main lobby.

Part 7 Reading Comprehension

Questions 19–23 refer to the following two e-mail messages.

To: Annabelle Pope
From: Henry Rice
Subject: Surgery

Hi Annabelle,

I was wondering if you could help me out with something. My doctor has recommended that I get knee replacement surgery. I am trying to identify the best hospital for this sort of procedure. My doctor says she usually recommends City Hospital, but I have heard that Upstate Hospital specializes in this kind of surgery. You had a similar procedure last year, didn't you? I think you broke your knee, or was it your elbow? Which hospital did you go to? Were you satisfied with the results of your treatment, and were you well cared for by the staff? I would appreciate the benefit of your advice. I need to make a decision soon since my doctor thinks this should be done before another month goes by. Thanks.

Henry

To: Henry Rice
From: Annabelle Pope
Subject: Re: Surgery

Hi Henry,

I am sorry you need surgery, but I am sure you will feel it is worth it. I had my procedure done at Upstate Hospital, and I would recommend that place to anyone. The procedure I had was similar to yours, except it was my hip, not my knee. My surgeon was excellent, and I received good care from all the staff. The mission of the hospital is to provide the highest level of care possible, and the entire staff works hard to fulfill that mission. I was originally told that I would need to be in the hospital for a week, but when it became clear that I wouldn't be recovered enough by that time, the doctor didn't hesitate to keep me there for an extra three days. They wouldn't permit me to go home until they were sure I was ready. I really think Upstate is the best hospital for your surgery. Let me know when it is scheduled, and I will visit you there.

Annabelle

19. What does Henry ask Annabelle to do?
    (A) Recommend a hospital.
    (B) Perform surgery.
    (C) Visit him in the hospital.
    (D) Talk to his doctor.

20. Why was Annabelle in the hospital last year?
    (A) For a broken knee.
    (B) For a broken elbow.
    (C) For a hip replacement.
    (D) For a knee replacement.

21. How long was Annabelle in the hospital?
    (A) Three days.
    (B) A week.
    (C) Ten days.
    (D) A month.

22. The word *results* in the first e-mail, line 9, is closest in meaning to
    (A) outcome
    (B) process
    (C) nature
    (D) price

23. The word *mission* in the second e-mail, line 7, is closest in meaning to
    (A) rule
    (B) goal
    (C) demand
    (D) requirement

Lesson 50

Pharmacy

WORDS TO LEARN

consult

control

convenient

detect

factor

interaction

limit

monitor

potential

sample

sense

volunteer

Study the following definitions and examples.

1. **consult** v., to seek advice or information of
   a. The doctor consulted with a specialist before writing a new prescription.
   b. May I consult with you about a drug interaction case I have?
2. **control** v., to exercise authority or power over
   a. To control the cost of this medication, you may get the generic version.
   b. Please take your medication every day to control your high blood pressure.
3. **convenient** adj., suited or favorable to one's purpose; easy to reach
   a. Is this a convenient location for you to pick up your prescription?
   b. It is convenient to have a pharmacy right across the street from my doctor's office.
4. **detect** v., to discover or ascertain
   a. My doctor put me through some simple tests to detect if I have asthma.
   b. I have to keep track of my sleep patterns to detect how many times I get up in the night.
5. **factor** n., a contribution to an accomplishment, a result, or a process
   a. Taking medications as directed is an important factor in getting well.
   b. Could my cat be a factor contributing to my asthma?
6. **interaction** n., a mutual activity
   a. My pharmacist was concerned about the interaction of the two medications I was prescribed.
   b. The interaction between the patient and the doctor showed a high level of trust.
7. **limit** n., the point beyond which something cannot proceed
   a. My prescription has a limit of three refills.
   b. My health plan authorization sets a limit on which health care providers I can see without their permission.
8. **monitor** v., to keep track of
   a. The nurse practitioner carefully monitors the number of medications her patients are taking.
   b. The patient had weekly appointments so that the doctor could monitor her progress.
9. **potential** adj., capable of being but not yet in existence; possible
   a. To avoid any potential side effects from the medication, be sure to tell your doctor all the drugs you are currently taking.
   b. Given the potential delay in getting reimbursed by the health plan, why don't we just fill one prescription today?
10. **sample** n., a portion, piece, or segment that is representative of a whole
    a. The pharmacist gave Myra a few free samples of the allergy medication.
    b. A sample of the population taking the new medicine was surveyed to determine whether it caused side effects.
11. **sense** n., a judgment; an intellectual interpretation
    a. The doctor had a good sense about what the problem was but wanted to get a second opinion.
    b. I got the sense it would be better to get my prescription filled right away.
12. **volunteer** v., to perform a service by choice or without being asked
    a. My doctor volunteered to call the drugstore, so my medication would be waiting for me.
    b. Since Tom was feeling so unwell, his son volunteered to pick up his prescription at the pharmacy for him.

WORD FAMILIES

verb	consult	Beatrice consulted her pharmacist about the number of different medications she is taking.
noun	consultation	Let me arrange a consultation with a specialist to discuss your heart problem and some possible medications.
adjective	consultative	This is a consultative process and you probably won't have a definitive answer immediately.

noun	convenience	The convenience of a 24-hour neighborhood pharmacy is not to be underestimated.
adjective	convenient	Many people shop there because of its convenient location.
adverb	conveniently	The pharmacy is conveniently located on my way home from work.

verb	detect	The laboratory test detected the presence of medication in his blood.
noun	detection	Early detection of diseases usually means that medications can be more effective.
adjective	detectable	After he took his medication faithfully for a few months and exercised more, Jack's disease was no longer detectable.

verb	limit	My health insurance company has severely limited the amount of money it will pay out for prescription medicine.
noun	limit	Even though that headache medicine does not require a prescription, there is a limit to how many times a day you should take it.
adjective	limited	The new drugstore on the corner really isn't convenient because of its limited hours of operation.

noun	potential	Be careful when taking this medication because it has the potential to make you feel sleepy.
adjective	potential	Margaret decided not to take the medicine the doctor had prescribed because of its potential side effects.
adverb	potentially	Many medications are potentially dangerous so it is important to take them exactly as prescribed by the doctor.

verb	volunteer	The pharmacist volunteers his services monthly at the free clinic for homeless people.
noun	volunteer	Volunteers bring filled prescriptions from the pharmacy to the homes of shut-ins.
adjective	voluntary	Your compliance with this new policy is completely voluntary, but we think it is in the public interest that you do so.

WORDS IN CONTEXT

Read the following passage and write the words in the blanks below.

consulting	detection	limit	samples
control	factors	monitor	sense
convenient	interactions	potential	volunteers

Yoko is having trouble with seasonal allergies this fall. After (1) _____ with her doctor, she decides to take medication on a regular basis to (2) _____ her symptoms. Her doctor recommends the medication he thinks will work best and offers her a handful of (3) _____ at no charge. For her long-term needs, Yoko will need to have a prescription filled. Her doctor (4) _____ to call the pharmacy Yoko uses to order a supply, which will (5) _____ the time she spends waiting for the prescription to be filled.

Yoko is new in town and does not know which pharmacy she wants to use. She knows that there is a drugstore near her apartment and one near where she works, but does not remember the operating hours for either. Yoko knows that (6) _____ hours and location are important (7) _____ in selecting a pharmacy. Although she can fill different prescriptions at different drugstores, it makes more (8) _____ to Yoko to fill all of her medications at one location.

Some drugs can have harmful (9) _____ when taken together. Usually, your doctor will prevent this sort of problem before it starts. But, if you see more than one doctor, it is hard to (10) _____ the various medications you are taking. Having all your prescriptions filled at one location increases the chances that the pharmacist will detect a (11) _____ drug interaction problem. This timely (12) _____ can save your life.

WORD PRACTICE

LISTENING COMPREHENSION

TRACK
51

Part 1 Photo

Look at the picture and listen to the sentences.
Choose the sentence that best describes the picture.

1. Ⓐ Ⓑ Ⓒ Ⓓ

Part 2 Question–Response

Listen to the question and the three responses. Choose the response that best answers the question.

2. Ⓐ Ⓑ Ⓒ   3. Ⓐ Ⓑ Ⓒ

Part 3 Conversation

Listen to the dialogue. Then read each question and choose the best answer.

4. Whom is the man talking to?
   (A) A doctor.
   (B) A pharmacist.
   (C) His wife.
   (D) His friend.

5. What is the man's problem?
   (A) Headache.
   (B) Backache.
   (C) Broken hand.
   (D) Broken nose.

6. When will the man fill the prescription?
   (A) Today.
   (B) Within two days.
   (C) On the way to work.
   (D) After trying the samples.

Part 4 Talk

Listen to the talk. Then read each question and choose the best answer.

7. What is a possible side effect of the medication?
   (A) Sleepiness.
   (B) Stomachaches.
   (C) Fatigue.
   (D) Headaches.

8. How often should the patient take the medication?
   (A) Once a day.
   (B) Two times a day.
   (C) Three times a day.
   (D) Four times a day.

9. Why should the patient call the doctor in a few days?
   (A) To request more days off work.
   (B) To report how the medication is working.
   (C) To get pills for his headaches.
   (D) To ask for more samples.

READING

Part 5 Incomplete Sentences

Choose the word that best completes the sentence.

10. Would you please schedule the patient for a medical _____ tomorrow afternoon?
    (A) consult   (C) consulting
    (B) consultation   (D) consultative

11. Your prescription will be ready in an hour, if that's _____ for you.
    (A) conveniences   (C) convenience
    (B) conveniently   (D) convenient

12. The doctor _____ a potential problem during the examination, so he wants me to consult a specialist.
    (A) detected   (C) controlled
    (B) limited   (D) monitored

13. My doctor has decided to _____ the amount of medication I am taking.
    (A) limit   (C) limiting
    (B) limited   (D) limits

14. Inform the pharmacist of any other medications you are taking to avoid any _____ drug interactions.
    (A) potentially   (C) potentiality
    (B) potential   (D) potency

15. We desperately need _____ to help at the free clinic next month.
    (A) voluntary   (C) volunteers
    (B) volunteer   (D) volunteerism

Part 6 Text Completion

CLOVERDALE PHARMACY
The neighborhood pharmacy that you can rely on!

Cloverdale is open 24 hours a day, seven days a week. Unlike other pharmacies with limited schedules, we're open all the time. You can rely on us in an emergency at any time of day. And, our schedule makes it _____ for busy working people to fill prescriptions after

      16. (A) convenient
           (B) convenience
           (C) conveniently
           (D) convention

work or on weekends.

You're always safe with us! When you fill a prescription at Cloverdale, we keep a careful record. This way, we can easily _____ the medications you are taking and inform you

      17. (A) are monitored
           (B) be monitored
           (C) to monitor
           (D) monitor

of any potentially harmful interactions.

Do you need help selecting over-the-counter medications? Our pharmacists are available to _____ with you and help you choose the medications that suit your needs.

18. (A) conduct
    (B) consult
    (C) construct
    (D) conjunct

Cloverdale Pharmacy. We're here to serve you.

Part 7 Reading Comprehension

Questions 19–23 refer to the following article.

Many people don't realize that their pharmacist is an important member of their health care team. If you always fill you prescriptions at the same pharmacy, then you will have a pharmacist who is familiar with your medical issues and can detect any possible problems with your medications. In fact, it is a good idea to volunteer information about medications you are already taking when you visit a new pharmacist. Then, she can add this information to your records and have a complete file of information. She can monitor the drugs you are taking and let you know of any potential interactions or harmful side effects.

If cost is an issue for you, your pharmacist can help. Ask her if there are any less expensive brands of your medication available. Or, you can request that she fill only half the prescription, to give you a chance to try out the medication before paying for the entire amount. You can also ask your doctor for a few free samples. Once you have ascertained that the prescribed medication is working for you, you can go ahead and ask your pharmacist to fill the prescription for you. When you pick up your prescription, don't forget to ask the pharmacist to explain to you how to take it if you have any doubts. She can also supply you with written instructions.

Your pharmacist can provide you with important support, but there is a limit to what she can do. If you suspect that you have a problem that requires medical attention, you should always consult your doctor right away.

19. What is the purpose of this article?
    (A) To explain the role of a pharmacist.
    (B) To help select medications.
    (C) To give instructions on taking medications.
    (D) To advertise a particular pharmacy.

20. What can you ask your pharmacist to do?
    (A) Recommend a good doctor.
    (B) Suggest different brands.
    (C) Write a prescription.
    (D) Give you medical attention.

21. What should you ask for when you pick up your prescription?
    (A) A cheaper brand.
    (B) Some free samples.
    (C) Instructions.
    (D) A discount.

22. The word *detect* in line 3 is closest in meaning to
    (A) repair
    (B) create
    (C) inform
    (D) discover

23. The word *potential* in line 8 is closest in meaning to
    (A) common
    (B) interesting
    (C) dangerous
    (D) possible

Word Review #10   Lessons 46–50 Health

Choose the word that best completes the sentence.

1. Your doctor's _____ are as important as his prescriptions.
   (A) recommend
   (B) recommended
   (C) recommending
   (D) recommendations

2. Dentists are as concerned with your dental _____ as with the condition of your teeth.
   (A) habits
   (B) habitual
   (C) habitually
   (D) habituated

3. To avoid _____ any additional charges, you should ask to be discharged from the hospital.
   (A) incur
   (B) incurs
   (C) incurred
   (D) incurring

4. It is as fast and efficient to _____ with your pharmacist as with your physician.
   (A) consult
   (B) consulting
   (C) consulted
   (D) consultation

5. Although an annual checkup is important, you should also make an _____ whenever you have a health concern.
   (A) appoint
   (B) appointed
   (C) appointment
   (D) appointments

6. A dentist can perform dental _____ as well as routine maintenance.
   (A) restore
   (B) restored
   (C) restoring
   (D) restoration

7. A good medical insurance policy will _____ preventive health programs as well as treatment.
   (A) emphasize
   (B) emphasis
   (C) emphasizing
   (D) emphasized

8. The most difficult part of hospitalization is being _____.
   (A) admit
   (B) admitted
   (C) admissions
   (D) admitting

9. A pharmacist will _____ the customer's medications.
   (A) monitor
   (B) monitors
   (C) monitoring
   (D) monitored

10. I don't understand most of what I read in a hospital's billing _____.
   (A) state
   (B) stated
   (C) stating
   (D) statement

Choose the one word or phrase that best completes each sentence.

The most important part of your health care is the _____ visit to your doctor.

11. (A) daily
    (B) monthly
    (C) annual
    (D) perennial

By visiting your doctor once a year, you can feel sure that any changes in your health will be detected. Your doctor might _____ lifestyle changes, such as diet

12. (A) recommend
    (B) recommends
    (C) to recommend
    (D) recommending

and exercise, that you will need to make in order to maintain your health. The best way to _____ serious disease, after all, is to maintain a healthy lifestyle.

13. (A) prevent
    (B) prevention
    (C) preventive
    (D) preventively

MEMO

To: All company staff
From: Human Resources Office
Re: Dental insurance

Dental insurance is now available to all company _____. We can offer you a policy that

14. (A) person
    (B) personal
    (C) personify
    (D) personnel

covers all the usual dental _____, such as cleanings and fillings. Unfortunately, surgery

15. (A) conveniences
    (B) procedures
    (C) appointments
    (D) irritations

and other complicated procedures will not be covered. If you are interested in applying for this insurance, please notify our office before the end of this month. We _____ you to take

16. (A) are encouraged
    (B) encouraging
    (C) encouraged
    (D) encourage

advantage of this opportunity to obtain affordable dental care for yourself and your family.

Your doctor has prescribed this medication to treat your symptoms. Take it as instructed by your doctor. It is most _____ when taken with meals. Consult

17. (A) effect
    (B) effective
    (C) effectively
    (D) effectiveness

with your doctor before taking any additional medications to avoid _____

18. (A) potent
    (B) potion
    (C) potential
    (D) potentially

harmful interactions. Possible side effects of this medication include sleepiness and _____ of the stomach.

19. (A) irritate
    (B) irritant
    (C) irritation
    (D) irritating

Answer Key

Lessons 1–5 General Business

Lesson 1 Contracts
Words in Context: 1. establish 2. agreement 3. parties
4. specifies 5. obligates 6. assurance 7. determine 8. provide
9. resolve 10. engaging 11. abide by 12. cancel
Word Practice: 1. B 2. A 3. A 4. C 5. A 6. D 7. A 8. A
9. B 10. A 11. A 12. B 13. D 14. B 15. D 16. D 17. B
18. D 19. A 20. B 21. C 22. A 23. D

Lesson 2 Marketing
Words in Context: 1. product 2. market 3. persuaded
4. consumers 5. attract 6. satisfied 7. current 8. inspiration
9. convince 10. compared 11. competes 12. fad
Word Practice: 1. C 2. A 3. B 4. C 5. D 6. A 7. D 8. C
9. B 10. C 11. A 12. C 13. A 14. D 15. B 16. C 17. A
18. D 19. B 20. A 21. C 22. D 23. B

Lesson 3 Warranties
Words in Context: 1. promise 2. required 3. frequently
4. consider 5. characteristics 6. variety 7. covers 8. implies
9. expire 10. protect 11. reputations 12. consequences
Word Practice: 1. A 2. B 3. A 4. C 5. B 6. A 7. B 8. A
9. D 10. D 11. B 12. D 13. C 14. A 15. D 16. A 17. B
18. C 19. A 20. D 21. D 22. B 23. A

Lesson 4 Business Planning
Words in Context: 1. develop 2. primary 3. avoid
4. substitute 5. strengthen 6. strategy 7. evaluation 8. offered
9. risks 10. gathering 11. demonstrate 12. address
Word Practice: 1. A 2. A 3. B 4. D 5. A 6. B 7. A 8. B
9. B 10. A 11. A 12. C 13. D 14. C 15. A 16. D 17. A
18. C 19. C 20. A 21. B 22. A 23. D

Lesson 5 Conferences
Words in Context: 1. associations 2. get in touch 3. take
part in 4. sessions 5. attending 6. select 7. arrangements
8. accommodate 9. hold 10. overcrowded 11. location
12. register
Word Practice: 1. D 2. B 3. B 4. C 5. D 6. C 7. A 8. D
9. A 10. B 11. C 12. B 13. A 14. A 15. D 16. A 17. D
18. C 19. B 20. B 21. C 22. D 23. A

Word Review #1: 1. C 2. D 3. D 4. D 5. A 6. B 7. A
8. B 9. A 10. A 11. D 12. B 13. C 14. B 15. A 16. C
17. B 18. D 19. C

Lessons 6–10 Office Issues

Lesson 6 Computers and the Internet
Words in Context: 1. shut down 2. warning 3. figure out
4. access 5. search 6. deleted 7. duplicate 8. ignore
9. display 10. failed 11. allocate 12. compatible
Word Practice: 1. C 2. A 3. A 4. D 5. A 6. C 7. B 8. C
9. D 10. A 11. B 12. B 13. B 14. B 15. C 16. B 17. A
18. D 19. C 20. C 21. D 22. B 23. D

Lesson 7 Office Technology
Words in Context: 1. in charge 2. durable 3. affordable
4. reduce 5. capacity 6. physical 7. initiates 8. stays on top
of 9. recurring 10. provider 11. as needed 12. stock
Word Practice: 1. A 2. B 3. C 4. D 5. B 6. A 7. D 8. B
9. C 10. D 11. C 12. A 13. B 14. D 15. B 16. A 17. C
18. D 19. A 20. C 21. D 22. B 23. A

Lesson 8 Office Procedures
Words in Context: 1. appreciation 2. made of 3. reinforced
4. casually 5. code 6. out of 7. verbalize 8. practices
9. outdated 10. been exposed to 11. brought in 12. glimpse
Word Practice: 1. B 2. C 3. C 4. B 5. A 6. D 7. A 8. B
9. C 10. A 11. B 12. D 13. D 14. A 15. B 16. C 17. C
18. A 19. B 20. C 21. B 22. C 23. A

Lesson 9 Electronics
Words in Context: 1. sharply 2. networks 3. facilitated
4. processing 5. popular 6. software 7. stored
8. revolutionized 9. devices 10. skills 11. technical
12. replaced
Word Practice: 1. C 2. C 3. B 4. A 5. C 6. D 7. A 8. C
9. D 10. C 11. D 12. B 13. A 14. C 15. A 16. B 17. C
18. C 19. B 20. D 21. B 22. A 23. B

Lesson 10 Correspondence
Words in Context: 1. proofed 2. revision 3. beforehand
4. assemble 5. folding 6. courier 7. express 8. distributed
9. layout 10. mention 11. complicated 12. petition
Word Practice: 1. C 2. B 3. C 4. B 5. C 6. C 7. A 8. B
9. D 10. A 11. B 12. A 13. A 14. B 15. C 16. D 17. A
18. D 19. D 20. C 21. A 22. B 23. C

Word Review #2: 1. C 2. D 3. B 4. D 5. B 6. A 7. B 8. B
9. C 10. B 11. D 12. B 13. D 14. A 15. C 16. B 17. D
18. A 19. B

Lessons 11–15 Personnel

Lesson 11 Job Advertising and Recruiting
Words in Context: 1. time-consuming 2. match 3. recruit 4. accomplishments 5. bring together 6. abundant 7. candidates 8. qualifications 9. coming up with 10. profile 11. commensurate 12. submit
Word Practice: 1. D 2. A 3. B 4. D 5. C 6. A 7. D 8. A 9. A 10. C 11. A 12. A 13. B 14. A 15. A 16. B 17. D 18. A 19. B 20. C 21. A 22. D 23. C

Lesson 12 Applying and Interviewing
Words in Context: 1. experts 2. confidence 3. weaknesses 4. constantly 5. follow up 6. abilities 7. apply 8. backgrounds 9. interview 10. called in 11. present 12. hesitant
Word Practice: 1. A 2. A 3. C 4. B 5. D 6. A 7. D 8. B 9. B 10. D 11. C 12. A 13. D 14. B 15. A 16. B 17. C 18. D 19. C 20. C 21. D 22. A 23. D

Lesson 13 Hiring and Training
Words in Context: 1. conducted 2. rejected 3. successfully 4. generate 5. hires 6. training 7. update 8. keep up with 9. set up 10. mentor 11. look up to 12. on track
Word Practice: 1. B 2. A 3. B 4. D 5. A 6. B 7. D 8. B 9. D 10. B 11. B 12. C 13. A 14. D 15. B 16. A 17. D 18. D 19. B 20. D 21. A 22. D 23. C

Lesson 14 Salaries and Benefits
Words in Context: 1. negotiated 2. benefits 3. compensated 4. delicate 5. aware 6. wage 7. flexibility 8. basis 9. raise 10. retirement 11. eligible 12. vested
Word Practice: 1. C 2. B 3. A 4. D 5. C 6. B 7. A 8. A 9. B 10. C 11. C 12. C 13. B 14. B 15. A 16. A 17. C 18. C 19. C 20. B 21. A 22. D 23. A

Lesson 15 Promotions, Pensions, and Awards
Words in Context: 1. recognizes 2. contributions 3. achievements/merits 4. promotions 5. merits/achievements 6. loyalty 7. obvious 8. look to 9. praised 10. value 11. look forward 12. dedicate
Word Practice: 1. C 2. A 3. C 4. D 5. C 6. A 7. B 8. C 9. C 10. C 11. C 12. C 13. C 14. B 15. A 16. D 17. B 18. A 19. C 20. D 21. B 22. A 23. B

Word Review #3: 1. A 2. A 3. B 4. C 5. D 6. C 7. B 8. B 9. D 10. B 11. A 12. B 13. D 14. D 15. A 16. D 17. C 18. B 19. C

Lessons 16–20 Purchasing

Lesson 16 Shopping
Words in Context: 1. bear 2. behavior 3. mandatory 4. strictly 5. items 6. expand 7. exploring 8. bargains 9. checkout 10. trend 11. merchandise 12. comfort
Word Practice: 1. C 2. B 3. B 4. A 5. B 6. D 7. B 8. C 9. D 10. C 11. A 12. D 13. A 14. C 15. C 16. C 17. C 18. D 19. C 20. B 21. A 22. D 23. A

Lesson 17 Ordering Supplies
Words in Context: 1. consistent 2. stationery 3. obtain 4. diverse 5. maintaining 6. essential 7. prerequisite 8. smooth 9. functioning 10. enterprise 11. source 12. quality
Word Practice: 1. C 2. C 3. C 4. B 5. D 6. D 7. B 8. A 9. B 10. C 11. C 12. C 13. C 14. B 15. A 16. B 17. D 18. B 19. A 20. C 21. D 22. A 23. D

Lesson 18 Shipping
Words in Context: 1. integral 2. catalog 3. shipping 4. minimize 5. receive 6. accurate 7. carrier 8. inventory 9. sufficient 10. fulfill 11. on hand 12. supplies
Word Practice: 1. C 2. A 3. A 4. A 5. B 6. C 7. D 8. D 9. A 10. A 11. C 12. A 13. A 14. C 15. B 16. B 17. D 18. A 19. D 20. A 21. C 22. B 23. C

Lesson 19 Invoices
Words in Context: 1. efficient 2. compiled 3. charges 4. customer 5. estimated 6. terms 7. imposed 8. dispute 9. discount 10. mistake 11. rectified 12. promptly
Word Practice: 1. A 2. A 3. C 4. D 5. C 6. C 7. C 8. D 9. C 10. B 11. B 12. C 13. D 14. A 15. A 16. A 17. D 18. C 19. C 20. D 21. B 22. A 23. C

Lesson 20 Inventory
Words in Context: 1. verifies 2. crucial 3. installed 4. running 5. subtracts 6. adjusted 7. automatically 8. scanning 9. reflect 10. tedious 11. discrepancies 12. disturbances
Word Practice: 1. A 2. A 3. C 4. B 5. B 6. D 7. D 8. D 9. B 10. B 11. A 12. A 13. D 14. D 15. A 16. A 17. A 18. B 19. B 20. C 21. B 22. C 23. A

Word Review #4: 1. A 2. B 3. A 4. A 5. C 6. C 7. B 8. A 9. D 10. B 11. D 12. B 13. A 14. C 15. D 16. B 17. A 18. C 19. D

Lessons 21–25 Financing and Budgeting

Lesson 21 Banking
Words in Context: 1. transact 2. borrow 3. mortgages
4. cautious 5. down payment 6. dividends 7. restrict 8. take out 9. balance 10. deductions 11. accept 12. signature
Word Practice: 1. D 2. A 3. C 4. D 5. A 6. A 7. B 8. A
9. C 10. A 11. D 12. B 13. B 14. C 15. D 16. C 17. B
18. A 19. C 20. B 21. D 22. A 23. C

Lesson 22 Accounting
Words in Context: 1. accumulated 2. budget 3. clients
4. outstanding 5. profitable 6. audited 7. accounting
8. building up 9. turnover 10. reconcile 11. debt 12. assets
Word Practice: 1. A 2. B 3. A 4. D 5. C 6. A 7. C 8. B
9. A 10. D 11. A 12. B 13. B 14. C 15. C 16. B 17. D
18. D 19. B 20. B 21. C 22. D 23. B

Lesson 23 Investments
Words in Context: 1. invest 2. resources 3. wise 4. portfolio
5. pull out 6. return 7. committed 8. long-term 9. fund
10. attitude 11. conservative (or aggressive) 12. aggressive (or conservative)
Word Practice: 1. A 2. A 3. C 4. B 5. A 6. D 7. D 8. B
9. A 10. C 11. B 12. A 13. A 14. C 15. D 16. C 17. D
18. C 19. B 20. C 21. B 22. A 23. D

Lesson 24 Taxes
Words in Context: 1. prepares 2. deadline 3. fill out 4. filed
5. spouse 6. joint 7. refund 8. calculated 9. owe 10. gave up
11. withhold 12. penalized
Word Practice: 1. D 2. A 3. C 4. B 5. D 6. D 7. A 8. D
9. A 10. A 11. B 12. B 13. D 14. B 15. C 16. C 17. C
18. B 19. B 20. C 21. D 22. A 23. D

Lesson 25 Financial Statements
Words in Context: 1. level 2. target 3. forecasts 4. overall
5. projected 6. desired 7. yield 8. translate 9. realistic
10. perspective 11. detailed 12. typical
Word Practice: 1. A 2. C 3. A 4. B 5. C 6. D 7. C 8. C
9. B 10. C 11. C 12. B 13. A 14. D 15. A 16. D 17. A
18. B 19. A 20. C 21. A 22. B 23. D

Word Review #5: 1. A 2. B 3. D 4. B 5. C 6. C 7. D
8. A 9. D 10. D 11. B 12. D 13. C 14. D 15. B 16. C
17. A 18. B 19. A

Lessons 26–30 Management Issues

Lesson 26 Property and Departments
Words in Context: 1. disruptive 2. adjacent 3. lobby
4. inconsiderate 5. collaboration 6. hampered 7. move up
8. scrutinized 9. opting 10. conducive 11. concentrate
12. open to
Word Practice: 1. A 2. A 3. C 4. D 5. B 6. C 7. D 8. C
9. A 10. B 11. B 12. A 13. C 14. A 15. C 16. B 17. C
18. D 19. A 20. C 21. D 22. B 23. C

Lesson 27 Board Meetings and Committees
Words in Context: 1. waste 2. agenda 3. matters 4. goals
5. lengthy 6. adhered to 7. brought up 8. priority 9. go
ahead 10. periodically 11. progress 12. concluded
Word Practice: 1. D 2. C 3. C 4. D 5. B 6. C 7. A 8. D
9. A 10. A 11. A 12. B 13. C 14. B 15. B 16. D 17. C
18. B 19. C 20. D 21. B 22. A 23. C

Lesson 28 Quality Control
Words in Context: 1. conform 2. defects 3. garment
4. inspect 5. throws out 6. enhance 7. repel 8. take back
9. brand 10. uniform 11. wrinkle 12. perceive
Word Practice: 1. C 2. B 3. B 4. D 5. A 6. B 7. D 8. B
9. D 10. C 11. C 12. A 13. C 14. C 15. A 16. A 17. C
18. D 19. B 20. D 21. C 22. A 23. B

Lesson 29 Product Development
Words in Context: 1. anxious 2. decade 3. supervisor
4. responsible 5. logical 6. systematic 7. ascertain 8. solve
9. researched 10. examining 11. experiments 12. assume
Word Practice: 1. B 2. C 3. A 4. A 5. C 6. B 7. D 8. C
9. B 10. A 11. A 12. C 13. B 14. B 15. B 16. C 17. D
18. B 19. A 20. D 21. C 22. D 23. A

Lesson 30 Renting and Leasing
Words in Context: 1. apprehensive 2. lease 3. Occupancy
4. indicator 5. fluctuations 6. due to 7. condition 8. lock
(themselves) into 9. get out of 10. circumstances 11. subject
12. tenant
Word Practice: 1. A 2. B 3. A 4. D 5. D 6. B 7. D 8. B
9. B 10. B 11. A 12. D 13. C 14. B 15. C 16. A 17. C
18. D 19. A 20. D 21. B 22. C 23. A

Word Review #6: 1. C 2. A 3. C 4. A 5. C 6. D 7. D
8. C 9. B 10. D 11. A 12. B 13. C 14. B 15. D 16. C
17. A 18. C 19. D

Lessons 31–35 Restaurants and Events

Lesson 31 Selecting a Restaurant
Words in Context: 1. secure 2. relies 3. guidance
4. suggestion 5. subjective 6. daring 7. appeal 8. delicious
9. majority 10. compromise 11. mix 12. familiar
Word Practice: 1. A 2. A 3. A 4. B 5. C 6. D 7. A 8. B
9. C 10. B 11. C 12. D 13. D 14. C 15. A 16. B 17. C
18. D 19. B 20. D 21. A 22. B 23. C

Lesson 32 Eating Out
Words in Context: 1. randomly 2. foreign 3. patrons
4. predict 5. remind 6. mix up 7. complete 8. judged
9. excite 10. flavor 11. ingredients 12. appetites
Word Practice: 1. B 2. B 3. C 4. A 5. B 6. D 7. D 8. C
9. C 10. A 11. C 12. D 13. C 14. A 15. D 16. B 17. B
18. A 19. D 20. A 21. C 22. B 23. B

Lesson 33 Ordering Lunch
Words in Context: 1. falls to 2. burdensome 3. multiple
4. narrow 5. individual 6. commonly 7. settled 8. delivered
9. pick up 10. impress 11. elegant 12. reasonably
Word Practice: 1. A 2. A 3. B 4. D 5. C 6. B 7. C 8. A
9. C 10. D 11. C 12. B 13. A 14. B 15. C 16. A 17. D
18. D 19. B 20. A 21. D 22. A 23. C

Lesson 34 Cooking as a Career
Words in Context: 1. outlet 2. drawn 3. profession
4. demanding 5. influx 6. incorporate 7. methods 8. themes
9. accustomed 10. relinquish 11. culinary 12. apprenticeship
Word Practice: 1. A 2. C 3. B 4. C 5. A 6. B 7. C 8. D
9. D 10. D 11. D 12. C 13. B 14. B 15. A 16. B 17. D
18. B 19. A 20. D 21. C 22. A 23. D

Lesson 35 Events
Words in Context: 1. event 2. coordinated 3. site 4. stage
5. exact 6. dimensions 7. regulations 8. lead time 9. ideally
10. assist 11. proximity 12. general
Word Practice: 1. D 2. B 3. C 4. B 5. C 6. C 7. D 8. B
9. A 10. C 11. A 12. B 13. A 14. C 15. B 16. D 17. A
18. C 19. D 20. A 21. D 22. B 23. C

Word Review #7: 1. C 2. D 3. B 4. A 5. D 6. C 7. C
8. C 9. D 10. B 11. C 12. A 13. D 14. B 15. D 16. B
17. C 18. D 19. A

Lessons 36–40 Travel

Lesson 36 General Travel
Words in Context: 1. agent 2. valid 3. itinerary 4. delayed
5. prohibited 6. luggage 7. embarkation 8. board 9. depart
10. beverage 11. announcements 12. claims
Word Practice: 1. A 2. A 3. B 4. D 5. C 6. A 7. B 8. B
9. A 10. D 11. C 12. B 13. A 14. B 15. A 16. A 17. C
18. B 19. C 20. B 21. B 22. D 23. D

Lesson 37 Airlines
Words in Context: 1. deal with 2. expensive 3. substantial
4. economical 5. scenery 6. destination 7. prospective
8. situation 9. excursion 10. equivalent 11. extending
12. distinguishable
Word Practice: 1. D 2. C 3. C 4. C 5. B 6. A 7. B 8. A
9. B 10. D 11. A 12. C 13. D 14. D 15. B 16. B 17. C
18. B 19. D 20. B 21. D 22. A 23. C

Lesson 38 Trains
Words in Context: 1. relatively 2. punctual 3. fares
4. directories 5. comprehensive 6. remote 7. operate
8. remainder 9. duration 10. deluxe 11. offset 12. entitle
Word Practice: 1. C 2. A 3. B 4. D 5. A 6. B 7. D 8. C
9. A 10. C 11. A 12. A 13. B 14. C 15. B 16. D 17. A
18. A 19. C 20. B 21. D 22. A 23. D

Lesson 39 Hotels
Words in Context: 1. preclude 2. rates 3. reservations
4. advance 5. notify 6. confirm 7. quoted 8. service
9. expect 10. housekeeper 11. chains 12. check in
Word Practice: 1. C 2. B 3. A 4. D 5. C 6. A 7. A 8. B
9. D 10. C 11. B 12. D 13. C 14. A 15. B 16. A 17. C
18. D 19. D 20. B 21. A 22. C 23. C

Lesson 40 Car Rentals
Words in Context: 1. tempted 2. nervous 3. coincided
4. disappointment 5. guaranteed 6. contacted 7. license
8. confusing 9. intended 10. tier 11. request 12. thrill
Word Practice: 1. C 2. B 3. B 4. D 5. D 6. C 7. D 8. C
9. A 10. D 11. C 12. A 13. C 14. D 15. A 16. B 17. A
18. C 19. C 20. B 21. A 22. D 23. B

Word Review #8: 1. D 2. C 3. A 4. D 5. C 6. D 7. A
8. C 9. D 10. B 11. B 12. A 13. D 14. C 15. A 16. B
17. D 18. A 19. B

Lessons 41–45 Entertainment

Lesson 41 Movies
Words in Context: 1. continues 2. entertaining 3. disperse 4. influence 5. descriptions 6. represent 7. successive 8. range 9. combines 10. released 11. attain 12. separate
Word Practice: 1. A 2. C 3. A 4. D 5. A 6. C 7. B 8. C 9. A 10. A 11. C 12. A 13. B 14. D 15. B 16. D 17. C 18. D 19. C 20. B 21. B 22. A 23. D

Lesson 42 Theater
Words in Context: 1. created 2. elements 3. performance 4. occurs 5. approach 6. action 7. experiences 8. dialogue 9. rehearsal 10. audience 11. reviews 12. sell out
Word Practice: 1. A 2. B 3. C 4. B 5. A 6. D 7. D 8. D 9. B 10. B 11. A 12. D 13. C 14. A 15. B 16. A 17. C 18. B 19. B 20. A 21. D 22. C 23. D

Lesson 43 Music
Words in Context: 1. reason 2. available 3. category 4. taste 5. divided 6. broad 7. disparate 8. urge 9. instinctive 10. lively 11. favorite 12. relax
Word Practice: 1. D 2. A 3. C 4. B 5. C 6. A 7. C 8. A 9. D 10. C 11. A 12. D 13. B 14. D 15. B 16. C 17. D 18. A 19. C 20. B 21. B 22. D 23. C

Lesson 44 Museums
Words in Context: 1. admire 2. spectrum 3. responded 4. expressing 5. significant 6. fashion 7. criticism 8. schedule 9. leisure 10. collected 11. specialize 12. acquire
Word Practice: 1. B 2. C 3. C 4. C 5. B 6. D 7. A 8. B 9. A 10. C 11. C 12. A 13. C 14. D 15. B 16. D 17. A 18. C 19. D 20. B 21. C 22. A 23. D

Lesson 45 Media
Words in Context: 1. subscribes 2. political 3. thoroughly 4. constitutes 5. disseminated 6. investigative 7. assignments 8. decisions 9. impact 10. links 11. constant 12. in-depth
Word Practice: 1. C 2. C 3. A 4. B 5. B 6. D 7. C 8. C 9. D 10. C 11. D 12. B 13. B 14. B 15. A 16. C 17. B 18. D 19. D 20. A 21. D 22. B 23. A

Word Review #9: 1. D 2. B 3. C 4. D 5. A 6. A 7. B 8. C 9. B 10. B 11. D 12. C 13. A 14. B 15. C 16. A 17. B 18. C 19. D

Lessons 46–50 Health

Lesson 46 Doctor's Office
Words in Context: 1. annually 2. effective 3. diagnosing 4. preventing 5. appointment 6. record 7. assessment 8. instruments 9. manage 10. recommend 11. refer 12. serious
Word Practice: 1. A 2. C 3. B 4. C 5. C 6. D 7. B 8. A 9. B 10. D 11. A 12. D 13. A 14. B 15. A 16. C 17. C 18. D 19. A 20. C 21. D 22. B 23. A

Lesson 47 Dentist's Office
Words in Context: 1. aware 2. catch up 3. regularly 4. encourage 5. habit 6. position 7. irritates 8. illuminates 9. overview 10. evident 11. restores 12. distraction
Word Practice: 1. B 2. C 3. A 4. A 5. A 6. C 7. B 8. C 9. D 10. D 11. C 12. A 13. B 14. C 15. B 16. B 17. C 18. C 19. D 20. A 21. D 22. B 23. C

Lesson 48 Health Insurance
Words in Context: 1. concerns 2. personnel 3. policy 4. portion 5. treatment 6. reimbursement 7. suitable 8. emphasize 9. alternatives 10. regardless 11. aspect 12. incurs
Word Practice: 1. A 2. C 3. B 4. D 5. D 6. B 7. A 8. B 9. D 10. A 11. C 12. C 13. B 14. D 15. B 16. C 17. A 18. C 19. B 20. A 21. B 22. B 23. D

Lesson 49 Hospitals
Words in Context: 1. mission 2. pertinent 3. results 4. authorization 5. identification 6. admission 7. procedures 8. surgeon 9. escort 10. accompany (or escort) 11. statement 12. designated
Word Practice: 1. D 2. C 3. A 4. D 5. A 6. C 7. A 8. C 9. B 10. B 11. A 12. B 13. D 14. C 15. A 16. D 17. B 18. B 19. A 20. C 21. C 22. A 23. B

Lesson 50 Pharmacy
Words in Context: 1. consulting 2. control 3. samples 4. volunteers 5. limit 6. convenient 7. factors 8. sense 9. interactions 10. monitor 11. potential 12. detection
Word Practice: 1. C 2. C 3. B 4. A 5. B 6. D 7. B 8. A 9. B 10. B 11. D 12. A 13. A 14. B 15. C 16. A 17. D 18. B 19. A 20. B 21. C 22. D 23. D

Word Review #10: 1. D 2. A 3. D 4. A 5. C 6. D 7. A 8. B 9. A 10. D 11. C 12. A 13. A 14. D 15. B 16. D 17. B 18. D 19. C

Word Index

The number indicates the lesson in which the word is taught.

Phrasal Verbs

Idioms

Appendix

Audioscripts for the Listening Comprehension Exercises

LESSON 1:
Contracts

Part 1: Photo

Number 1. Look at the picture marked Number 1.
- (A) He's having a party.
- (B) He's signing the agreement.
- (C) He's reading the contract provisions.
- (D) He's putting on his glasses.

Part 2: Question–Response

Number 2.

Do you know why the meeting was cancelled?
- (A) Yes, they couldn't agree on a time to meet.
- (B) No, the meeting wasn't cancelled.
- (C) You aren't obligated to attend the meeting.

Number 3.

Haven't you resolved that problem yet?
- (A) We're working on it.
- (B) We have both letters.
- (C) You have my assurance.

Part 3: Short Conversation

Numbers 4 through 6 relate to the following conversation.

[M] Do you think we will ever resolve our difficulties with the computer company? They keep charging us for extra services that they haven't provided.

[W] They've assured me several times that they will correct our bills, but they haven't done it yet.

[M] Last month they charged us for repair services that we never ordered. Maybe we should cancel their services now and find another provider.

[W] No, we signed an agreement to use their services for only a year. There's just two months left on that contract, then we can sign with a different company.

Part 4: Talk

Questions 7 through 9 relate to the following recording.

The last provision in the contract states that if either party determines it is in his best interest to cancel the contract, he is obligated to inform the other immediately of his intention. If you both agree, we can specify that the canceling party must communicate his intent at least thirty days prior to cancellation. All the rest seems to be in order. I can have my assistant write up the agreement and have it ready for the two of you to sign at the end of the week.

LESSON 2:
Marketing

Part 1: Photo

Number 1. Look at the picture marked Number 1.
- (A) The clerk is competing with others.
- (B) The shoppers are comparing prices.
- (C) The man is not attracting a crowd.
- (D) The consumer is convincing the sales person.

Part 2: Question–Response

Number 2.

Aren't pop-up ads on the Internet just a fad?
- (A) No, they're here to stay.
- (B) I put up with a lot.
- (C) She's not fat.

Number 3.

Was the customer satisfied with our work?
- (A) All our work is customized.
- (B) Yes, he was quite satisfied.
- (C) I found a new customer today.

Part 3: Short Conversation

Numbers 4 through 6 relate to the following conversation.

[W] With a new store opening across the street, we'll have to work harder to compete in our market. We need to attract more customers to our store and our products.

[M] Perhaps our ads could show some of our satisfied customers and have them talk about their experiences shopping with us. Ads like that are often persuasive.

[W] Where do you get your inspiration? That's such a great idea! I'll call a photographer to come over and shoot pictures of people shopping in our store.

Part 4: Talk

Questions 7 through 9 relate to the following recording.

To attract new customers, we must first convince them that we offer something worthwhile. We need to inspire them to try our services, just once, so that they can make their own comparison. Their experience will persuade them that we are better than their competition. But what is it that we offer that makes us unique? What do you think we offer that the competition does not? We will discuss these questions during our workshop this afternoon, but our task doesn't stop there. When you go home tonight, I want each of you to think about how you can best promote our company's products, so that when you meet with our store clients you give us the best representation possible.

LESSON 3:
Warranties

Part 1: Photo

Number 1. Look at the picture marked Number 1.
  (A)   There is a variety of books for sale.
  (B)   The list of requirements is on the table.
  (C)   The price is clearly marked on the cover.
  (D)   The books are protected from the rain.

Part 2: Question–Response

Number 2.

When does the warranty expire?
  (A)   I always check the warranty.
  (B)   Three years from date of purchase.
  (C)   That's the implication.

Number 3.

What are the consequences of not registering your purchase?
  (A)   If you don't register, you won't receive any recall notices.
  (B)   Consequently, we quit the company.
  (C)   Our company purchased more this year than last.

Part 3: Short Conversation

Numbers 4 through 6 relate to the following conversation.

[M] Your car comes with a basic one-year, thirty-thousand-mile warranty, but you might want to consider purchasing a two-year, sixty-thousand-mile extended warranty. Both guarantee full protection as long as you have the car serviced by an approved mechanic.

[W] What are the consequences if I choose not to use an approved mechanic?

[M] The terms of the warranty require you to choose a mechanic from our approved list in order to be covered.

[W] Then I'll use an approved mechanic for now, but I won't purchase the extended warranty. Then I can use my own mechanic when the basic warranty expires.

Part 4: Talk

Questions 7 through 9 relate to the following recording.

We frequently receive items that are still under warranty, but we don't automatically repair them. Don't forget: a warranty is only valid if the product has been used according to the manufacturer's directions. Oftentimes a buyer will drop a machine or use it for something other than what it's intended for. Consequently, they're not covered. A common characteristic of this type of return is that it's cracked or smashed, or shows an unusual pattern of wear. Remember, we promise our customers that all our products will operate smoothly every time when handled according to the directions enclosed in each package. All defective products returned within thirty days of purchase will get a complete refund. Products returned after that time are sent to us for repair.

LESSON 4:
Business Planning

Part 1: Photo

Number 1. Look at the picture marked Number 1.
- (A)   The managers are planning a strategy.
- (B)   The president is dressing for dinner.
- (C)   The primary shape is round.
- (D)   The demonstrators are avoiding the meeting.

Part 2: Question–Response

Number 2.

Have you addressed the cost of rent in your business plan?
- (A)   Yes, we've planned for all our costs.
- (B)   No, we don't know his new address.
- (C)   We meant to finish the plan last night.

Number 3.

In what ways has the restaurant grown or developed?
- (A)   Its own vegetables in the back gardens.
- (B)   It's now a national chain.
- (C)   It is taller and stronger.

Part 3: Short Conversation

Numbers 4 through 6 relate to the following conversation.

[W] Alexa is developing a business plan. I told her you might be able to help her with the market research.

[M] I'd be happy to offer to help with that. I'm very proud of her. Going into business for yourself can be risky but very rewarding.

[W] I know she is very serious about careful planning to avoid making obvious mistakes.

[M] Yes, she has the right approach. The most important strategy for success is to start with a sound business plan.

Part 4: Talk

Questions 7 through 9 relate to the following recording.

Now let's turn to page seventeen of the business plan. This section addresses our strategy for long-term development of the company. In order to minimize risk over the long haul, we hope to grow only as quickly as the company can support. In other words, we want to avoid more borrowing so that the primary funding for growth comes from profits. We believe that this is the best way to develop a strong company that will not be seriously harmed by temporary downturns in the market. On page eighteen you will see our evaluation method outlined. The first phase of the evaluation of our business plan is set to begin early next year.

LESSON 5:
Conferences

Part 1: Photo

Number 1. Look at the picture marked Number 1.
- (A)   The attendees are registering at the desk.
- (B)   The organizers are selecting their seats.
- (C)   The banquet room is overcrowded.
- (D)   The participants are attending a session.

Part 2: Question–Response

Number 2.

How many will attend the conference?
- (A)   On Thursday.
- (B)   At least one hundred folks.
- (C)   We've made the arrangements.

Number 3.

Was the room overcrowded?
- (A)   The crowds were excited.
- (B)   Yes, and it was very hot, too.
- (C)   No, it was room number twelve.

Part 3: Short Conversation

Numbers 4 through 6 relate to the following conversation.

[M] Has the committee selected a site for our conference next year?

[W] Not yet. It's difficult to find a site that can accommodate a group of our size. We don't want our sessions to be overcrowded.

[M] That's true. And if our projections are correct, we can expect around 500 people to attend. But we need to have a site selected by the end of next month.

[W] We have some possibilities in mind. We'll know soon if any of them will work out.

Part 4: Talk

Questions 7 through 9 relate to the following recording.

All conference facilities need to provide reasonable accommodation for people with disabilities. Disabled individuals need to be able to take part in every session that is being offered. In case a session is held in an off-site location, we are not responsible for providing accommodation. But for any event held at our facility, we need to make the necessary arrangements for disabled participants. Most areas of our facility are handicapped accessible, but in some situations we need to make further accommodations. For example, conference planners are asked to get in touch with us ahead of time if any attendees will require special interpreters for the hearing impaired. To facilitate this, conference planners usually ask attendees to request interpreters at the time that they register for the conference.

LESSON 6:
Computers and
the Internet

Part 1: Photo

Number 1. Look at the picture marked Number 1.
- (A)   The computers are in the display window.
- (B)   The duplicate photos are on the table.
- (C)   The computers are shut down.
- (D)   The programs are deleted.

Part 2: Question–Response

Number 2.

How can I access the information?
- (A)   You'll find it if you search the website.
- (B)   Yes, it's very important information.
- (C)   No, I wasn't impressed.

Number 3.

Do you want to duplicate it, or delete it?
- (A)   Oh, I definitely need a copy.
- (B)   I'll do it double time.
- (C)   Deleted files go into the recycle bin.

Part 3: Short Conversation

Numbers 4 through 6 relate to the following conversation.

[M] I can't figure this out. When I tried to access my e-mail program, the monitor went black.

[W] It sounds like there's a problem with the display.

[M] Let me shut down the computer and then try one more time.

[W] If that fails to work, you should call in a repairperson right away. You shouldn't ignore a problem like this.

Part 4: Talk

Questions 7 through 9 relate to the following recording.

I strongly urge you to read the manual before attempting to run this software program. You may be tempted to ignore this advice. But I'm warning you all: it is not likely that you will be able to figure out this program on your own. This is especially important for owners of our competitors' products that aren't compatible with this program. Your computer could crash or shut down without warning. In fact, when you start working with this program, make sure you have duplicate files so, in case of system failure, you will not lose your work. Remember, if your system fails, all your files could be deleted. But if you have duplicated the files onto an external hard drive, you will have no trouble accessing them when you need them.

LESSON 7:
Office Technology

Part 1: Photo

Number 1. Look at the picture marked Number 1.
(A)   He's using the computer keyboard.
(B)   He's reducing the size of his office.
(C)   He's stocking the supplies.
(D)   He's signing his initials on his desk.

Part 2: Question–Response

Number 2.

Do you think we can afford the additional support?
(A)   Office morale seems fine.
(B)   It's already in the budget.
(C)   They're in stock.

Number 3.

Who's in charge of the photocopier?
(A)   It has twice the capacity.
(B)   The warranty has expired.
(C)   The office manager stays on top of it.

Part 3: Short Conversation

Numbers 4 through 6 relate to the following conversation.

[M] As part of the company's cost-saving initiative, we must have approval on all new purchases.

[W] Who will be in charge of approvals?

[M] Each of the department heads has been asked to stay on top of purchases. All purchase orders will have to be signed by one of them.

[W] Well, that's annoying. I just can't see it as a good idea. It adds one more step to the ordering process and could cause delays.

Part 4: Talk

Questions 7 through 9 relate to the following recording.

We have had a few problems with ordering these units on an as-needed basis. The first problem is that nobody seems to take the initiative to place the order with the provider. That's because when they're ordering just one recorder, they feel it isn't worth their time. So even though their need is recurring, they don't feel that the effort is justified. Here's where a more aggressive provider could help us out, by anticipating our needs and staying on top of them. In fact, I have looked into the matter and discovered a provider that could meet this need. It's the John Able and Sons Company. I don't know if any of you are familiar with them. Their products are quite affordable. I suggest we look into making our orders from this company in the future.

LESSON 8:
Office Procedures

Part 1: Photo

Number 1. Look at the picture marked Number 1.
(A)   The crew is cleaning the glass.
(B)   The workers are not dressed casually.
(C)   The golfers are practicing their game.
(D)   The waiters are bringing in food.

Part 2: Question–Response

Number 2.

Can young workers really appreciate what it meant to publish a book before computers were around?
- (A) They're working hard.
- (B) Our youngest employee is a published author.
- (C) Of course they can't.

Number 3.

What is silicon made of?
- (A) The sale is still on.
- (B) We're out of intercoms.
- (C) Sand.

Part 3: Short Conversation

Numbers 4 through 6 relate to the following conversation.

[M] I appreciate the fact that you have taken time out of your schedule to come and talk to me.

[W] I want to make sure that you understand the practices of the company.

[M] It seems difficult for other employees to give me a verbal explanation of the practices, although they definitely are familiar with them.

[W] Everything is outlined in writing in the Employee Handbook. You can look through that later to reinforce what we will talk about today.

Part 4: Talk

Questions 7 through 9 relate to the following recording.

This training is designed to reinforce and strengthen your current computer skills. We really don't have the time to introduce these programs from the start, and we'll only have limited time for practice today. What we want to do is verbally cover the main functions of the program and make sure that you're all exposed to some of the features of the newer version. So, at least you'll get a glimpse of what the newer version of the program has to offer. OK, let's get started. I promised to finish before noon, when lunch will be served for everyone in the board room.

TRACK
10

LESSON 9:
Electronics

Part 1: Photo

Number 1. Look at the picture marked Number 1.
- (A) The calculators are stored in the closet.
- (B) The computers are linked by a network.
- (C) The technician is replacing a part.
- (D) The worker is reading the software manual.

Part 2: Question–Response

Number 2.

How long will it take to replace the hard drive?
- (A) Hard drives are expensive.
- (B) Our technicians have the skills, don't worry.
- (C) A few hours.

Number 3.

Can you understand the technical section?
- (A) That's good advice, thanks.
- (B) I hope so—I'm the technician.
- (C) On page thirteen.

Part 3: Short Conversation

Numbers 4 through 6 relate to the following conversation.

[W] Unfortunately, I don't have the skills to retrieve this file, and I really need it. I was counting on using it to complete my project proposal.

[M] Maybe I can help you out. I'm new at this too, but I do know a few things. Are your files stored on the network?

[W] No, they're stored on the company ftp site.

[M] Yes, there's a special process you have to use, but I'm not sure I can figure it out. You'd better ask someone in the IT department to help you.

Part 4: Talk

Questions 7 through 9 relate to the following recording.

Downloading software is a simple process. You can download a file from a remote server, or you can simply download it from the company network. Once you've done it, you'll see how easy the process is. It really takes no technical skills and, indeed, everyday folks do it every day. Today we are going to practice downloading software from a website. To facilitate the process, I have outlined the steps here on this chart. If you get lost, just look up here and follow the steps. Technically speaking, this is a very simple process. Now, you all have your computers turned on and connected to the Internet, right? Then the next thing you'll do is type in the following web address.

LESSON 10:
Correspondence

Part 1: Photo

Number 1. Look at the picture marked Number 1.
  (A)   He's assembling the computer.
  (B)   He's folding the magazine in half.
  (C)   He's revising his notes.
  (D)   He's displaying the layout.

Part 2: Question–Response

Number 2.

Has the newsletter been distributed yet?
  (A)   No, he isn't feeling better yet.
  (B)   Yes, it was sent out this morning.
  (C)   Express mail is the fastest way to distribute it.

Number 3.

How long will it take to assemble the documents?
  (A)   I always fold the documents first.
  (B)   They're about ten pages long.
  (C)   Not more than thirty minutes.

Part 3: Short Conversation

Numbers 4 through 6 relate to the following conversation.

[M] I have the documents for tomorrow's meeting all ready. I proofed them last night and copied them this morning. Now all I need is your help in assembling them.

[W] You should have asked me beforehand. I'm too busy to do it now.

[M] I mentioned to you that I would need your help today. These have to be finished before the end of the afternoon.

[W] I'm sorry, but I don't remember your mentioning it. Why don't you ask my assistant to help you with the folding and stapling?

Part 4: Talk

Questions 7 through 9 relate to the following recording.

Tired of waiting in line? Try our new express, self-service Courier Center. You can purchase stamps, weigh parcels, look up ZIP codes, even send registered mail. The Courier Center is located in the lobby at the Fourth Street entrance. It's open from six A.M. until eight P.M. daily. Closed Sunday. Postal staff are always on hand to show you how to use the services. Mention this announcement to them and receive a free city-wide ZIP code directory.

LESSON 11:
Job Advertising
and Recruiting

Part 1: Photo

Number 1. Look at the picture marked Number 1.
  (A)   The job profile is posted on the board.
  (B)   The qualifications are listed on the wall.
  (C)   The harvest this season is abundant.
  (D)   The candidate is checking the job listings in the newspaper.

Part 2: Question–Response

Number 2.

Which candidate mentioned her father's fish boat?
(A)   The first one.
(B)   She fishes for a living.
(C)   Her father sells oats.

Number 3.

What recent accomplishment are you most proud of?
(A)   I need to resend this package.
(B)   I won the employee-of-the-month award in May.
(C)   I found it most time-consuming.

Part 3: Short Conversation

Numbers 4 through 6 relate to the following conversation.

[M] Have you come up with any ideas for finishing your job search?

[W] It's been very time-consuming and draining, but I think it's finally coming to an end. And it's about time, too. I've been at this for five months now.

[M] Does this mean that you've found the job that's the perfect match?

[W] Maybe. I'm very hopeful about a position I interviewed for yesterday. I know I have all the qualifications.

Part 4: Talk

Questions 7 through 9 relate to the following recording.

Candidates are asked to submit a current résumé and letter of interest. Your résumé should list your qualifications for the job you are applying for. It should also list specific accomplishments in past jobs or in school. Your letter of interest should also outline your long-term career goals. If you bring together a picture of your past, your current goals, and your future, your profile will be more cohesive to our hirers. We are currently recruiting for entry-level positions in our accounting department. Salaries are competitive and commensurate with experience.

TRACK
13

LESSON 12:
Applying and
Interviewing

Part 1: Photo

Number 1. Look at the picture marked Number 1.
(A)   The applicant is called in for an interview.
(B)   The expert is putting on his coat.
(C)   The sick cat is hiding its weakness.
(D)   The room is ready for a party.

Part 2: Question–Response

Number 2.

Can I apply for this job online?
(A)   Yes, the instructions for applicants are on our website.
(B)   No, that rule doesn't apply to this situation.
(C)   The applications are due next week.

Number 3.

Are you ready for the written test?
(A)   The test is administered by computer.
(B)   My score was sent in the mail.
(C)   Not quite, I don't have a pencil.

Part 3: Short Conversation

Numbers 4 through 6 relate to the following conversation.

[W] Do you remember the first time I applied for a job? I had absolutely no confidence in myself.

[M] And look where you are now—a widely respected expert in the field of computer networks.

[W] Isn't it interesting how we change and grow. I was hesitant to go on my first job interview because I didn't think I could present myself well. I was sure no one would hire me.

[M] And now you're asked to speak at conferences all over the country. In fact, I'd like to ask you to help me out with planning a workshop I have to give next week.

Part 4: Talk

Questions 7 through 9 relate to the following recording.

Thank you for calling the Salvo Human Resources Department Job Hotline.

Salvo is currently looking to hire people with a background in Asian Languages as well as software design. To hear about this special opportunity, press one. To listen to job descriptions for all of our current job openings, press two. To request an application, press three. To follow up on your application status, press four. To learn the location of a Salvo Employment Presentation in a city near you, press five. Please have a pen and paper by the phone and be ready to record the relevant information.

LESSON 13:
Hiring and Training

Part 1: Photo

Number 1. Look at the picture marked Number 1.
- (A)   The conductor is signaling the train.
- (B)   The trainer is conducting a session.
- (C)   The applicant is setting up an interview.
- (D)   The employees are rejecting the contract.

Part 2: Question–Response

Number 2.

You don't think this will generate a lot of extra paperwork, do you?
- (A)   No. In fact, I think it will reduce paperwork.
- (B)   Yes, the papers have arrived.
- (C)   I already turned on the generator.

Number 3.

Do you think that Lena looks up to Virginia?
- (A)   Lena's application was rejected.
- (B)   Virginia was her mentor, so it's natural that she would.
- (C)   The team will update us on Thursday.

Part 3: Short Conversation

Numbers 4 through 6 relate to the following conversation.

[M] How has the week of training gone so far? I've been concerned that the group is too big.

[W] We do have a large group of trainees, but we've been able to stay on track and get a lot accomplished.

[M] Everyone is commenting on the amount of excitement that your program has generated.

[W] Yes, we're quite pleased with our success so far. Well, I have to get going. I need to set up the meeting room for this afternoon's session. See you later.

Part 4: Talk

Questions 7 through 9 relate to the following recording.

Welcome to our first annual mentors training program. You have been selected by your coworkers for this program because they look up to you. And that's an honor. So congratulations to all of you for being here. Today we're going to start by generating a list of characteristics that make a successful mentor. I'd like you all to take a few minutes to think back to a mentor you've known or worked with. What made that person a good mentor? In order to stay on track with our schedule, we'll take no more than five minutes for this first activity. So, please begin listing your ideas now, and when I say stop it will be time to share with the group.

LESSON 14:
Salaries and Benefits

Part 1: Photo

Number 1. Look at the picture marked Number 1.
- (A)   He's washing his hands.
- (B)   He's negotiating a salary raise.
- (C)   He's counting his wages.
- (D)   He's paying with a check.

Part 2: Question–Response

Number 2.

Who is eligible to participate in the retirement plan?
- (A) She has already retired.
- (B) Employees who've been with us for at least three months.
- (C) You need to be aware of these benefits.

Number 3.

When will I get a raise?
- (A) Your first salary review will be in six months.
- (B) Lift it a little bit higher, please.
- (C) Usually four to six percent of your current salary.

Part 3: Short Conversation

Numbers 4 through 6 relate to the following conversation.

[M] We can't seem to make ends meet with my hourly wage.

[W] I think it's time for you to ask for a raise.

[M] I don't want to ask for too much compensation. I'm getting health insurance, after all, and I've only been working there for six months.

[W] But, you've been working hard. You should get regular wage increases. You deserve it. You deserve paid vacation and life insurance, too.

Part 4: Talk

Questions 7 through 9 relate to the following recording.

Please open your Employee Handbook to page seven. This section deals with your salary and salary increases. You will have an annual salary review. The average raise is 4.2 percent a year, just above the cost of living. Also, be aware that not all employees get a raise. Compensation is based solely on performance and your contribution to the company, and, sure enough, each year we find that some employees are not eligible for a raise. We have a clearly outlined review process in place, which your supervisor will go over with you. Let's take a look at benefits. Each employee gets ten days of paid vacation a year in addition to major national holidays. You also get five days of sick leave annually.

LESSON 15: Promotions, Pensions, and Rewards

TRACK
16

Part 1: Photo

Number 1. Look at the picture marked Number 1.
- (A) The librarian is dedicating her novel to her boss.
- (B) The promoter is putting away a book.
- (C) The employee is receiving a book as an award.
- (D) The manager is recognizing his old workers.

Part 2: Question–Response

Number 2.

Has she proven her loyalty?
- (A) She's been with us for forty-seven years.
- (B) Loyalty deserves praise.
- (C) No, she hasn't completed it.

Number 3.

Where is the dedication ceremony going to be held?
- (A) The ceremony was full of fanfare.
- (B) Nobody questions her dedication.
- (C) At the flag pole, in the parking lot.

Part 3: Short Conversation

Numbers 4 through 6 relate to the following conversation.

[M] I'm looking forward to the awards ceremony tonight.

[W] So am I. I hope Darrell finally gets some recognition for all the work that he has done.

[M] He certainly has been very productive in the last few months.

[W] He has always been a hard worker. His dedication to his job is impressive, and he is certainly one of the company's most loyal employees.

Part 4: Talk

Questions 7 through 9 relate to the following recording.

Everyone enjoys receiving recognition for the work that they do. Today, we will honor two employees who have been working for the company ever since we opened our doors in 1985. Their loyalty to the company is an honor for us. No value can be placed on these employees; they are priceless to us. Since they began working with us, they have been promoted to ever higher positions, not because of their connections or degrees, but because of the contributions they have made to the company. In other words, they have been promoted for their merit. These high achievers are a credit to our company, and I am very pleased to be able to honor them here tonight. Mr. Louis Boitano and Ms. Gina Minot, please come up to the front to receive your awards.

LESSON 16:
Shopping

Part 1: Photo

Number 1. Look at the picture marked Number 1.
- (A) They're putting the merchandise on the shelves.
- (B) They're pushing their cart to the check-out.
- (C) They're examining the items for sale.
- (D) They're behaving in an unusual way.

Part 2: Question–Response

Number 2.

I'll go wait in the checkout line.
- (A) Check this out, it's really fancy.
- (B) I'll be there in a minute.
- (C) You always find good bargains.

Number 3.

Which items are you returning?
- (A) The computer itemizes them.
- (B) All of them.
- (C) I'll come back.

Part 3: Short Conversation

Numbers 4 through 6 relate to the following conversation.

[M] In my psychology class we're studying consumer behavior. I've just spent three weeks watching what people buy.

[W] I'm sure you found that people hunt for bargains to save money. Economics is what drives people.

[M] Actually, shoppers report that they buy the brands they know best and feel most comfortable with, regardless of price.

[W] Well, now, that's interesting. I suppose all that marketing of brand names is really worthwhile for the manufacturers.

Part 4: Talk

Questions 7 through 9 relate to the following recording.

Attention shoppers. If you're looking for a true bargain, visit aisle seven for our sale on winter boots. All footwear is marked ten to forty percent off, this week only. At these prices, items won't last long, so hurry and save now. While you're at it, why not explore our other winter merchandise? We have coats, scarves, hats, and lots of other items to keep you toasty warm and comfortable during the chilly winter weather. When you're in the checkout aisle, don't forget to ask for a frequent shopper card. Every time you visit the store and make a purchase, your card is marked. After ten visits, you will be eligible for a free gift! This is our way of saying, "Thank you for shopping with us."

LESSON 17:
Ordering Supplies

Part 1: Photo

Number 1. Look at the picture marked Number 1.
- (A) She's obtaining supplies from the cabinet.
- (B) She's polishing her desk smoothly.
- (C) She's using office stationery for her correspondence.
- (D) She's buying quality toys.

Part 2: Question–Response

Number 2.

Is an order form essential?
- (A)   The essence is in there.
- (B)   You can order twenty-four hours a day.
- (C)   It's a prerequisite for all orders.

Number 3.

What is the function of this stamp?
- (A)   You need to obtain a signature.
- (B)   We need a one-dollar stamp.
- (C)   It shows that the order has been received.

Part 3: Short Conversation

Numbers 4 through 6 relate to the following conversation.

[M] Do you know of a wholesale source for glassware?

[W] As a matter of fact, I know of a supplier who sells better-quality wine glasses. It's a new enterprise called Crystal Company.

[M] I'm actually looking for a diverse range of glassware, but I can check their website to find out about their product line.

[W] That's a good idea. Phone me to let me know what you find out. I'll be out the rest of today, but we can talk over the weekend.

Part 4: Talk

Questions 7 through 9 relate to the following recording.

As you all know, we had a little slip up in our order with Margatel last week. Now, Margatel is one of our biggest clients. They order more than fifty thousand dollars worth of stationery alone each year. It is essential that we · maintain a smooth relationship with Margatel, or some of us may end up out on the street. So let's see if we can find the source of this mix-up, and then we'll go about setting it straight. First, according to our records, Carla, you took the order on January nineteenth for forty boxes of business envelopes and thirty boxes of manila envelopes. Is this correct? And the order was supposed to be shipped out on the twenty-first.

LESSON 18:
Shipping

Part 1: Photo

Number 1. Look at the picture marked Number 1.
- (A)   The goods are scanned in the catalog.
- (B)   The supplies are being counted by hand.
- (C)   The trucks are loading at the shipping dock.
- (D)   The carriers are using bicycles for deliveries.

Part 2: Question–Response

Number 2.

Are these numbers accurate?
- (A)   They've been checked and double-checked.
- (B)   The numbers were written down.
- (C)   The spillage was minimal.

Number 3.

How many items are listed in the catalog?
- (A)   About three hundred fifty.
- (B)   It is sufficiently clear.
- (C)   To fulfill customer's wishes.

Part 3: Short Conversation

Numbers 4 through 6 relate to the following conversation.

[M] We are completely out of packing supplies and cannot prepare anymore boxes today.

[W] It's your job to make certain that you have enough packing materials to fulfill orders. Remember, those boxes have to be addressed and shipped out before the end of the week.

[M] I thought we had enough boxes on hand, but I was wrong. Anyhow, I can pick up some more tomorrow.

[W] As long as they're ready to send by Friday.

Part 4: Talk

Questions 7 through 9 relate to the following recording.

A quick review of our catalog shows the variety and quality of the merchandise we carry, but it does nothing to draw attention to our competitive pricing. Competitive pricing is integral to our success. Customers want to minimize costs and maximize value. Remember our motto: we supply the best, you pay the least. In the future, our catalogs will reflect this motto by comparing our prices with those of our competitors. For selected items throughout the catalog, we will show the prices charged by competitors for the same or similar items. Some people may question this information, but it is guaranteed to be as accurate as possible. We will rely on careful research to obtain the pricing information we publish. Remember, honesty is the best policy. This information on competitors' pricing will first appear in next winter's catalog, available in January.

LESSON 19:
Invoices

Part 1: Photo

Number 1. Look at the picture marked Number 1.
- (A) She's looking over the orders.
- (B) She's talking to the customers.
- (C) She's ordering more paper by phone.
- (D) She's asking a clerk for a discount.

Part 2: Question–Response

Number 2.

Why were there so many mistakes in yesterday's orders?
- (A) We had two temps working here.
- (B) Seven mistakes.
- (C) Because we improved our system.

Number 3.

How much was the discount?
- (A) I've compiled the data.
- (B) They placed the order.
- (C) Fifteen percent.

Part 3: Short Conversation

Numbers 4 through 6 relate to the following conversation.

[M] I've compiled a list of office supplies we need to order immediately. The order should go out as soon as possible as these are essential items.

[W] Don't worry. I'll deal with it promptly.

[M] Please check the supply room before you send out the order, just to be sure I didn't make any mistakes. And when you receive the invoice, check it over carefully to make sure all the charges are accurate.

[W] Relax. I'll take care of everything efficiently. I'll check the supply closet today and send the order out first thing tomorrow, and I'll make sure all the charges on the invoice are right.

Part 4: Talk

Questions 7 through 9 relate to the following recording.

According to the terms of payment, a customer is eligible for a discount only if the entire invoice is paid upon completion of service. Prompt payment is much more efficient because we don't have to bill the customer. Also, as soon as we receive payment, it becomes capital. We estimate that prompt payments save us about 15 percent for each project. This is a significant amount of money for the company. Therefore, it is greatly to our advantage to encourage prompt payment as much as we possibly can.

LESSON 20:
Inventory

Part 1: Photo

Number 1. Look at the picture marked Number 1.
- (A) He's verifying the number of items in stock.
- (B) He's adjusting the height of the boxes.
- (C) He's disturbing the order of the shelves.
- (D) He's scanning the goods by computer.

Part 2: Question–Response

Number 2.

Shall we set it to be done automatically, or shall we do them all by hand?
(A)   Automatically.
(B)   They were hand delivered.
(C)   Set it on the counter, please.

Number 3.

Have they installed the new computers yet?
(A)   The computers run the jet.
(B)   No, they aren't all that tall.
(C)   Yes, and they're working beautifully.

Part 3: Short Conversation

Numbers 4 through 6 relate to the following conversation.

[M] Even though the computer says we have five of these bedspreads left, I'd like you to go to the stockroom and verify that for me.

[W] If the computer says we have five, why would there be any discrepancy?

[M] Sometimes there are adjustments to the inventory. I don't want to tell this customer that we have a bedspread if we are out of stock.

[W] All right. I'll check the stockroom myself and let you know right away.

Part 4: Talk

Questions 7 through 9 relate to the following recording.

We verify the computer's count with a physical inventory every year in January. It's a tedious process, but it's crucial to keeping our records straight. Even the physical counting leaves us with some discrepancies, but we feel that it more closely reflects our numbers. The physical count also puts us two steps closer to figuring out any huge discrepancies. Remember, in the long run any discrepancy is a liability. So, although we have to close everything down and stop running the business for the three days that it takes to complete the inventory, it is well worth the effort that it takes.

TRACK 22

LESSON 21:
Banking

Part 1: Photo

Number 1. Look at the picture marked number 1.
(A)   She's signing papers at the bank.
(B)   She's buying a new wallet.
(C)   She's borrowing money from a friend.
(D)   She's making a transaction at an ATM.

Part 2: Question–Response

Number 2.

How much money did you take out of your bank account?
(A)   I took out only 100 dollars.
(B)   That accountant charges a lot for his services.
(C)   Yes, I took the money to the bank.

Number 3.

What do you want to borrow so much money for?
(A)   It didn't cost so much money.
(B)   I earned all that money myself.
(C)   I want to buy a car.

Part 3: Short Conversation

Numbers 4 through 6 relate to the following conversation.

[W] Since you have an account with this bank, all we require in order to cash your check is a photo ID. Your driver's license would do.

[M] I've lost my driver's license, but my signature is on file. Is that enough?

[W] I'm sorry, but we have to be cautious. We can only accept a photo ID for transactions like this. You could, however, deposit the check in your account. It would take just seven business days to clear, then the funds would be available to you.

[M] All right, then, I'll do that. Then I'll go downtown and get a new driver's license.

Part 4: Talk

Questions 7 through 9 relate to the following recording.

To qualify for a mortgage, you have to be able to make a down payment of ten percent. You also have to show that you have been at your current job for at least one year and at your current address for three or more years. It's also a good idea to have some extra money in a savings account. Your account balance should be equivalent to about three months of your normal take-home salary. All these things assure the lender that you will be able to make your monthly mortgage payments.

TRACK
23

LESSON 22:
Accounting

Part 1: Photo

Number 1. Look at the picture marked number 1.
  (A)   The auditor is looking over the books.
  (B)   Snow is accumulating on the ground.
  (C)   The employee turnover is high.
  (D)   She is meeting her clients in her office.

Part 2: Question–Response

Number 2.

Do you have any outstanding debts?
  (A)   Yes, I understand all about debts.
  (B)   Yes, I still owe money on my car.
  (C)   Yes, he's a very upstanding citizen.

Number 3.

What assets do you have?
  (A)   I own my house and I have some money in the bank.
  (B)   I felt quite upset by the news.
  (C)   I don't have an assistant.

Part 3: Short Conversation

Numbers 4 through 6 relate to the following conversation.

[W] I have a one o'clock appointment with a client today. I should be back at the office before five.

[M] Is this the client you are trying to save from all his debt?

[W] That's the one! How he accumulated so much debt, I'll never understand. I've worked out a budget for him for the coming year and plan to present it to him this afternoon.

[M] Good luck! I know you've put a good deal of work into that, and I hope your client finds it acceptable.

Part 4: Talk

Questions 7 through 9 relate to the following recording.

The most important factor in making your accounting firm profitable is to build up a solid list of clients. You want your clients to continue bringing their accounting business to you year after year and to avoid the problem of client turnover. Also, keep in mind that charging higher fees does not mean that you will make more money. If your clients feel that your fees are fair, they will recommend your services to their friends and colleagues. Finally, never forget what your most valuable asset is. It's easy to spend money on office equipment and rental fees for your space, but these are not the things that attract clients. It is important to make sure you have a team of excellent accountants on your staff. A qualified staff is the most valuable asset any accounting firm can have.

TRACK
24

LESSON 23:
Investments

Part 1: Photo

Number 1. Look at the picture marked Number 1.
  (A)   The brokers are bidding aggressively.
  (B)   He's returning the products to the storeroom.
  (C)   The supplies are out of stock.
  (D)   He's making a phone call.

Part 2: Question–Response

Number 2.

Who can give me advice about my portfolio?
- (A) My stockbroker can help you with your investments.
- (B) It's a very nice portfolio.
- (C) I think you made a wise choice.

Number 3.

Will I get a good return on this investment?
- (A) Please return it to me when you've finished.
- (B) I'm sorry, we don't accept returns.
- (C) You should earn at least a fifteen percent return.

Part 3: Short Conversation

Numbers 4 through 6 relate to the following conversation.

[M] In order to minimize risk, investors should maintain a diverse portfolio by putting their money in various industry investments.

[W] You mean we should invest in natural resources as well as in manufacturing industries?

[M] Perhaps. Unless you are very aggressive, you don't want to put all your eggs in one basket. In fact, I have made close to a million dollars in the past ten years by following the strategy of maintaining a diverse portfolio.

[W] That's quite impressive. You know, I was thinking of pulling all my money out of the stock market, but now I think I'll stay in and follow your advice.

Part 4: Talk

Questions 7 through 9 relate to the following recording.

Have you thought about how you will fund your children's college education? Don't wait until they are in high school. The time to begin saving is when your children are still small. A good way to start is by investing some of your income in the stock market. You will get a good return on your money there. The best strategy is to commit a certain amount of your monthly income to your stock investments. Even after just two or three years, you should start to see your investment grow. By the time your children are ready for college, you'll be ready to pay for it.

LESSON 24:
Taxes

Part 1: Photo

Number 1. Look at the picture marked number 1.
- (A) She's filling out a form.
- (B) She's preparing dinner.
- (C) She's filing her nails.
- (D) She's calculating the total.

Part 2: Question–Response

Number 2.

How much do I owe?
- (A) About 125 dollars.
- (B) I own two cars.
- (C) I paid what I owed.

Number 3.

When do I have to file my income taxes?
- (A) It's only about a mile from here.
- (B) We received an incoming fax.
- (C) The deadline is April 15th.

Part 3: Short Conversation

Numbers 4 through 6 relate to the following conversation.

[M] I'm no good with numbers, so my spouse usually files our taxes. She does all the calculations and fills out the forms.

[W] You're lucky, then. I usually have to pay an accountant to prepare my taxes, and even then I sometimes miss the deadline.

[M] I did that once. Last year was the one time I filed our taxes, but I did it two months after the deadline and had to pay a huge penalty.

[W] Yes, the penalty is ten percent of what you owe, isn't it? I guess that's why your spouse is the one who usually files your taxes.

Part 4: Talk

Questions 7 through 9 relate to the following recording.

You will be getting a refund check of four hundred sixty dollars, and you can expect to receive it in eight to ten weeks. While I know that it's nice to get a refund check, I always tell my clients that it's better for your finances to avoid overpaying taxes in the first place. If you'd like, I can do some calculations which will show exactly how much you should ask your employer to withhold from your check in the future, and I'd only charge a small fee for this service.

LESSON 25:
Financial Statements

Part 1: Photo

Number 1. Look at the picture marked number 1.
  (A)   The graph shows stock market yields.
  (B)   The levels on the chart don't change.
  (C)   He's writing the translation with a pen.
  (D)   The bank is open now.

Part 2: Question–Response

Number 2.

What is our projected income for next year?
  (A)   We expect several projects to come in.
  (B)   It can't be protected.
  (C)   It'll probably be slightly higher than this year.

Number 3.

Is this an accurate translation of the statement?
  (A)   Yes, the translator did an excellent job.
  (B)   No, we don't need eight translators.
  (C)   The transportation in this area is not adequate.

Part 3: Short Conversation

Numbers 4 through 6 relate to the following conversation.

[W] I'm developing a projected financial statement for my business. I'll use it to see what kind of profits I can expect to yield this year.

[M] That's great. It'll also help you forecast periods where you might have financial problems.

[W] Yes. I'm sure it will be worth the effort for several reasons. I hope to have it finished soon—by the end of this week, in fact.

[M] I'm sure you'll have no problem with that. If you like, I can look over the details when it's finished and check your calculations and make any necessary corrections.

Part 4: Talk

Questions 7 through 9 relate to the following recording.

Many small businesses fail because of poor financial advice. Remember, a small business is no different from a large company in that financial planning is the key to success. Therefore, creating a projected financial statement is the first and most important step one should take when starting up a small business. It is realistic to expect your small business to become profitable during its first five years, but typically not during the first year. With this in mind, you can set reasonable targets and project expenses for the first year or two of your business. This will help you know what funds you need to raise in order to get and keep your business going.

LESSON 26:
Property and Departments

Part 1: Photo

Number 1. Look at the picture marked number 1.
  (A)   They're scrutinizing the drawing.
  (B)   They're disrupting the plans.
  (C)   They're concentrating on the newspaper.
  (D)   They're buying pens in the lobby.

Part 2: Question–Response

Number 2.

Where is your new office?
  (A)   It's adjacent to the lobby.
  (B)   I moved up to a new position.
  (C)   I'm open to it.

Number 3.

Is your boss open to new ideas?
  (A)   Yes, I like to keep the window open.
  (B)   Yes, it opens early every day.
  (C)   Yes, she always listens to my proposals.

Part 3: Short Conversation

Numbers 4 through 6 relate to the following conversation.

[M] I hear the remodeling of the office lobby will start soon. I hope the new lobby ends up more conducive to conversation than our current lobby is.

[W] I've spent a lot of time scrutinizing the plans for the new lobby, and I'm quite pleased. I think it will be everything you hope for.

[M] Good. And I hope the remodeling work doesn't take too long. I am afraid it will be disruptive to our business.

[W] It shouldn't take more than a few weeks. It will be finished by the middle of next month.

Part 4: Talk

Questions 7 through 9 relate to the following recording.

The design of an office can contribute a great deal to employee productivity. It is important to plan your office space so that it is conducive to collaboration, yet at the same time allows staff members to concentrate on their work. Many companies opt for a design that includes several smaller offices adjacent to a lobby rather than one large one, as they find the level of activity in an open office is often disruptive to work. At the same time, it is also important to include at least one larger work room so that staff members can work collaboratively. Such spaces would be used for meetings, team work on projects, and the like.

LESSON 27:
Board Meetings and Committees

TRACK 28

Part 1: Photo

Number 1. Look at the picture marked number 1.
  (A)   They're all wearing glasses.
  (B)   They're putting paper in the wastebasket.
  (C)   They're concluding their breakfast.
  (D)   They're checking the agenda.

Part 2: Question–Response

Number 2.

Do your staff members meet periodically?
  (A)   They read several newspapers and magazines.
  (B)   I haven't seen him for quite a long period.
  (C)   We have a meeting every Friday.

Number 3.

How did the meeting go?
  (A)   It was right after lunch.
  (B)   It was in the boardroom.
  (C)   It was a real waste of time.

Part 3: Short Conversation

Numbers 4 through 6 relate to the following conversation.

[M] That meeting was such a waste of time.

[W] You're right. It was too lengthy, and we didn't accomplish anything.

[M] We were in there for three hours, and no one even brought up the most important matters on the agenda. Next time there's one of these meetings, remind me not to attend it.

[W] I'm with you. I don't plan to go to another one of these meetings, either.

Part 4: Talk

Questions 7 through 9 relate to the following recording.

In order to keep everyone from feeling that this meeting is a waste of time, I've developed the following guidelines. Please adhere to them. One: Please discuss only the items on the agenda. This is not the time to bring up irrelevant or personal matters. Two: Please do not make unnecessarily lengthy speeches. Make your point as quickly and clearly as possible. Three: My goal is to conclude this meeting by four thirty. We will be able to do this if we all follow the guidelines. Thank you for your cooperation.

LESSON 28:
Quality Control

Part 1: Photo

Number 1. Look at the picture marked number 1.
- (A)   She's trying on a new garment.
- (B)   She's taking back damaged goods to the store.
- (C)   She's inspecting the products for defects.
- (D)   She's throwing out her uniform.

Part 2: Question–Response

Number 2.

Which brand is better?
- (A)   I love the music that band plays.
- (B)   Most of our customers prefer this one.
- (C)   No, I don't understand this letter.

Number 3.

Is this coat water repellent?
- (A)   Yes, this water tastes excellent.
- (B)   Yes, it will keep you very dry.
- (C)   Yes, you can wash it with soap and water.

Part 3: Short Conversation

Numbers 4 through 6 relate to the following conversation.

[M] What does the company do with garments that have defects in them?

[W] If the defects aren't too bad, we change the brand name and sell them in discount stores. You can find our skirts all over the country under different names.

[M] That's certainly more profitable than throwing them away. Do many of your garments end up that way?

[W] We find that about fifteen percent of them end up with defects. We sell our skirts at all the better women's clothing stores, so they have to conform to high standards.

Part 4: Talk

Questions 7 through 9 relate to the following recording.

We assure you that all our products go through strict quality control. All defective products are thrown out before they leave the factory. You can be sure that all our products that reach the store have been thoroughly inspected to make sure they conform to our high quality standards. If for any reason, however, you perceive a defect in one of our products or are not completely satisfied with it for any reason at all, you can take it back to the store for a one hundred percent refund, no questions asked.

LESSON 29:
Product Development

Part 1: Photo

Number 1. Look at the picture marked number 1.
- (A)   She's ascertaining the time of the flight.
- (B)   She's examining the contents of the test tube.
- (C)   She's experimenting with a new way home.
- (D)   She's solving a crossword puzzle.

Part 2: Question–Response

Number 2.

How long have you worked as a supervisor?
- (A)   I like it very much.
- (B)   He doesn't have an advisor.
- (C)   For almost a decade.

Number 3.

What kind of responsibilities does Jim have at his new job?
- (A)   He supervises the entire department.
- (B)   He's a fairly responsive person.
- (C)   He's responding very well.

Part 3: Short Conversation

Numbers 4 through 6 relate to the following conversation.

[W] We need to examine the data for our Binky doll sales before we decide how to modify it.

[M] Several companies have successfully experimented with modifications such as bright colors and noisemakers.

[W] Consumers today are anxious about inflation so our next modification should be to make the doll cheaper. I think if we lower the price by fifteen percent, we can increase sales by thirty percent or more.

[M] Maybe so, but you can't just assume those figures. You need to do some systematic price and sales research first.

Part 4: Talk

Questions 7 through 9 relate to the following recording.

This product has been on the market for over two decades, and it continues to sell well. Researchers aren't sure of the reason for this. They have examined hundreds of pages of market data but haven't ascertained an exact reason for the product's popularity. Is it the low price or the wide availability? Perhaps it is the consumers' familiarity with it. Researchers don't know which factors are responsible, but consumers continue to buy the product as it enters its twenty-second year on the market. In fact, it is the most popular product of its kind for teenagers, and far outsells similar products aimed at men, women, and children.

LESSON 30:
Renting and Leasing

Part 1: Photo

Number 1. Look at the picture marked number 1.
- (A)   The building is not occupied.
- (B)   The windows are in very poor condition.
- (C)   The store is closed due to bad weather.
- (D)   The parking lot is crowded with cars.

Part 2: Question–Response

Number 2.

Who are the occupants on the second floor?
- (A)   They'll take occupancy next week.
- (B)   Two lawyer's offices.
- (C)   No, we only occupy the first floor.

Number 3.

Is the building in good condition?
- (A)   Yes, the landlord keeps it in good repair.
- (B)   Yes, it's near all the bus routes.
- (C)   Yes, all the tenants are very nice.

Part 3: Short Conversation

Numbers 4 through 6 relate to the following conversation.

[M] I understand that we may be able to get out of this unfortunate circumstance.

[W] Yes, under certain conditions a clause in your contract may not be valid.

[M] I'll pay you whatever it takes to get us out of this legally. I don't want to be subjected to any lawsuit.

[W] You don't need to be apprehensive about that. Due to the poorly written clause, you have the option to get out of the contract if you decide to do so by the end of the month.

Part 4: Talk

Questions 7 through 9 relate to the following recording.

Before you sign a lease on a space for your business, make sure you have chosen the best location. Look for the indicators of a neighborhood that is good for business. Are there other, successful businesses occupying spaces nearby? Is there access to public transportation? Is the area attractive to customers and clients? If the conditions don't look right for your business, look into other options. Don't lock yourself into a long-term lease on a space that isn't right for you. Once you have found the best space for your business, then you can look at signing a long-term lease. Rental rates often fluctuate. If you sign a lease for five years, then you are guaranteed a rent you can afford.

LESSON 31:
Selecting a Restaurant

Part 1: Photo

Number 1. Look at the picture marked number 1.
- (A) The waiter is suggesting dessert.
- (B) The customers are relying on the menu.
- (C) The waiter is mixing the salad.
- (D) The customers are arriving at the restaurant.

Part 2: Question–Response

Number 2.

How can I secure reservations at such a popular restaurant?
- (A) Call early in the day.
- (B) You can feel secure at that restaurant.
- (C) I can recommend a popular restaurant.

Number 3.

How can I choose a good restaurant?
- (A) Look in the restaurant guide.
- (B) I never refuse food at a restaurant.
- (C) Yes, it's a very good restaurant.

Part 3: Short Conversation

Numbers 4 through 6 relate to the following conversation.

[W] The woman who writes the weekly restaurant reviews for the local newspaper has published a guide to local restaurants.

[M] That won't be too helpful. I don't think the same food appeals to her as appeals to me.

[W] I know what you mean. There's a lot of subjectivity in reviewing restaurants.

[M] Yes, I usually don't bother reading the reviews. I often eat out on weekends, but I rely on my coworkers to suggest good places to eat. They're familiar with a lot of the restaurants in the city.

Part 4: Talk

Questions 7 through 9 relate to the following recording.

Good afternoon. I am calling from the Patio Terrace Restaurant about your request for a reservation. I have secured a reservation for you at 8:30 P.M. tomorrow evening. Please arrive on time. We have a bar where you can enjoy appetizers and mixed drinks before dinner. If that idea appeals to you, I suggest arriving at seven thirty or eight o'clock. We have a parking lot in back for the exclusive use of our customers. Are you familiar with our location, or will you need directions?

LESSON 32:
Eating Out

Part 1: Photo

Number 1. Look at the picture marked number 1.
- (A) The chef is adding ingredients to the desserts.
- (B) The restaurant patrons are eating outside.
- (C) The customer is reminding the waiter to bring the drinks.
- (D) The waiter is wearing a hat.

Part 2: Question–Response

Number 2.

What kinds of flavors does the chef use?
- (A)   I don't like this kind of food.
- (B)   She uses a blend of Asian spices.
- (C)   Yes, the food is very flavorful.

Number 3.

Can you judge a restaurant just by looking at the menu?
- (A)   No, the judge didn't like that restaurant.
- (B)   No, I haven't looked at the menu yet.
- (C)   No, I think you have to eat there first.

Part 3: Short Conversation

Numbers 4 through 6 relate to the following conversation.

[M] This restaurant reminds me of the one we visited on vacation last year. I think they use many of the same ingredients in the dishes.

[W] You're right. The flavor of the dishes is similar. The food here is really quite tasty.

[M] It's fantastic. Let's not forget where this restaurant is so we can come back again and try some more dishes.

[W] This place just opened up last week, I think, but the food is so delicious I predict that it will have a lot of patrons very soon.

Part 4: Talk

Questions 7 through 9 relate to the following recording.

I'm sorry for the delay. I'm sure you thought I'd forgotten your order. The problem is, we have a new assistant chef, and he's mixed up everything in the kitchen. It will take a while longer for your meal to be ready, but we want to keep all our patrons happy so I'd be happy to bring you some free appetizers while you wait. It won't be too much longer. Your food should be on the table in about fifteen minutes or so. And I predict that when you finally get your meal, you'll judge that our chef's cooking is worth the wait.

TRACK 34

LESSON 33:
Ordering Lunch

Part 1: Photo

Number 1. Look at the picture marked number 1.
- (A)   She's settling the bill.
- (B)   She's writing a list.
- (C)   She's making a delivery.
- (D)   She's picking up the order.

Part 2: Question–Response

Number 2.

Does your restaurant have free delivery?
- (A)   Yes, deliveries are free on orders of ten dollars or more.
- (B)   Yes, we charge a fee for that service.
- (C)   Yes, we make deliveries after three.

Number 3.

Would you like that order delivered, or will you pick it up?
- (A)   Yes, please pick it up.
- (B)   I'll pick it up in half an hour.
- (C)   Pick up after yourself.

Part 3: Short Conversation

Numbers 4 through 6 relate to the following conversation.

[M] Will you please arrange for an elegant lunch to be delivered to the office during the regional manager's visit?

[W] That's such an annoying burden. It always falls to me to arrange these things. Why don't you just go to a restaurant?

[M] I need to show our impressive sales data during lunch and can't show slides at a restaurant.

[W] All right, then. I'll call the restaurant soon, and I'll ask for the lunch to be delivered by one o'clock. I suppose you'll want it served in the conference room.

Part 4: Talk

Questions 7 through 9 relate to the following recording.

Don't settle for uninteresting food and slow service. Order your next lunch from the Parkside Café, where speedy service is guaranteed. We're here to meet the needs of busy business people like you, and ordering from us is so easy. Simply make your selection from our list of made-to-order sandwiches and salads, then call in your order, and it will be ready to be picked up in ten minutes, guaranteed. Or have your meal delivered directly to your office. Our delivery fee is just fifteen percent of the price of your order. We handle both individual and group orders.

LESSON 34:
Cooking as a Career

Part 1: Photo

Number 1. Look at the picture marked number 1.
- (A) The chef is instructing the apprentices.
- (B) The professionals are chopping the food.
- (C) The customers are demanding menus.
- (D) The designers are incorporating fish motifs into the décor.

Part 2: Question–Response

Number 2.

How did you decide to enter the cooking profession?
- (A) Yes, I'm still looking for a profession.
- (B) The kitchen door is to your right.
- (C) I've always wanted to work in a restaurant.

Number 3.

How do you plan to draw new customers to the restaurant?
- (A) Yes, I'm accustomed to eating here.
- (B) We will expand the menu and offer new specials.
- (C) We saw several new customers there.

Part 3: Short Conversation

Numbers 4 through 6 relate to the following conversation.

[W] There's been a large influx of new chefs recently. And they're all demanding high salaries.

[M] Good chefs manage to draw customers into restaurants, so they're worth the salaries they're paid.

[W] Yes, the good ones are. For a skilled, professional chef, cooking can be quite a profitable career.

[M] I suppose you're right, though I can't see becoming a chef myself. I have no interest in practicing the culinary arts. But I do enjoy the results of a good chef's work. Let's plan to eat out more often.

Part 4: Talk

Questions 7 through 9 relate to the following recording.

Are you trying to decide on a profession? Don't forget to consider a career in the culinary arts. Many people find professional cooking to be an excellent outlet for their creativity. It's a demanding but exciting career with numerous opportunities. It is important to become well-trained in this profession. Don't be fooled into thinking that an apprenticeship is enough. People who plan to become chefs should enroll in an accredited culinary school. There they will learn the methods used by the best restaurants all around the world. Graduates of culinary schools become chefs, caterers, cooking instructors, and more. Join the many creative people who have been drawn to the cooking profession. You'll never be bored!

LESSON 35:
Events

Part 1: Photo

Number 1. Look at the picture marked number 1.
- (A) The exact number of guests is ten.
- (B) The location is ideal for a playground.
- (C) The regulations limit parking at night.
- (D) The banquet is staged in the ballroom.

Part 2: Question–Response

Number 2.

Can you give me a general idea of the number of guests you expect?
- (A) That's the ideal number.
- (B) About 150 people will attend.
- (C) Generally, I have good expectations.

Number 3.

How much lead time will we need?
- (A) The event should last about three or four hours.
- (B) I was the leader last time.
- (C) The hall has to be reserved a month in advance.

Part 3: Short Conversation

Numbers 4 through 6 relate to the following conversation.

[M] I've found the ideal site for our wedding reception. The dimensions are just right, and the manager will assist us with coordinating all the details.

[W] But you didn't tell me where it is.

[M] It's at the Berkshire Country Club. It's exactly what we wanted, and there's plenty of parking. I want you to see it right away because we have to sign the contract before the end of the week.

[W] That won't be hard. I'm free all day. Let's go look at it now.

Part 4: Talk

Questions 7 through 9 relate to the following recording.

I am coordinating the plans for our next big event, the year-end office party. Tom is assisting me, and we have already had several meetings. The event isn't until next month, so we've given ourselves plenty of lead time. Right now we're looking for a site that is in close proximity to the office and isn't too small to stage our event. You all know that the event is informal and that there won't be any ceremony or speeches. However, we will need to have more than just a general idea of how many will attend. We'll need an exact count by the end of the week, so please let us know soon if you plan to attend.

LESSON 36:
General Travel

Part 1: Photo

Number 1. Look at the picture marked number 1.
- (A) The luggage has not been claimed.
- (B) The suitcases are on the airplane.
- (C) The passengers are boarding with their bags.
- (D) The suits are hanging on the line.

Part 2: Question–Response

Number 2.

When does the train depart?
- (A) In fifteen minutes.
- (B) From Gate fifteen.
- (C) In another part of the station.

Number 3.

Will a meal be served during the flight?
- (A) Yes, I reserved your flight.
- (B) No, just beverages and a snack.
- (C) Their service is all right.

Part 3: Short Conversation

Numbers 4 through 6 relate to the following conversation.

[W] Would you care for another beverage?

[M] Is there time? According to my itinerary, we should be landing soon.

[W] You must have missed the announcement. We've been delayed and won't be landing for another hour.

[M] An hour? But I was supposed to be ready to board my connecting flight by three o'clock. I'll never make it on time. Now I'll have to change my whole itinerary.

Part 4: Talk

Questions 7 through 9 relate to the following recording.

Welcome to flight one fifteen. We will begin embarkation in five minutes. Please have a valid passport and ticket ready to show the flight attendant as you board. The itinerary for our trip today includes a thirty-minute stop in Chicago before we continue on to Los Angeles. We are scheduled for takeoff in twenty minutes, and since the captain has announced that he expects no delays in our trip, we should be departing on time. Please remember that once you are on board the plane, use of cell phones is prohibited until after we have taken off. We will begin our beverage service soon after takeoff, and lunch will be served later on. Have a pleasant flight.

LESSON 37:
Airlines

Part 1: Photo

Number 1. Look at the picture marked number 1.
  (A)   The sky is crowded with airplanes.
  (B)   The pilot is dealing with bad weather.
  (C)   The city can be distinguished in the background.
  (D)   The airplane is arriving at its destination.

Part 2: Question–Response

Number 2.

How can we keep expenses down?
  (A)   You're right, it's too expensive to keep.
  (B)   We can use the elevator.
  (C)   We can fly in economy class.

Number 3.

How long can you extend your stay?
  (A)   It's a long way away.
  (B)   I can't spend any more money.
  (C)   I can stay three more days.

Part 3: Short Conversation

Numbers 4 through 6 relate to the following conversation.

[M] The airfares to Australia are quite expensive, and I know you need to economize. Let me see what I can do to get you a better airfare.

[W] I'll really need a substantial discount to make my trip possible.

[M] I understand your situation. Now, if you are willing to change your destination and fly into Melbourne rather than Sydney, that would save you some money. And if you extend your trip by just two days, I think I can work out a really good fare for you.

[W] Fine, fine. The only important thing is that I need to arrive by next Sunday.

Part 4: Talk

Questions 7 through 9 relate to the following recording.

Thank you for calling Travel Time Travel Agency, your place for economically-priced airline tickets. If your destination is within this country, press one. If your destination is in another country, press two. If you would like to make hotel reservations or travel arrangements other than purchasing airline tickets, press three. We're sorry, information on special excursion rates is not currently available because our computer system is down. Please call back later to find out if the situation has changed.

LESSON 38:
Trains

Part 1: Photo

Number 1. Look at the picture marked number 1.
  (A)   They're checking the directory.
  (B)   They're paying their fare.
  (C)   They're promptly boarding the train.
  (D)   They're using the remainder of their ticket.

Part 2: Question–Response

Number 2.

Why is the fare to London so high?
(A)   Because this is a deluxe train.
(B)   The weather in London is unusually fair.
(C)   We already said good-bye.

Number 3.

Do you think the train will be punctual?
(A)   Yes, it's always fun to ride the train.
(B)   No, it will be several minutes late.
(C)   Everything functions well.

Part 3: Short Conversation

Numbers 4 through 6 relate to the following conversation.

[W] According to the directory, the next train to New York leaves at ten. Do you think it'll leave punctually?

[M] I think so. The trains have to operate on time or people won't want to ride them. I see here that the ten o'clock train arrives in New York at 1:30. That's a relatively short trip.

[W] But it's long enough for me to get hungry. Let's buy some snacks now so we'll have something to eat on the trip.

[M] There's no time. It's almost ten now, and we have to buy our tickets before we get on the train, or we'll pay a higher fare on board.

Part 4: Talk

Questions 7 through 9 relate to the following recording.

People often ask if the higher fares charged on the new high-speed trains are offset by the savings in time. The answer is yes. In fact, the duration of a high-speed train trip in some cases is not much more than a plane trip, and the fare is always cheaper than a plane ticket. Unfortunately, these trains operate out of far fewer cities than do planes and the traditional slower trains. On the other hand, all tickets on high-speed trains are first class. This means that your fare entitles you to a deluxe ride in a comfortable seat from which you can enjoy the scenery as it moves past your window. Unlike first-class plane tickets, however, meals are not usually included in the price of your train ticket. You have to pay extra for food.

TRACK 40

LESSON 39:
Hotels

Part 1: Photo

Number 1. Look at the picture marked number 1.
(A)   The guests are checking into the hotel.
(B)   The housekeeper is cleaning the room.
(C)   This room has been serviced and is ready for occupancy.
(D)   The reservations agent is quoting a high rate.

Part 2: Question–Response

Number 2.

What rate do you charge for a double room?
(A)   Yes, you could change to a double room.
(B)   It costs eighty-five dollars a night.
(C)   This hotel has great rooms.

Number 3.

What time should we check in?
(A)   Before nine o'clock.
(B)   We only take credit cards.
(C)   At the registration desk.

Part 3: Short Conversation

Numbers 4 through 6 relate to the following conversation.

[W] What is our hotel chain's policy on canceling reservations?

[M] If we are notified of a cancellation at least twenty-four hours in advance of check-in time, we refund the deposit.

[W] That's good news because I just talked to a customer who wants to cancel and expects to have his deposit returned.

[M] That should be no problem. Just call the customer back and tell him we will remove the charge from his credit card.

Part 4: Talk

Questions 7 through 9 relate to the following recording.

Welcome to the Palm Garden Hotel chain. As a hotel employee, many opportunities await you. You may be starting out as housekeepers, but any one of you could advance to manager as you gain experience. Our goal at the Palm Garden Hotels is to provide the highest level of service possible. Our customers pay high rates to stay at our hotels, and they expect an advanced level of service in return. This goal, quite naturally, precludes anything but a professional attitude on the part of our employees. We expect the highest level of service from all of you. Now, we are ready to start our tour of the hotel. We'll begin right next door in the dining room, then move on to the kitchen. This way, please.

LESSON 40:
Car Rentals

Part 1: Photo

Number 1. Look at the picture marked number 1.
- (A)   He's disappointed in the movie.
- (B)   He's showing his driver's license.
- (C)   He's contacting the agency to rent a car.
- (D)   He's tempted to have more cake.

Part 2: Question–Response

Number 2.

Can I request collision insurance with my rental car?
- (A)   No, we haven't made a decision.
- (B)   Yes, we can provide you with that insurance.
- (C)   It's the best car we have.

Number 3.

How many car rental agencies have you contacted?
- (A)   We asked for a compact car.
- (B)   I've only called two or three.
- (C)   Each agency has its own contract.

Part 3: Short Conversation

Numbers 4 through 6 relate to the following conversation.

[W] Would you like collision insurance on your rental car? It's optional, though we do recommend it.

[M] I doubt that we'll have an accident, but I'd feel less nervous with the insurance.

[W] No one ever intends to have an accident, of course, but most customers opt for the insurance when they rent from us. Let me just check the price . . . . OK, the cost of insurance for this car is just thirty dollars.

[M] Fine. Here's my credit card. You can charge everything on that.

Part 4: Talk

Questions 7 through 9 relate to the following recording.

If you are traveling to another country and intend to rent a car while there, there are several things to do before you leave. First, get an international driver's license. Then contact your local car rental agency to find out if they have offices abroad. If so, you can arrange to rent your car through them and avoid the confusion of signing a contract in a foreign language. This way, when you arrive and pick up your car, you won't be disappointed. It is tempting when you pick up your rental car to jump right in and drive away. Don't do this. First, check the car carefully for signs of damage. If you see any, point them out to the agent. You don't want to have to pay for damage that you didn't cause.

LESSON 41:
Movies

Part 1: Photo

Number 1. Look at the picture marked number 1.
- (A)   There are four separate movie posters on the wall.
- (B)   The film description is read to the moviegoers.
- (C)   The pedestrians are being entertained.
- (D)   The fans are continuing to buy tickets.

Part 2: Question–Response

Number 2.

When will the movie be released?
- (A)   It'll be reviewed in next Friday's paper.
- (B)   It'll be over in about 30 minutes.
- (C)   It'll be in theaters next month.

Number 3.

How would you describe that movie?
- (A)   It was the most romantic film I've ever seen.
- (B)   I'd move it over here.
- (C)   We decided it together.

Part 3: Short Conversation

Numbers 4 through 6 relate to the following conversation.

[W] Sam Peterson is one of my favorite actors. I thought his latest movie was even more entertaining than his previous ones. It's easy to see how he's been influenced by situation comedies on television.

[M] He certainly has developed a broader range of styles over the past two years.

[W] Yes, though I prefer him in his recent comedies more than in his earlier movies. I guess I just like comedy movies more than dramas or mysteries. I like to laugh.

[M] I think he's brilliant in all his movies, and I have no doubt that his success will continue. He's already made three movies this year, and another will be released before the end of this month.

Part 4: Talk

Questions 7 through 9 relate to the following recording.

On next week's show we'll interview a big name in the entertainment industry, Maria Moreno. Ms. Moreno's combined beauty and talent have made her popular everywhere. She's attained worldwide fame over the last several years through her outstanding performances in several hit movies. Her impressive acting abilities range from the comedic to the dramatic. Ms. Moreno will describe for us her latest movie, which has recently finished production and will be released next month. We'll also talk about the directors and fellow actors who have influenced her career.

TRACK 43

LESSON 42:
Theater

Part 1: Photo

Number 1. Look at the picture marked number 1.
- (A)   The dancer is rehearsing for a performance.
- (B)   The audience is entering the theater.
- (C)   The reviewer is watching the action.
- (D)   The actor is approaching the musician.

Part 2: Question–Response

Number 2.

Do you think tickets will sell out quickly?
- (A)   Yes, they'll sell them at the box office.
- (B)   Yes, it's a very popular play.
- (C)   Yes, I'll tell them about the tickets.

Number 3.

How long did the performance last?
- (A)   No, it was first.
- (B)   It was very well-done.
- (C)   About an hour and a half.

Part 3: Short Conversation

Numbers 4 through 6 relate to the following conversation.

[M] Did you read the review of the new musical comedy in yesterday's paper?

[W] Yes, it sounds great, doesn't it? They say the charming dialogue among the characters is very funny. Would you like to see it?

[M] Yes, but I've heard the tickets are sold out for the entire five-week run. I can't believe it.

[W] Well, that often occurs when a play is really great. And, I have a surprise for you. I already got tickets. I called the theater last Friday and got them. We're going to see the Sunday afternoon performance.

Part 4: Talk

Questions 7 through 9 relate to the following recording.

Audiences can't stop talking about the Shakespeare Theater's production of *Romeo and Juliet*. Reviewers have praised the director's creative new approach to this timeless story. Shouldn't you see it for yourself? Performances are at eight o'clock Thursday through Sunday evenings and at two o'clock on Saturday and Sunday afternoons. Order your tickets by e-mail: tickets@shakespeare.org. Call 656-9025 for prices and other information, or visit our website at www.shakespeare.org to read play reviews. Tickets are expected to sell out quickly, so order yours today. See *Romeo and Juliet* and experience the magic of live theater.

LESSON 43: Music

Part 1: Photo

Number 1. Look at the picture marked number 1.
  (A)   The critic is tasting the new dish.
  (B)   The fans are urging the team to win.
  (C)   The nurse is recommending relaxation.
  (D)   The orchestra is playing the conductor's favorite music.

Part 2: Question–Response

Number 2.

Is there a reason that you don't like opera?
  (A)   Yes, I find it really boring.
  (B)   The opera season begins in December.
  (C)   No, I don't.

Number 3.

What are your musical preferences?
  (A)   The musical instruments are in the next room.
  (B)   The library has a good reference collection.
  (C)   I like jazz and classical music.

Part 3: Short Conversation

Numbers 4 through 6 relate to the following conversation.

[M] I looked for some good music on that website you recommended, but I couldn't find anything I liked. Most of what they had was pretty uninteresting—just the usual boring stuff.

[W] I'm sorry. I guess your tastes just don't match mine. I've found a lot of music there that I really enjoy. What are you looking for that's so urgent?

[M] My friend is having a dance party tomorrow night and he asked me to put together the music for it. I only have till tomorrow to do this and I'm still looking for something that will really inspire people to get out there and dance.

[W] Relax. You've got the whole Internet available to you. You should be able to find what you need. Why don't you ask your friend Bill for some ideas of where to look? He knows more about this than I do.

Part 4: Talk

Questions 7 through 9 relate to the following recording.

Welcome to the Music Appreciation class. I know you are all here to broaden your tastes in music and to discover which types of music you prefer most. We'll do that by looking at several categories of music and disparate composers' styles. We'll also look at the development of musical instruments throughout history. The textbook for this class is available at the college bookstore, and I urge you to buy it and start reading it right away. At the end of the semester, we'll have the opportunity to attend a concert of the City Symphony Orchestra. Unfortunately, I am not able to obtain free tickets for you, but I can get them at a twenty-five percent discount so you'll only have to pay thirty dollars each. Please let me know before you leave class today whether or not you are interested in this opportunity.

LESSON 44:
Museums

Part 1: Photo

Number 1. Look at the picture marked number 1.
- (A) The secretary is keeping a schedule.
- (B) The artist is expressing himself by drawing.
- (C) The carpenter is working leisurely.
- (D) The critic is admiring her collection.

Part 2: Question–Response

Number 2.

Which artist do you admire most?
- (A) Painting is the hardest to do.
- (B) We hired a photographer.
- (C) Picasso is my favorite.

Number 3.

Have you seen the museum's sculpture collection?
- (A) Yes, your coats are over there.
- (B) Yes, I can give you directions to the museum.
- (C) Yes, they have some amazing pieces of sculpture.

Part 3: Short Conversation

Numbers 4 through 6 relate to the following conversation.

[M] Art historians say that this painting is a significant contribution to the field. Do you like it?

[W] I have to admit that art history was never my strong subject, so I'm not sure what my opinion's worth. I can say that I'm drawn to the painting, but I'm never sure I can tell what abstract art is trying to express.

[M] Neither can I, but I still think it's a beautiful painting. I admire the use of color.

[W] Well, yes. Fortunately, the museum's collection covers a wide spectrum of styles. They've acquired some really interesting pieces. It's certainly worth the price of admission.

Part 4: Talk

Questions 7 through 9 relate to the following recording.

Thank you for calling the National Museum of Art. Our collection of newly acquired paintings is on view this month in the main gallery. Also opening this month is a special exhibit of prints entitled "Clothing Fashions of the Early Twentieth Century." Next month begins our winter lecture series. The series this year includes specialists in African sculpture, nineteenth-century painting, and several well-known art critics. To hear the lecture series schedule, press one. To hear the schedule of guided tours, press two. To speak with an operator, please stay on the line.

LESSON 45:
Media

Part 1: Photo

Number 1. Look at the picture marked number 1.
- (A) The magazine reader is subscribing to a journal.
- (B) The newspaper journalist is choosing a story.
- (C) The TV reporter is covering an assignment.
- (D) The e-columnist is adding a link online.

Part 2: Question–Response

Number 2.

Why do you subscribe to that newspaper?
- (A) I decided to buy the newspaper.
- (B) Yes, I write for that newspaper.
- (C) Because it's the best newspaper around.

Number 3.

Who did you assign that story to?
- (A) I gave the assignment to Mr. Lee.
- (B) I've already signed the papers.
- (C) I didn't see the signs.

Part 3: Short Conversation

Numbers 4 through 6 relate to the following conversation.

[M] Would you choose to work for television instead of a newspaper?

[W] Never! Newspapers can cover a story much more thoroughly than television news shows can.

[M] That's certainly a decisive answer. But I suppose your thirteen years as an investigative reporter for a newspaper gives you the authority to answer the question.

[W] Yes. It's clear that newspapers can offer in-depth news in ways that television just can't. It's important for you, as a journalism student, to understand that.

Part 4: Talk

Questions 7 through 9 relate to the following recording.

Coming up next on the six o'clock news we'll bring you in-depth coverage of the investigation into the fraud allegedly committed by the president of the National Industrial Company over the past twelve months. We'll have commentary on whether or not the president's alleged actions constitute a crime which should be prosecuted in court, then we'll look at the impact this controversy could have on our national economy. Remember, you heard it first on the Channel Five Six O'clock News, your link to what's happening in the world. The news tonight will be reported by James Smith, substituting for Mary Milo who is away on a special assignment.

LESSON 46:
Doctor's Office

Part 1: Photo

Number 1. Look at the picture marked number 1.
(A)   He's diagnosing a patient.
(B)   He's making an appointment to play golf.
(C)   He's recommending a restaurant.
(D)   He's playing a musical instrument.

Part 2: Question–Response

Number 2.

What is the most effective way to prevent heart disease?
(A)   Yes, I feel at ease.
(B)   He was born with a heart defect.
(C)   Diet and exercise are the best way.

Number 3.

What is that instrument for?
(A)   No, I only use three instruments.
(B)   It's for listening to your heart.
(C)   Yes, I used it before.

Part 3: Short Conversation

Numbers 4 through 6 relate to the following conversation.

[W] I'm recommending that you see a specialist at the university hospital for another test.

[M] That sounds serious. Am I OK?

[W] Don't worry. I often refer patients to specialists who have more experience than I do with the latest diagnostic methods. But you should make your appointment soon, before the end of this month, if possible.

[M] I'll call today. You'll give me a copy of my medical record to take with me, won't you, Doctor?

Part 4: Talk

Questions 7 through 9 relate to the following recording.

Dr. Sato's office has an opening for an experienced office manager. Responsibilities include keeping track of the doctor's appointments, managing patients' medical and insurance records, and overseeing the work of two office assistants who answer the phones and make appointments. The successful candidate will be an effective organizer and have a serious attitude. Previous experience in a doctor's office is required. Benefits include competitive salary and three weeks vacation annually. Please send a résumé and two letters of recommendation to Dr. Sato before the first of next month.

LESSON 47:
Dentist's Office

Part 1: Photo

Number 1. Look at the picture marked number 1.
(A)   The neighbors are catching up on the news.
(B)   The dental technician is restoring the whiteness to his teeth.
(C)   The plumber checks the drains regularly.
(D)   The dietician is encouraging good eating habits.

Part 2: Question–Response

Number 2.

Can you restore my broken tooth?
(A)   Yes, I'll remove it.
(B)   Yes, the store is open tonight.
(C)   Yes, I can fix it.

Number 3.

Can you adjust the position of the chair?
(A)   I can change it if you're uncomfortable.
(B)   The chair belongs to me.
(C)   I think the air feels fine.

Part 3: Short Conversation

Numbers 4 through 6 relate to the following conversation.

[W] A quick overview of your dental records shows that there is cause for concern. You need to make more regular dental appointments if you want to have a healthy mouth.

[M] I don't care about cavities. I just want you to restore the shine to my teeth.

[W] Then I encourage you to kick the habits of smoking and drinking coffee. They both dull the teeth. We can also schedule an appointment for a special cleaning to whiten your teeth.

[M] That's a good idea. I'd like to do it as soon as possible. Can we do it next week?

Part 4: Talk

Questions 7 through 9 relate to the following recording.

Would you like to illuminate the room with your smile? It can be done. Most people aren't aware of how easy and inexpensive it is to restore the whiteness to your teeth. Our product can be used at home without the need to visit the dentist. Just apply the product to your teeth every night after your regular tooth brushing. It's that simple. Maintain your usual cleaning habits, and after just a few days, your teeth will start to look whiter. Unlike similar products, ours is guaranteed not to irritate sensitive gums. Why wait? Visit our website at www.whiterteeth.com and order your supply today. You'll see why our company has the highest sales of all dental product companies in the nation.

LESSON 48:
Health Insurance

Part 1: Photo

Number 1. Look at the picture marked number 1.
(A)   The patient is concerned about her weight.
(B)   The doctor is measuring the medicine.
(C)   The woman's salary is too high.
(D)   The clerk is weighing the vegetables.

Part 2: Question–Response

Number 2.

Will my insurance policy cover my elective surgery?
(A)   Yes, it covers emergencies.
(B)   You can select any surgeon on the list.
(C)   No, you have to pay for that yourself.

Number 3.

Who was in charge of choosing an insurance policy for our company?
(A)   It's charged against your monthly salary.
(B)   The Director of Personnel chose it.
(C)   We can't make any changes.

Part 3: Short Conversation

Numbers 4 through 6 relate to the following conversation.

[M] Does the health plan allow me to see a specialist immediately, or do I have to see my primary care provider first?

[W] If you go without your primary provider's referral, you will incur a higher percentage of the total cost.

[M] Then I would pay an increased portion of the bill. But if I go through my primary care provider first, it will take a lot longer to get to the specialist because the soonest I can get an appointment with the primary care provider is three weeks from now.

[W] I still think it's your best alternative. If you follow the usual procedure and see your primary care provider first, you'll save yourself a lot of headaches as well as money.

Part 4: Talk

Questions 7 through 9 relate to the following recording.

In response to the concerns many of our personnel have expressed about the cost of our current health plan, we have decided to make an alternative plan available to anyone who is interested. This plan offers fewer benefits, but those who opt for it will incur fewer costs. I would like to emphasize that even though we have chosen this alternative to help people save money, it is available to everyone regardless of what your salary is or how long you have worked at the company. We have spent several months searching for an alternative health insurance policy, and I am happy to say we have finally found one that will suit our needs in all aspects. If you are interested in switching to the new plan, please let Human Resources know within the next two weeks. The new policy will go into effect at the beginning of next year.

LESSON 49:
Hospitals

Part 1: Photo

Number 1. Look at the picture marked number 1.
  (A)   The escort's leading the group.
  (B)   The guard's authorizing the visitors.
  (C)   The musician's following the procedures.
  (D)   The physician's identifying the medicine.

Part 2: Question–Response

Number 2.

When will I be permitted to go home?
  (A)   Because you're in good health now.
  (B)   You'll be admitted to the hospital next week.
  (C)   You can leave tomorrow morning.

Number 3.

When will I find out my test results?
  (A)   Some time next week.
  (B)   They look very good.
  (C)   I found them in the drawer.

Part 3: Short Conversation

Numbers 4 through 6 relate to the following conversation.

[W] I'm not at all happy with the care my husband received here. Is there someone designated to handle complaints?

[M] Our mission is to deliver complete satisfaction. What is your problem?

[W] The hospital identified my husband incorrectly in the computer system, and now all his records are mixed up. They almost gave him the wrong medication twice, and now they want to charge us for surgery when he only came in for some tests.

[M] If you will permit me to take a look at your statement. . . . Yes, I think I see what the problem is. Exactly how is your husband's name spelled?

Part 4: Talk

Questions 7 through 9 relate to the following recording.

I've gotten the lab results from the tests we did last week and, as I expected, you'll have to be admitted to the hospital for surgery. I've already sent the form to the insurance company. It's not unusual for it to take seven or eight days to receive their authorization, so I'd like to schedule the procedure for ten days from now. You should expect a hospital stay of two or three days. I'll prepare the pertinent paperwork for you to give to the admitting nurse.

TRACK
51

LESSON 50:
Pharmacy

Part 1: Photo

Number 1. Look at the picture marked number 1.
  (A)   The consultant is greeting the doctor.
  (B)   The volunteers are cleaning the shelves.
  (C)   The pharmacist is checking the samples.
  (D)   The patient is limiting his activity.

Part 2: Question–Response

Number 2.

Is there a limited number of refills I can have on this prescription?
  (A)   Yes, I can fill it before three o'clock.
  (B)   Yes, you can have this prescription.
  (C)   Yes, you only get two.

Number 3.

What are the potential side effects of this medication?
  (A)   It's one of the most effective medications I've seen.
  (B)   It can cause sleepiness in some people.
  (C)   No, it isn't essential.

Part 3: Short Conversation

Numbers 4 through 6 relate to the following conversation.

[W] These pills should control your backache. You should detect improvement within two days.

[M] But my wife used a different medication for her back pain, and it really worked for her.

[W] Just because a certain pill worked for a relative or friend doesn't mean it'll work for you. Everybody is different, and there are different factors that determine how a medication will work. I can't just hand out the same pills to everyone.

[M] No, I guess that wouldn't make sense. OK, I'll try these samples, and if they work, I'll go ahead and fill the prescription you wrote.

Part 4: Talk

Questions 7 through 9 relate to the following recording.

The medication I'd like to prescribe for you is one of the most effective drugs for controlling sleeping problems and should also help alleviate your headaches. It's very convenient to use. You just take it once a day, about thirty minutes before you go to bed. I'll give you a few free samples to try out. Call me in four or five days to let me know how it's working. But I'm sure you'll be happy with it and want to fill the prescription. The only potential side effect it has is stomachaches, and it shouldn't have any interactions with your other medications. There's also no limit to the length of time you can use it. You can just keep on taking it as long as you feel a need.

NOTES

MP3 Track Listing

Track Number	Track Title
1	Introduction
2	Lesson 1: Contracts
3	Lesson 2: Marketing
4	Lesson 3: Warranties
5	Lesson 4: Business Planning
6	Lesson 5: Conferences
7	Lesson 6: Computers and the Internet
8	Lesson 7: Office Technology
9	Lesson 8: Office Procedures
10	Lesson 9: Electronics
11	Lesson 10: Correspondence
12	Lesson 11: Job Advertising and Recruiting
13	Lesson 12: Applying and Interviewing
14	Lesson 13: Hiring and Training
15	Lesson 14: Salaries and Benefits
16	Lesson 15: Promotions, Pensions, and Awards
17	Lesson 16: Shopping
18	Lesson 17: Ordering Supplies
19	Lesson 18: Shipping
20	Lesson 19: Invoices
21	Lesson 20: Inventory
22	Lesson 21: Banking
23	Lesson 22: Accounting
24	Lesson 23: Investments
25	Lesson 24: Taxes
26	Lesson 25: Financial Statements
27	Lesson 26: Property and Departments
28	Lesson 27: Board Meetings and Committees
29	Lesson 28: Quality Control
30	Lesson 29: Product Development
31	Lesson 30: Renting and Leasing
32	Lesson 31: Selecting a Restaurant
33	Lesson 32: Eating Out
34	Lesson 33: Ordering Lunch
35	Lesson 34: Cooking as a Career
36	Lesson 35: Events
37	Lesson 36: General Travel
38	Lesson 37: Airlines
39	Lesson 38: Trains
40	Lesson 39: Hotels
41	Lesson 40: Car Rentals
42	Lesson 41: Movies
43	Lesson 42: Theater
44	Lesson 43: Music
45	Lesson 44: Museums
46	Lesson 45: Media
47	Lesson 46: Doctor's Office
48	Lesson 47: Dentist's Office
49	Lesson 48: Health Insurance
50	Lesson 49: Hospitals
51	Lesson 50: Pharmacy

BARRON'S LICENSING AGREEMENT/DISCLAIMER OF WARRANTY
For books including one or more Audio CDs and/or CD-ROMs

Ownership of Rights. The disc(s) in the plastic sleeve was/were created for Barron's Educational Series, Inc., and the editorial contents therein remain the intellectual property of Barron's. Users may not reproduce the disc(s), authorize or permit the disc(s) reproduction, transmit the disc(s), or permit any portion thereof to be transmitted for any purpose whatsoever.

License. Barron's hereby grants to the consumer of this product the limited license to use same solely for personal use. Any other use shall be in violation of Barron's rights to the aforesaid intellectual property and in violation of Barron's copyright interest in such disc(s).

Limited Warranty. Disclaimer of Implied Warranties. If the disc(s) fail(s) to function in a satisfactory manner, Barron's sole liability to any purchaser or user shall be limited to refunding the price paid for same by said purchaser or user. Barron's makes no other warranties, express or implied, with respect the disc(s). *Barron's specifically disclaims any warranty of fitness for a particular purpose or of merchantability.*

Consequential Damages. Barron's shall not be liable under any circumstances for indirect, incidental, special, or consequential damages resulting from the purchase or use of the disc(s).